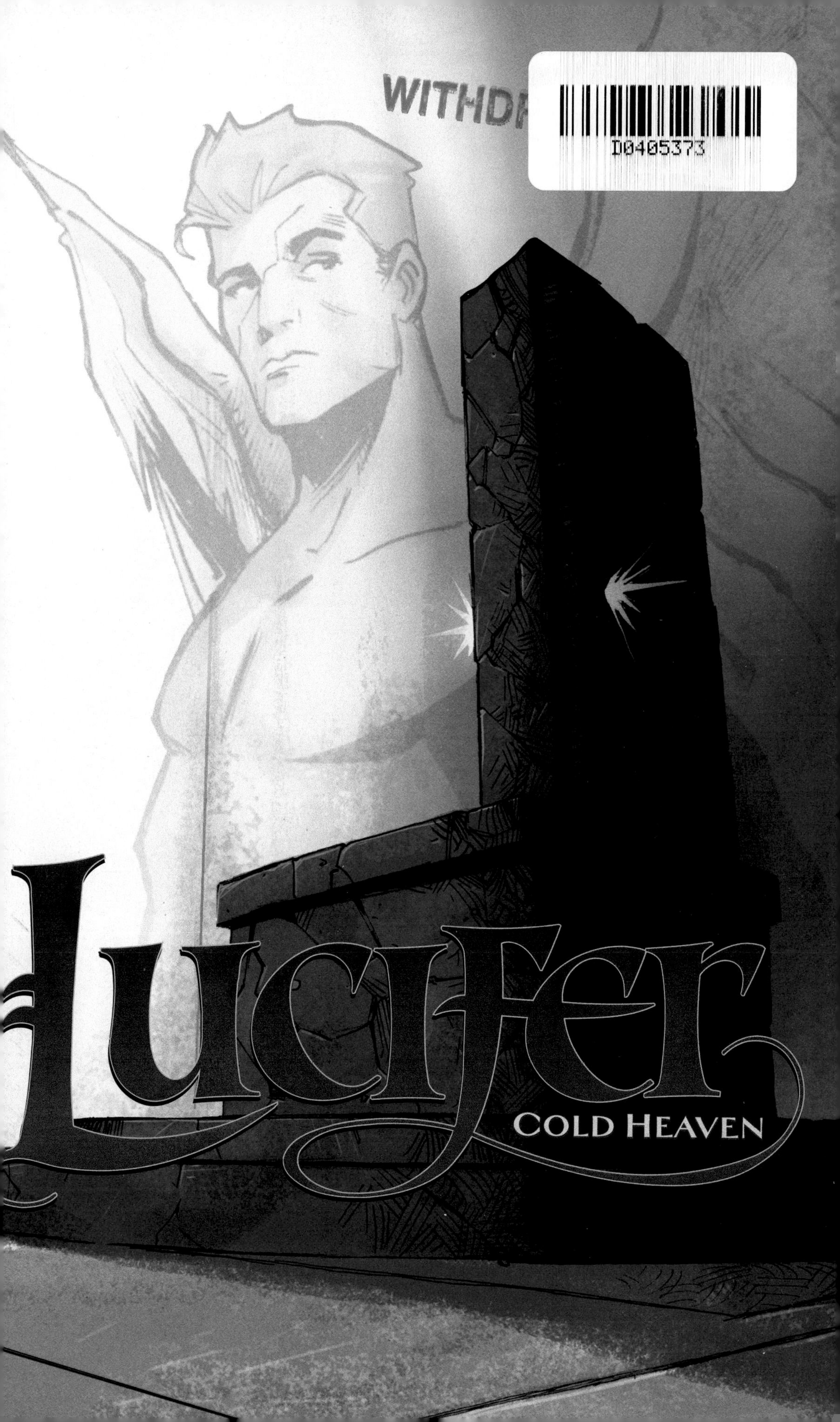
Lucifer
COLD HEAVEN

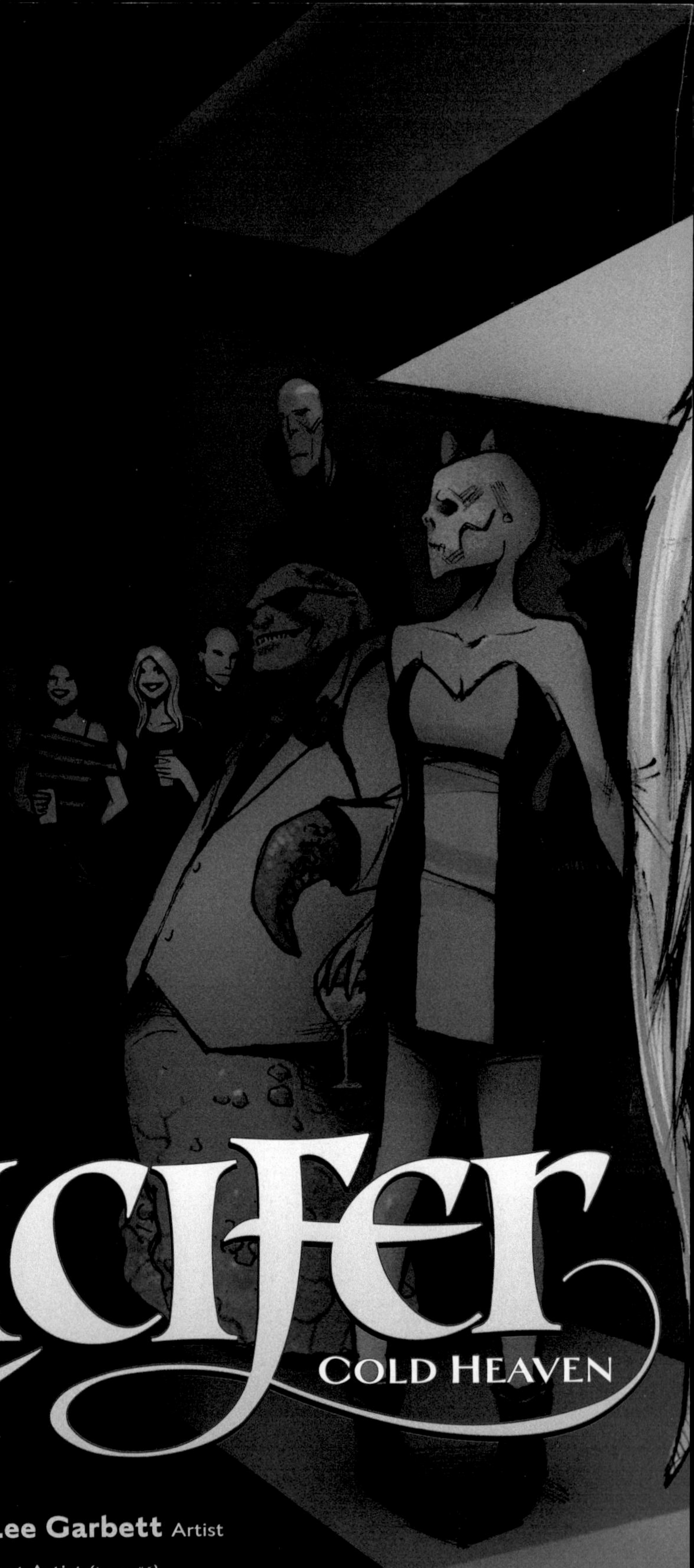

Lucifer

Cold Heaven

Holly Black Writer **Lee Garbett** Artist

Stephanie Hans Guest Artist *(Issue #6)*

Antonio Fabela Colorist *(Issues #1-5)*

Todd Klein Letterer **Dave Johnson** Collection Cover

Dave Johnson *(Issues #1-5)* **Christopher Moeller** *(Issue #6)* Original Series Covers

Based on characters created by **NEIL GAIMAN, SAM KIETH and MIKE DRINGENBERG**

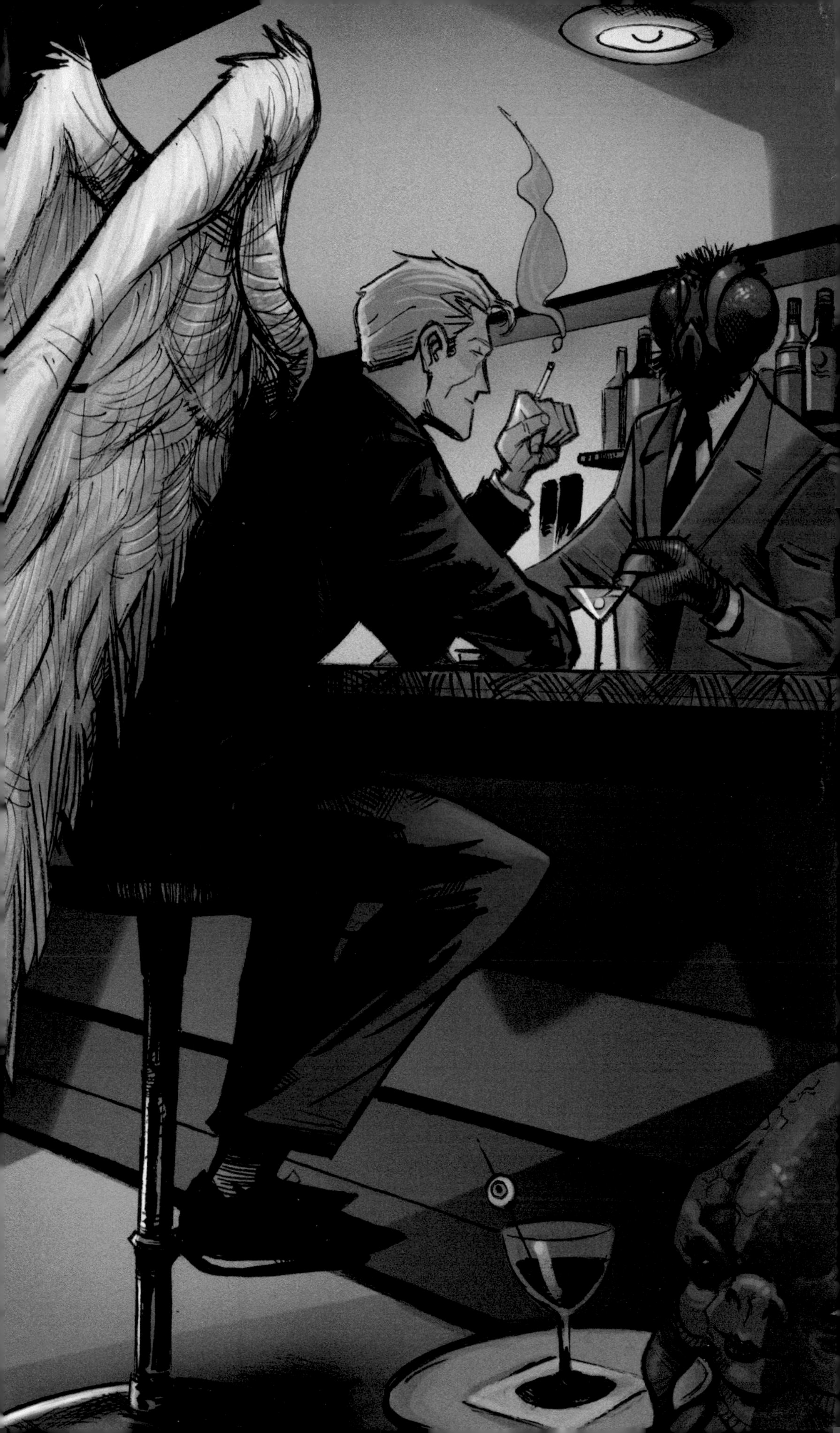

ELLIE PYLE Editor – Original Series

MOLLY MAHAN Associate Editor – Original Series

JEB WOODARD Group Editor – Collected Editions

SCOTT NYBAKKEN Editor – Collected Edition

STEVE COOK Design Director – Books

CURTIS KING JR. Publication Design

SHELLY BOND VP & Executive Editor – Vertigo

DIANE NELSON President

DAN DIDIO and **JIM LEE** Co-Publishers

GEOFF JOHNS Chief Creative Officer

AMIT DESAI Senior VP – Marketing & Global Franchise Management

NAIRI GARDINER Senior VP – Finance

SAM ADES VP – Digital Marketing

BOBBIE CHASE VP – Talent Development

MARK CHIARELLO Senior VP – Art, Design & Collected Editions

JOHN CUNNINGHAM VP – Content Strategy

ANNE DEPIES VP – Strategy Planning & Reporting

DON FALLETTI VP – Manufacturing Operations

LAWRENCE GANEM VP – Editorial Administration & Talent Relations

ALISON GILL Senior VP – Manufacturing & Operations

HANK KANALZ Senior VP – Editorial Strategy & Administration

JAY KOGAN VP – Legal Affairs

DEREK MADDALENA Senior VP – Sales & Business Development

JACK MAHAN VP – Business Affairs

DAN MIRON VP – Sales Planning & Trade Development

NICK NAPOLITANO VP – Manufacturing Administration

CAROL ROEDER VP – Marketing

EDDIE SCANNELL VP – Mass Account & Digital Sales

COURTNEY SIMMONS Senior VP – Publicity & Communications

JIM (SKI) SOKOLOWSKI VP – Comic Book Specialty & Newsstand Sales

SANDY YI Senior VP – Global Franchise Management

LUCIFER VOL. 1: COLD HEAVEN

Published by DC Comics. Compilation and all new material Copyright © 2016 DC Comics. All Rights Reserved.

Originally published in single magazine form as LUCIFER 1-6. Copyright © 2015, 2016 DC Comics. All Rights Reserved. All characters, their distinctive likenesses and related elements featured in this publication are trademarks of DC Comics. VERTIGO is a trademark of DC Comics. The stories, characters and incidents featured in this publication are entirely fictional. DC Comics does not read or accept unsolicited submissions of ideas, stories or artwork.

DC Comics
2900 West Alameda Avenue, Burbank, CA 91505
Printed in the USA. First Printing.
ISBN: 978-1-4012-6193-1

Library of Congress Cataloging-in-Publication Data

Names: Black, Holly, author. | Garbett, Lee, illustrator. | Hans, Stephanie, illustrator. | Fabela, Antonio, illustrator. | Klein, Todd, illustrator. | Moeller, Christopher, illustrator.
Title: Lucifer. Volume 1, Cold Heaven / Holly Black, writer ; Lee Garbett, artist ; Stephanie Hans, guest artist (issue Nº6) ; Antonio Fabela, colorist ; Todd Klein, letterer ; Dave Johnson, cover art ; Dave Johnson (issues Nº1-5), Christopher Moeller (issue Nº6), original series covers.
Other titles: Cold Heaven
Description: Burbank, CA : DC Comics, [2016]
Identifiers: LCCN 2016021796 | ISBN 9781401261931 (paperback)
Subjects: LCSH: Devil—Comic books, strips, etc. | Angels—Comic books, strips, etc. | BISAC: COMICS & GRAPHIC NOVELS / Superheroes.
Classification: LCC PN6728.L79 B57 2016 | DDC 741.5/973—dc23
LC record available at https://lccn.loc.gov/2016021796

PEFC Certified

Printed on paper from sustainably managed forests and controlled sources

PEFC/29-31-75   www.pefc.org

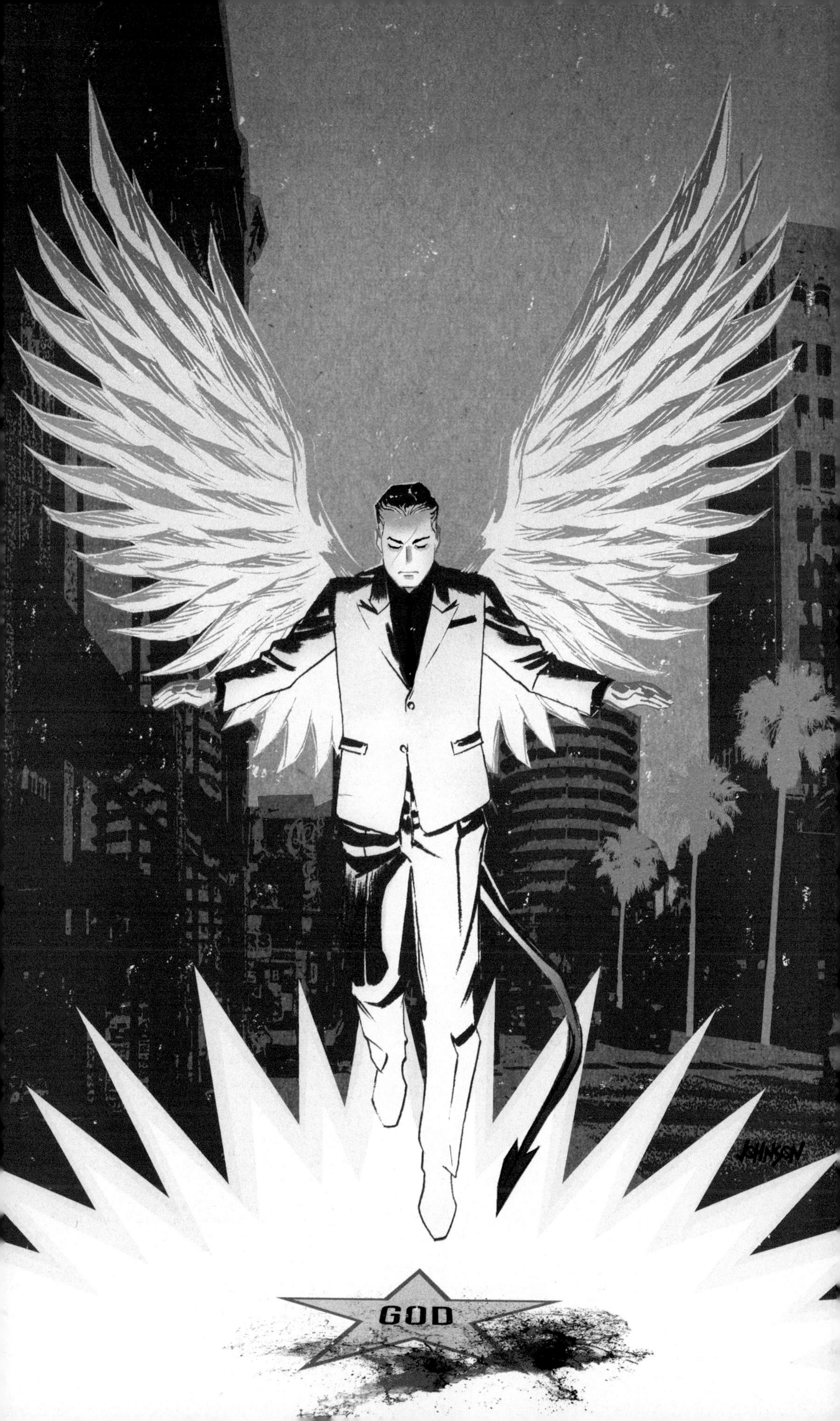
JOHNSON
GOD

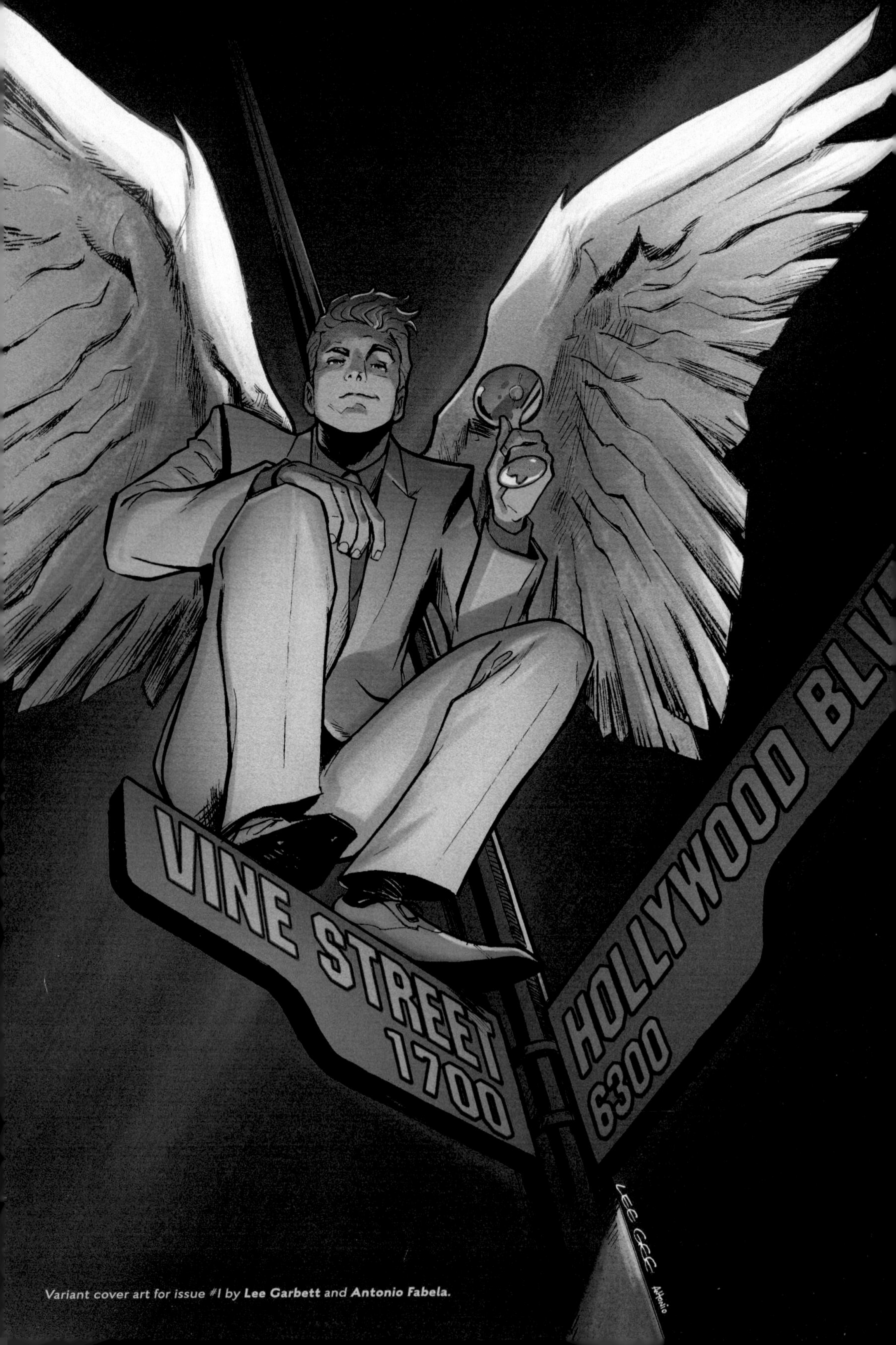
VINE STREET
1700
HOLLYWOOD BLV
6300

*Variant cover art for issue #1 by **Lee Garbett** and **Antonio Fabela**.*

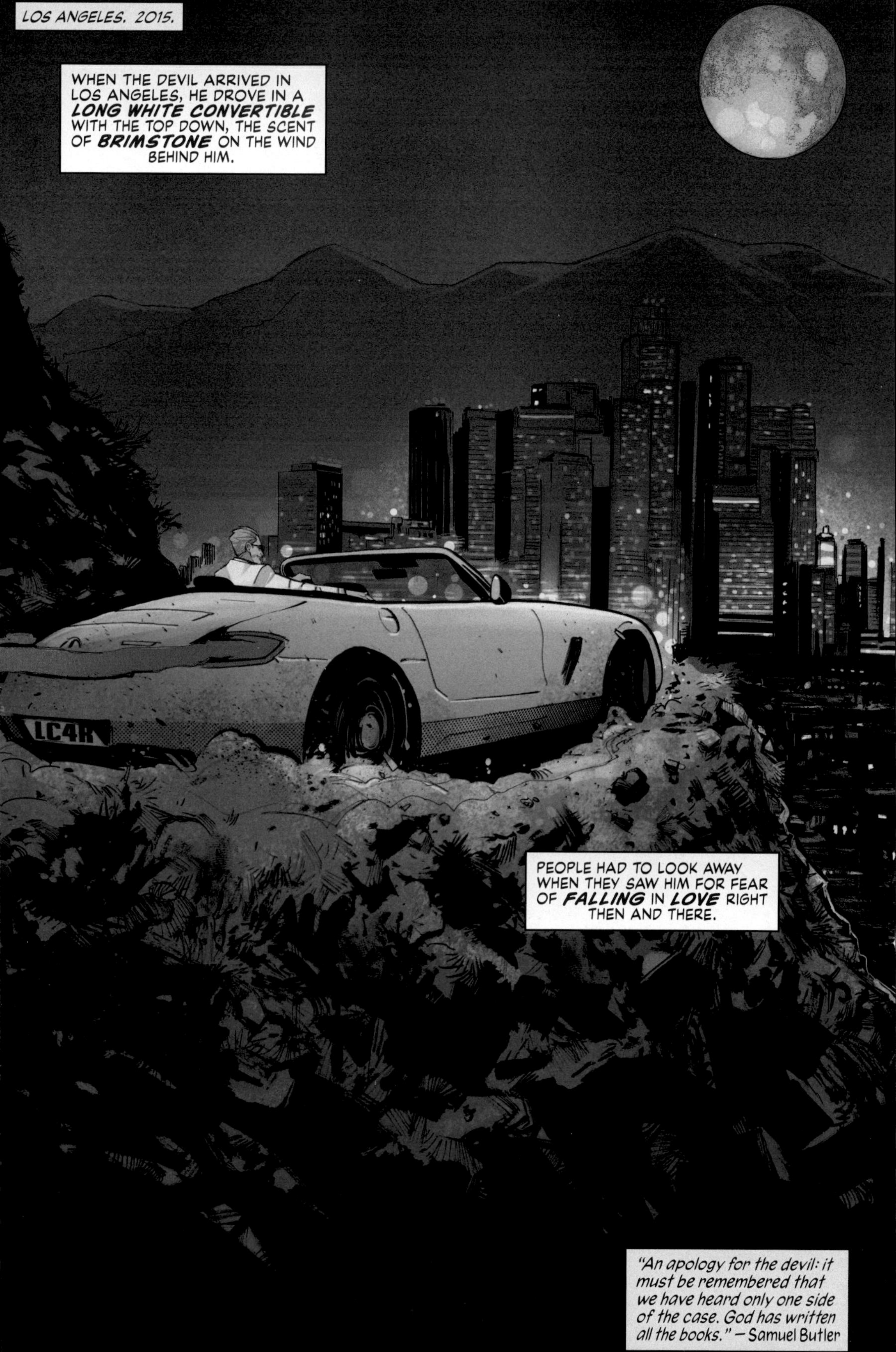
LOS ANGELES. 2015.
WHEN THE DEVIL ARRIVED IN LOS ANGELES, HE DROVE IN A LONG WHITE CONVERTIBLE WITH THE TOP DOWN, THE SCENT OF BRIMSTONE ON THE WIND BEHIND HIM.
LC4R
PEOPLE HAD TO LOOK AWAY WHEN THEY SAW HIM FOR FEAR OF FALLING IN LOVE RIGHT THEN AND THERE.
"An apology for the devil: it must be remembered that we have heard only one side of the case. God has written all the books." – Samuel Butler

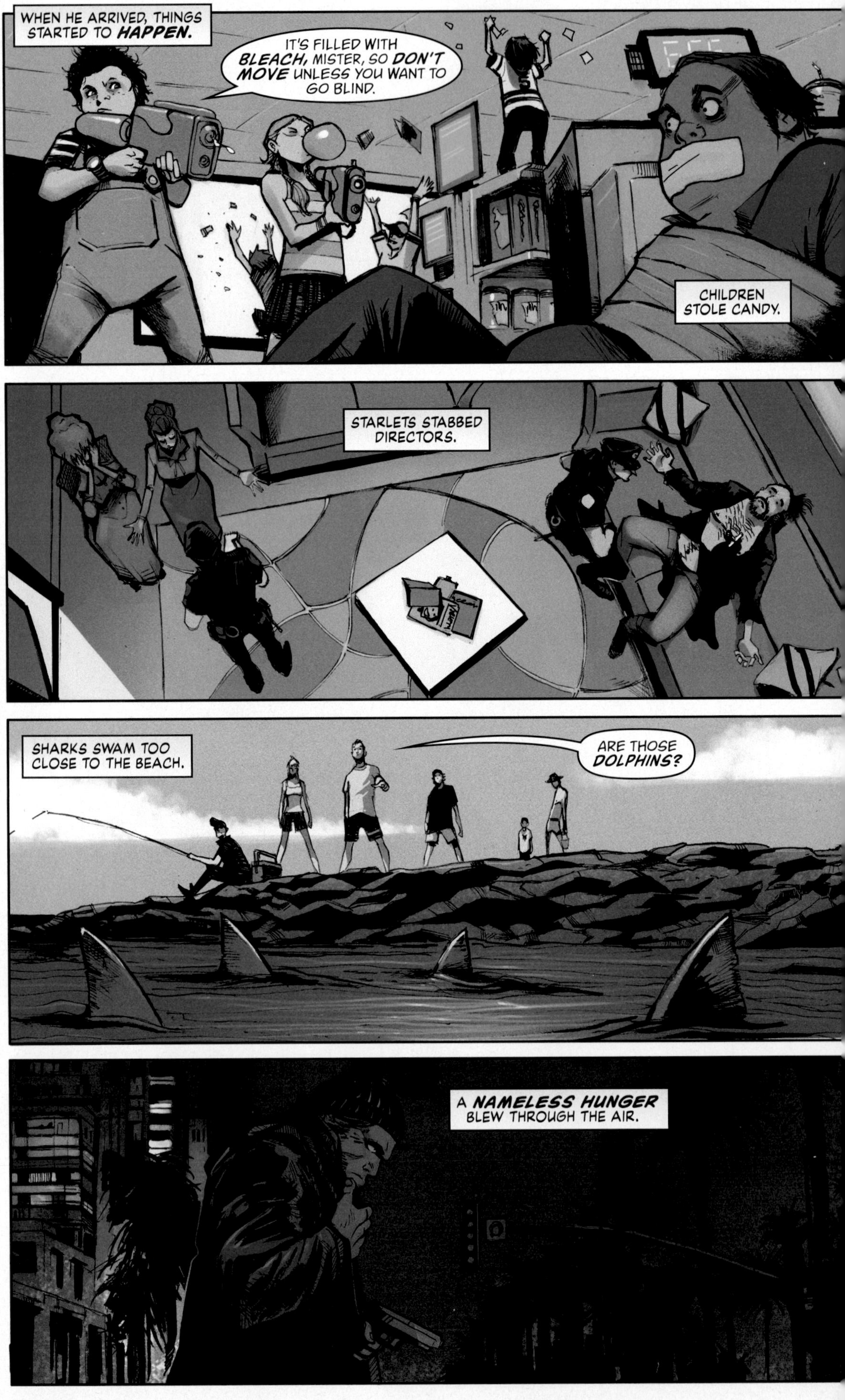
WHEN HE ARRIVED, THINGS STARTED TO HAPPEN.
IT'S FILLED WITH BLEACH, MISTER, SO DON'T MOVE UNLESS YOU WANT TO GO BLIND.
CHILDREN STOLE CANDY.
STARLETS STABBED DIRECTORS.
SHARKS SWAM TOO CLOSE TO THE BEACH.
ARE THOSE DOLPHINS?
A NAMELESS HUNGER BLEW THROUGH THE AIR.

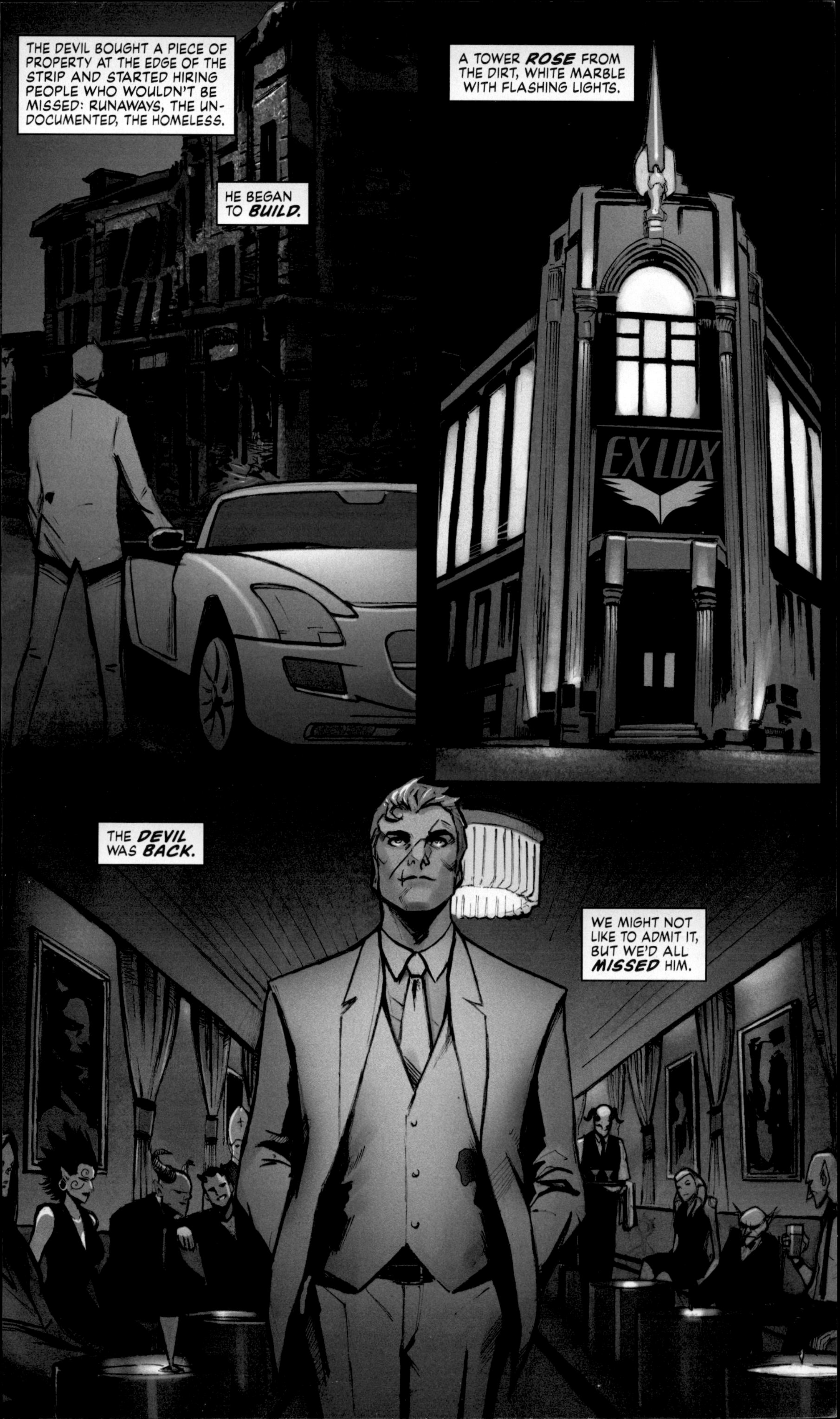
THE DEVIL BOUGHT A PIECE OF PROPERTY AT THE EDGE OF THE STRIP AND STARTED HIRING PEOPLE WHO WOULDN'T BE MISSED: RUNAWAYS, THE UN-DOCUMENTED, THE HOMELESS.
HE BEGAN TO BUILD.
A TOWER ROSE FROM THE DIRT, WHITE MARBLE WITH FLASHING LIGHTS.
EX LUX
THE DEVIL WAS BACK.
WE MIGHT NOT LIKE TO ADMIT IT, BUT WE'D ALL MISSED HIM.

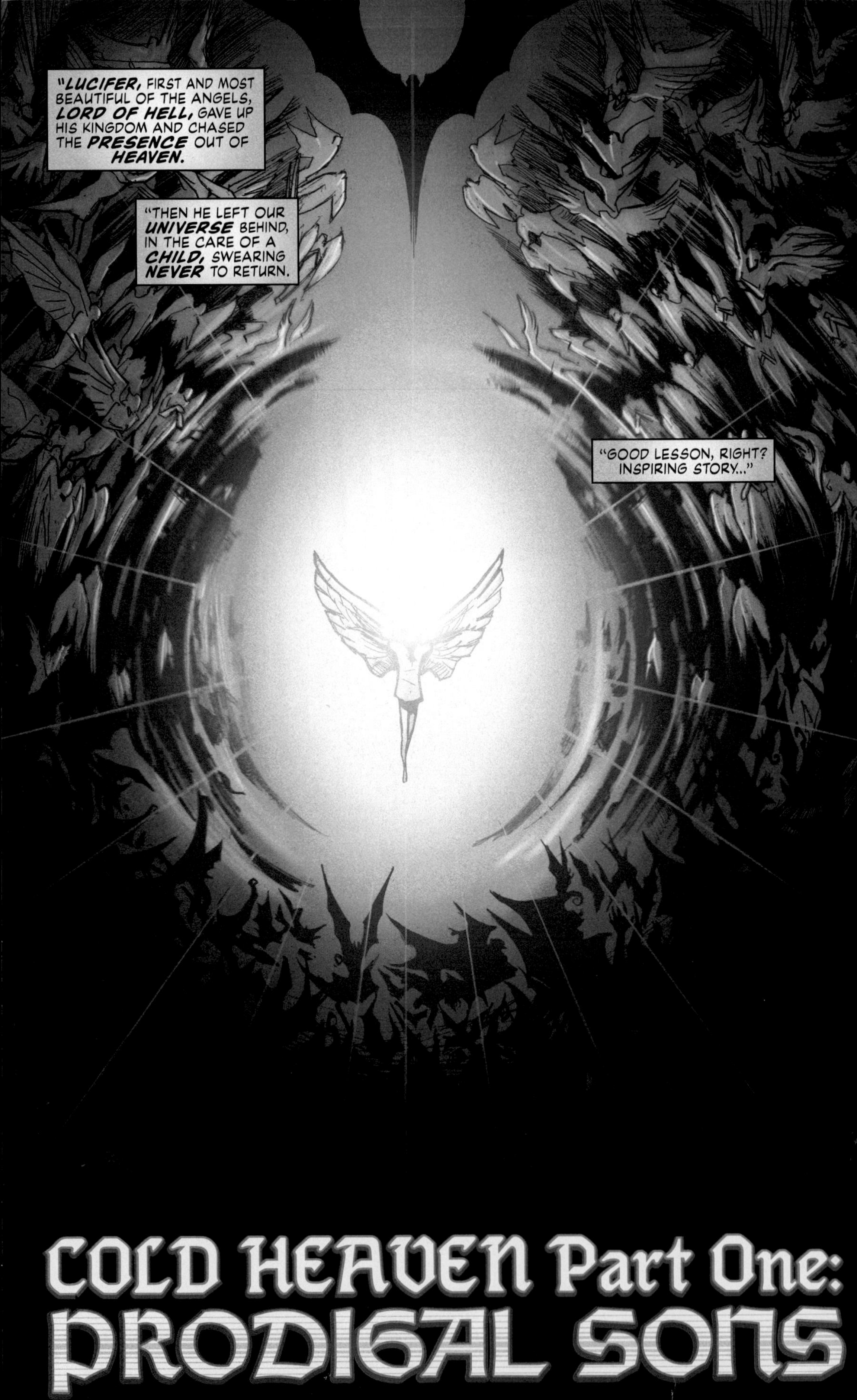
"LUCIFER, FIRST AND MOST BEAUTIFUL OF THE ANGELS, LORD OF HELL, GAVE UP HIS KINGDOM AND CHASED THE PRESENCE OUT OF HEAVEN.
"THEN HE LEFT OUR UNIVERSE BEHIND, IN THE CARE OF A CHILD, SWEARING NEVER TO RETURN.
"GOOD LESSON, RIGHT? INSPIRING STORY..."
COLD HEAVEN Part One:
PRODIGAL SONS

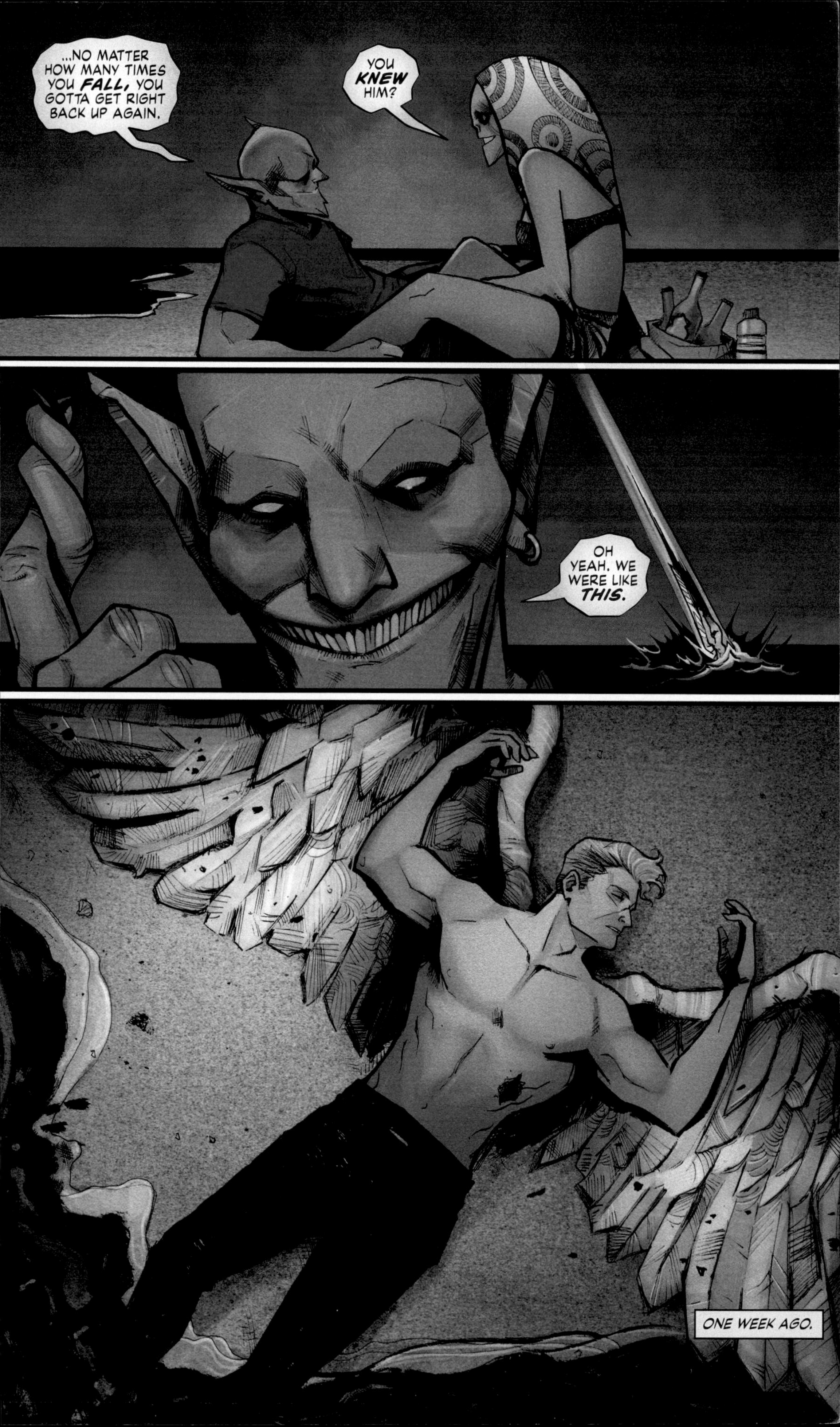
...NO MATTER HOW MANY TIMES YOU FALL, YOU GOTTA GET RIGHT BACK UP AGAIN.
YOU KNEW HIM?
OH YEAH. WE WERE LIKE THIS.
ONE WEEK AGO.

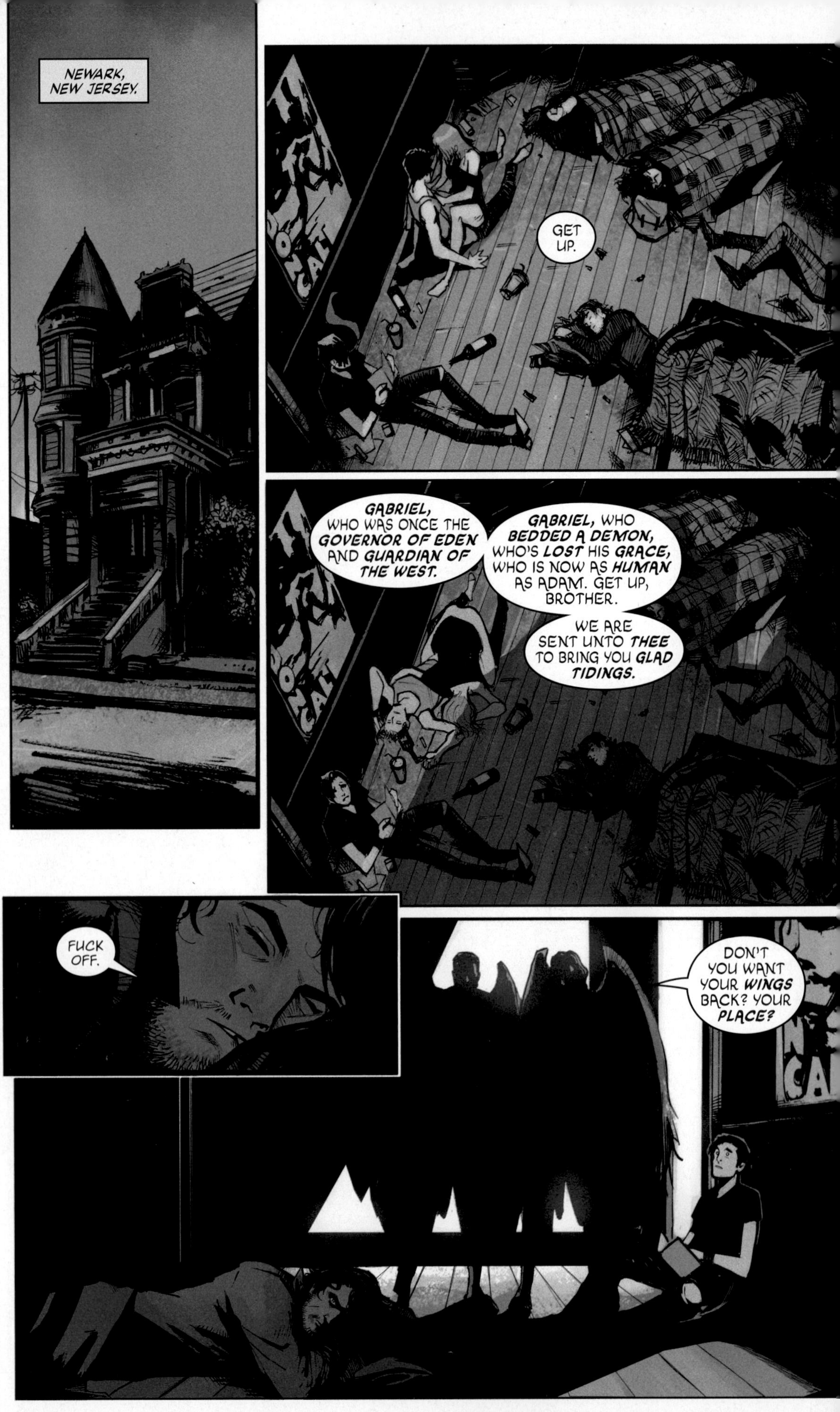
NEWARK, NEW JERSEY.
GET UP.
GABRIEL, WHO WAS ONCE THE GOVERNOR OF EDEN AND GUARDIAN OF THE WEST.
GABRIEL, WHO BEDDED A DEMON, WHO'S LOST HIS GRACE, WHO IS NOW AS HUMAN AS ADAM. GET UP, BROTHER.
WE ARE SENT UNTO THEE TO BRING YOU GLAD TIDINGS.
FUCK OFF.
DON'T YOU WANT YOUR WINGS BACK? YOUR PLACE?

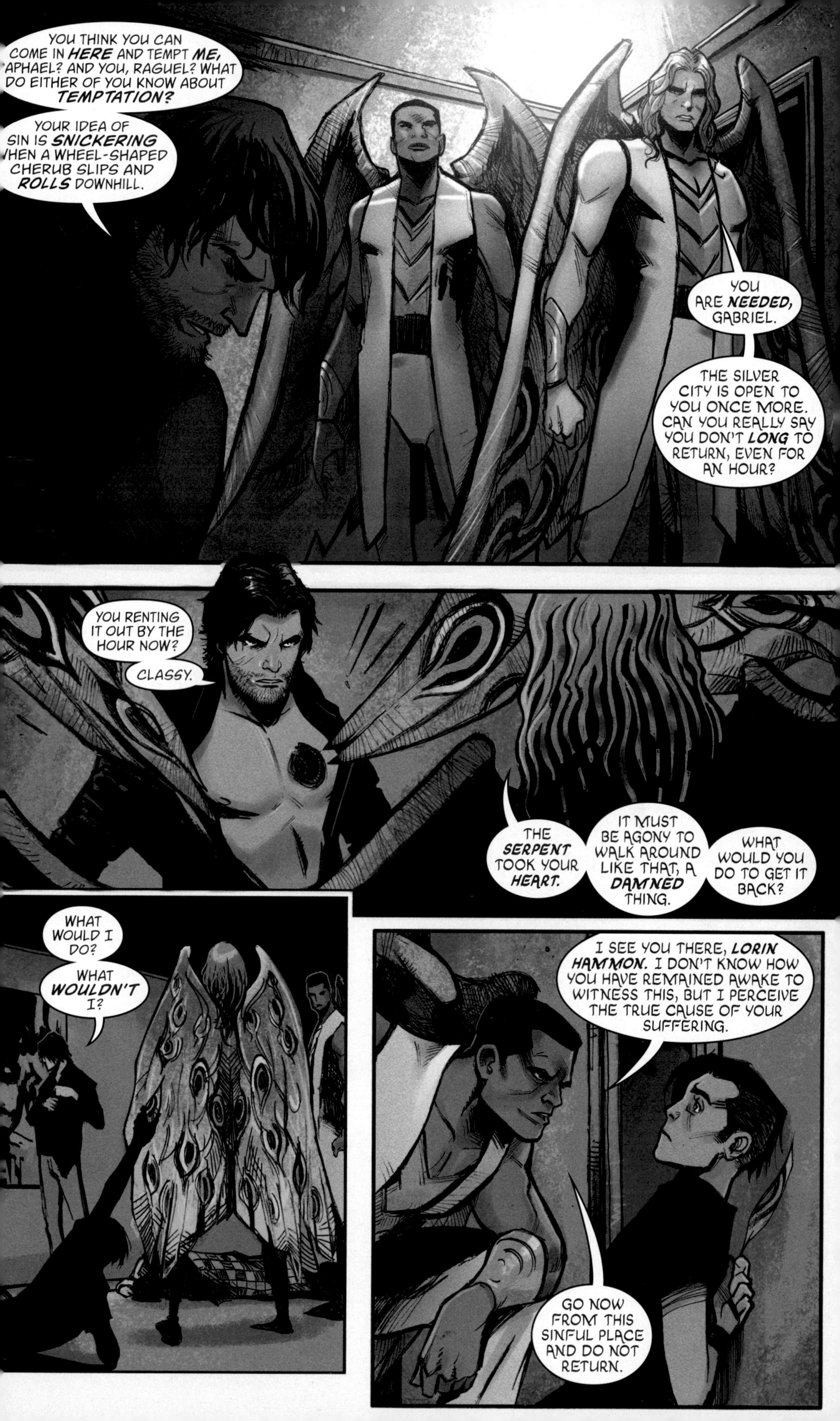

YOU THINK YOU CAN COME IN HERE AND TEMPT ME, RAPHAEL? AND YOU, RAGUEL? WHAT DO EITHER OF YOU KNOW ABOUT TEMPTATION?
YOUR IDEA OF SIN IS SNICKERING WHEN A WHEEL-SHAPED CHERUB SLIPS AND ROLLS DOWNHILL.
YOU ARE NEEDED, GABRIEL.
THE SILVER CITY IS OPEN TO YOU ONCE MORE. CAN YOU REALLY SAY YOU DON'T LONG TO RETURN, EVEN FOR AN HOUR?
YOU RENTING IT OUT BY THE HOUR NOW?
CLASSY.
THE SERPENT TOOK YOUR HEART.
IT MUST BE AGONY TO WALK AROUND LIKE THAT, A DAMNED THING.
WHAT WOULD YOU DO TO GET IT BACK?
WHAT WOULD I DO?
WHAT WOULDN'T I?
I SEE YOU THERE, LORIN HAMMON. I DON'T KNOW HOW YOU HAVE REMAINED AWAKE TO WITNESS THIS, BUT I PERCEIVE THE TRUE CAUSE OF YOUR SUFFERING.
GO NOW FROM THIS SINFUL PLACE AND DO NOT RETURN.

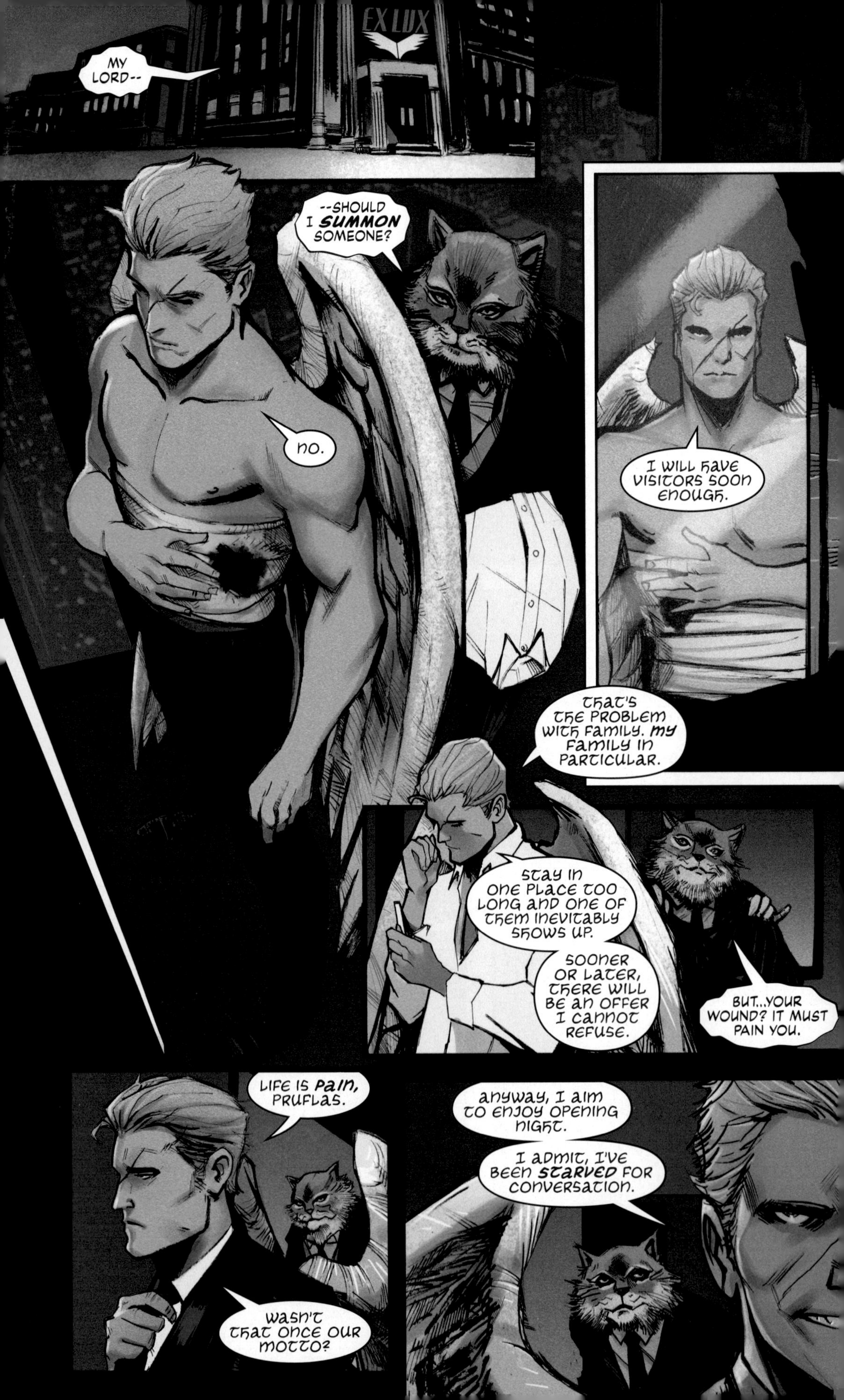
EX LUX
MY LORD--
--SHOULD I SUMMON SOMEONE?
no.
I WILL HAVE VISITORS SOON ENOUGH.
THAT'S THE PROBLEM WITH FAMILY. MY FAMILY IN PARTICULAR.
STAY IN ONE PLACE TOO LONG AND ONE OF THEM INEVITABLY SHOWS UP.
SOONER OR LATER, THERE WILL BE AN OFFER I CANNOT REFUSE.
BUT...YOUR WOUND? IT MUST PAIN YOU.
LIFE IS PAIN, PRUFLAS.
WASN'T THAT ONCE OUR MOTTO?
ANYWAY, I AIM TO ENJOY OPENING NIGHT.
I ADMIT, I'VE BEEN STARVED FOR CONVERSATION.

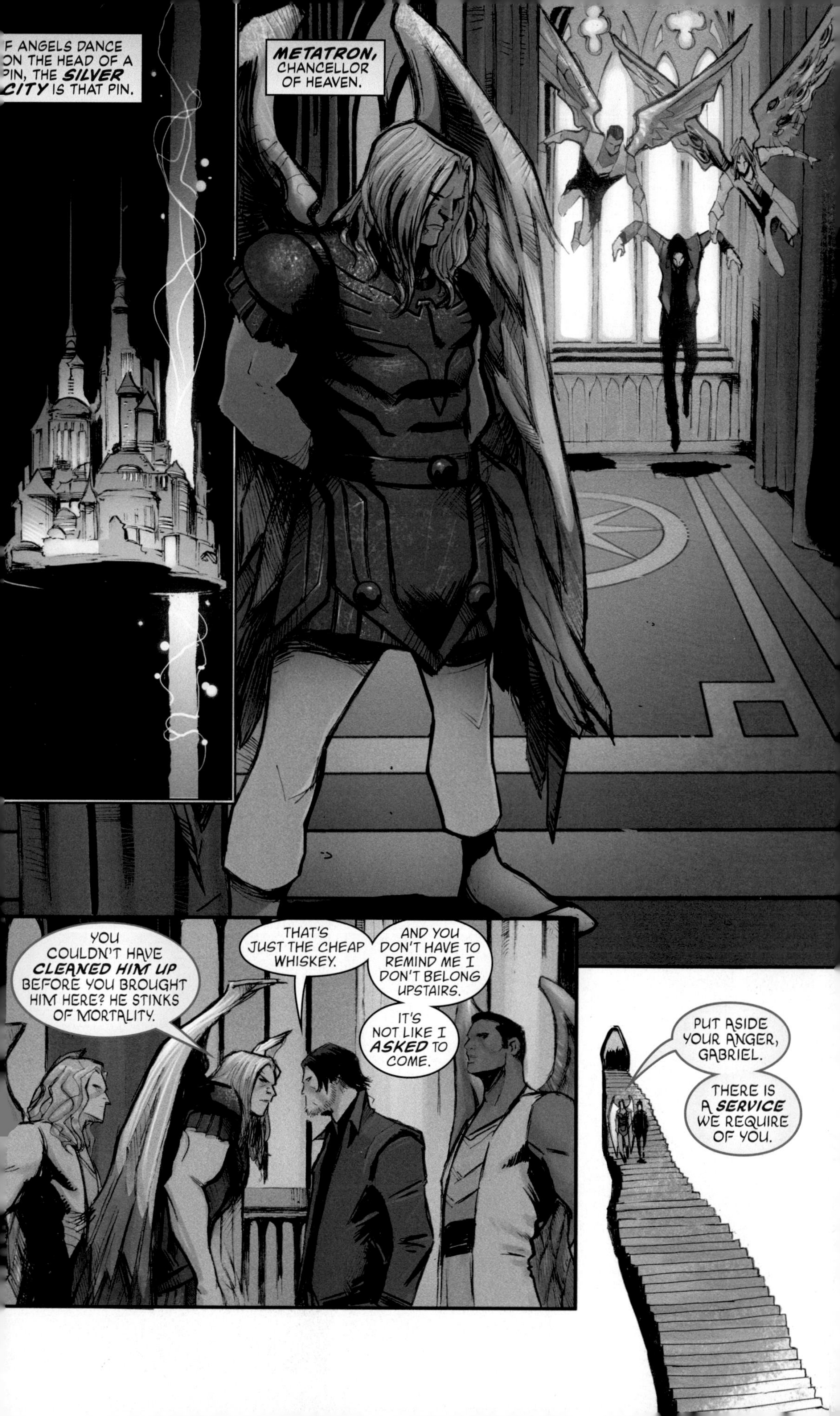
F ANGELS DANCE ON THE HEAD OF A PIN, THE SILVER CITY IS THAT PIN.
METATRON, CHANCELLOR OF HEAVEN.
YOU COULDN'T HAVE CLEANED HIM UP BEFORE YOU BROUGHT HIM HERE? HE STINKS OF MORTALITY.
THAT'S JUST THE CHEAP WHISKEY.
AND YOU DON'T HAVE TO REMIND ME I DON'T BELONG UPSTAIRS.
IT'S NOT LIKE I ASKED TO COME.
PUT ASIDE YOUR ANGER, GABRIEL.
THERE IS A SERVICE WE REQUIRE OF YOU.

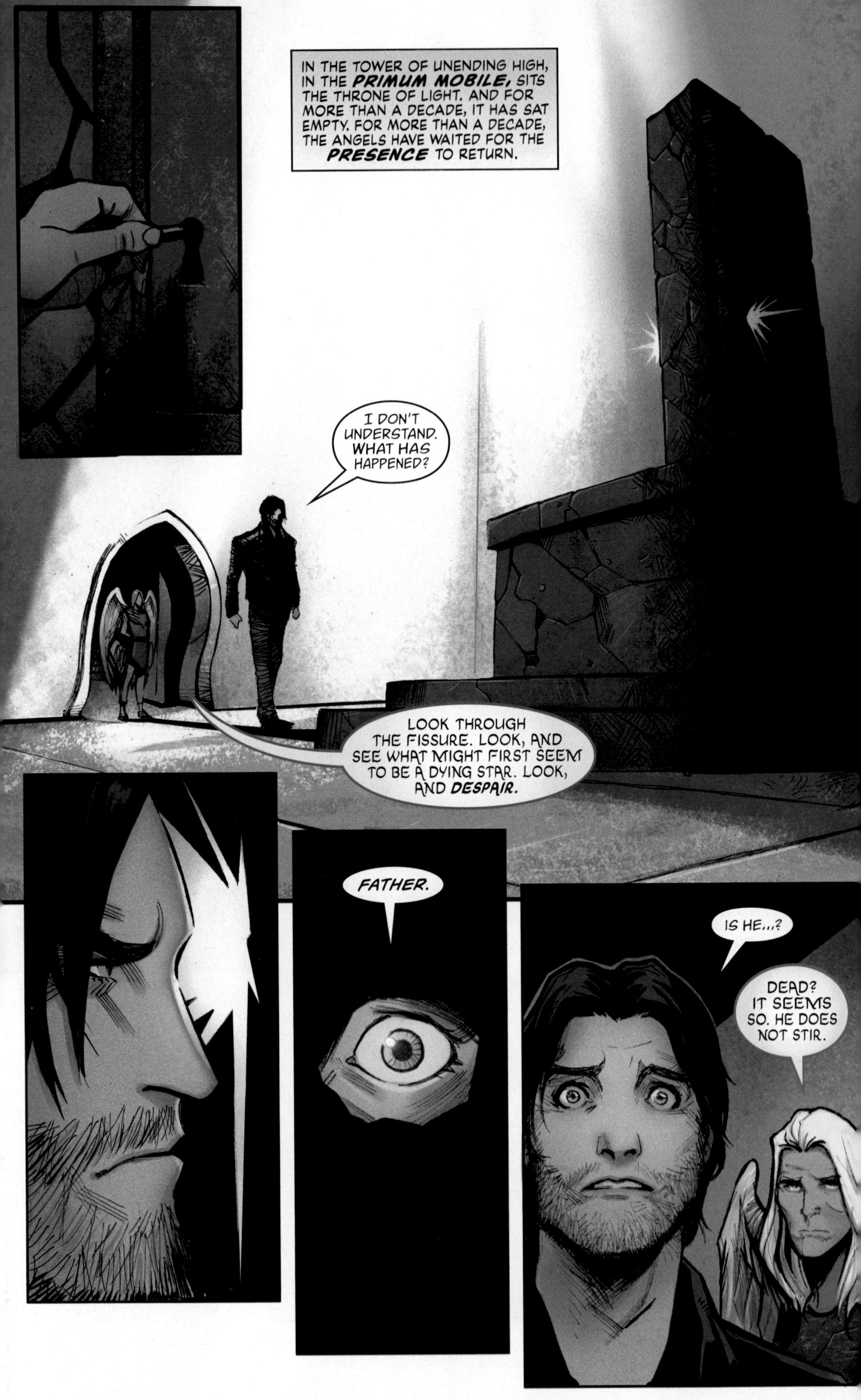
IN THE TOWER OF UNENDING HIGH, IN THE **PRIMUM MOBILE,** SITS THE THRONE OF LIGHT. AND FOR MORE THAN A DECADE, IT HAS SAT EMPTY. FOR MORE THAN A DECADE, THE ANGELS HAVE WAITED FOR THE **PRESENCE** TO RETURN.
I DON'T UNDERSTAND. WHAT HAS HAPPENED?
LOOK THROUGH THE FISSURE. LOOK, AND SEE WHAT MIGHT FIRST SEEM TO BE A DYING STAR. LOOK, AND **DESPAIR.**
FATHER.
IS HE...?
DEAD? IT SEEMS SO. HE DOES NOT STIR.

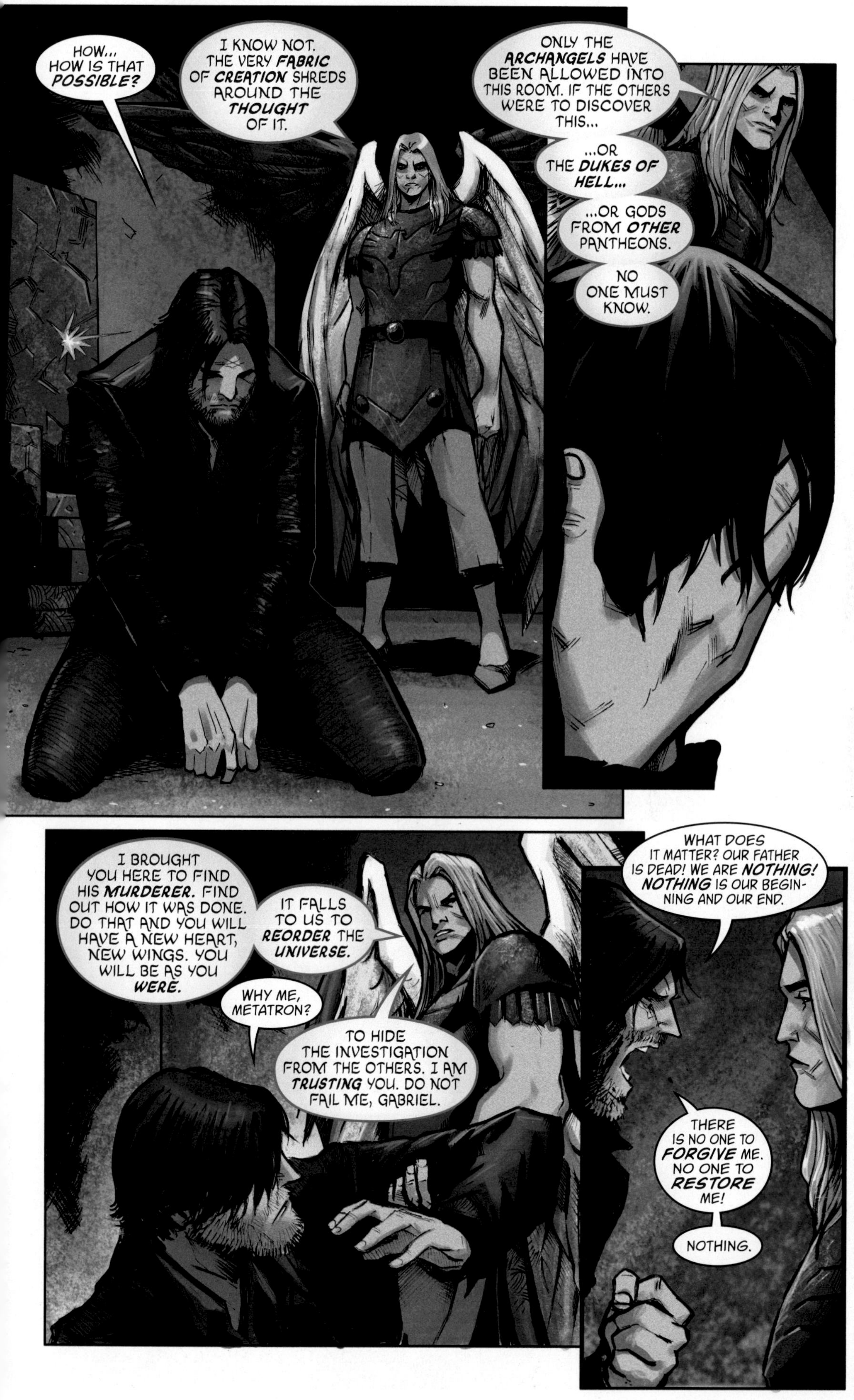
HOW... HOW IS THAT POSSIBLE?
I KNOW NOT. THE VERY FABRIC OF CREATION SHREDS AROUND THE THOUGHT OF IT.
ONLY THE ARCHANGELS HAVE BEEN ALLOWED INTO THIS ROOM. IF THE OTHERS WERE TO DISCOVER THIS...
...OR THE DUKES OF HELL...
...OR GODS FROM OTHER PANTHEONS.
NO ONE MUST KNOW.
I BROUGHT YOU HERE TO FIND HIS MURDERER. FIND OUT HOW IT WAS DONE. DO THAT AND YOU WILL HAVE A NEW HEART, NEW WINGS. YOU WILL BE AS YOU WERE.
IT FALLS TO US TO REORDER THE UNIVERSE.
WHY ME, METATRON?
TO HIDE THE INVESTIGATION FROM THE OTHERS. I AM TRUSTING YOU. DO NOT FAIL ME, GABRIEL.
WHAT DOES IT MATTER? OUR FATHER IS DEAD! WE ARE NOTHING! NOTHING IS OUR BEGIN-NING AND OUR END.
THERE IS NO ONE TO FORGIVE ME. NO ONE TO RESTORE ME!
NOTHING.

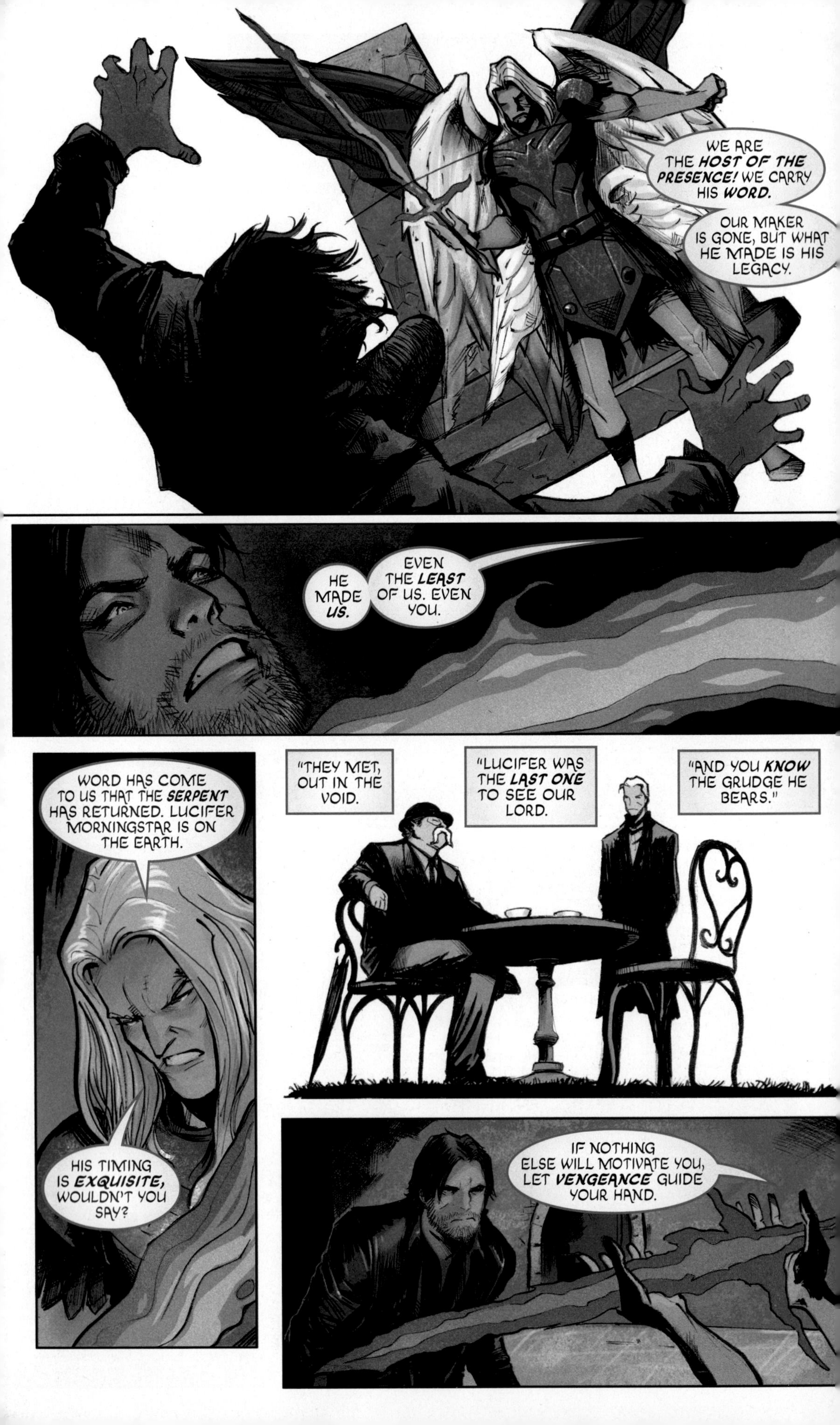
WE ARE THE HOST OF THE PRESENCE! WE CARRY HIS WORD.
OUR MAKER IS GONE, BUT WHAT HE MADE IS HIS LEGACY.
HE MADE US.
EVEN THE LEAST OF US. EVEN YOU.
WORD HAS COME TO US THAT THE SERPENT HAS RETURNED. LUCIFER MORNINGSTAR IS ON THE EARTH.
HIS TIMING IS EXQUISITE, WOULDN'T YOU SAY?
"THEY MET, OUT IN THE VOID.
"LUCIFER WAS THE LAST ONE TO SEE OUR LORD.
"AND YOU KNOW THE GRUDGE HE BEARS."
IF NOTHING ELSE WILL MOTIVATE YOU, LET VENGEANCE GUIDE YOUR HAND.

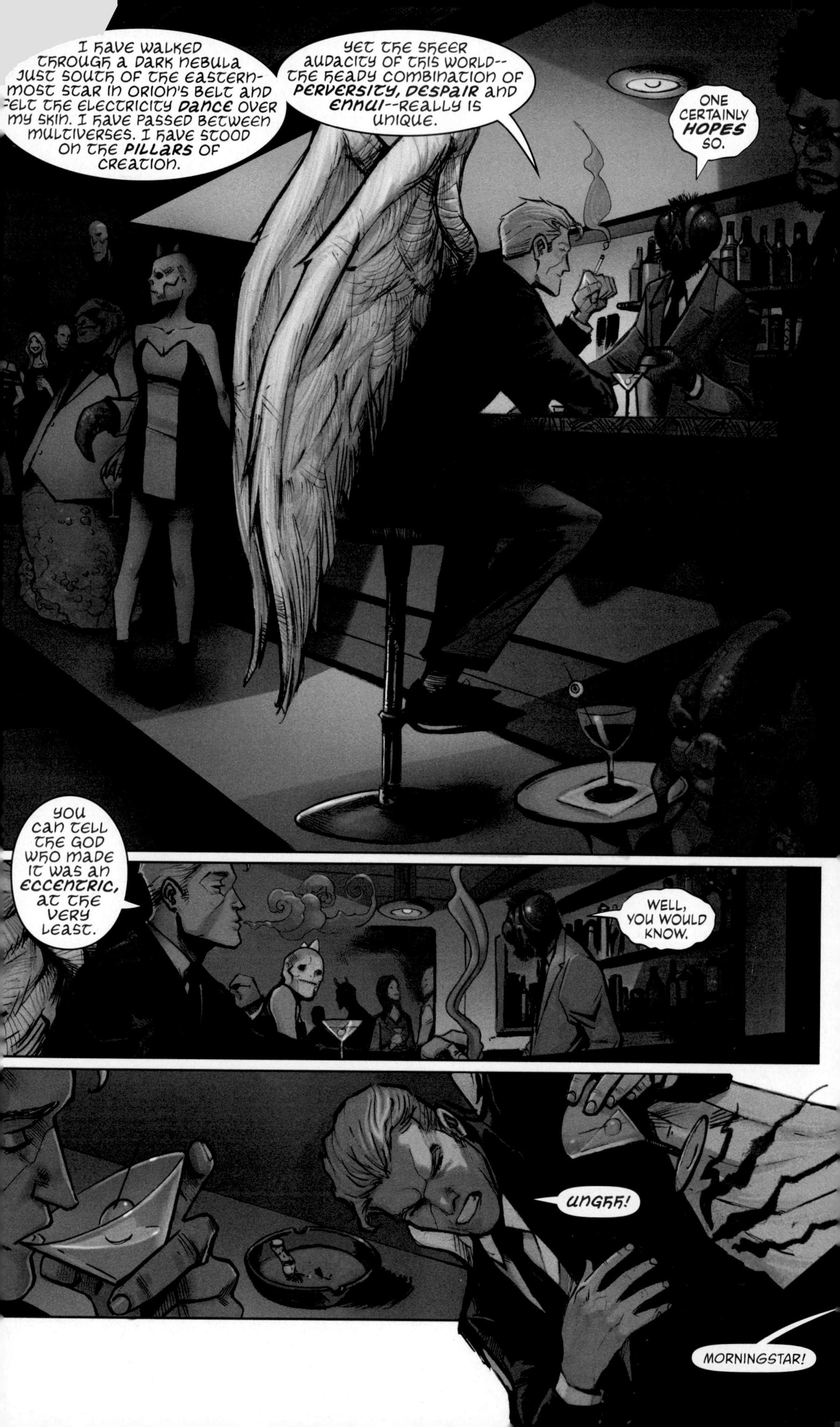
I HAVE WALKED THROUGH A DARK NEBULA JUST SOUTH OF THE EASTERN-MOST STAR IN ORION'S BELT AND FELT THE ELECTRICITY DANCE OVER MY SKIN. I HAVE PASSED BETWEEN MULTIVERSES. I HAVE STOOD ON THE PILLARS OF CREATION.
YET THE SHEER AUDACITY OF THIS WORLD--THE HEADY COMBINATION OF PERVERSITY, DESPAIR AND ENNUI--REALLY IS UNIQUE.
ONE CERTAINLY HOPES SO.
YOU CAN TELL THE GOD WHO MADE IT WAS AN ECCENTRIC, AT THE VERY LEAST.
WELL, YOU WOULD KNOW.
UNGHH!
MORNINGSTAR!

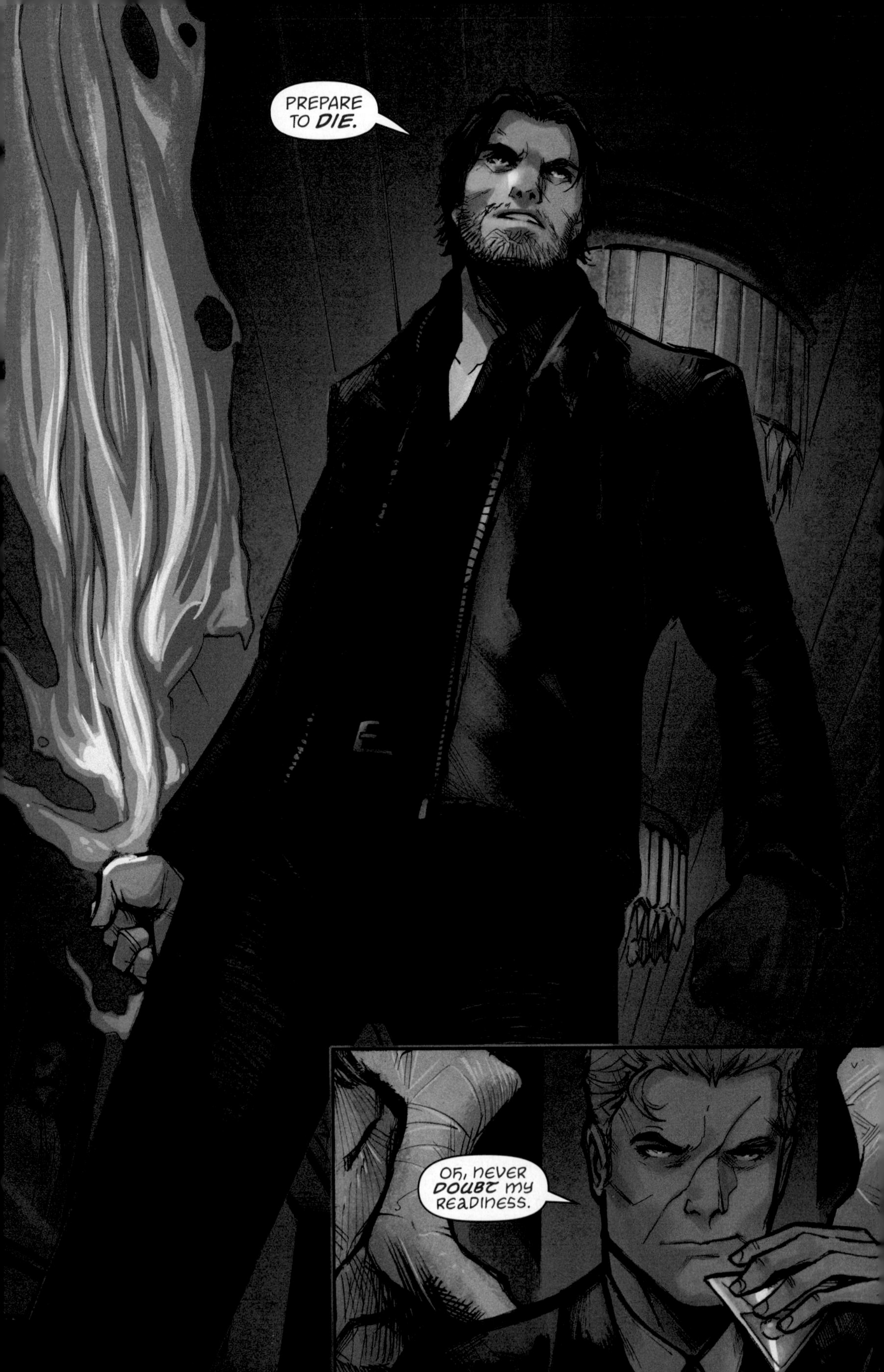
PREPARE TO DIE.
OH, NEVER DOUBT MY READINESS.

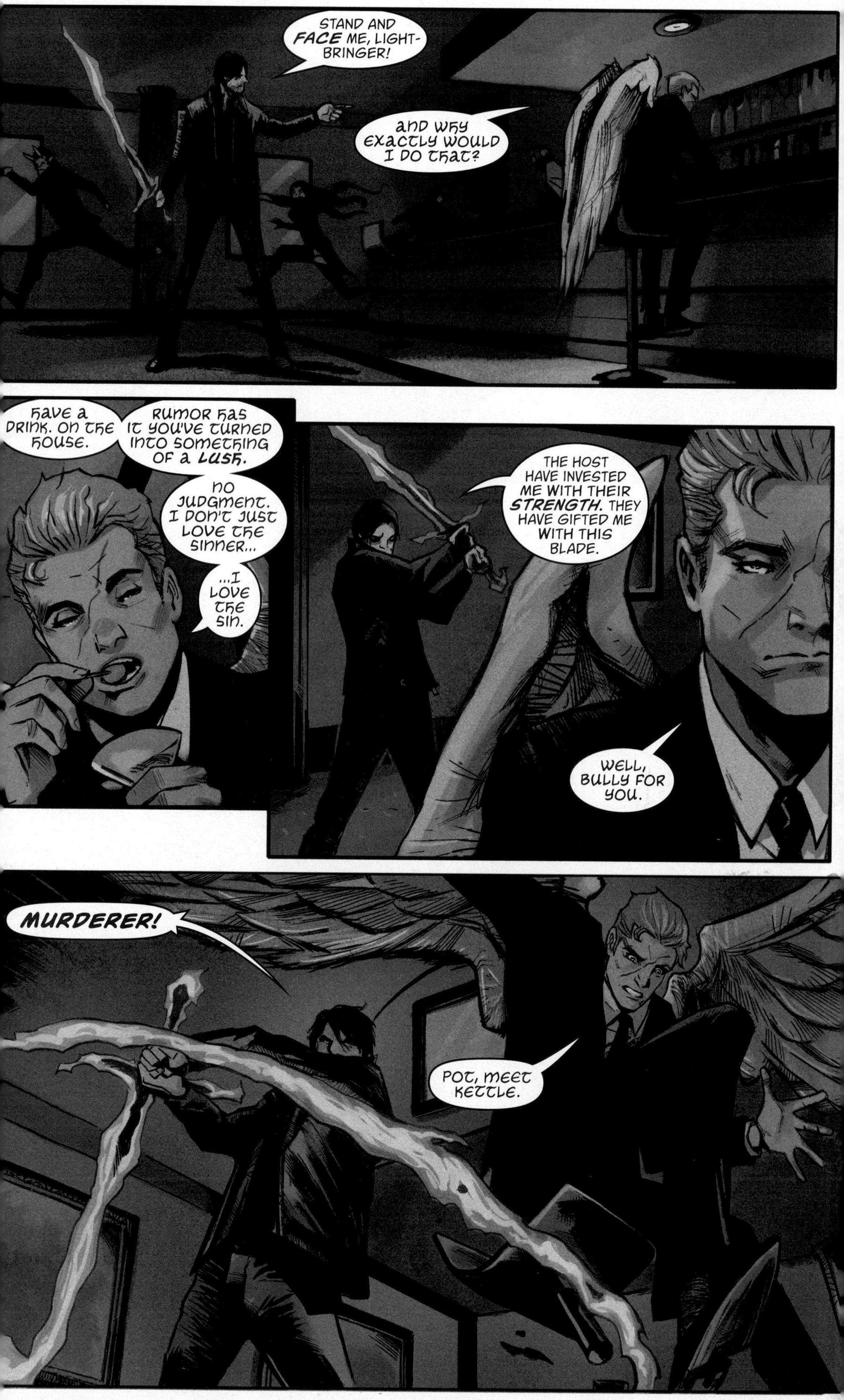
STAND AND FACE ME, LIGHT-BRINGER!
AND WHY EXACTLY WOULD I DO THAT?
HAVE A DRINK. ON THE HOUSE.
RUMOR HAS IT YOU'VE TURNED INTO SOMETHING OF A LUSH.
NO JUDGMENT. I DON'T JUST LOVE THE SINNER...
...I LOVE THE SIN.
THE HOST HAVE INVESTED ME WITH THEIR STRENGTH. THEY HAVE GIFTED ME WITH THIS BLADE.
WELL, BULLY FOR YOU.
MURDERER!
POT, MEET KETTLE.

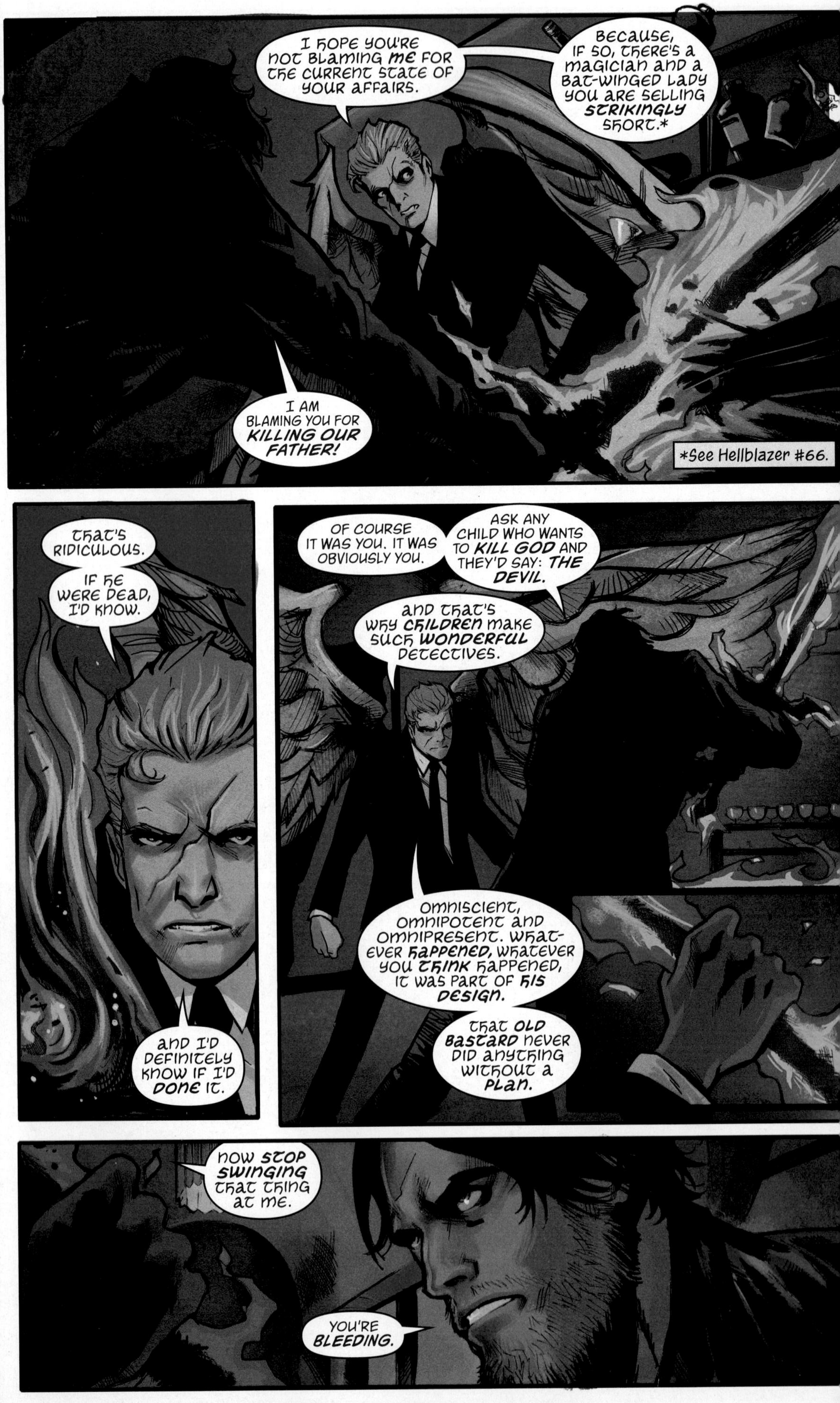
I HOPE YOU'RE NOT BLAMING ME FOR THE CURRENT STATE OF YOUR AFFAIRS.
BECAUSE, IF SO, THERE'S A MAGICIAN AND A BAT-WINGED LADY YOU ARE SELLING STRIKINGLY SHORT.*
I AM BLAMING YOU FOR KILLING OUR FATHER!
*See Hellblazer #66.
THAT'S RIDICULOUS.
IF HE WERE DEAD, I'D KNOW.
AND I'D DEFINITELY KNOW IF I'D DONE IT.
OF COURSE IT WAS YOU. IT WAS OBVIOUSLY YOU.
ASK ANY CHILD WHO WANTS TO KILL GOD AND THEY'D SAY: THE DEVIL.
AND THAT'S WHY CHILDREN MAKE SUCH WONDERFUL DETECTIVES.
OMNISCIENT, OMNIPOTENT AND OMNIPRESENT. WHAT-EVER HAPPENED, WHATEVER YOU THINK HAPPENED, IT WAS PART OF HIS DESIGN.
THAT OLD BASTARD NEVER DID ANYTHING WITHOUT A PLAN.
NOW STOP SWINGING THAT THING AT ME.
YOU'RE BLEEDING.

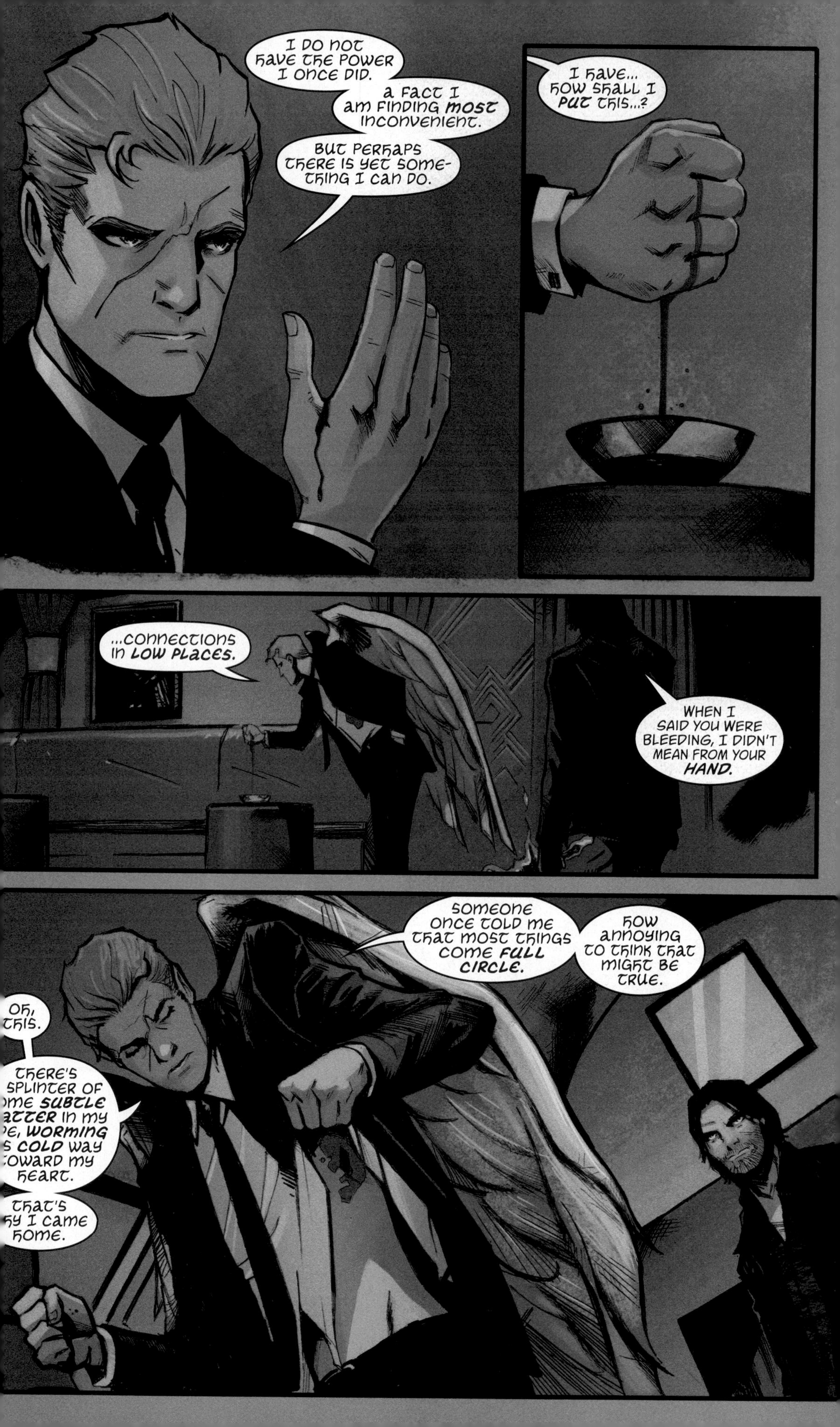
I DO NOT HAVE THE POWER I ONCE DID.
A FACT I AM FINDING MOST INCONVENIENT.
BUT PERHAPS THERE IS YET SOME-THING I CAN DO.
I HAVE... HOW SHALL I PUT THIS...?
...CONNECTIONS IN LOW PLACES.
WHEN I SAID YOU WERE BLEEDING, I DIDN'T MEAN FROM YOUR HAND.
SOMEONE ONCE TOLD ME THAT MOST THINGS COME FULL CIRCLE.
HOW ANNOYING TO THINK THAT MIGHT BE TRUE.
OH, THIS.
THERE'S SPLINTER OF OME SUBTLE ATTER IN MY E, WORMING S COLD WAY TOWARD MY HEART.
THAT'S HY I CAME HOME.

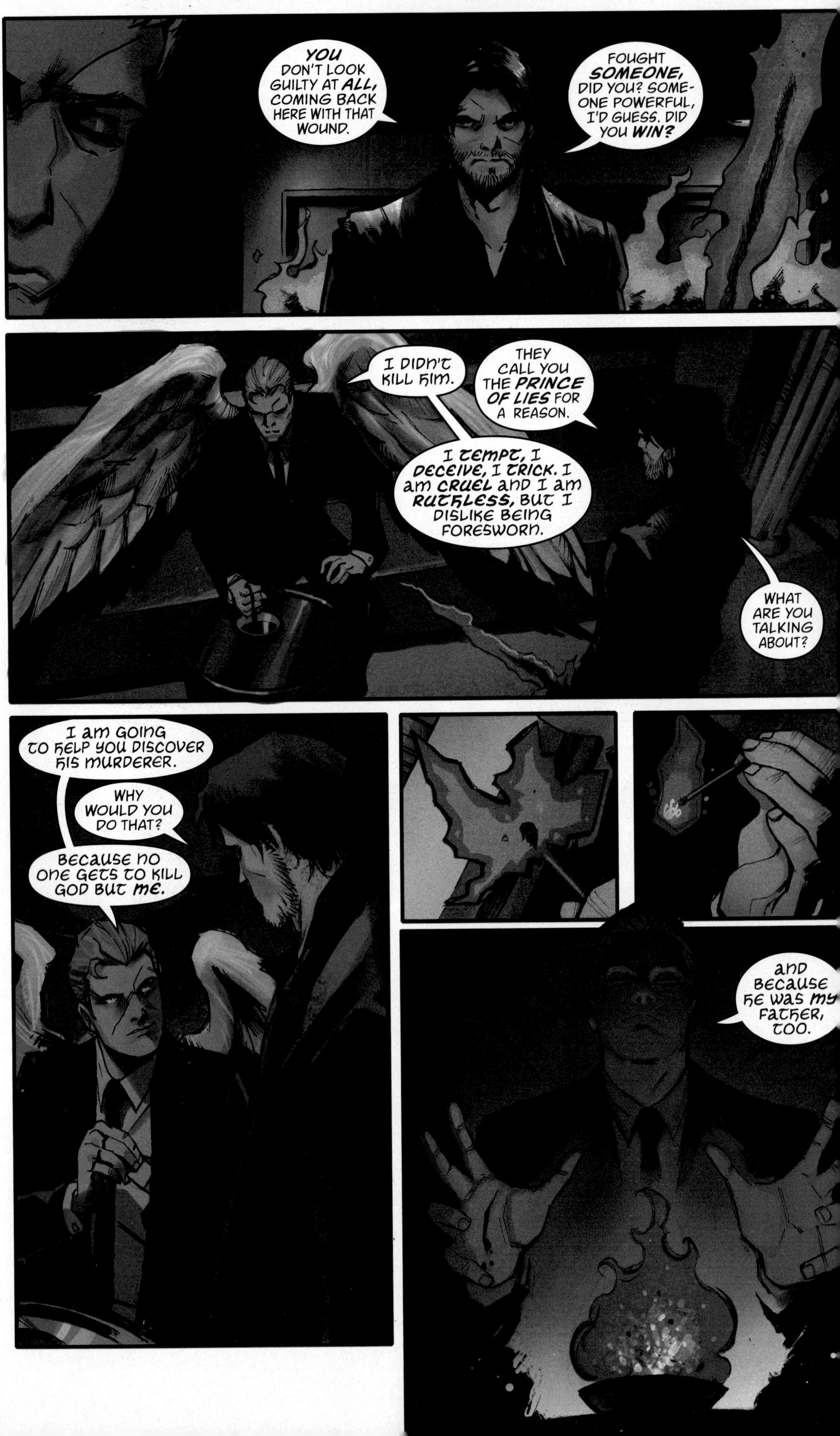
YOU DON'T LOOK GUILTY AT ALL, COMING BACK HERE WITH THAT WOUND.
FOUGHT SOMEONE, DID YOU? SOME-ONE POWERFUL, I'D GUESS. DID YOU WIN?
I DIDN'T KILL HIM.
THEY CALL YOU THE PRINCE OF LIES FOR A REASON.
I TEMPT, I DECEIVE, I TRICK. I AM CRUEL AND I AM RUTHLESS, BUT I DISLIKE BEING FORESWORN.
WHAT ARE YOU TALKING ABOUT?
I AM GOING TO HELP YOU DISCOVER HIS MURDERER.
WHY WOULD YOU DO THAT?
BECAUSE NO ONE GETS TO KILL GOD BUT ME.
AND BECAUSE HE WAS MY FATHER, TOO.

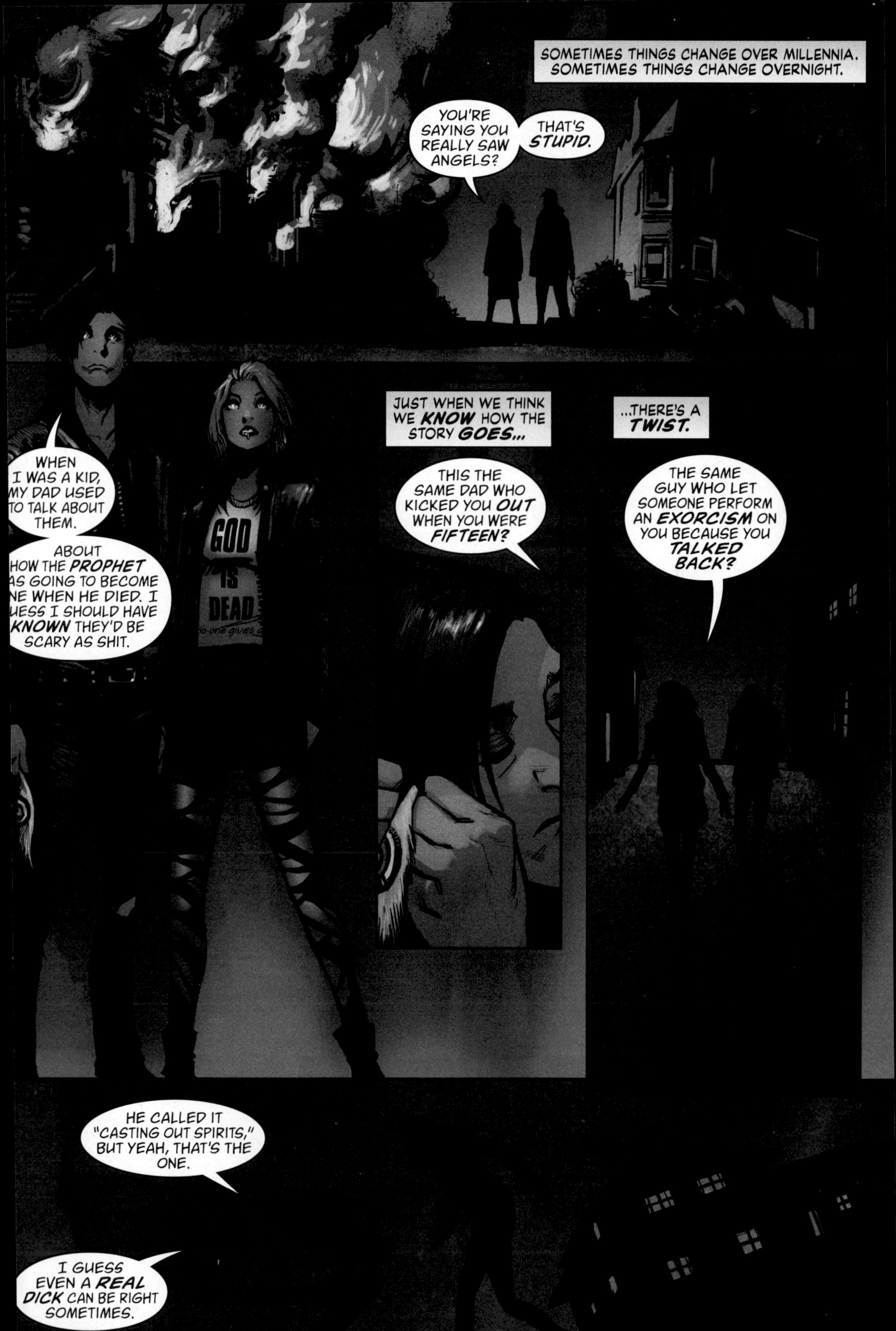
SOMETIMES THINGS CHANGE OVER MILLENNIA. SOMETIMES THINGS CHANGE OVERNIGHT.
YOU'RE SAYING YOU REALLY SAW ANGELS?
THAT'S STUPID.
WHEN I WAS A KID, MY DAD USED TO TALK ABOUT THEM.
ABOUT HOW THE PROPHET AS GOING TO BECOME NE WHEN HE DIED. I UESS I SHOULD HAVE KNOWN THEY'D BE SCARY AS SHIT.
GOD IS DEAD
JUST WHEN WE THINK WE KNOW HOW THE STORY GOES...
THIS THE SAME DAD WHO KICKED YOU OUT WHEN YOU WERE FIFTEEN?
...THERE'S A TWIST.
THE SAME GUY WHO LET SOMEONE PERFORM AN EXORCISM ON YOU BECAUSE YOU TALKED BACK?
HE CALLED IT "CASTING OUT SPIRITS," BUT YEAH, THAT'S THE ONE.
I GUESS EVEN A REAL DICK CAN BE RIGHT SOMETIMES.

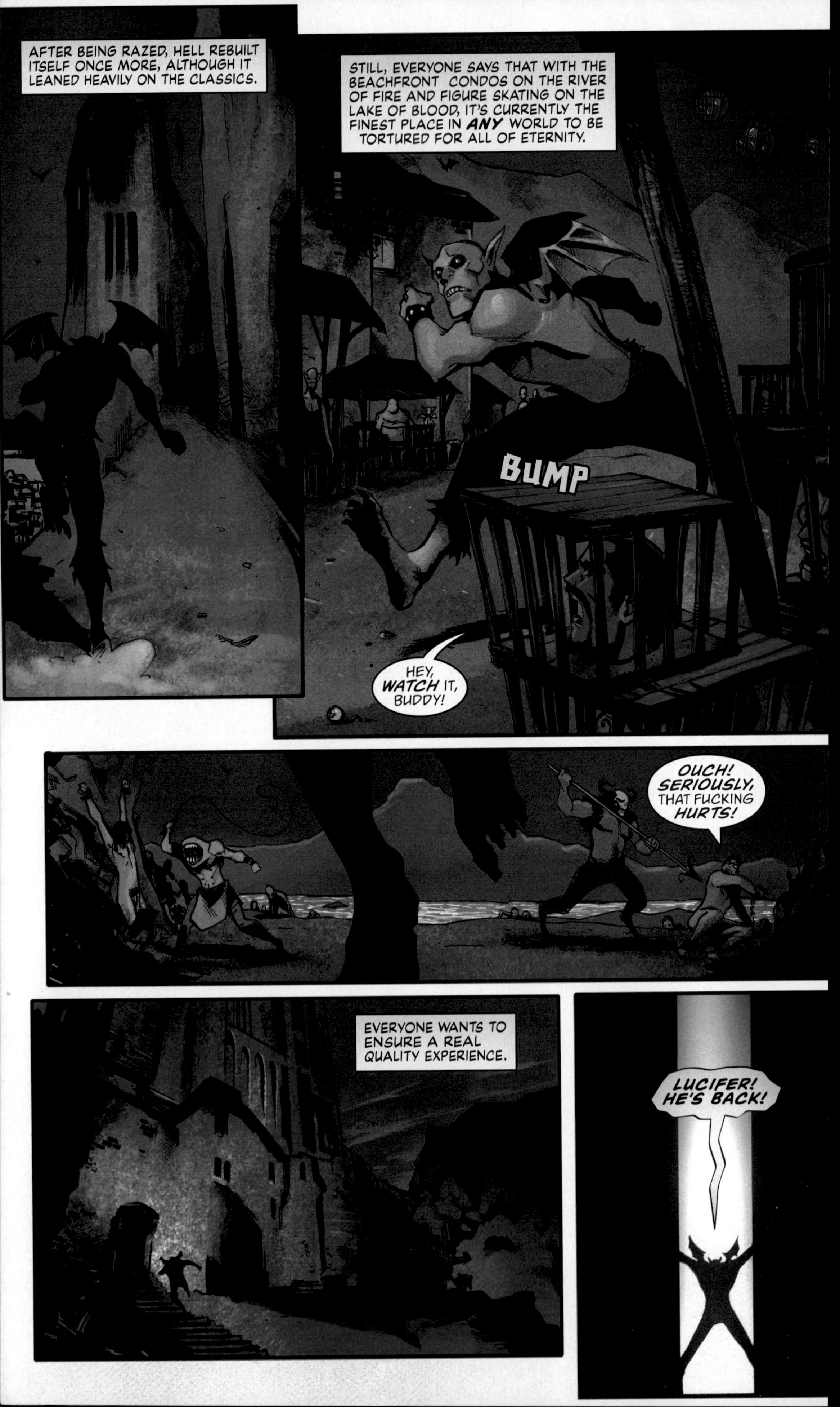

AFTER BEING RAZED, HELL REBUILT ITSELF ONCE MORE, ALTHOUGH IT LEANED HEAVILY ON THE CLASSICS.
STILL, EVERYONE SAYS THAT WITH THE BEACHFRONT CONDOS ON THE RIVER OF FIRE AND FIGURE SKATING ON THE LAKE OF BLOOD, IT'S CURRENTLY THE FINEST PLACE IN ANY WORLD TO BE TORTURED FOR ALL OF ETERNITY.
BUMP
HEY, WATCH IT, BUDDY!
OUCH! SERIOUSLY, THAT FUCKING HURTS!
EVERYONE WANTS TO ENSURE A REAL QUALITY EXPERIENCE.
LUCIFER! HE'S BACK!

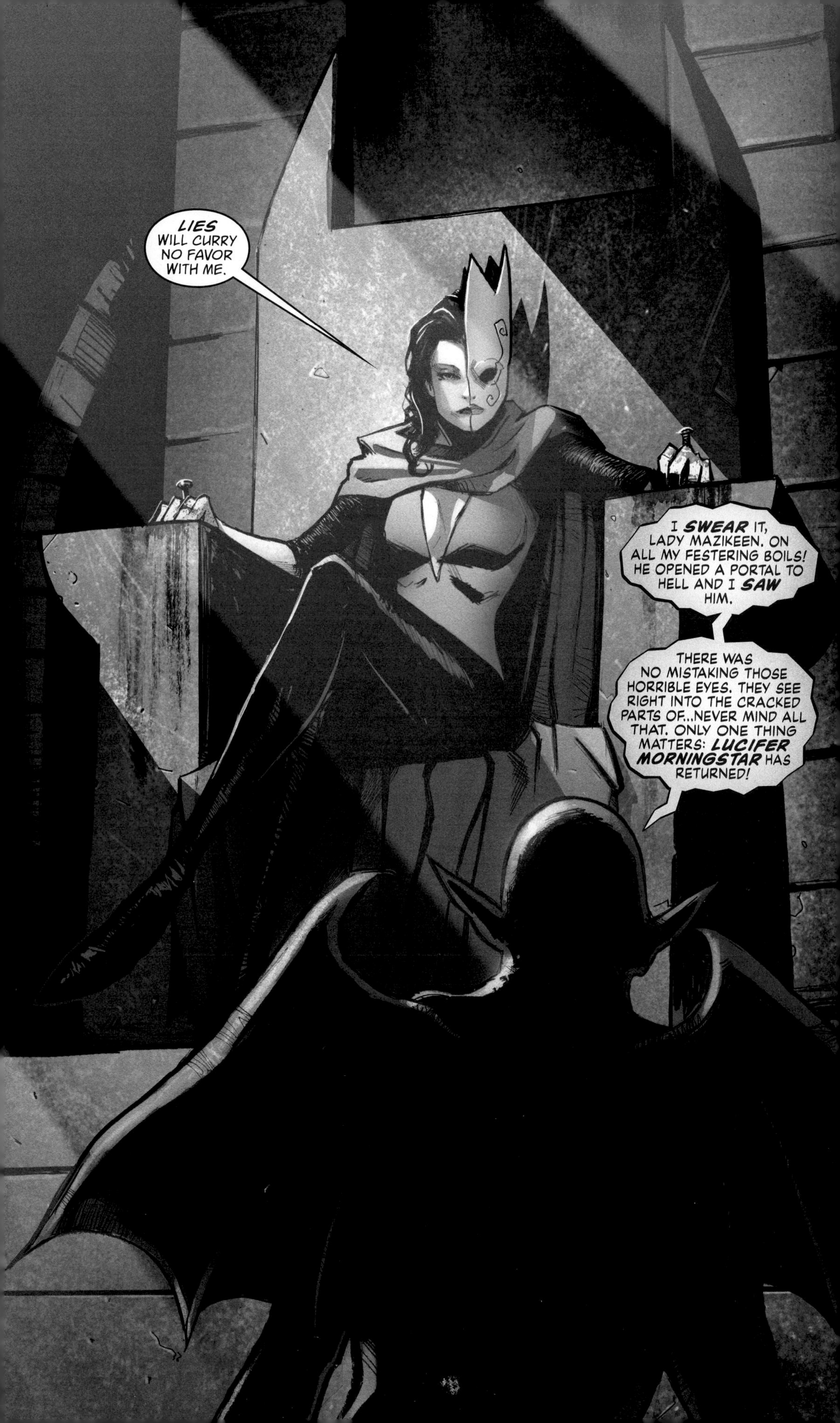
LIES WILL CURRY NO FAVOR WITH ME.
I SWEAR IT, LADY MAZIKEEN, ON ALL MY FESTERING BOILS! HE OPENED A PORTAL TO HELL AND I SAW HIM.
THERE WAS NO MISTAKING THOSE HORRIBLE EYES. THEY SEE RIGHT INTO THE CRACKED PARTS OF...NEVER MIND ALL THAT. ONLY ONE THING MATTERS: LUCIFER MORNINGSTAR HAS RETURNED!

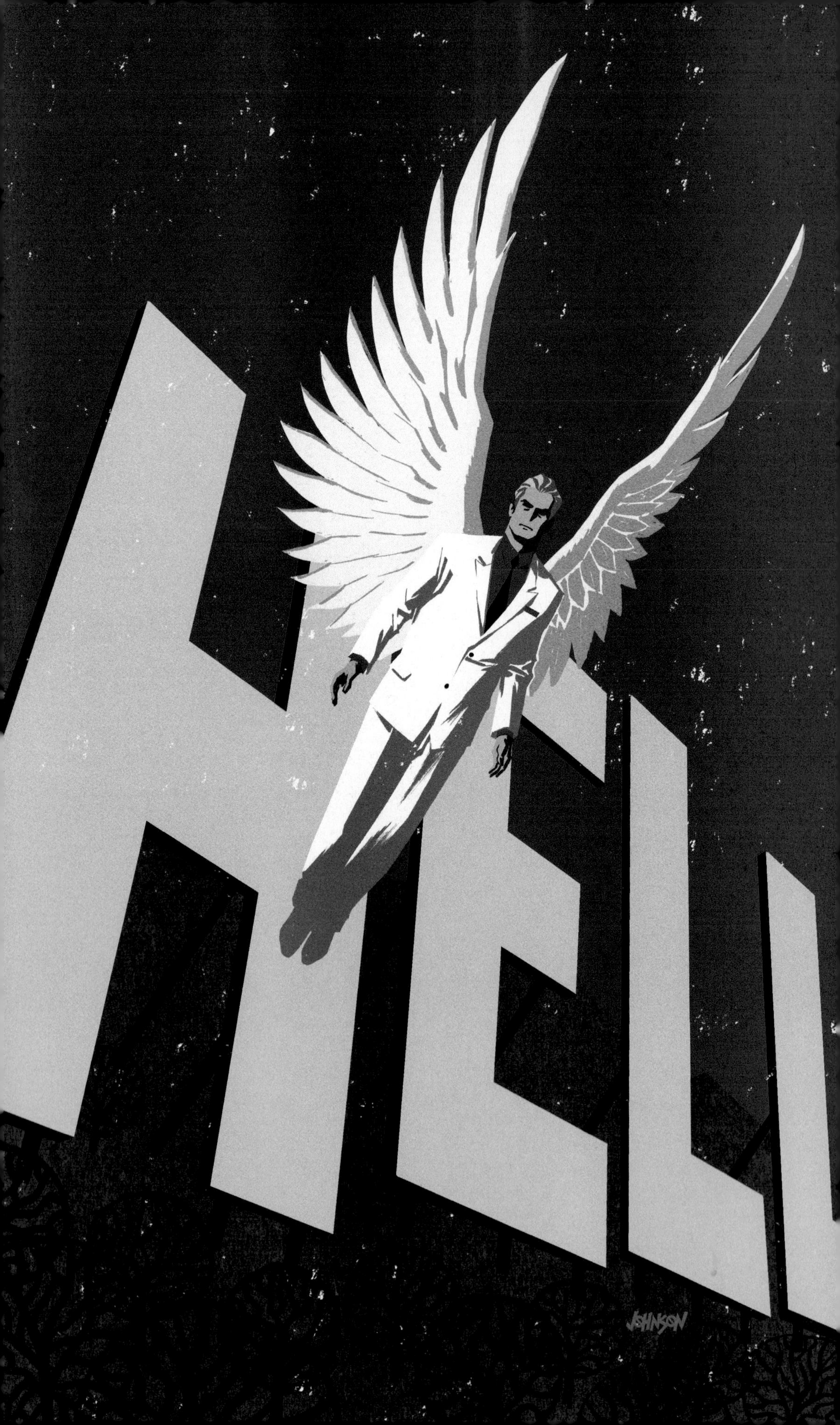
HELL
JOHNSON

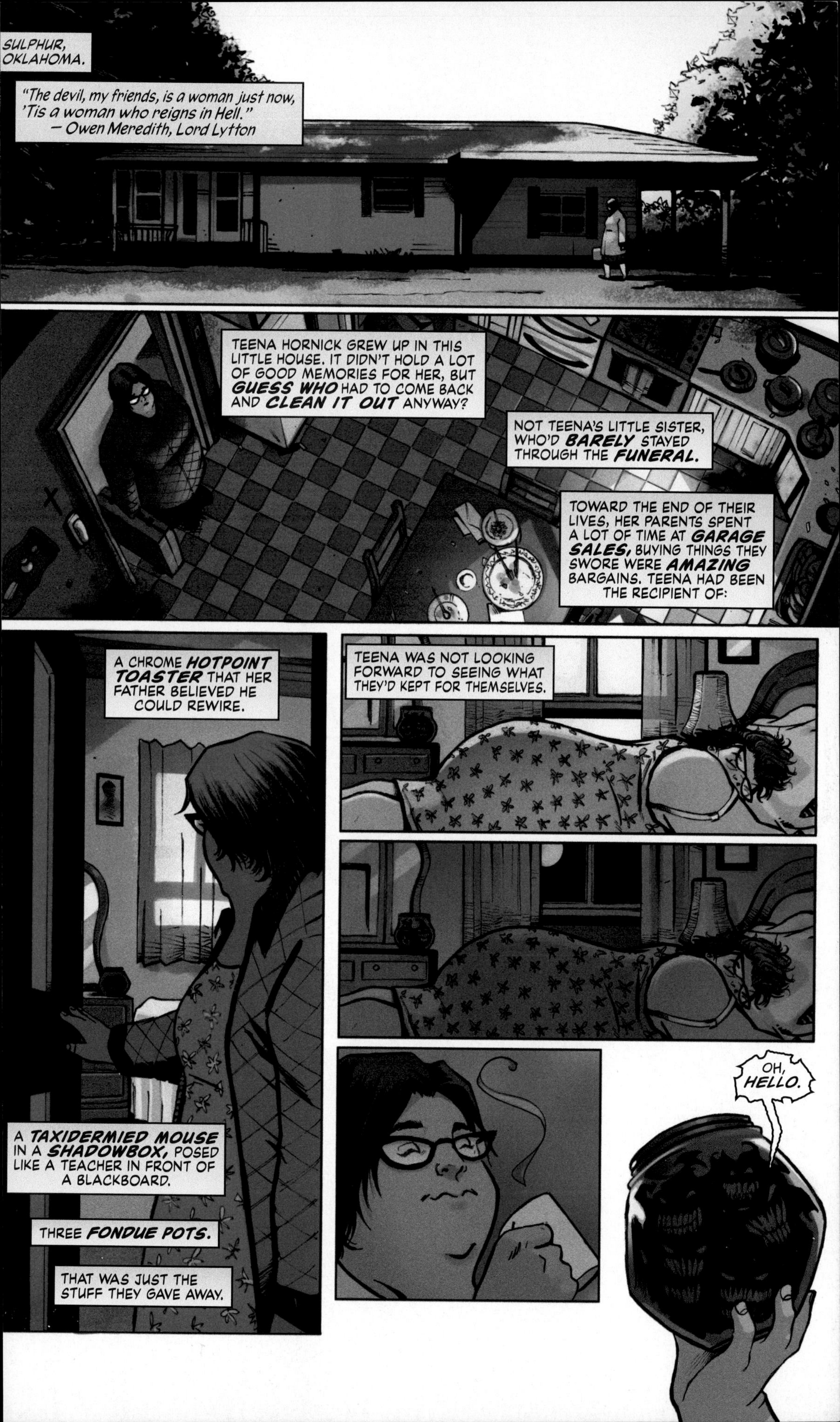
SULPHUR, OKLAHOMA.
"The devil, my friends, is a woman just now, 'Tis a woman who reigns in Hell." — Owen Meredith, Lord Lytton
TEENA HORNICK GREW UP IN THIS LITTLE HOUSE. IT DIDN'T HOLD A LOT OF GOOD MEMORIES FOR HER, BUT GUESS WHO HAD TO COME BACK AND CLEAN IT OUT ANYWAY?
NOT TEENA'S LITTLE SISTER, WHO'D BARELY STAYED THROUGH THE FUNERAL.
TOWARD THE END OF THEIR LIVES, HER PARENTS SPENT A LOT OF TIME AT GARAGE SALES, BUYING THINGS THEY SWORE WERE AMAZING BARGAINS. TEENA HAD BEEN THE RECIPIENT OF:
A CHROME HOTPOINT TOASTER THAT HER FATHER BELIEVED HE COULD REWIRE.
A TAXIDERMIED MOUSE IN A SHADOWBOX, POSED LIKE A TEACHER IN FRONT OF A BLACKBOARD.
THREE FONDUE POTS.
THAT WAS JUST THE STUFF THEY GAVE AWAY.
TEENA WAS NOT LOOKING FORWARD TO SEEING WHAT THEY'D KEPT FOR THEMSELVES.
OH, HELLO.

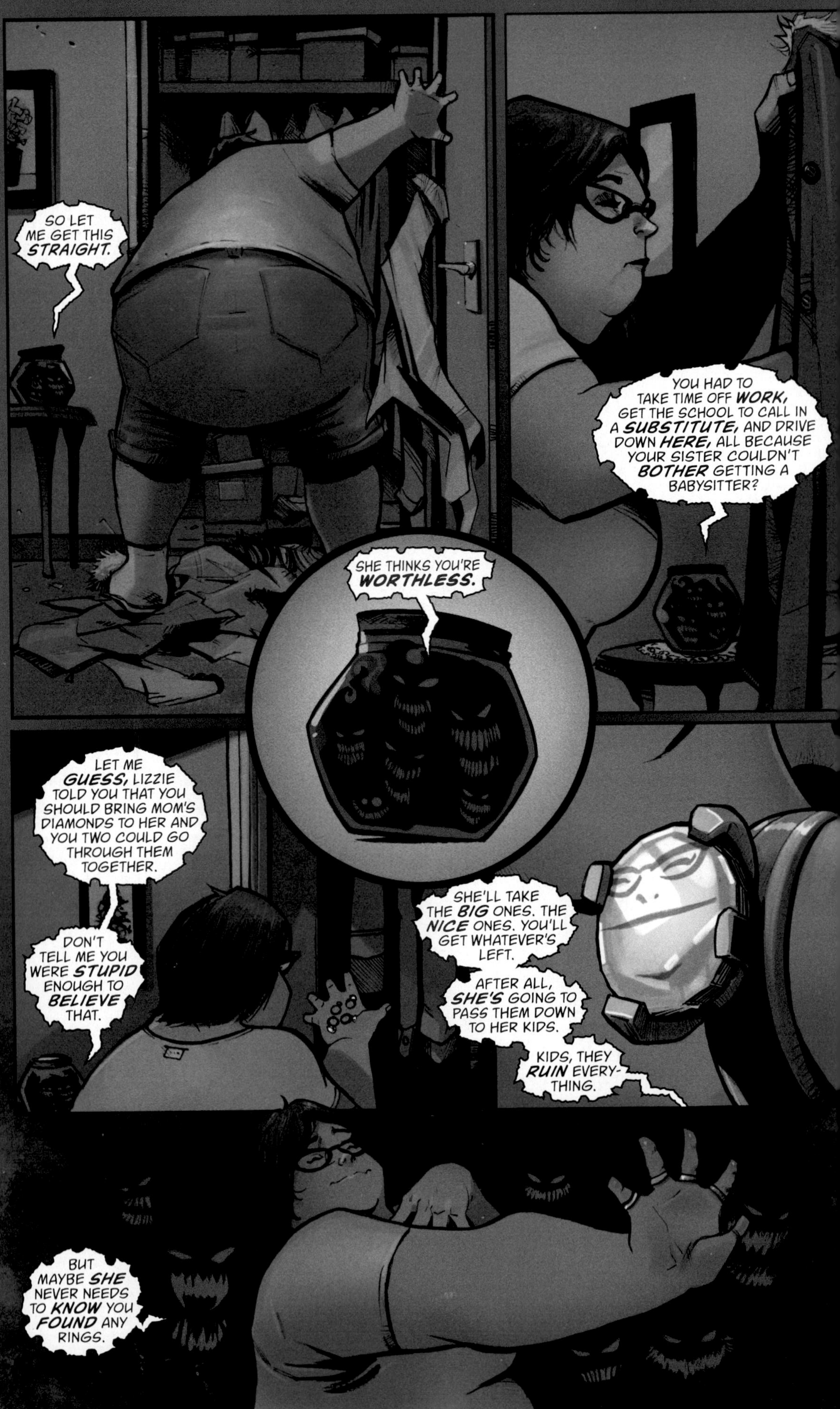
SO LET ME GET THIS STRAIGHT.
YOU HAD TO TAKE TIME OFF WORK, GET THE SCHOOL TO CALL IN A SUBSTITUTE, AND DRIVE DOWN HERE, ALL BECAUSE YOUR SISTER COULDN'T BOTHER GETTING A BABYSITTER?
SHE THINKS YOU'RE WORTHLESS.
LET ME GUESS, LIZZIE TOLD YOU THAT YOU SHOULD BRING MOM'S DIAMONDS TO HER AND YOU TWO COULD GO THROUGH THEM TOGETHER.
DON'T TELL ME YOU WERE STUPID ENOUGH TO BELIEVE THAT.
SHE'LL TAKE THE BIG ONES. THE NICE ONES. YOU'LL GET WHATEVER'S LEFT.
AFTER ALL, SHE'S GOING TO PASS THEM DOWN TO HER KIDS.
KIDS, THEY RUIN EVERY-THING.
BUT MAYBE SHE NEVER NEEDS TO KNOW YOU FOUND ANY RINGS.

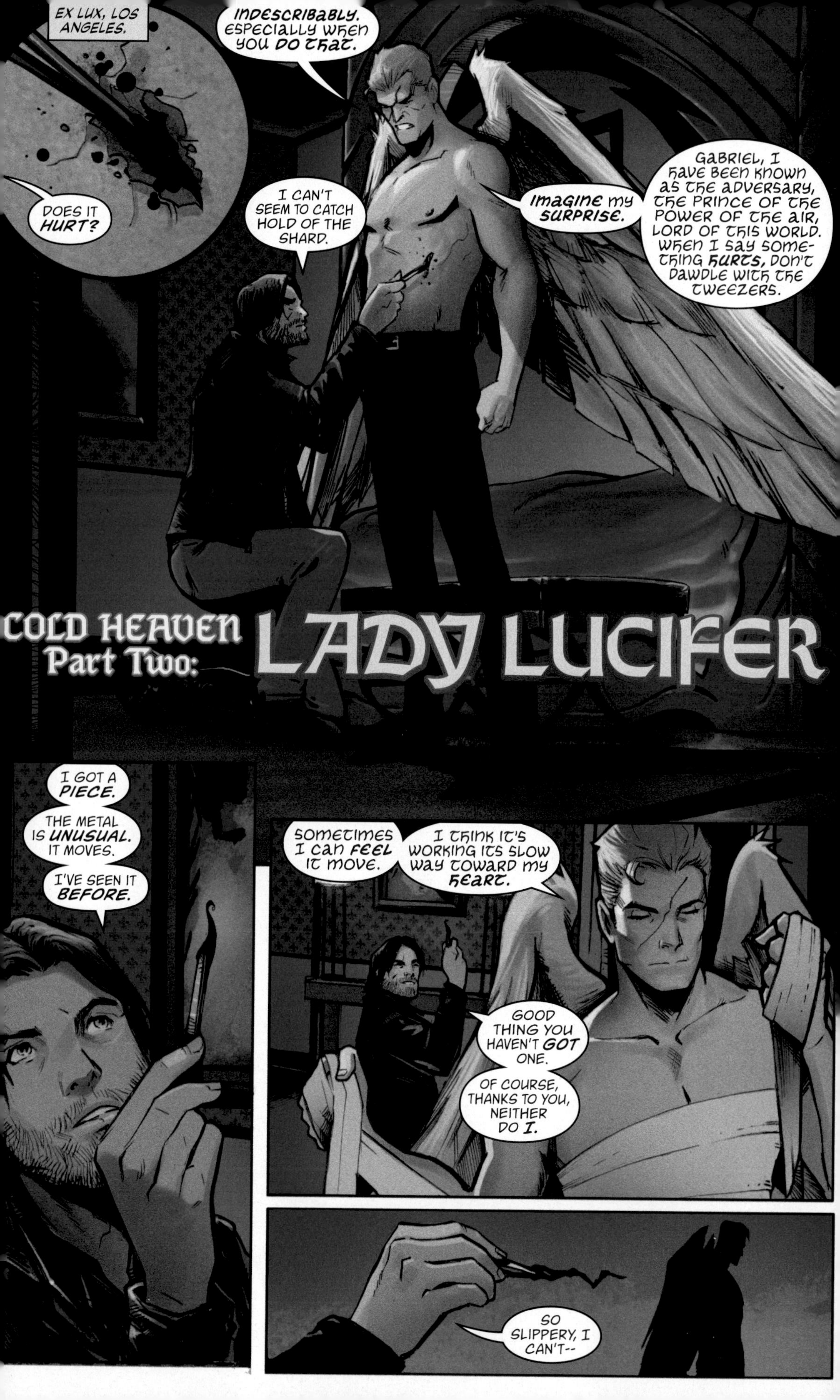

EX LUX, LOS ANGELES.
DOES IT HURT?
INDESCRIBABLY. ESPECIALLY WHEN YOU DO THAT.
I CAN'T SEEM TO CATCH HOLD OF THE SHARD.
IMAGINE MY SURPRISE.
GABRIEL, I HAVE BEEN KNOWN AS THE ADVERSARY, THE PRINCE OF THE POWER OF THE AIR, LORD OF THIS WORLD. WHEN I SAY SOMETHING HURTS, DON'T DAWDLE WITH THE TWEEZERS.
COLD HEAVEN Part Two: LADY LUCIFER
I GOT A PIECE.
THE METAL IS UNUSUAL. IT MOVES.
I'VE SEEN IT BEFORE.
SOMETIMES I CAN FEEL IT MOVE.
I THINK IT'S WORKING ITS SLOW WAY TOWARD MY HEART.
GOOD THING YOU HAVEN'T GOT ONE.
OF COURSE, THANKS TO YOU, NEITHER DO I.
SO SLIPPERY, I CAN'T--

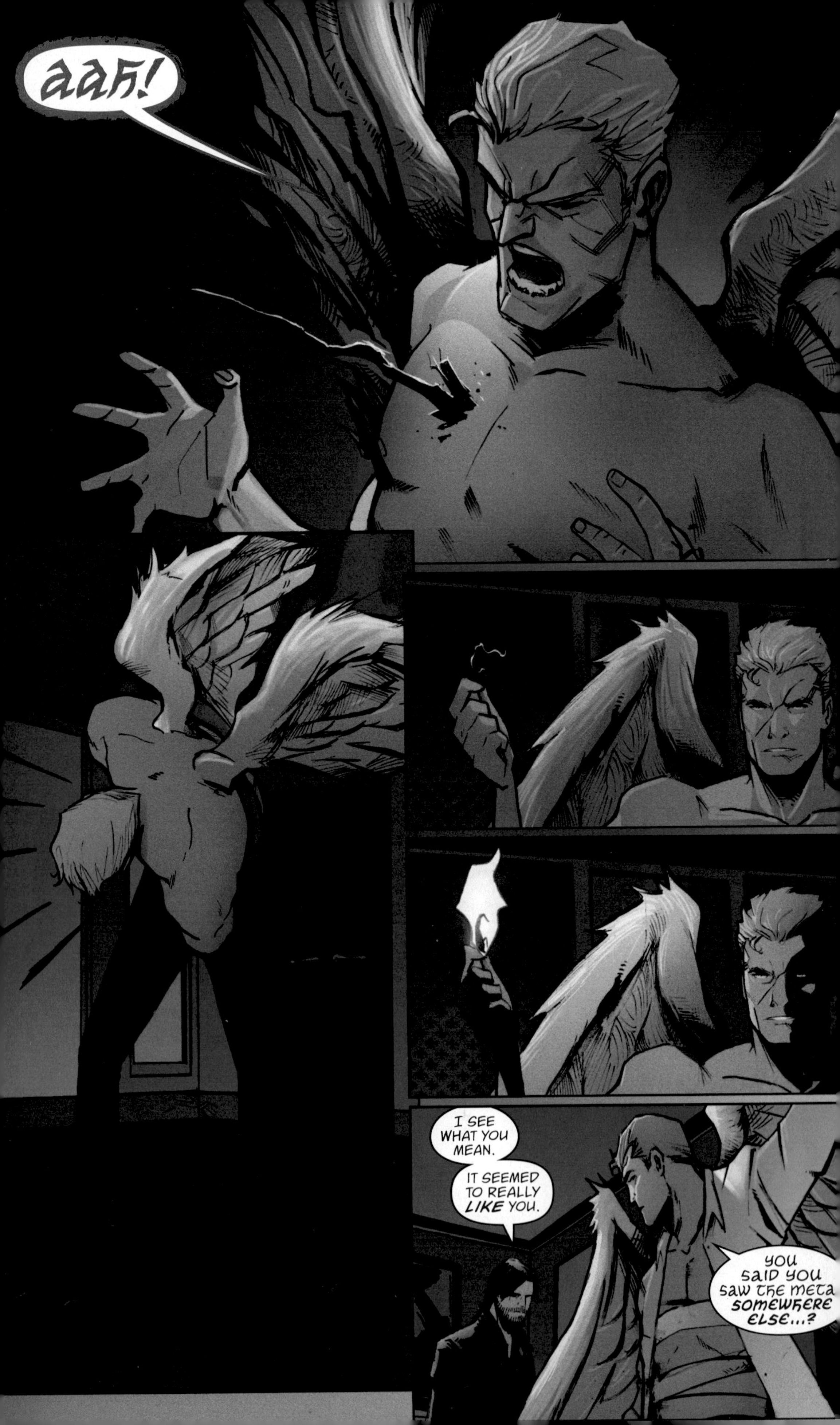
AAH!
I SEE WHAT YOU MEAN.
IT SEEMED TO REALLY *LIKE* YOU.
YOU SAID YOU SAW THE META *SOMEWHERE ELSE...?*

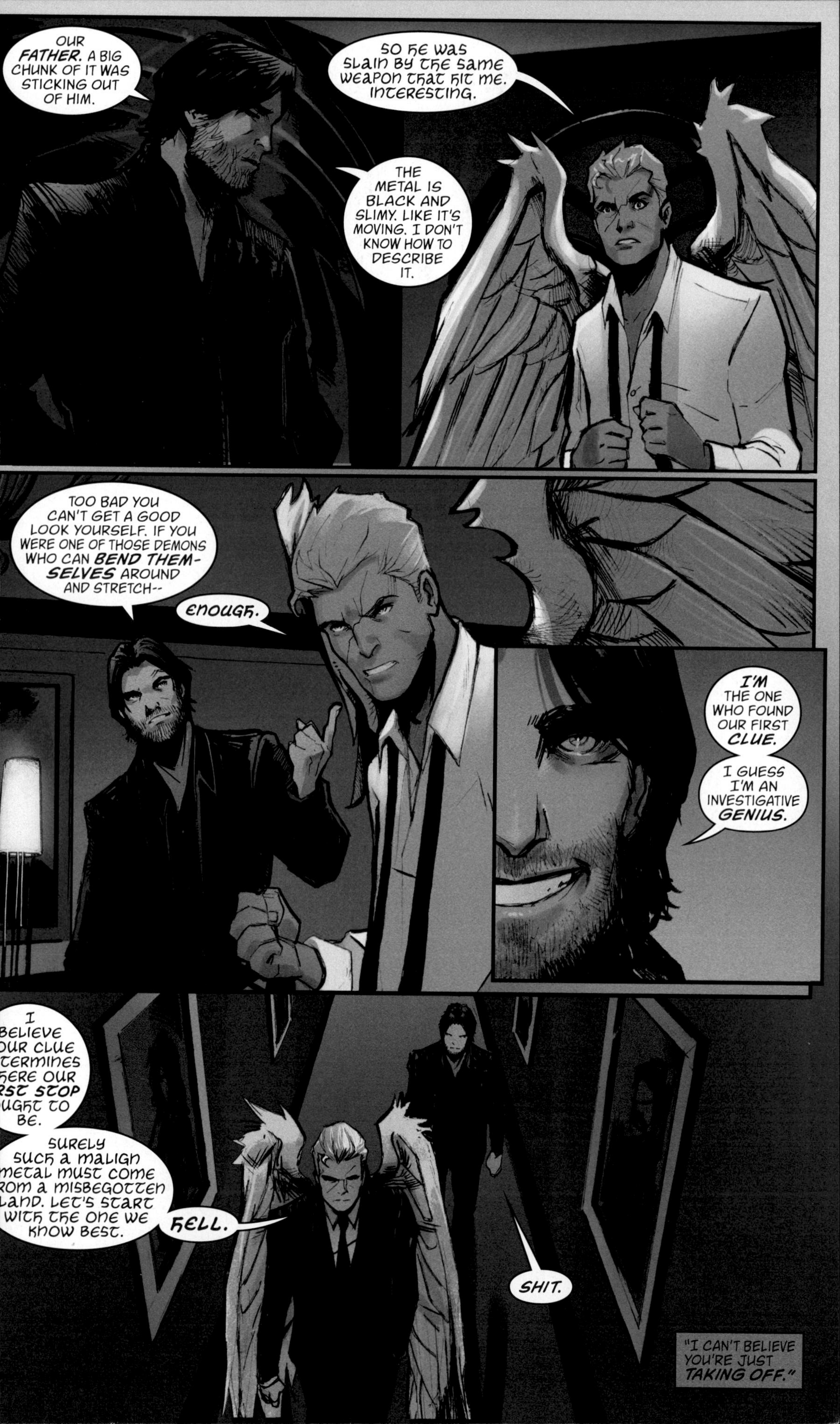
OUR FATHER. A BIG CHUNK OF IT WAS STICKING OUT OF HIM.
SO HE WAS SLAIN BY THE SAME WEAPON THAT HIT ME. INTERESTING.
THE METAL IS BLACK AND SLIMY. LIKE IT'S MOVING. I DON'T KNOW HOW TO DESCRIBE IT.
TOO BAD YOU CAN'T GET A GOOD LOOK YOURSELF. IF YOU WERE ONE OF THOSE DEMONS WHO CAN BEND THEM-SELVES AROUND AND STRETCH--
ENOUGH.
I'M THE ONE WHO FOUND OUR FIRST CLUE.
I GUESS I'M AN INVESTIGATIVE GENIUS.
I BELIEVE OUR CLUE DETERMINES WHERE OUR FIRST STOP OUGHT TO BE.
SURELY SUCH A MALIGN METAL MUST COME FROM A MISBEGOTTEN LAND. LET'S START WITH THE ONE WE KNOW BEST.
HELL.
SHIT.
"I CAN'T BELIEVE YOU'RE JUST TAKING OFF."

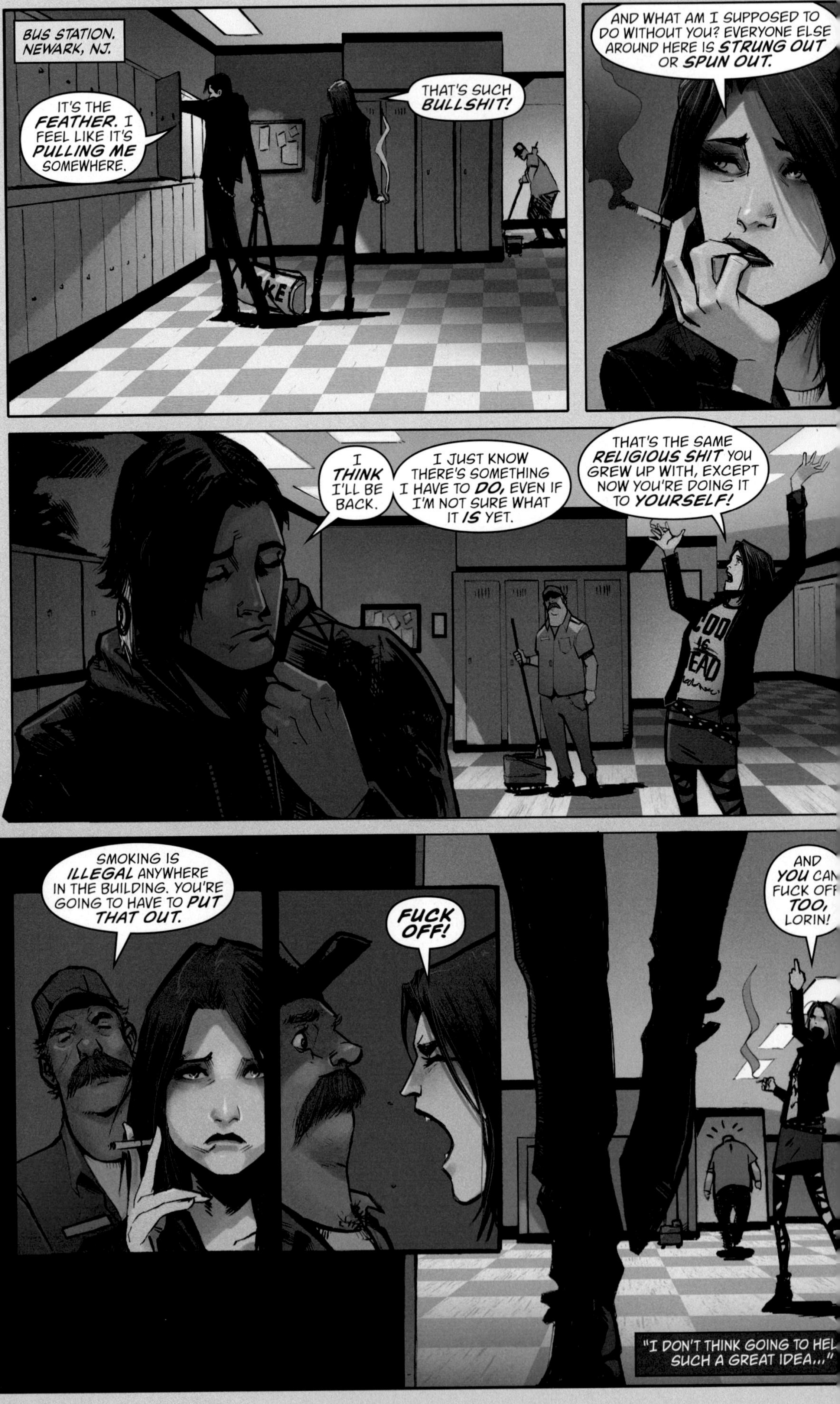
BUS STATION. NEWARK, NJ.
IT'S THE FEATHER. I FEEL LIKE IT'S PULLING ME SOMEWHERE.
THAT'S SUCH BULLSHIT!
AND WHAT AM I SUPPOSED TO DO WITHOUT YOU? EVERYONE ELSE AROUND HERE IS STRUNG OUT OR SPUN OUT.
I THINK I'LL BE BACK.
I JUST KNOW THERE'S SOMETHING I HAVE TO DO, EVEN IF I'M NOT SURE WHAT IT IS YET.
THAT'S THE SAME RELIGIOUS SHIT YOU GREW UP WITH, EXCEPT NOW YOU'RE DOING IT TO YOURSELF!
SMOKING IS ILLEGAL ANYWHERE IN THE BUILDING. YOU'RE GOING TO HAVE TO PUT THAT OUT.
FUCK OFF!
AND YOU CAN FUCK OFF TOO, LORIN!
"I DON'T THINK GOING TO HEL SUCH A GREAT IDEA..."

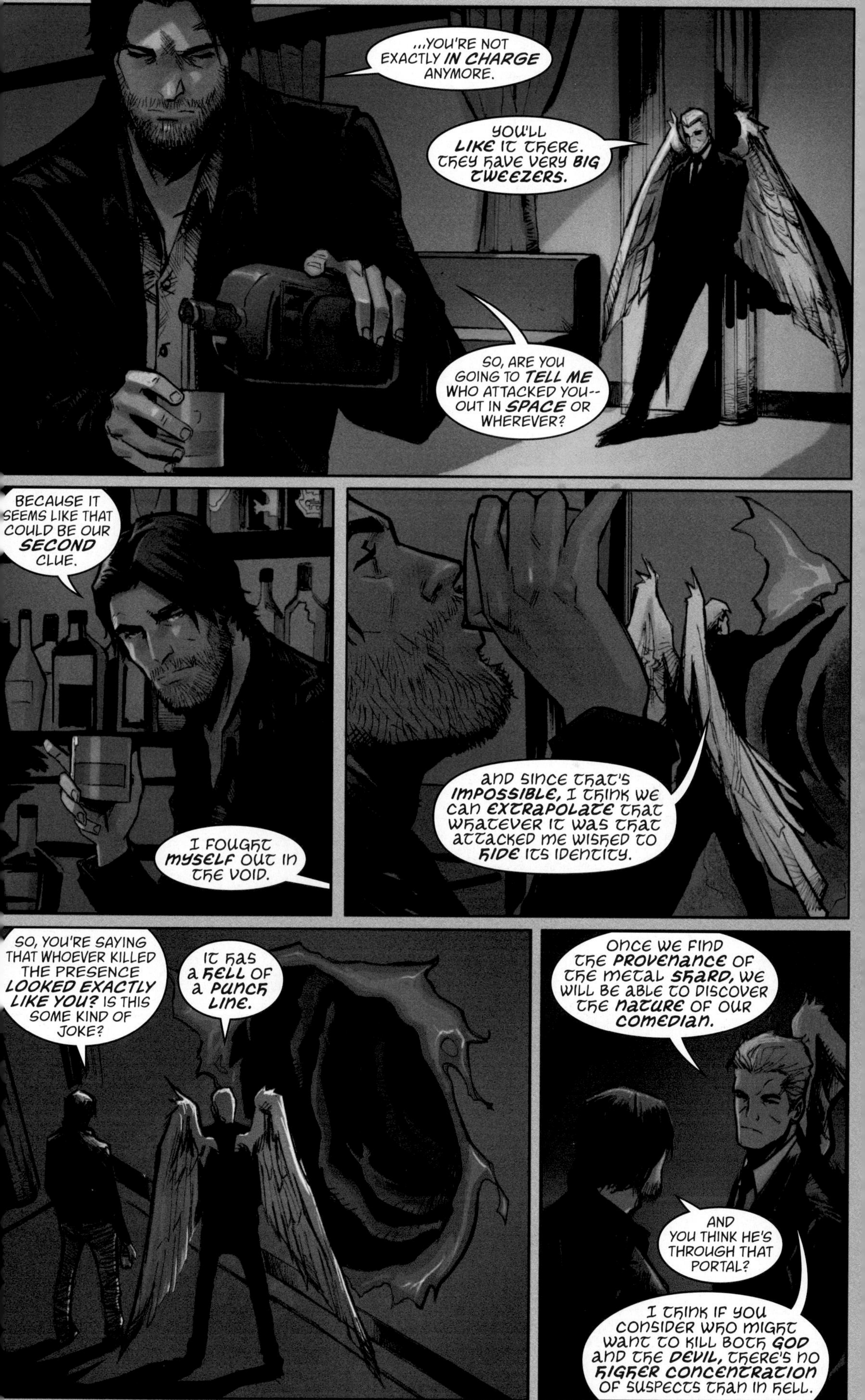
...YOU'RE NOT EXACTLY IN CHARGE ANYMORE.
YOU'LL LIKE IT THERE. THEY HAVE VERY BIG TWEEZERS.
SO, ARE YOU GOING TO TELL ME WHO ATTACKED YOU-- OUT IN SPACE OR WHEREVER?
BECAUSE IT SEEMS LIKE THAT COULD BE OUR SECOND CLUE.
I FOUGHT MYSELF OUT IN THE VOID.
AND SINCE THAT'S IMPOSSIBLE, I THINK WE CAN EXTRAPOLATE THAT WHATEVER IT WAS THAT ATTACKED ME WISHED TO HIDE ITS IDENTITY.
SO, YOU'RE SAYING THAT WHOEVER KILLED THE PRESENCE LOOKED EXACTLY LIKE YOU? IS THIS SOME KIND OF JOKE?
IT HAS A HELL OF A PUNCH LINE.
ONCE WE FIND THE PROVENANCE OF THE METAL SHARD, WE WILL BE ABLE TO DISCOVER THE NATURE OF OUR COMEDIAN.
AND YOU THINK HE'S THROUGH THAT PORTAL?
I THINK IF YOU CONSIDER WHO MIGHT WANT TO KILL BOTH GOD AND THE DEVIL, THERE'S NO HIGHER CONCENTRATION OF SUSPECTS THAN IN HELL.

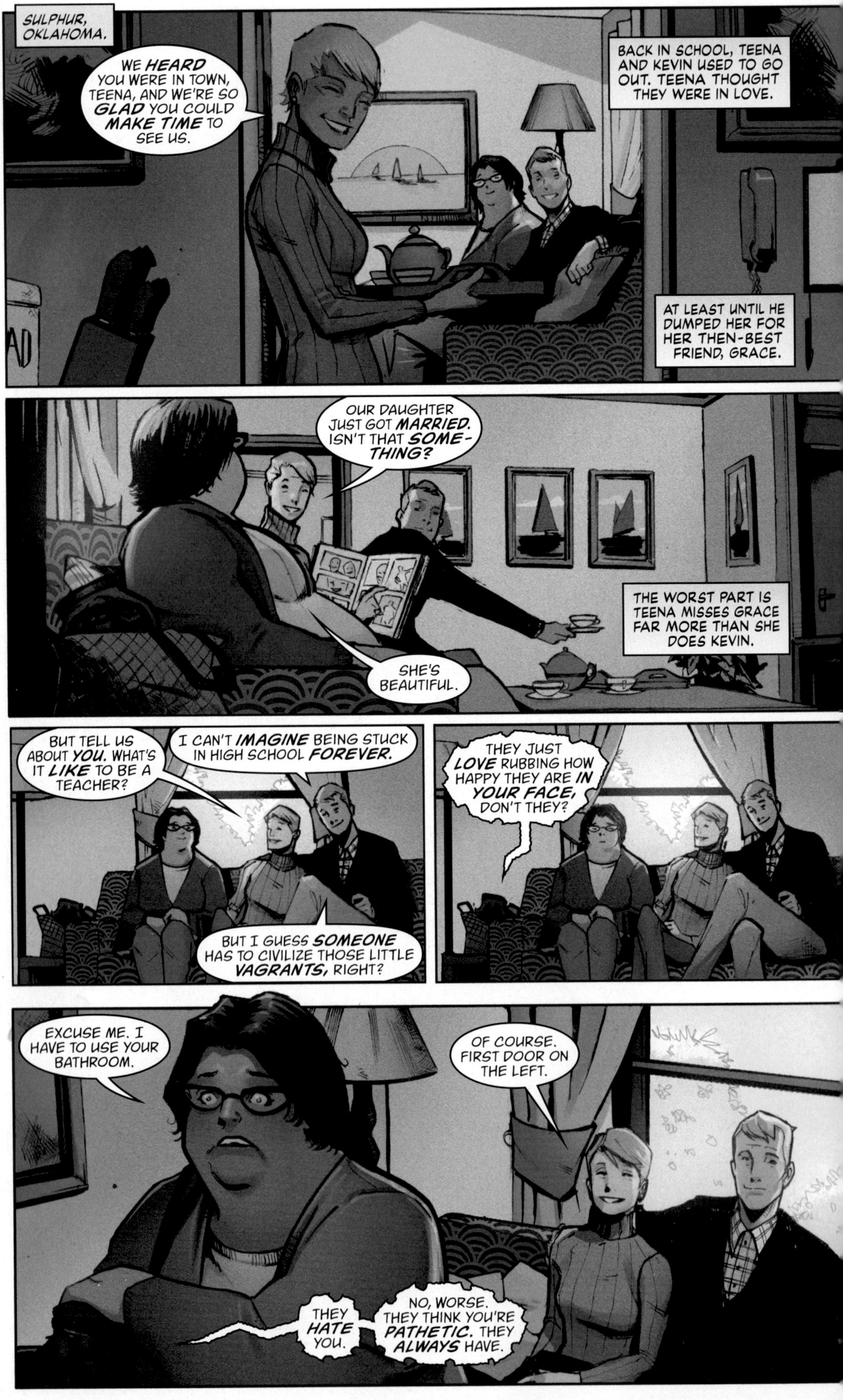
SULPHUR, OKLAHOMA.
WE HEARD YOU WERE IN TOWN, TEENA, AND WE'RE SO GLAD YOU COULD MAKE TIME TO SEE US.
BACK IN SCHOOL, TEENA AND KEVIN USED TO GO OUT. TEENA THOUGHT THEY WERE IN LOVE.
AT LEAST UNTIL HE DUMPED HER FOR HER THEN-BEST FRIEND, GRACE.
OUR DAUGHTER JUST GOT MARRIED. ISN'T THAT SOME-THING?
THE WORST PART IS TEENA MISSES GRACE FAR MORE THAN SHE DOES KEVIN.
SHE'S BEAUTIFUL.
BUT TELL US ABOUT YOU. WHAT'S IT LIKE TO BE A TEACHER?
I CAN'T IMAGINE BEING STUCK IN HIGH SCHOOL FOREVER.
BUT I GUESS SOMEONE HAS TO CIVILIZE THOSE LITTLE VAGRANTS, RIGHT?
THEY JUST LOVE RUBBING HOW HAPPY THEY ARE IN YOUR FACE, DON'T THEY?
EXCUSE ME. I HAVE TO USE YOUR BATHROOM.
OF COURSE. FIRST DOOR ON THE LEFT.
THEY HATE YOU.
NO, WORSE. THEY THINK YOU'RE PATHETIC. THEY ALWAYS HAVE.

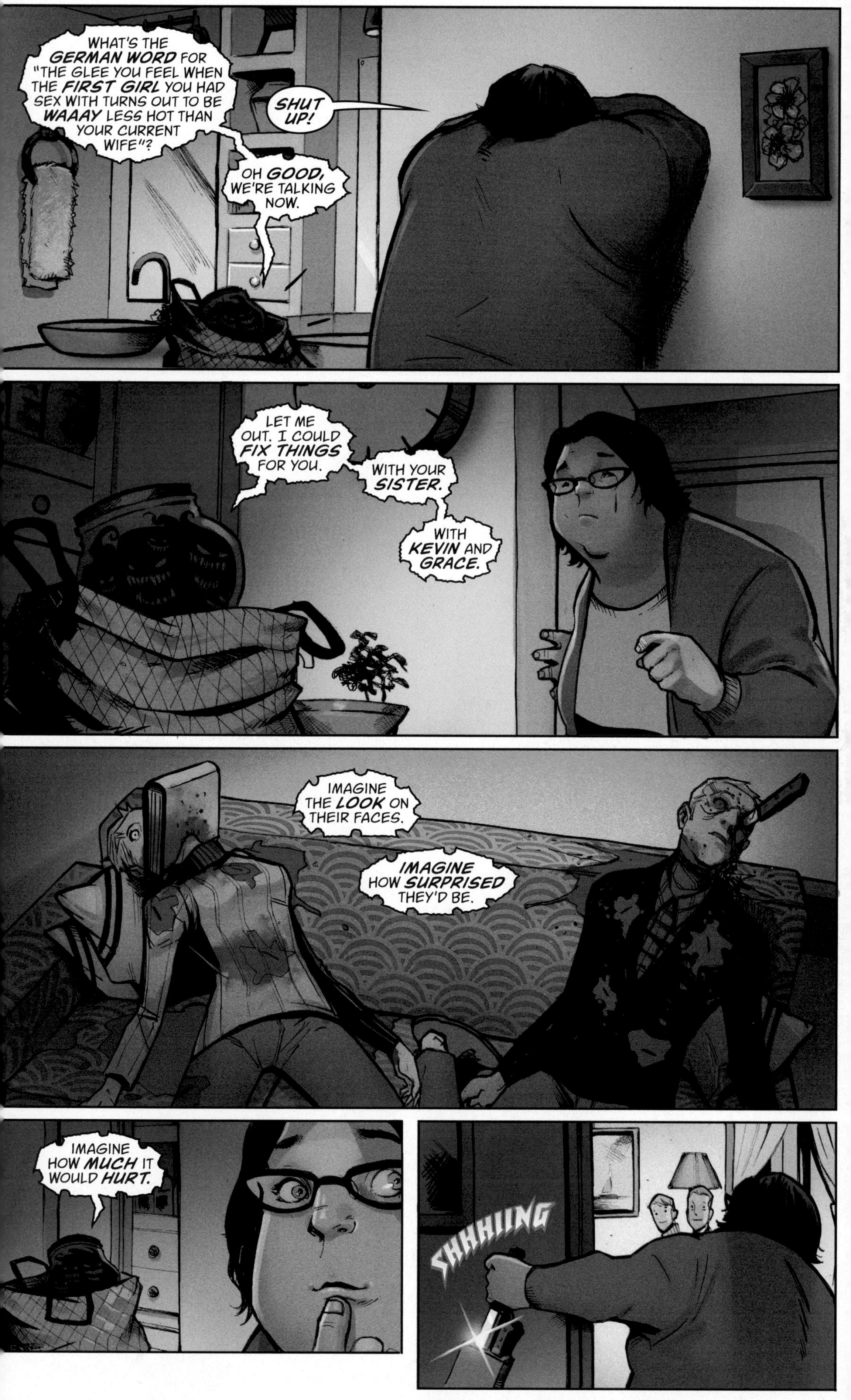

WHAT'S THE GERMAN WORD FOR "THE GLEE YOU FEEL WHEN THE FIRST GIRL YOU HAD SEX WITH TURNS OUT TO BE WAAAY LESS HOT THAN YOUR CURRENT WIFE"?
SHUT UP!
OH GOOD, WE'RE TALKING NOW.
LET ME OUT. I COULD FIX THINGS FOR YOU.
WITH YOUR SISTER.
WITH KEVIN AND GRACE.
IMAGINE THE LOOK ON THEIR FACES.
IMAGINE HOW SURPRISED THEY'D BE.
IMAGINE HOW MUCH IT WOULD HURT.
SHHHIING

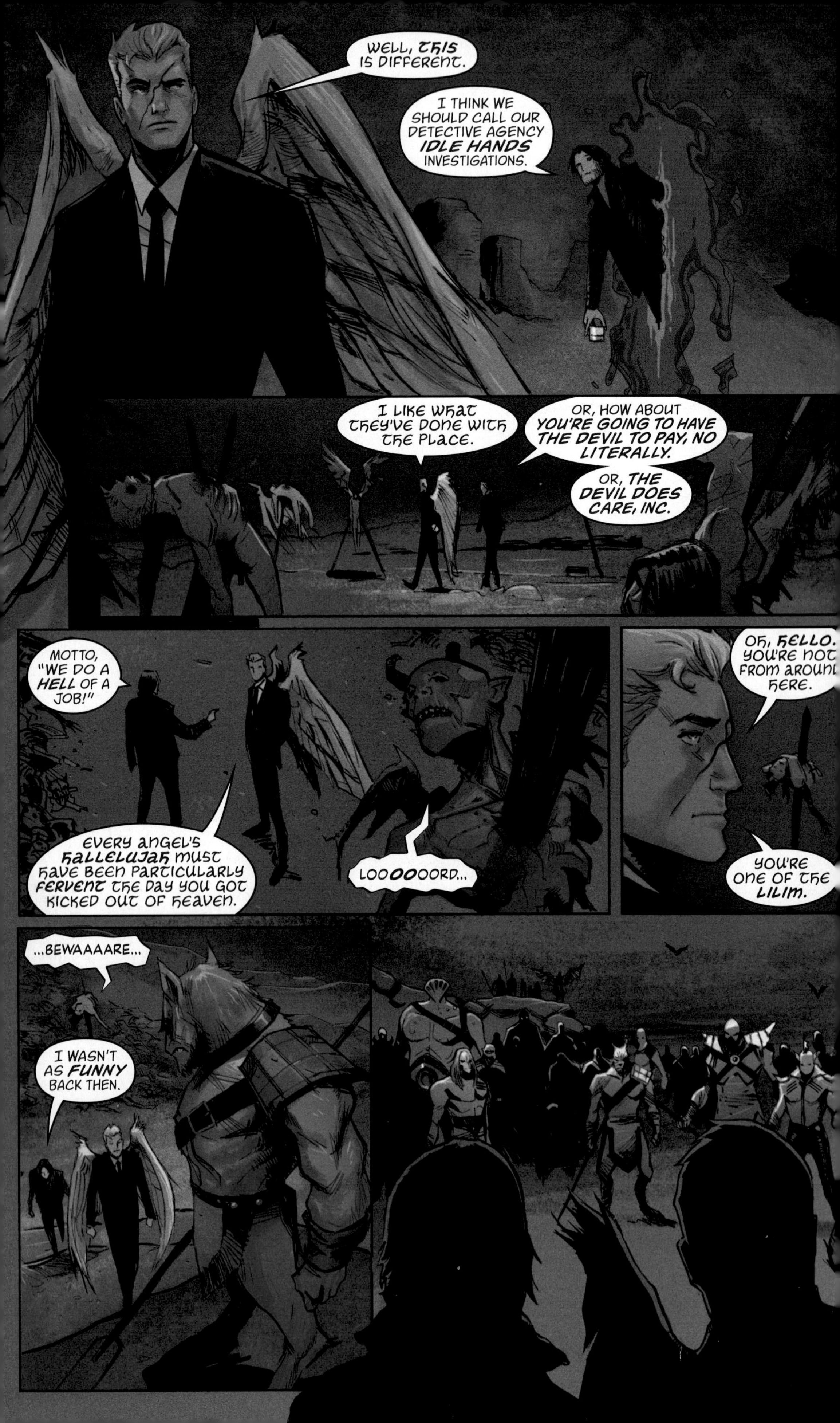
WELL, THIS IS DIFFERENT.
I THINK WE SHOULD CALL OUR DETECTIVE AGENCY IDLE HANDS INVESTIGATIONS.
I LIKE WHAT THEY'VE DONE WITH THE PLACE.
OR, HOW ABOUT YOU'RE GOING TO HAVE THE DEVIL TO PAY, NO LITERALLY.
OR, THE DEVIL DOES CARE, INC.
MOTTO, "WE DO A HELL OF A JOB!"
EVERY ANGEL'S HALLELUJAH MUST HAVE BEEN PARTICULARLY FERVENT THE DAY YOU GOT KICKED OUT OF HEAVEN.
LOOOOOORD...
OH, HELLO. YOU'RE NOT FROM AROUN HERE.
YOU'RE ONE OF THE LILIM.
...BEWAAAARE...
I WASN'T AS FUNNY BACK THEN.

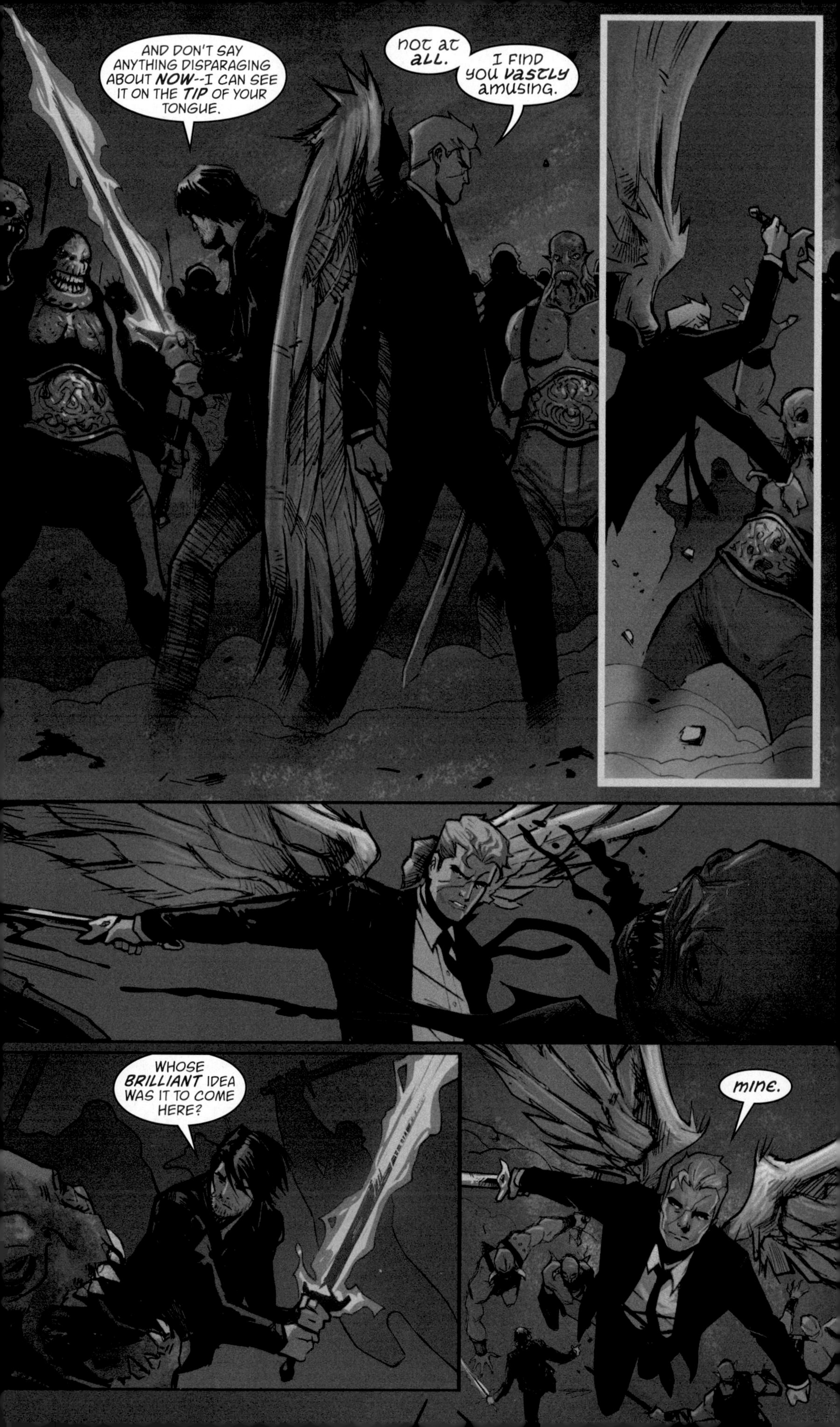
AND DON'T SAY ANYTHING DISPARAGING ABOUT NOW--I CAN SEE IT ON THE TIP OF YOUR TONGUE.
not at all.
I FIND YOU VASTLY amusing.
WHOSE BRILLIANT IDEA WAS IT TO COME HERE?
mine.

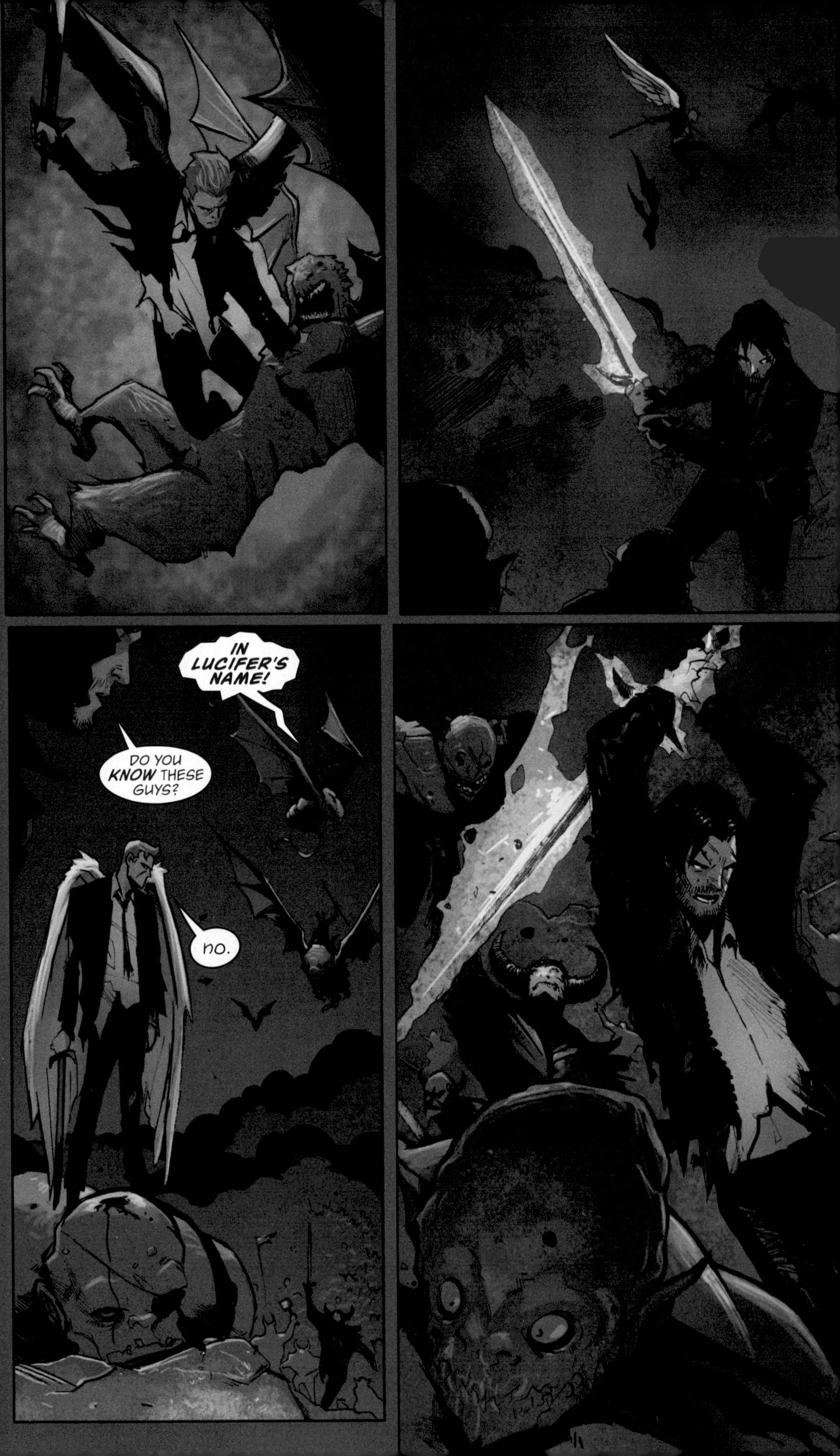
IN LUCIFER'S NAME!
DO YOU KNOW THESE GUYS?
no.

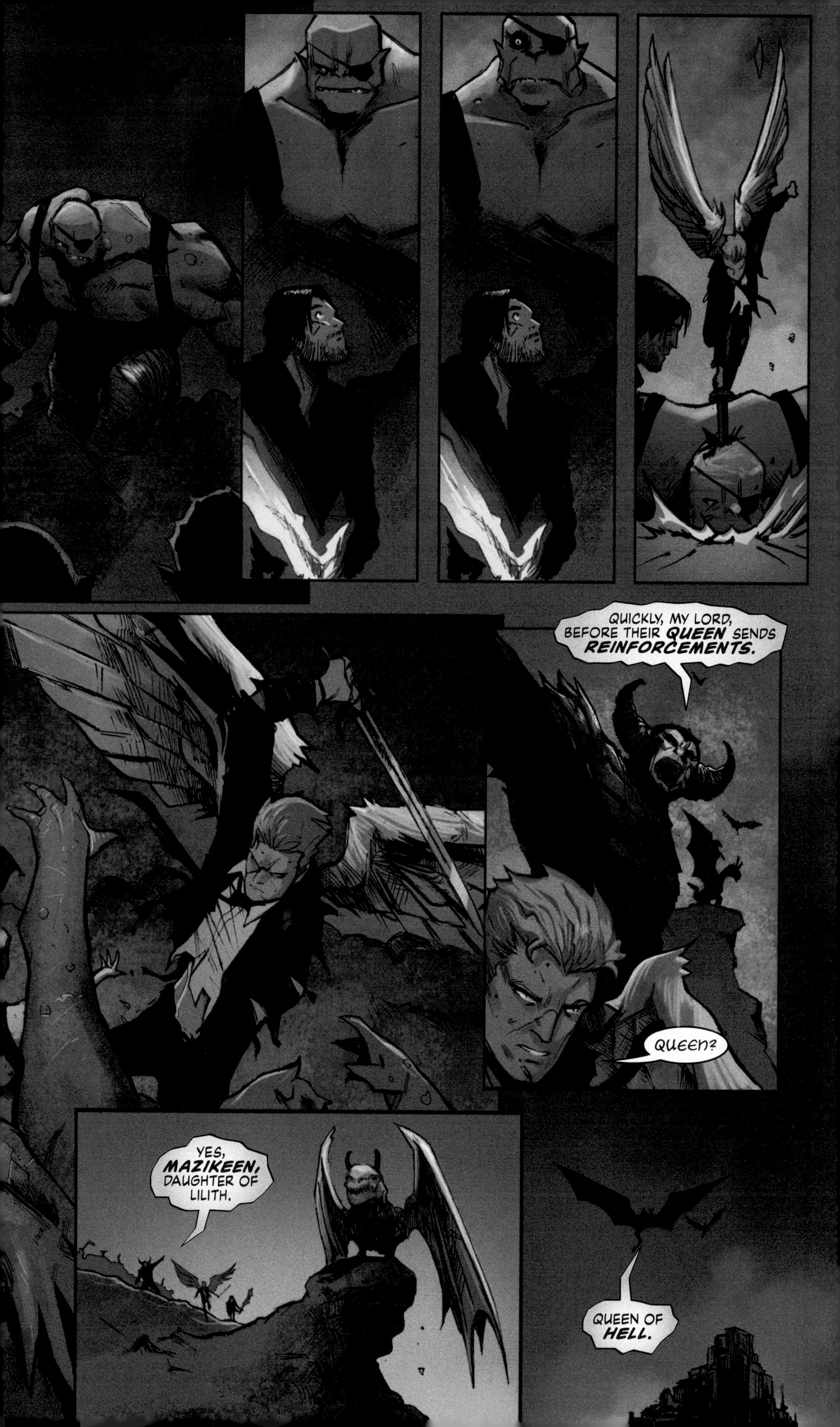
QUICKLY, MY LORD, BEFORE THEIR QUEEN SENDS REINFORCEMENTS.
QUEEN?
YES, MAZIKEEN, DAUGHTER OF LILITH.
QUEEN OF HELL.

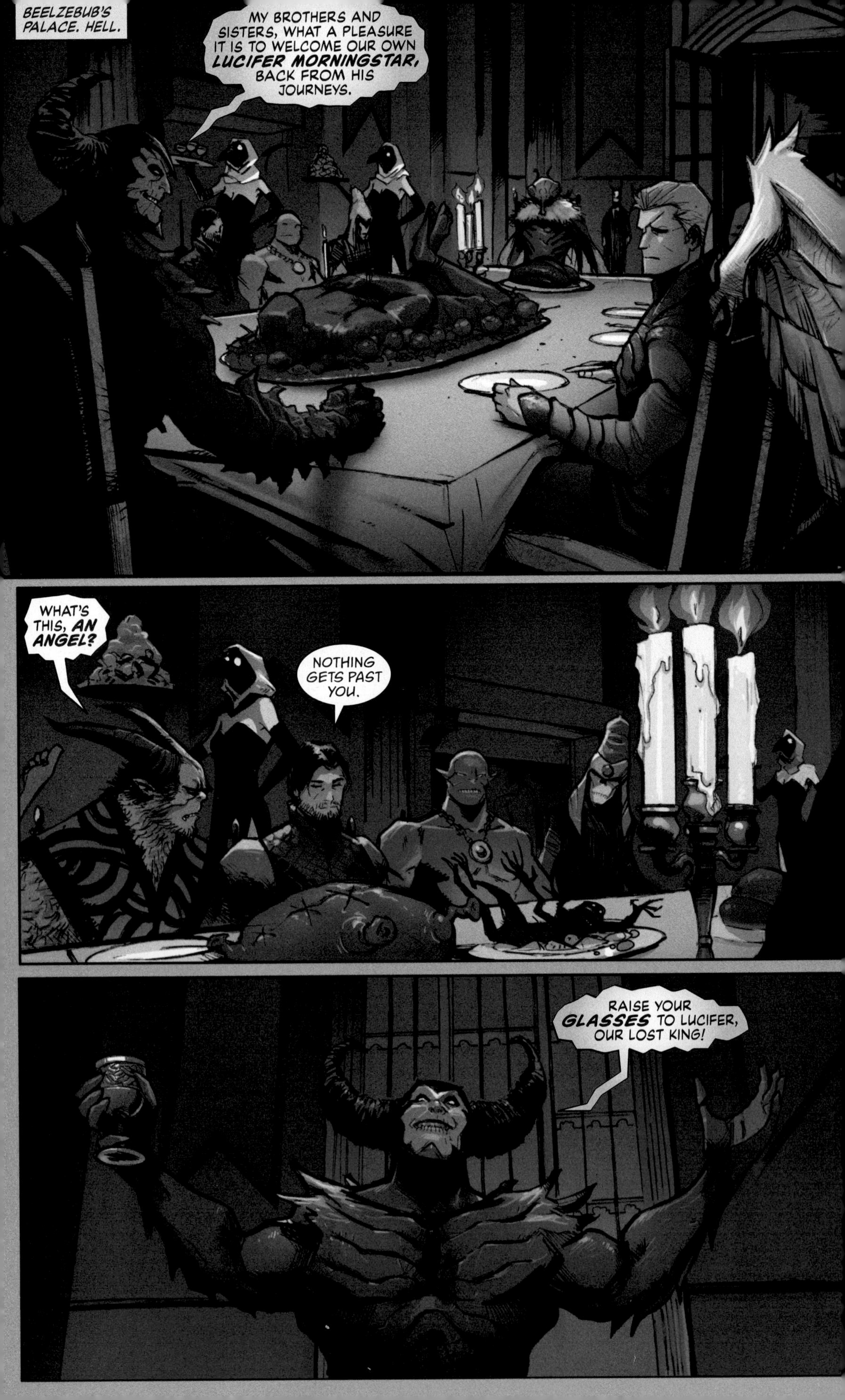
BEELZEBUB'S PALACE. HELL.
MY BROTHERS AND SISTERS, WHAT A PLEASURE IT IS TO WELCOME OUR OWN LUCIFER MORNINGSTAR, BACK FROM HIS JOURNEYS.
WHAT'S THIS, AN ANGEL?
NOTHING GETS PAST YOU.
RAISE YOUR GLASSES TO LUCIFER, OUR LOST KING!

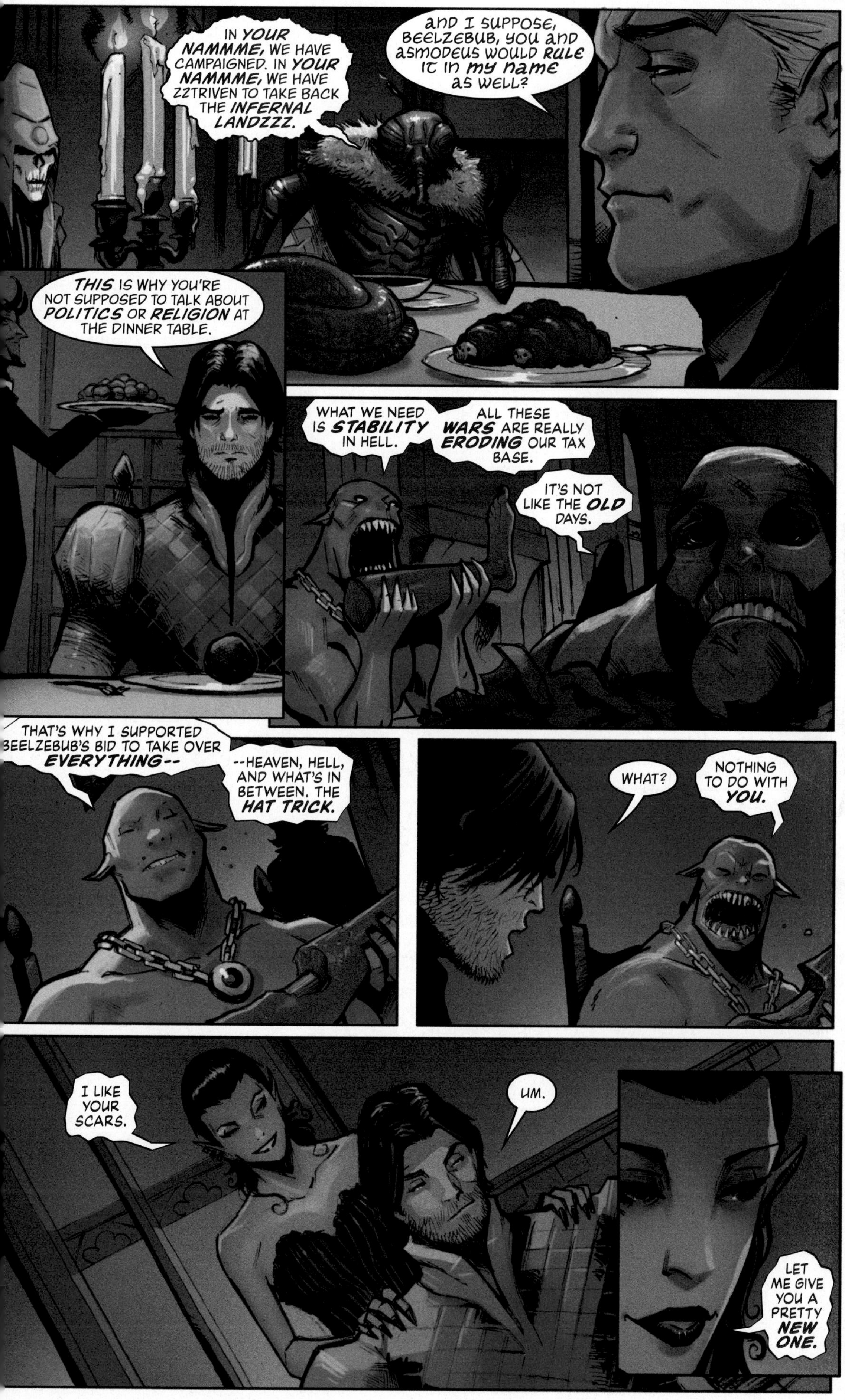

IN YOUR NAMMME, WE HAVE CAMPAIGNED. IN YOUR NAMMME, WE HAVE ZZTRIVEN TO TAKE BACK THE INFERNAL LANDZZZ.
AND I SUPPOSE, BEELZEBUB, YOU AND ASMODEUS WOULD RULE IT IN MY NAME AS WELL?
THIS IS WHY YOU'RE NOT SUPPOSED TO TALK ABOUT POLITICS OR RELIGION AT THE DINNER TABLE.
WHAT WE NEED IS STABILITY IN HELL.
ALL THESE WARS ARE REALLY ERODING OUR TAX BASE.
IT'S NOT LIKE THE OLD DAYS.
THAT'S WHY I SUPPORTED BEELZEBUB'S BID TO TAKE OVER EVERYTHING--
--HEAVEN, HELL, AND WHAT'S IN BETWEEN. THE HAT TRICK.
WHAT?
NOTHING TO DO WITH YOU.
I LIKE YOUR SCARS.
UM.
LET ME GIVE YOU A PRETTY NEW ONE.

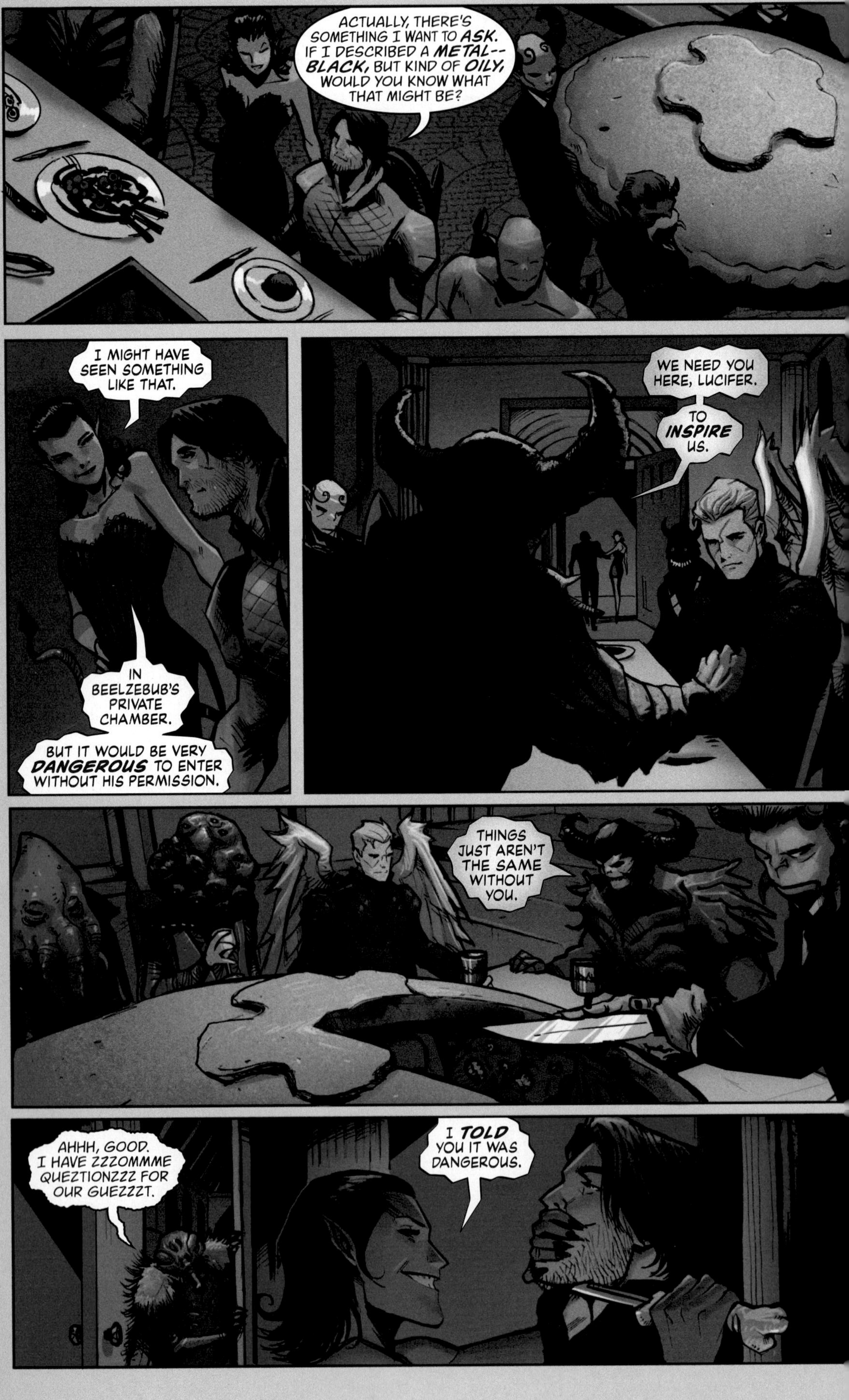
ACTUALLY, THERE'S SOMETHING I WANT TO ASK. IF I DESCRIBED A METAL-- BLACK, BUT KIND OF OILY, WOULD YOU KNOW WHAT THAT MIGHT BE?
I MIGHT HAVE SEEN SOMETHING LIKE THAT.
IN BEELZEBUB'S PRIVATE CHAMBER.
BUT IT WOULD BE VERY DANGEROUS TO ENTER WITHOUT HIS PERMISSION.
WE NEED YOU HERE, LUCIFER.
TO INSPIRE US.
THINGS JUST AREN'T THE SAME WITHOUT YOU.
AHHH, GOOD. I HAVE ZZZOMMME QUEZTIONZZZ FOR OUR GUEZZZT.
I TOLD YOU IT WAS DANGEROUS.

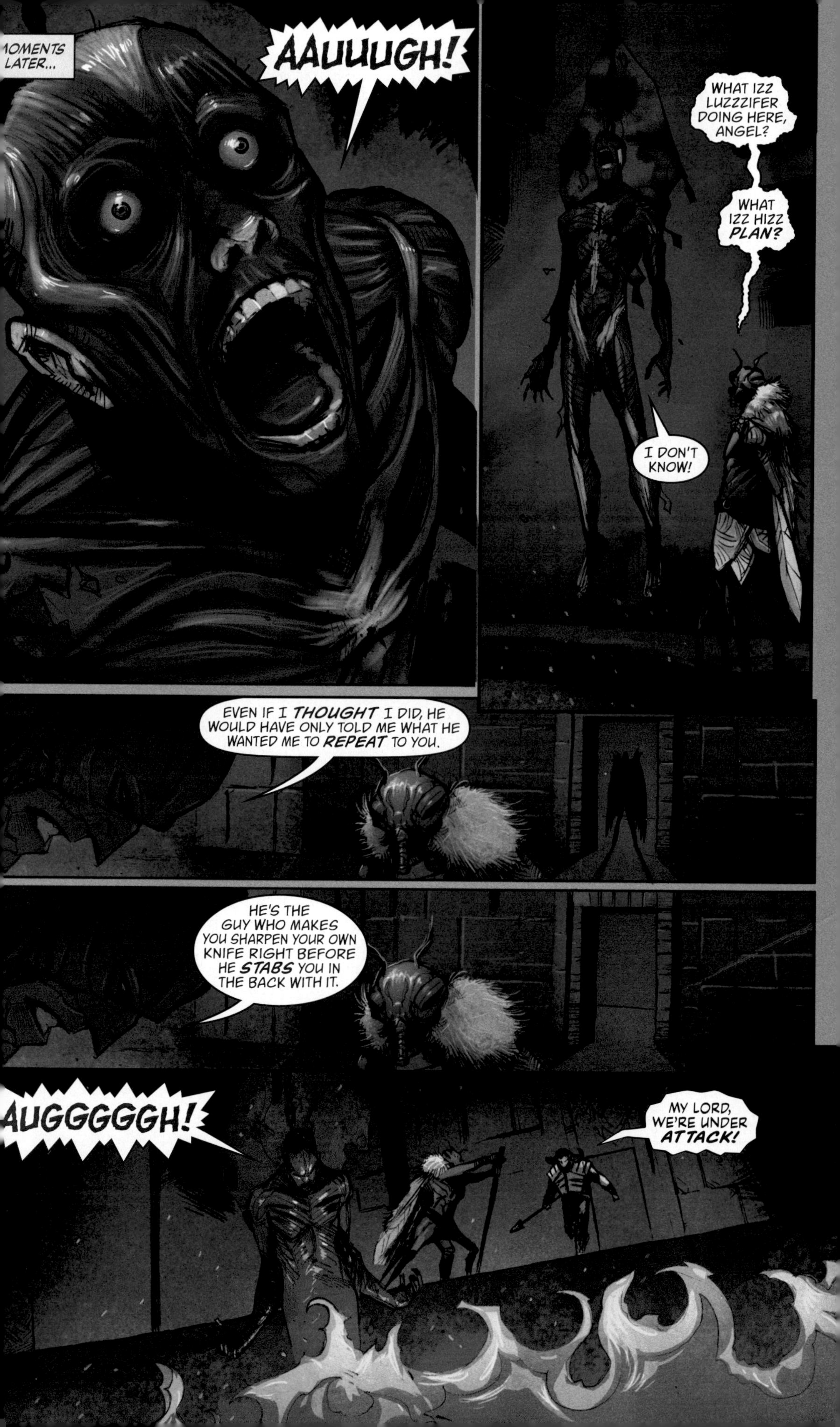

MOMENTS LATER...
AAUUUGH!
WHAT IZZ LUZZZIFER DOING HERE, ANGEL?
WHAT IZZ HIZZ *PLAN?*
I DON'T KNOW!
EVEN IF I *THOUGHT* I DID, HE WOULD HAVE ONLY TOLD ME WHAT HE WANTED ME TO *REPEAT* TO YOU.
HE'S THE GUY WHO MAKES YOU SHARPEN YOUR OWN KNIFE RIGHT BEFORE HE *STABS* YOU IN THE BACK WITH IT.
AUGGGGGH!
MY LORD, WE'RE UNDER *ATTACK!*

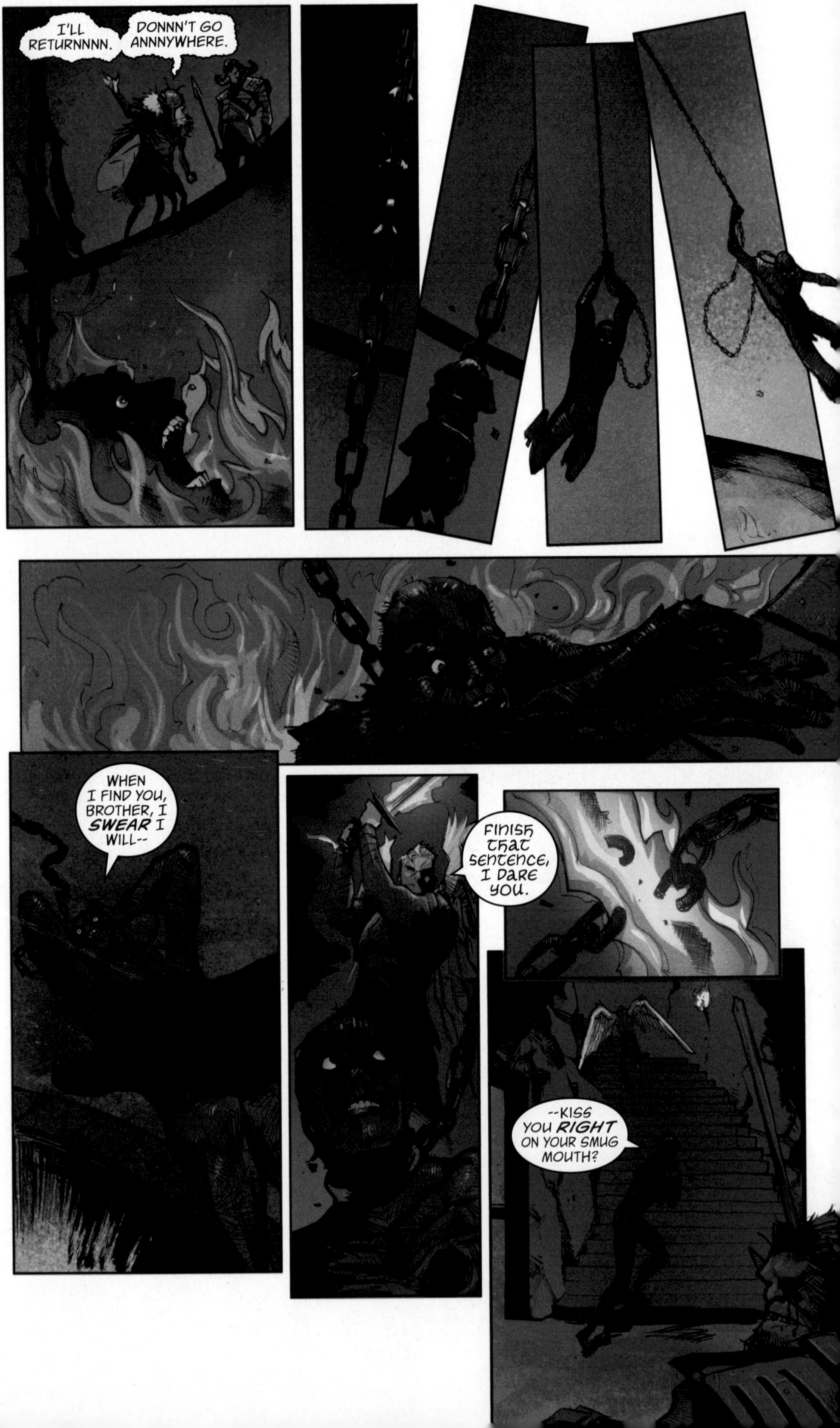
I'LL RETURNNNN.
DONNN'T GO ANNNYWHERE.
WHEN I FIND YOU, BROTHER, I **SWEAR** I WILL--
FINISH THAT SENTENCE, I DARE YOU.
--KISS YOU **RIGHT** ON YOUR SMUG MOUTH?

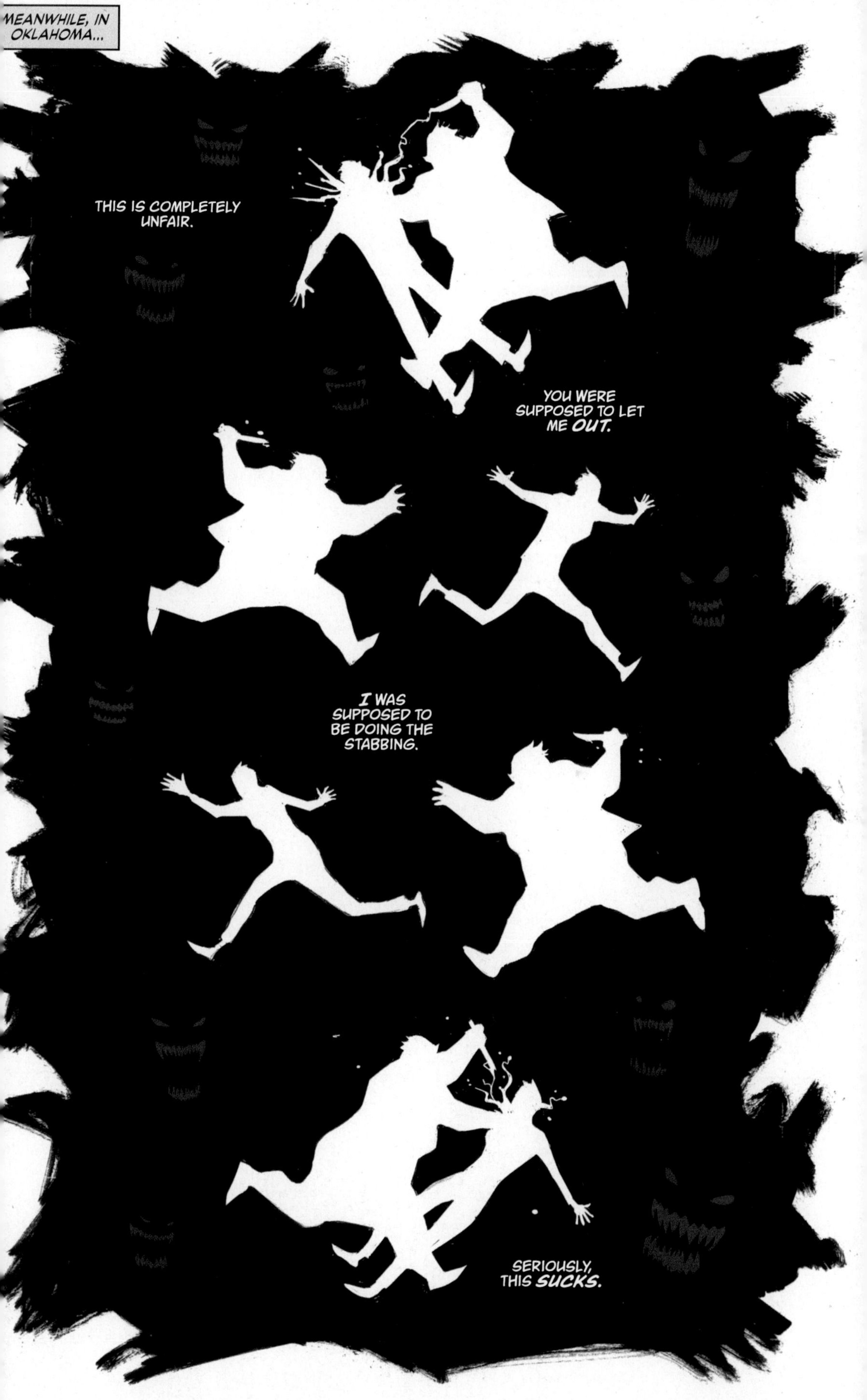
MEANWHILE, IN OKLAHOMA...
THIS IS COMPLETELY UNFAIR.
YOU WERE SUPPOSED TO LET ME OUT.
I WAS SUPPOSED TO BE DOING THE STABBING.
SERIOUSLY, THIS SUCKS.

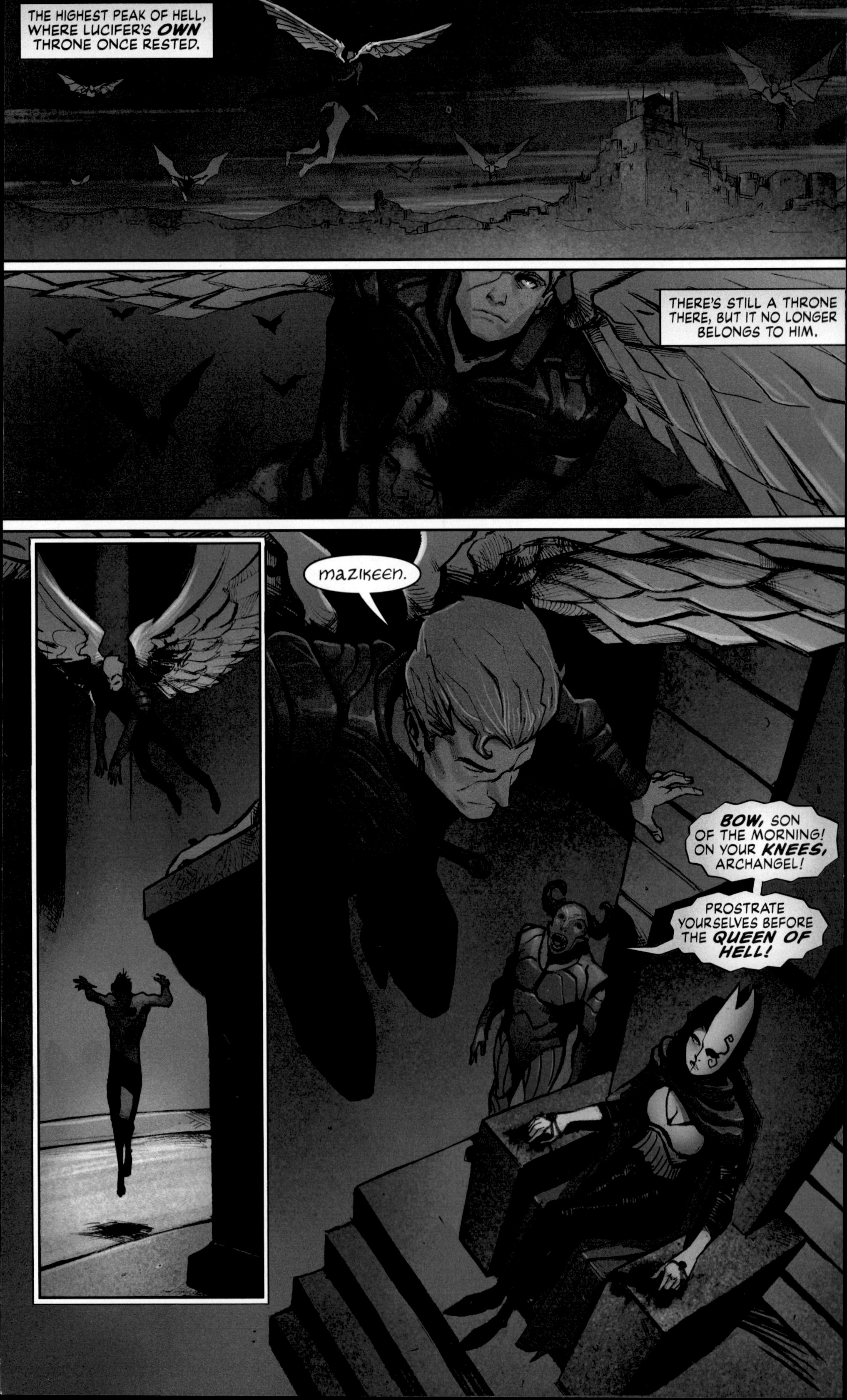

THE HIGHEST PEAK OF HELL, WHERE LUCIFER'S OWN THRONE ONCE RESTED.
THERE'S STILL A THRONE THERE, BUT IT NO LONGER BELONGS TO HIM.
mazikeen.
BOW, SON OF THE MORNING! ON YOUR KNEES, ARCHANGEL!
PROSTRATE YOURSELVES BEFORE THE QUEEN OF HELL!

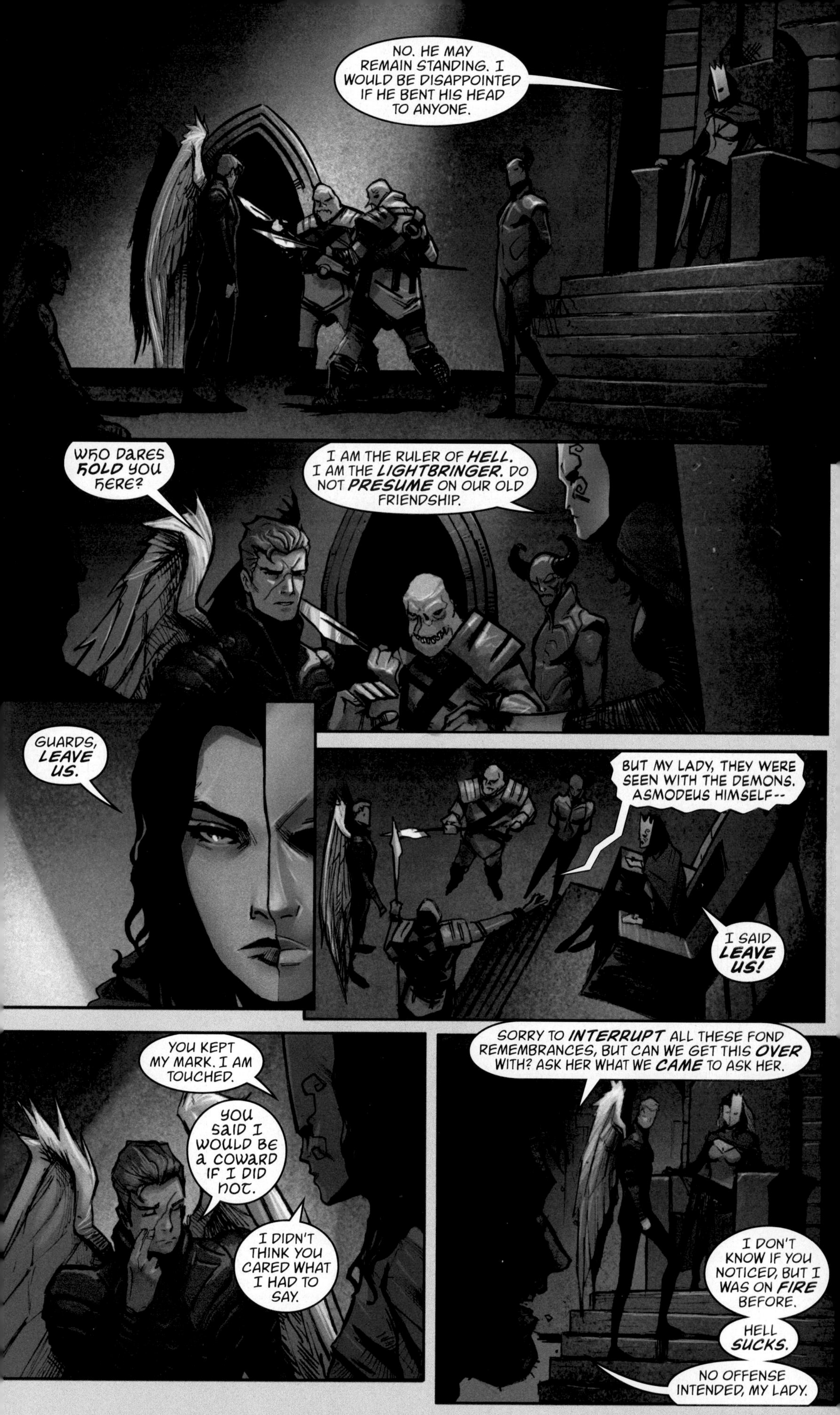
NO. HE MAY REMAIN STANDING. I WOULD BE DISAPPOINTED IF HE BENT HIS HEAD TO ANYONE.
WHO DARES HOLD YOU HERE?
I AM THE RULER OF HELL. I AM THE LIGHTBRINGER. DO NOT PRESUME ON OUR OLD FRIENDSHIP.
GUARDS, LEAVE US.
BUT MY LADY, THEY WERE SEEN WITH THE DEMONS. ASMODEUS HIMSELF--
I SAID LEAVE US!
YOU KEPT MY MARK. I AM TOUCHED.
YOU SAID I WOULD BE A COWARD IF I DID NOT.
I DIDN'T THINK YOU CARED WHAT I HAD TO SAY.
SORRY TO INTERRUPT ALL THESE FOND REMEMBRANCES, BUT CAN WE GET THIS OVER WITH? ASK HER WHAT WE CAME TO ASK HER.
I DON'T KNOW IF YOU NOTICED, BUT I WAS ON FIRE BEFORE.
HELL SUCKS.
NO OFFENSE INTENDED, MY LADY.

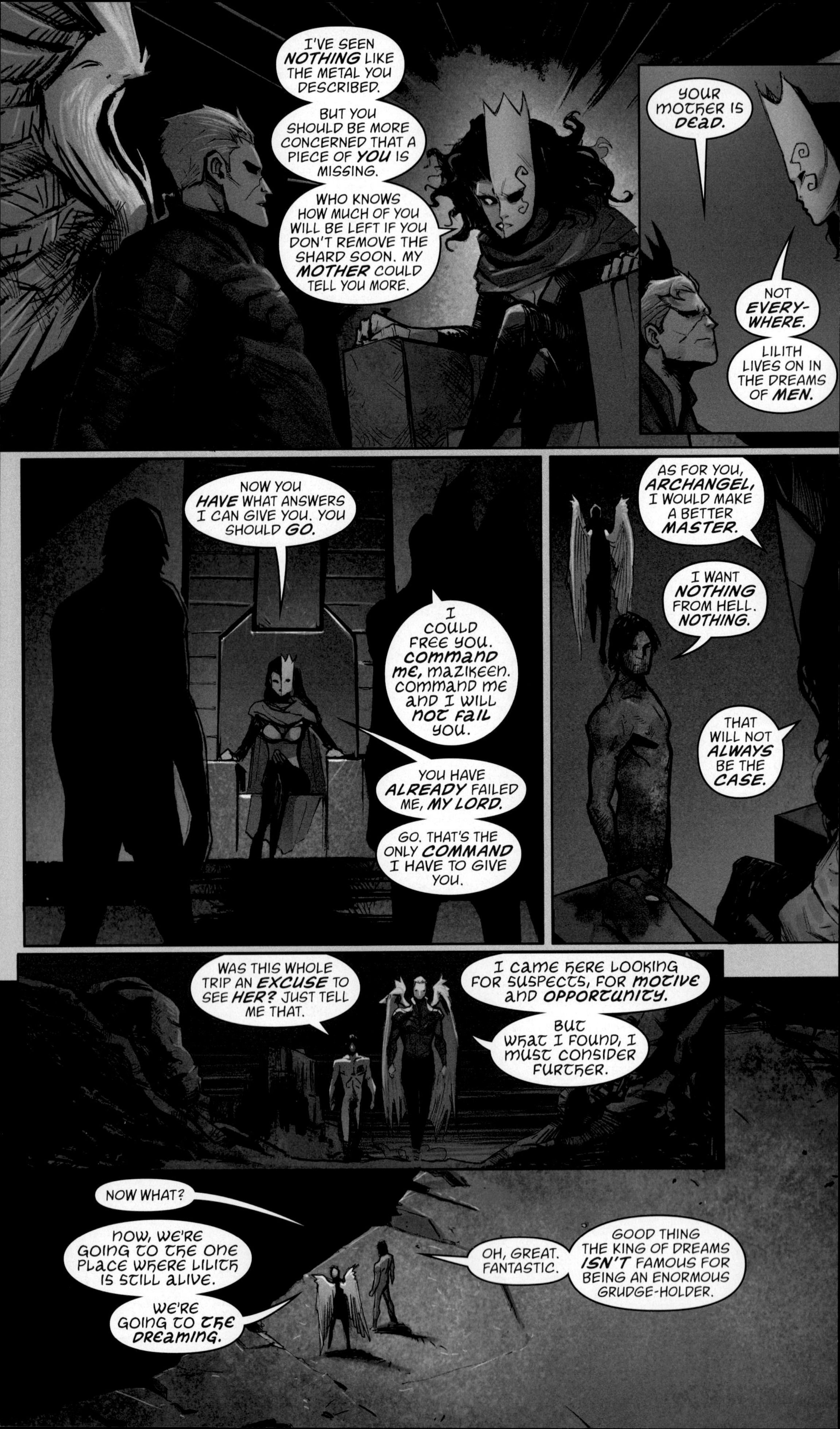
I'VE SEEN NOTHING LIKE THE METAL YOU DESCRIBED.
BUT YOU SHOULD BE MORE CONCERNED THAT A PIECE OF YOU IS MISSING.
WHO KNOWS HOW MUCH OF YOU WILL BE LEFT IF YOU DON'T REMOVE THE SHARD SOON. MY MOTHER COULD TELL YOU MORE.
YOUR MOTHER IS DEAD.
NOT EVERY-WHERE.
LILITH LIVES ON IN THE DREAMS OF MEN.
NOW YOU HAVE WHAT ANSWERS I CAN GIVE YOU. YOU SHOULD GO.
I COULD FREE YOU. COMMAND ME, MAZIKEEN. COMMAND ME AND I WILL NOT FAIL YOU.
YOU HAVE ALREADY FAILED ME, MY LORD.
GO. THAT'S THE ONLY COMMAND I HAVE TO GIVE YOU.
AS FOR YOU, ARCHANGEL, I WOULD MAKE A BETTER MASTER.
I WANT NOTHING FROM HELL. NOTHING.
THAT WILL NOT ALWAYS BE THE CASE.
WAS THIS WHOLE TRIP AN EXCUSE TO SEE HER? JUST TELL ME THAT.
I CAME HERE LOOKING FOR SUSPECTS, FOR MOTIVE AND OPPORTUNITY.
BUT WHAT I FOUND, I MUST CONSIDER FURTHER.
NOW WHAT?
NOW, WE'RE GOING TO THE ONE PLACE WHERE LILITH IS STILL ALIVE.
WE'RE GOING TO THE DREAMING.
OH, GREAT. FANTASTIC.
GOOD THING THE KING OF DREAMS ISN'T FAMOUS FOR BEING AN ENORMOUS GRUDGE-HOLDER.

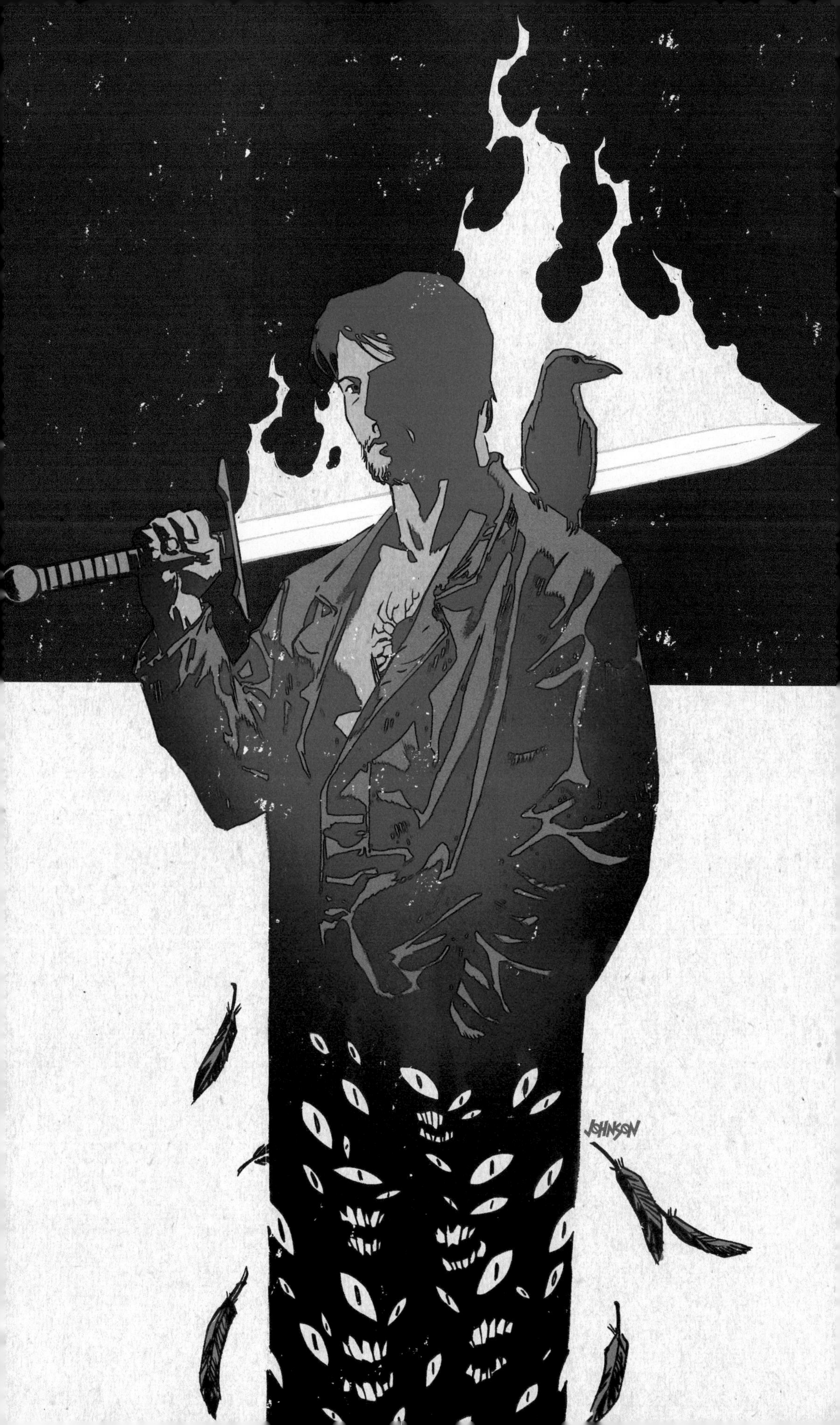
JOHNSON

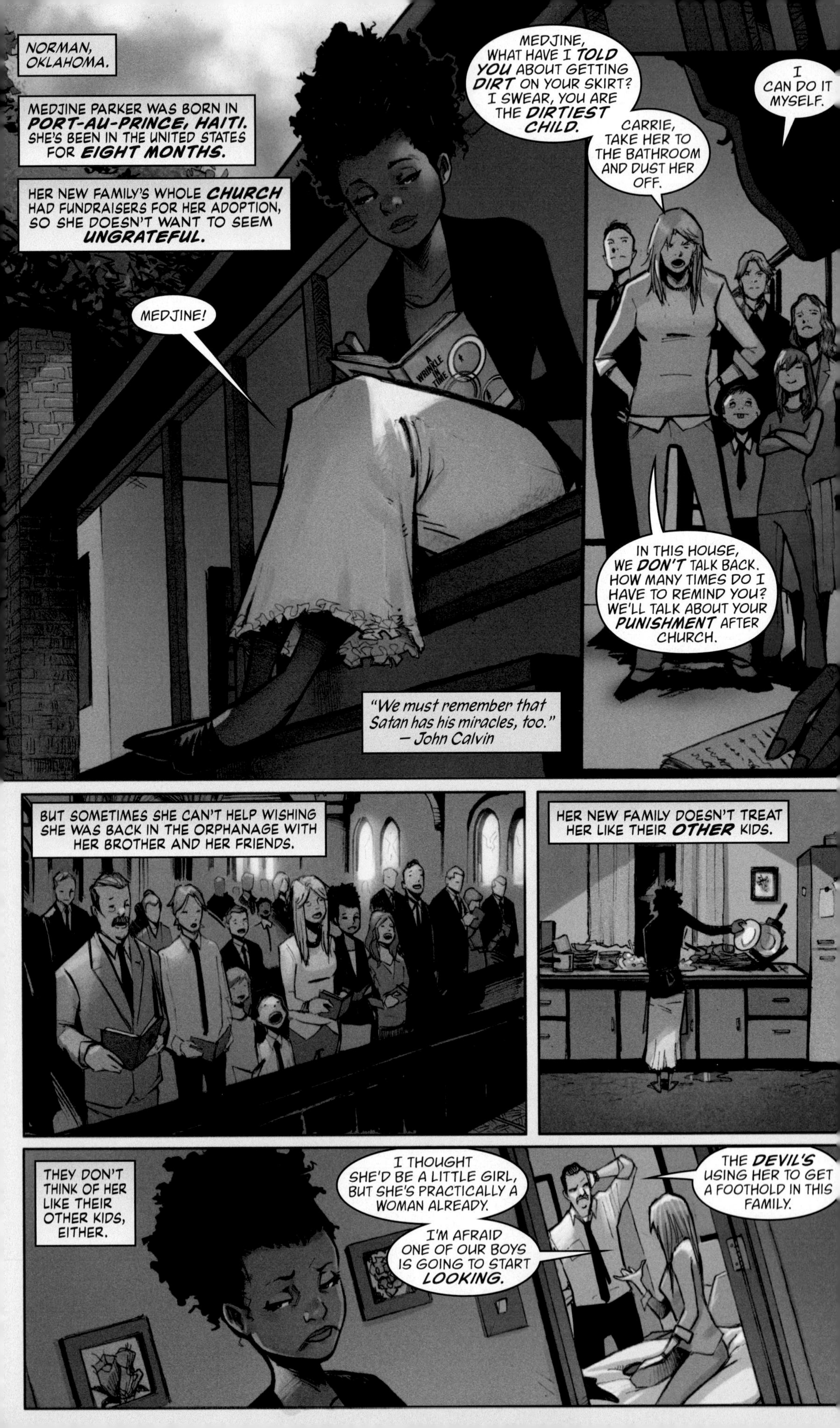
NORMAN, OKLAHOMA.
MEDJINE PARKER WAS BORN IN PORT-AU-PRINCE, HAITI. SHE'S BEEN IN THE UNITED STATES FOR EIGHT MONTHS.
HER NEW FAMILY'S WHOLE CHURCH HAD FUNDRAISERS FOR HER ADOPTION, SO SHE DOESN'T WANT TO SEEM UNGRATEFUL.
MEDJINE!
A WRINKLE IN TIME
"We must remember that Satan has his miracles, too." — John Calvin
MEDJINE, WHAT HAVE I TOLD YOU ABOUT GETTING DIRT ON YOUR SKIRT? I SWEAR, YOU ARE THE DIRTIEST CHILD.
CARRIE, TAKE HER TO THE BATHROOM AND DUST HER OFF.
I CAN DO IT MYSELF.
IN THIS HOUSE, WE DON'T TALK BACK. HOW MANY TIMES DO I HAVE TO REMIND YOU? WE'LL TALK ABOUT YOUR PUNISHMENT AFTER CHURCH.
BUT SOMETIMES SHE CAN'T HELP WISHING SHE WAS BACK IN THE ORPHANAGE WITH HER BROTHER AND HER FRIENDS.
HER NEW FAMILY DOESN'T TREAT HER LIKE THEIR OTHER KIDS.
THEY DON'T THINK OF HER LIKE THEIR OTHER KIDS, EITHER.
I THOUGHT SHE'D BE A LITTLE GIRL, BUT SHE'S PRACTICALLY A WOMAN ALREADY.
I'M AFRAID ONE OF OUR BOYS IS GOING TO START LOOKING.
THE DEVIL'S USING HER TO GET A FOOTHOLD IN THIS FAMILY.

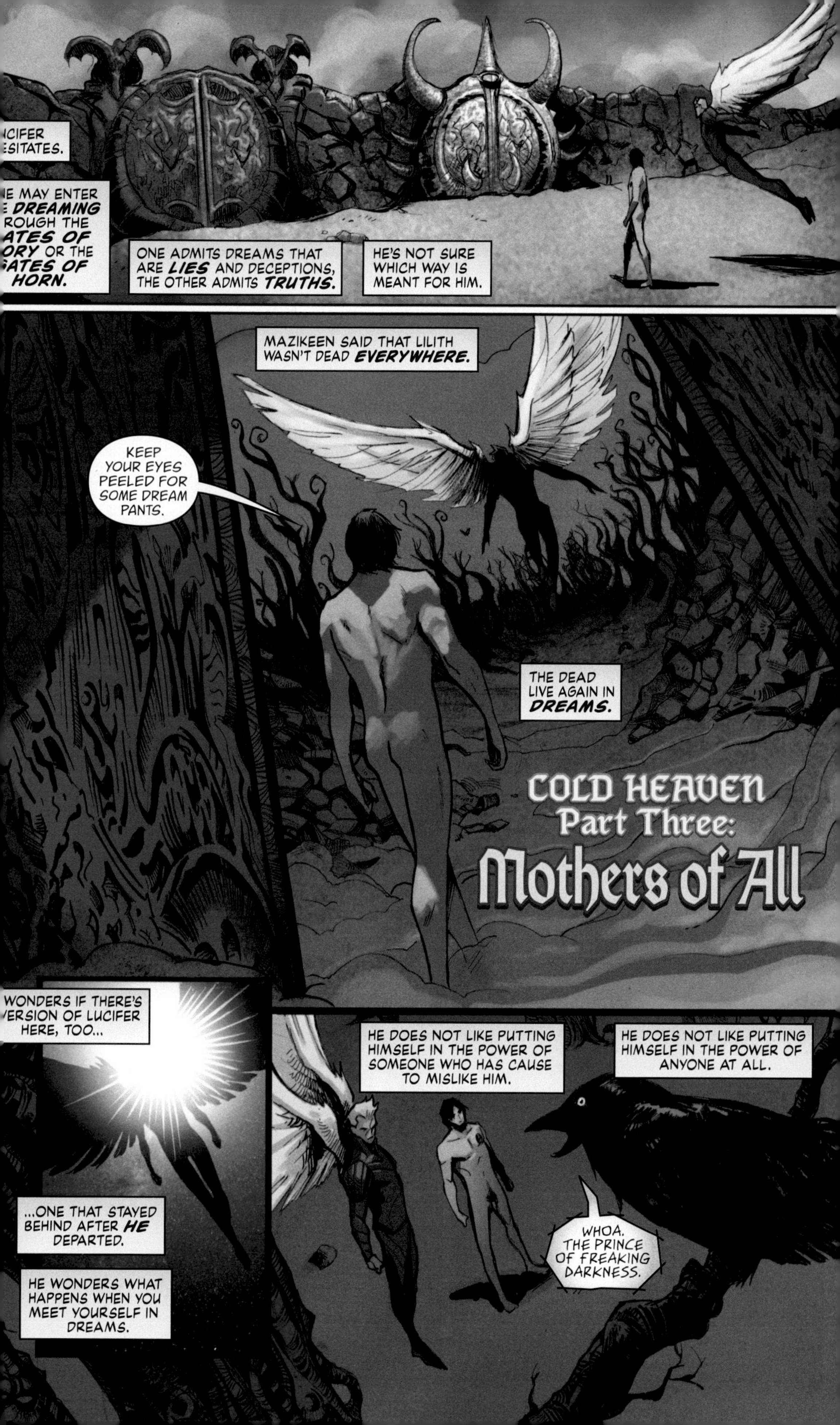

ICIFER ESITATES.
IE MAY ENTER E DREAMING ROUGH THE ATES OF ORY OR THE ATES OF HORN.
ONE ADMITS DREAMS THAT ARE LIES AND DECEPTIONS, THE OTHER ADMITS TRUTHS.
HE'S NOT SURE WHICH WAY IS MEANT FOR HIM.
MAZIKEEN SAID THAT LILITH WASN'T DEAD EVERYWHERE.
KEEP YOUR EYES PEELED FOR SOME DREAM PANTS.
THE DEAD LIVE AGAIN IN DREAMS.
COLD HEAVEN Part Three:
Mothers of All
WONDERS IF THERE'S VERSION OF LUCIFER HERE, TOO...
...ONE THAT STAYED BEHIND AFTER HE DEPARTED.
HE WONDERS WHAT HAPPENS WHEN YOU MEET YOURSELF IN DREAMS.
HE DOES NOT LIKE PUTTING HIMSELF IN THE POWER OF SOMEONE WHO HAS CAUSE TO MISLIKE HIM.
HE DOES NOT LIKE PUTTING HIMSELF IN THE POWER OF ANYONE AT ALL.
WHOA. THE PRINCE OF FREAKING DARKNESS.

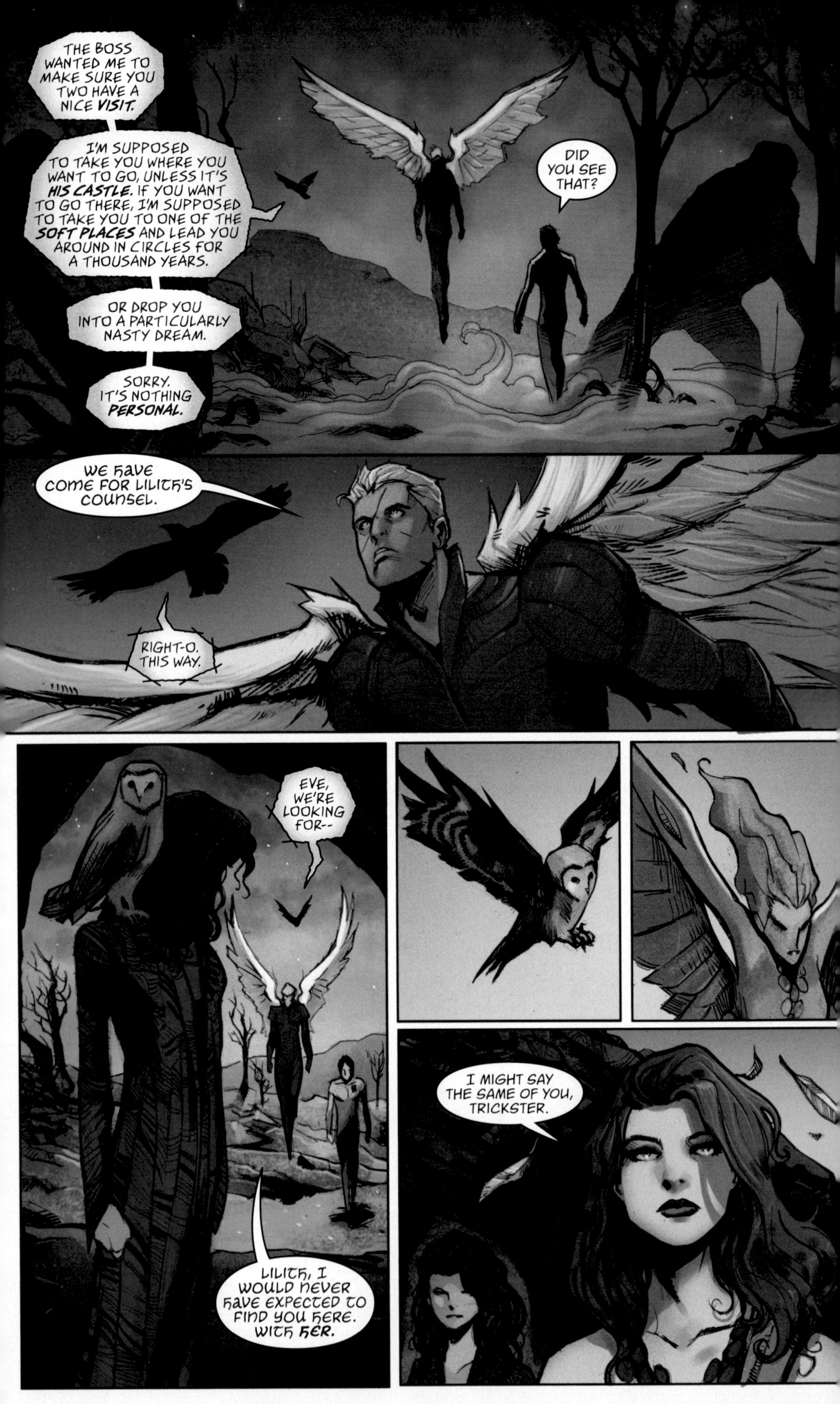
THE BOSS WANTED ME TO MAKE SURE YOU TWO HAVE A NICE VISIT.
I'M SUPPOSED TO TAKE YOU WHERE YOU WANT TO GO, UNLESS IT'S HIS CASTLE. IF YOU WANT TO GO THERE, I'M SUPPOSED TO TAKE YOU TO ONE OF THE SOFT PLACES AND LEAD YOU AROUND IN CIRCLES FOR A THOUSAND YEARS.
OR DROP YOU INTO A PARTICULARLY NASTY DREAM.
SORRY. IT'S NOTHING PERSONAL.
DID YOU SEE THAT?
WE HAVE COME FOR LILITH'S COUNSEL.
RIGHT-O. THIS WAY.
EVE, WE'RE LOOKING FOR--
LILITH, I WOULD NEVER HAVE EXPECTED TO FIND YOU HERE. WITH HER.
I MIGHT SAY THE SAME OF YOU, TRICKSTER.

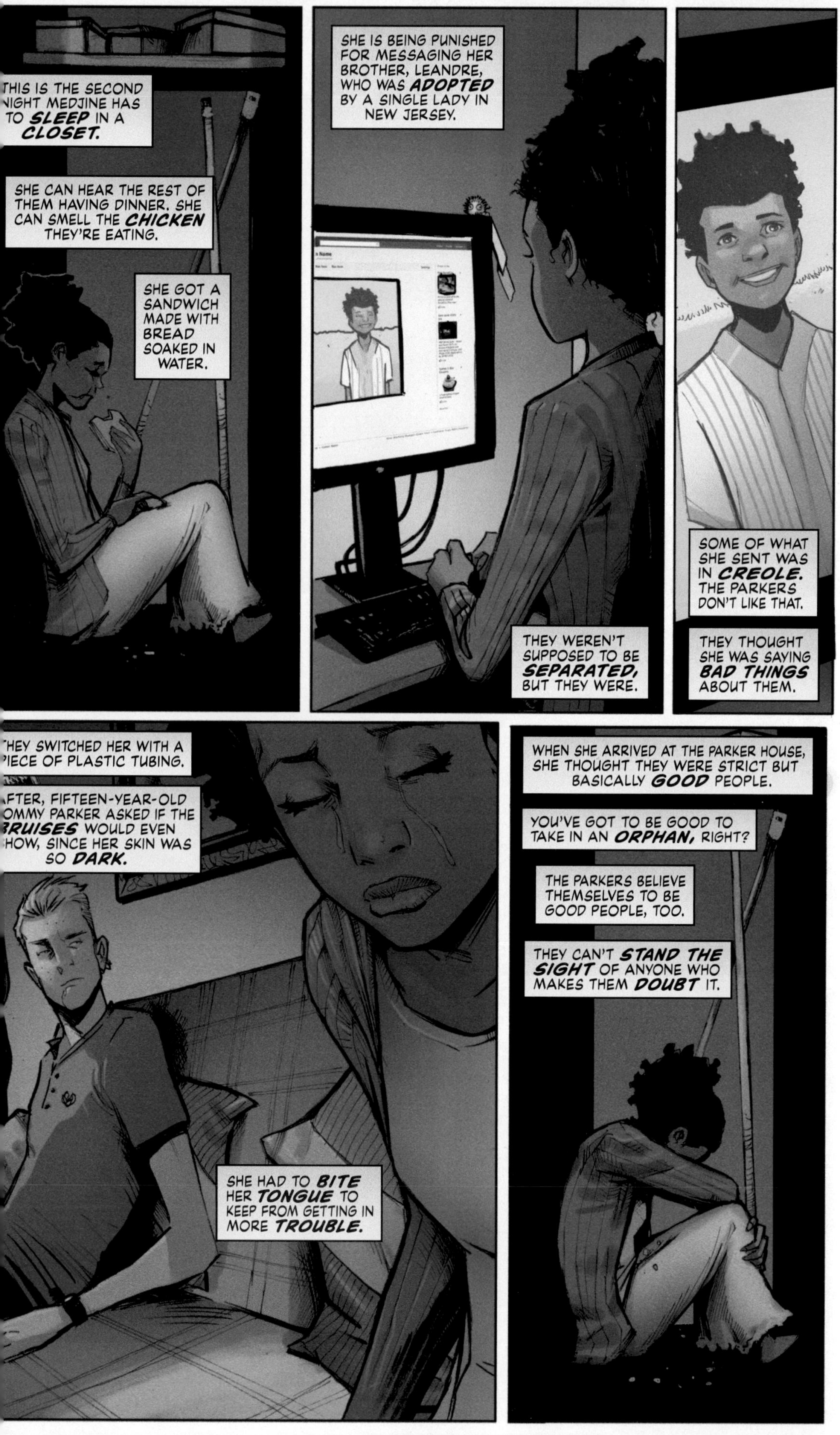

THIS IS THE SECOND NIGHT MEDJINE HAS TO SLEEP IN A CLOSET.
SHE CAN HEAR THE REST OF THEM HAVING DINNER. SHE CAN SMELL THE CHICKEN THEY'RE EATING.
SHE GOT A SANDWICH MADE WITH BREAD SOAKED IN WATER.
SHE IS BEING PUNISHED FOR MESSAGING HER BROTHER, LEANDRE, WHO WAS ADOPTED BY A SINGLE LADY IN NEW JERSEY.
THEY WEREN'T SUPPOSED TO BE SEPARATED, BUT THEY WERE.
SOME OF WHAT SHE SENT WAS IN CREOLE. THE PARKERS DON'T LIKE THAT.
THEY THOUGHT SHE WAS SAYING BAD THINGS ABOUT THEM.
THEY SWITCHED HER WITH A PIECE OF PLASTIC TUBING.
AFTER, FIFTEEN-YEAR-OLD TOMMY PARKER ASKED IF THE BRUISES WOULD EVEN SHOW, SINCE HER SKIN WAS SO DARK.
SHE HAD TO BITE HER TONGUE TO KEEP FROM GETTING IN MORE TROUBLE.
WHEN SHE ARRIVED AT THE PARKER HOUSE, SHE THOUGHT THEY WERE STRICT BUT BASICALLY GOOD PEOPLE.
YOU'VE GOT TO BE GOOD TO TAKE IN AN ORPHAN, RIGHT?
THE PARKERS BELIEVE THEMSELVES TO BE GOOD PEOPLE, TOO.
THEY CAN'T STAND THE SIGHT OF ANYONE WHO MAKES THEM DOUBT IT.

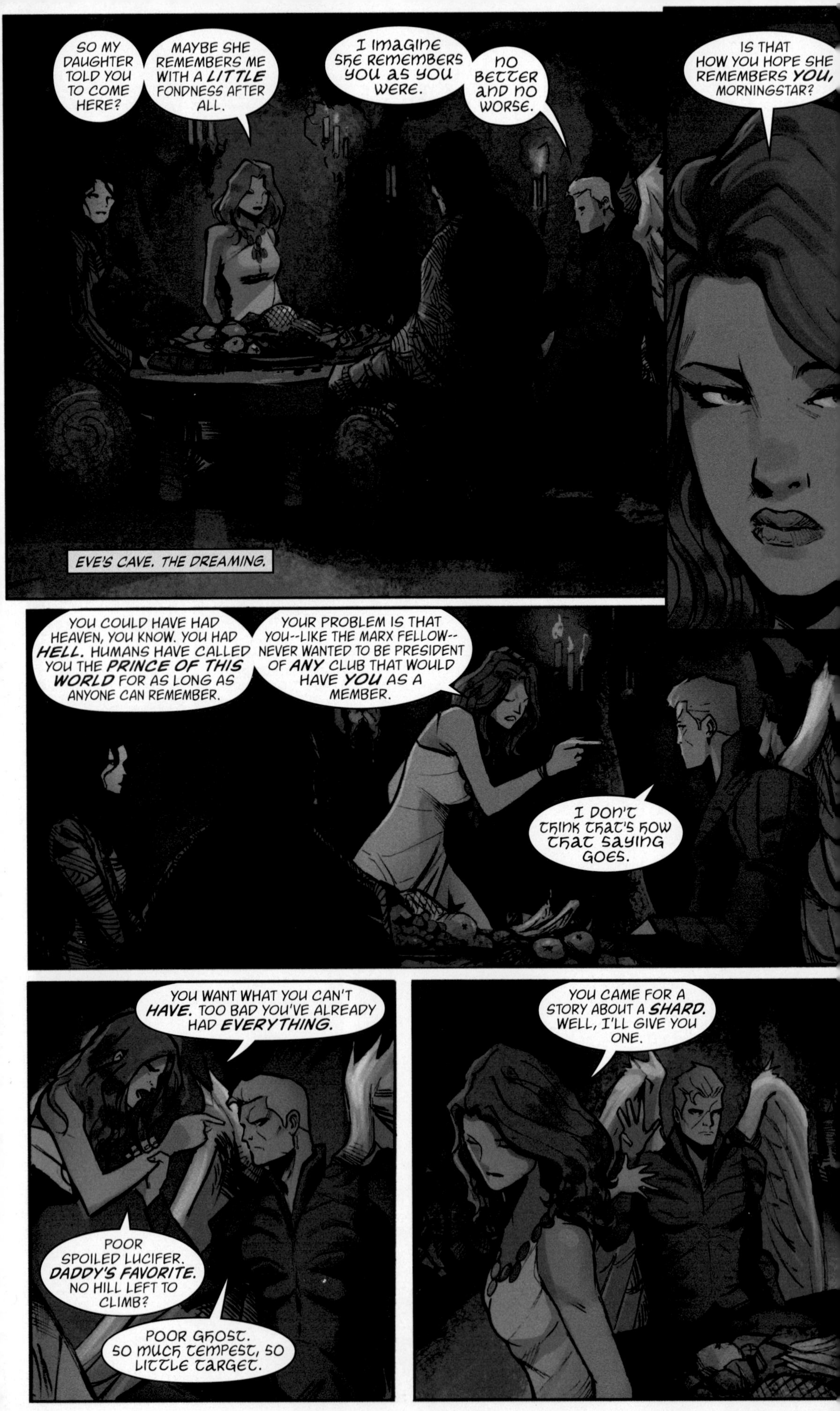

SO MY DAUGHTER TOLD YOU TO COME HERE?
MAYBE SHE REMEMBERS ME WITH A *LITTLE* FONDNESS AFTER ALL.
I IMAGINE SHE REMEMBERS YOU AS YOU WERE.
NO BETTER AND NO WORSE.
IS THAT HOW YOU HOPE SHE REMEMBERS *YOU,* MORNINGSTAR?
EVE'S CAVE. THE DREAMING.
YOU COULD HAVE HAD HEAVEN, YOU KNOW. YOU HAD *HELL.* HUMANS HAVE CALLED YOU THE *PRINCE OF THIS WORLD* FOR AS LONG AS ANYONE CAN REMEMBER.
YOUR PROBLEM IS THAT YOU--LIKE THE MARX FELLOW--NEVER WANTED TO BE PRESIDENT OF *ANY* CLUB THAT WOULD HAVE *YOU* AS A MEMBER.
I DON'T THINK THAT'S HOW THAT SAYING GOES.
YOU WANT WHAT YOU CAN'T *HAVE.* TOO BAD YOU'VE ALREADY HAD *EVERYTHING.*
POOR SPOILED LUCIFER. *DADDY'S FAVORITE.* NO HILL LEFT TO CLIMB?
POOR GHOST. SO MUCH TEMPEST, SO LITTLE TARGET.
YOU CAME FOR A STORY ABOUT A *SHARD.* WELL, I'LL GIVE YOU ONE.

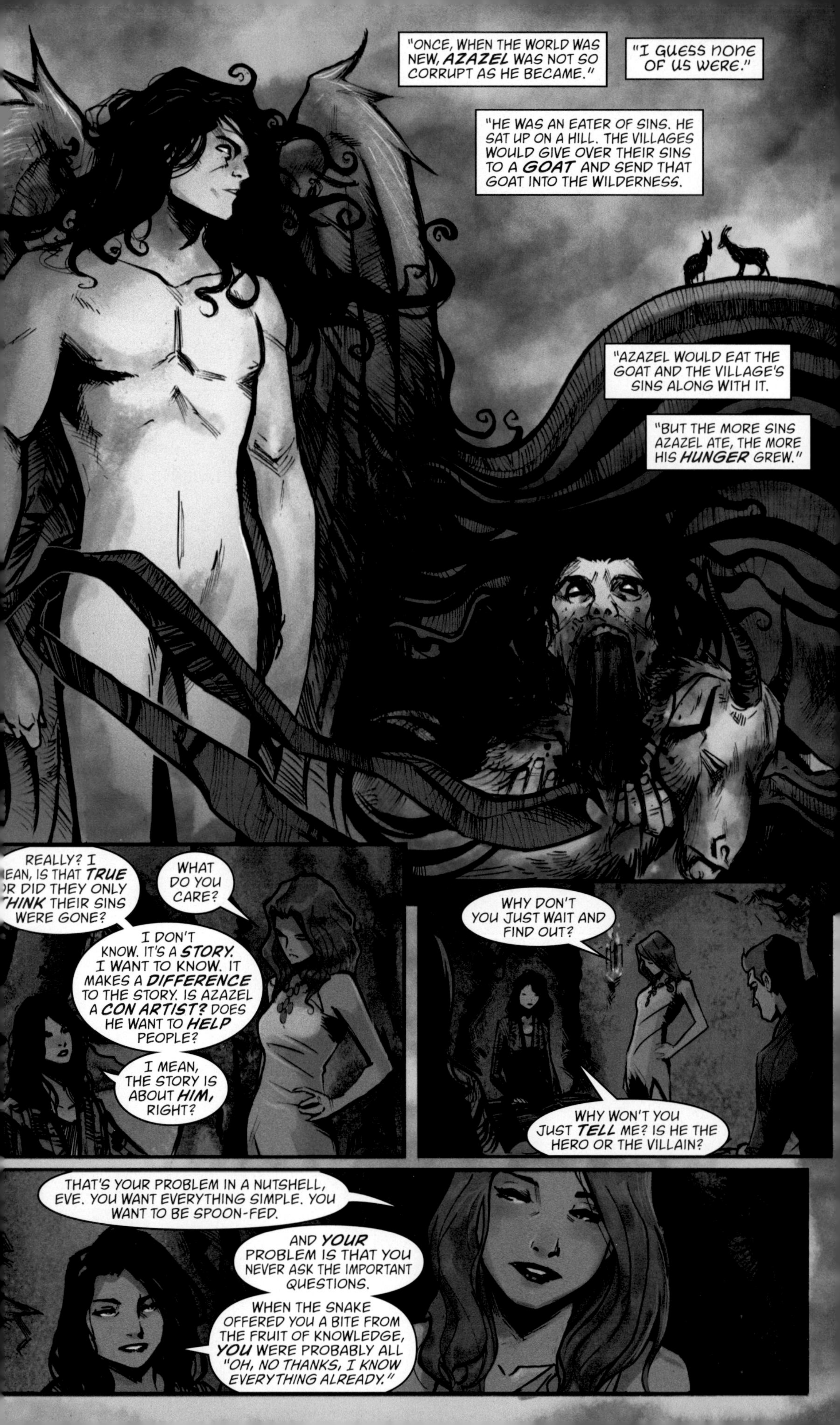
"ONCE, WHEN THE WORLD WAS NEW, AZAZEL WAS NOT SO CORRUPT AS HE BECAME."
"I GUESS NONE OF US WERE."
"HE WAS AN EATER OF SINS. HE SAT UP ON A HILL. THE VILLAGES WOULD GIVE OVER THEIR SINS TO A GOAT AND SEND THAT GOAT INTO THE WILDERNESS.
"AZAZEL WOULD EAT THE GOAT AND THE VILLAGE'S SINS ALONG WITH IT.
"BUT THE MORE SINS AZAZEL ATE, THE MORE HIS HUNGER GREW."
REALLY? I MEAN, IS THAT TRUE OR DID THEY ONLY THINK THEIR SINS WERE GONE?
WHAT DO YOU CARE?
I DON'T KNOW. IT'S A STORY. I WANT TO KNOW. IT MAKES A DIFFERENCE TO THE STORY. IS AZAZEL A CON ARTIST? DOES HE WANT TO HELP PEOPLE?
I MEAN, THE STORY IS ABOUT HIM, RIGHT?
WHY DON'T YOU JUST WAIT AND FIND OUT?
WHY WON'T YOU JUST TELL ME? IS HE THE HERO OR THE VILLAIN?
THAT'S YOUR PROBLEM IN A NUTSHELL, EVE. YOU WANT EVERYTHING SIMPLE. YOU WANT TO BE SPOON-FED.
AND YOUR PROBLEM IS THAT YOU NEVER ASK THE IMPORTANT QUESTIONS.
WHEN THE SNAKE OFFERED YOU A BITE FROM THE FRUIT OF KNOWLEDGE, YOU WERE PROBABLY ALL "OH, NO THANKS, I KNOW EVERYTHING ALREADY."

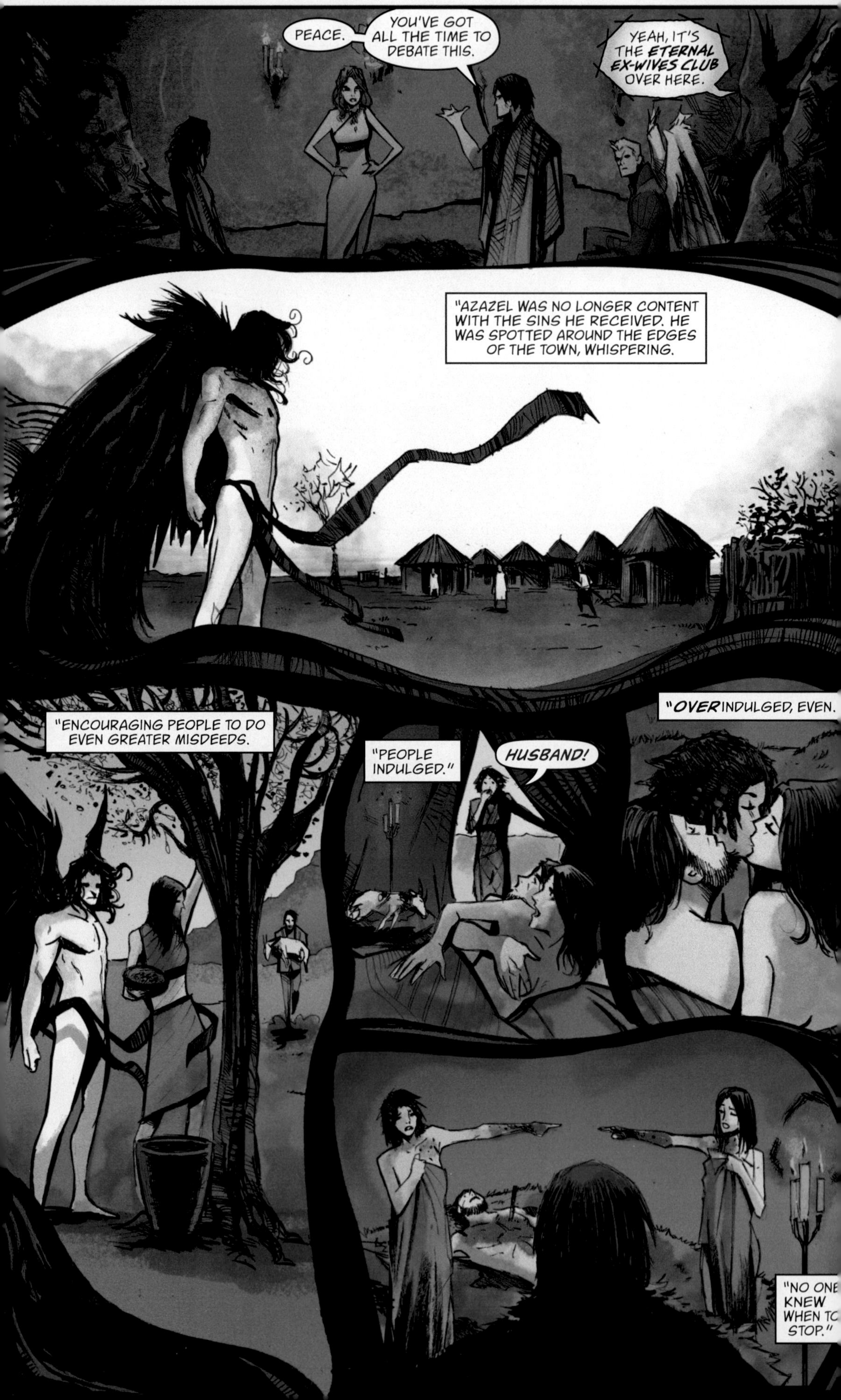
PEACE.
YOU'VE GOT ALL THE TIME TO DEBATE THIS.
YEAH, IT'S THE ETERNAL EX-WIVES CLUB OVER HERE.
"AZAZEL WAS NO LONGER CONTENT WITH THE SINS HE RECEIVED. HE WAS SPOTTED AROUND THE EDGES OF THE TOWN, WHISPERING.
"ENCOURAGING PEOPLE TO DO EVEN GREATER MISDEEDS.
"PEOPLE INDULGED."
HUSBAND!
"OVERINDULGED, EVEN.
"NO ONE KNEW WHEN TO STOP."

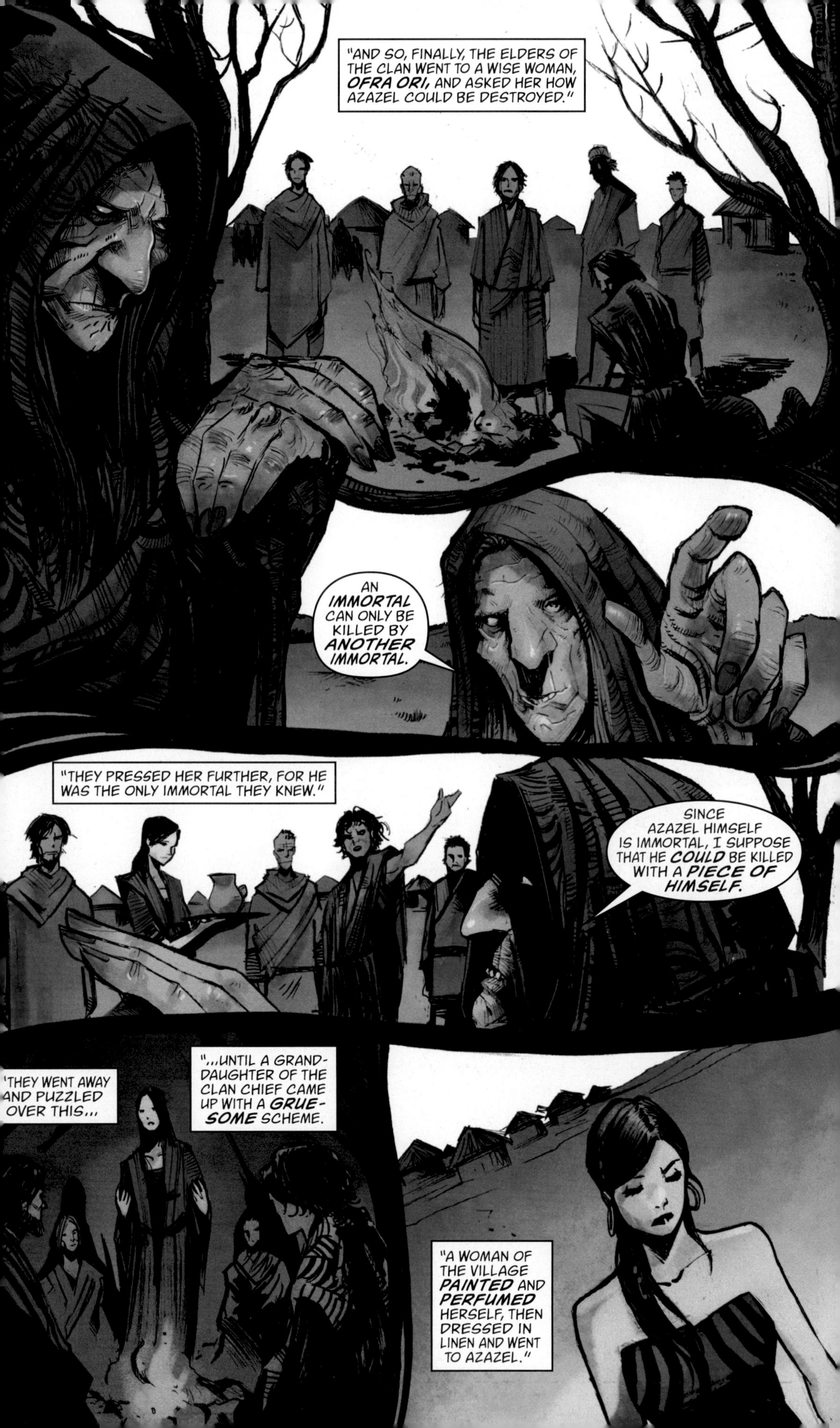
"AND SO, FINALLY, THE ELDERS OF THE CLAN WENT TO A WISE WOMAN, OFRA ORI, AND ASKED HER HOW AZAZEL COULD BE DESTROYED."
AN IMMORTAL CAN ONLY BE KILLED BY ANOTHER IMMORTAL.
"THEY PRESSED HER FURTHER, FOR HE WAS THE ONLY IMMORTAL THEY KNEW."
SINCE AZAZEL HIMSELF IS IMMORTAL, I SUPPOSE THAT HE COULD BE KILLED WITH A PIECE OF HIMSELF.
"THEY WENT AWAY AND PUZZLED OVER THIS...
"...UNTIL A GRAND-DAUGHTER OF THE CLAN CHIEF CAME UP WITH A GRUESOME SCHEME.
"A WOMAN OF THE VILLAGE PAINTED AND PERFUMED HERSELF, THEN DRESSED IN LINEN AND WENT TO AZAZEL."

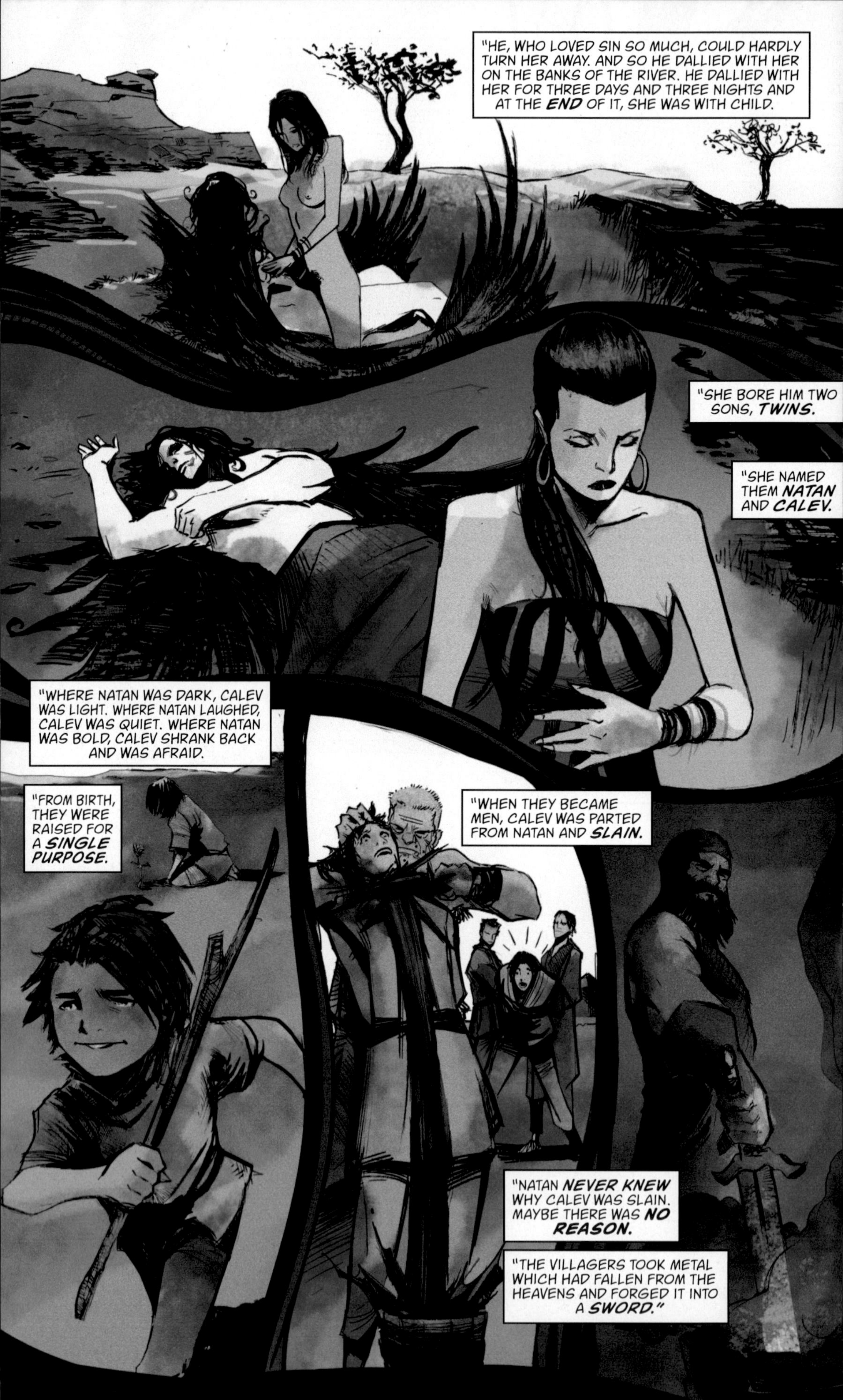
"HE, WHO LOVED SIN SO MUCH, COULD HARDLY TURN HER AWAY. AND SO HE DALLIED WITH HER ON THE BANKS OF THE RIVER. HE DALLIED WITH HER FOR THREE DAYS AND THREE NIGHTS AND AT THE END OF IT, SHE WAS WITH CHILD.
"SHE BORE HIM TWO SONS, TWINS.
"SHE NAMED THEM NATAN AND CALEV.
"WHERE NATAN WAS DARK, CALEV WAS LIGHT. WHERE NATAN LAUGHED, CALEV WAS QUIET. WHERE NATAN WAS BOLD, CALEV SHRANK BACK AND WAS AFRAID.
"FROM BIRTH, THEY WERE RAISED FOR A SINGLE PURPOSE.
"WHEN THEY BECAME MEN, CALEV WAS PARTED FROM NATAN AND SLAIN.
"NATAN NEVER KNEW WHY CALEV WAS SLAIN. MAYBE THERE WAS NO REASON.
"THE VILLAGERS TOOK METAL WHICH HAD FALLEN FROM THE HEAVENS AND FORGED IT INTO A SWORD."

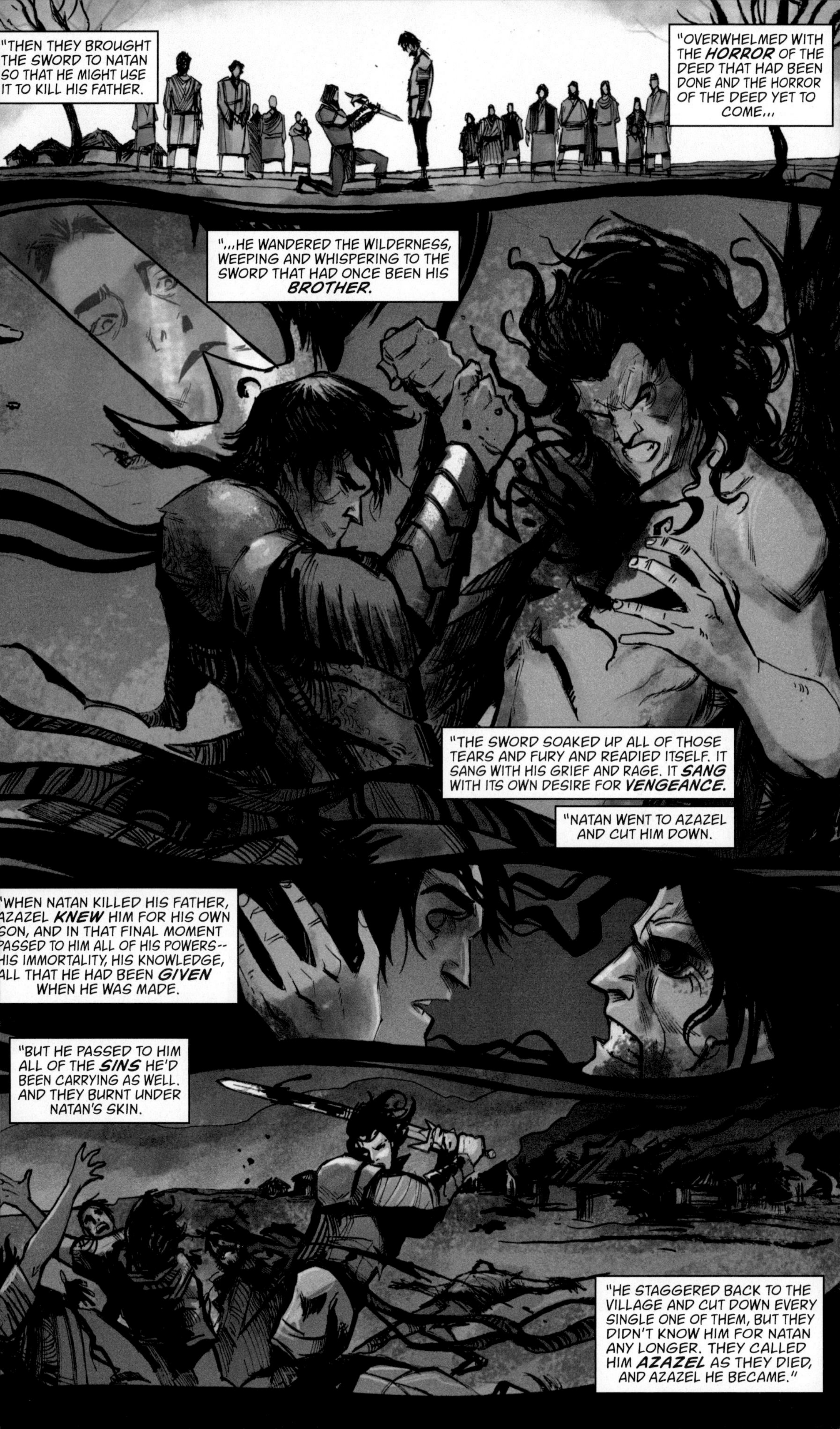
"THEN THEY BROUGHT THE SWORD TO NATAN SO THAT HE MIGHT USE IT TO KILL HIS FATHER.
"OVERWHELMED WITH THE HORROR OF THE DEED THAT HAD BEEN DONE AND THE HORROR OF THE DEED YET TO COME...
"...HE WANDERED THE WILDERNESS, WEEPING AND WHISPERING TO THE SWORD THAT HAD ONCE BEEN HIS BROTHER.
"THE SWORD SOAKED UP ALL OF THOSE TEARS AND FURY AND READIED ITSELF. IT SANG WITH HIS GRIEF AND RAGE. IT SANG WITH ITS OWN DESIRE FOR VENGEANCE.
"NATAN WENT TO AZAZEL AND CUT HIM DOWN.
"WHEN NATAN KILLED HIS FATHER, AZAZEL KNEW HIM FOR HIS OWN SON, AND IN THAT FINAL MOMENT PASSED TO HIM ALL OF HIS POWERS--HIS IMMORTALITY, HIS KNOWLEDGE, ALL THAT HE HAD BEEN GIVEN WHEN HE WAS MADE.
"BUT HE PASSED TO HIM ALL OF THE SINS HE'D BEEN CARRYING AS WELL. AND THEY BURNT UNDER NATAN'S SKIN.
"HE STAGGERED BACK TO THE VILLAGE AND CUT DOWN EVERY SINGLE ONE OF THEM, BUT THEY DIDN'T KNOW HIM FOR NATAN ANY LONGER. THEY CALLED HIM AZAZEL AS THEY DIED, AND AZAZEL HE BECAME."

"THE LORD SAID TO RAPHAEL: 'BIND AZAZEL HAND AND FOOT, AND CAST HIM INTO THE *DARKNESS*. MAKE AN OPENING IN THE DESERT, WHICH IS IN DUDAEL, AND CAST HIM THEREIN.'

"'PLACE UPON HIM ROUGH AND JAGGED ROCKS, AND COVER HIM WITH DARKNESS, AND LET HIM ABIDE THERE FOR EVER. AND ON THE DAY OF THE GREAT JUDGMENT HE SHALL BE CAST INTO THE FIRE.'

"AT LEAST THAT'S HOW THE BOOK OF *ENOCH* REMEMBERS IT.

"AND SO HE WAS, UNTIL HIS FLESH WORE AWAY AND HE REMEMBERED HIMSELF TO BE *NATAN* NO LONGER, BUT KNEW HIMSELF TO BE *AZAZEL*."

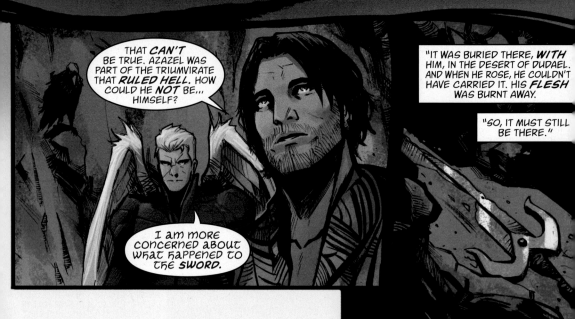

THAT *CAN'T* BE TRUE. AZAZEL WAS PART OF THE TRIUMVIRATE THAT *RULED HELL*. HOW COULD HE *NOT* BE... HIMSELF?

I AM MORE CONCERNED ABOUT WHAT HAPPENED TO THE *SWORD*.

"IT WAS BURIED THERE, *WITH* HIM, IN THE DESERT OF DUDAEL. AND WHEN HE ROSE, HE COULDN'T HAVE CARRIED IT. HIS *FLESH* WAS BURNT AWAY.

"SO, IT MUST STILL BE THERE."

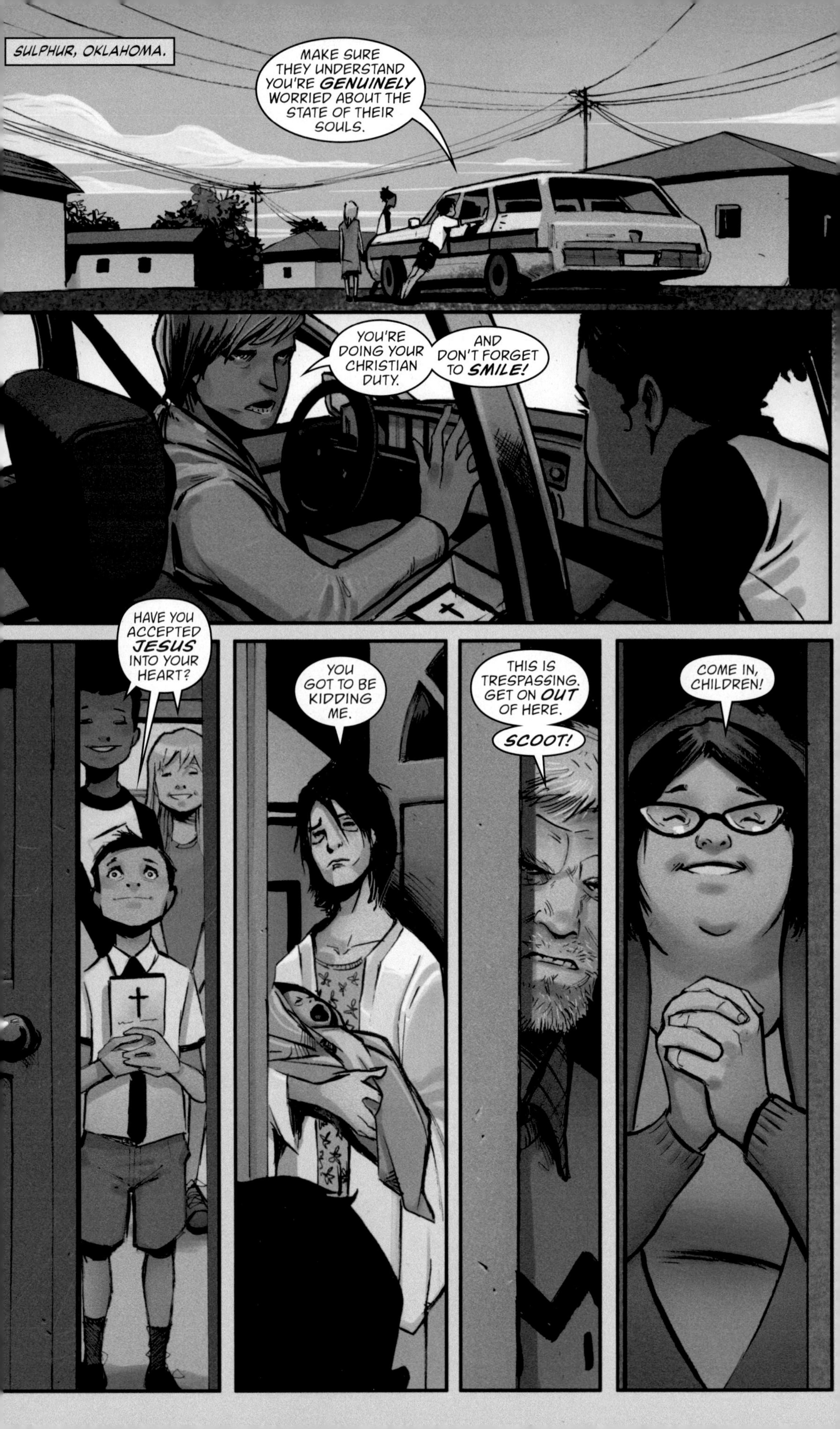
SULPHUR, OKLAHOMA.
MAKE SURE THEY UNDERSTAND YOU'RE GENUINELY WORRIED ABOUT THE STATE OF THEIR SOULS.
YOU'RE DOING YOUR CHRISTIAN DUTY.
AND DON'T FORGET TO SMILE!
HAVE YOU ACCEPTED JESUS INTO YOUR HEART?
YOU GOT TO BE KIDDING ME.
THIS IS TRESPASSING. GET ON OUT OF HERE.
SCOOT!
COME IN, CHILDREN!

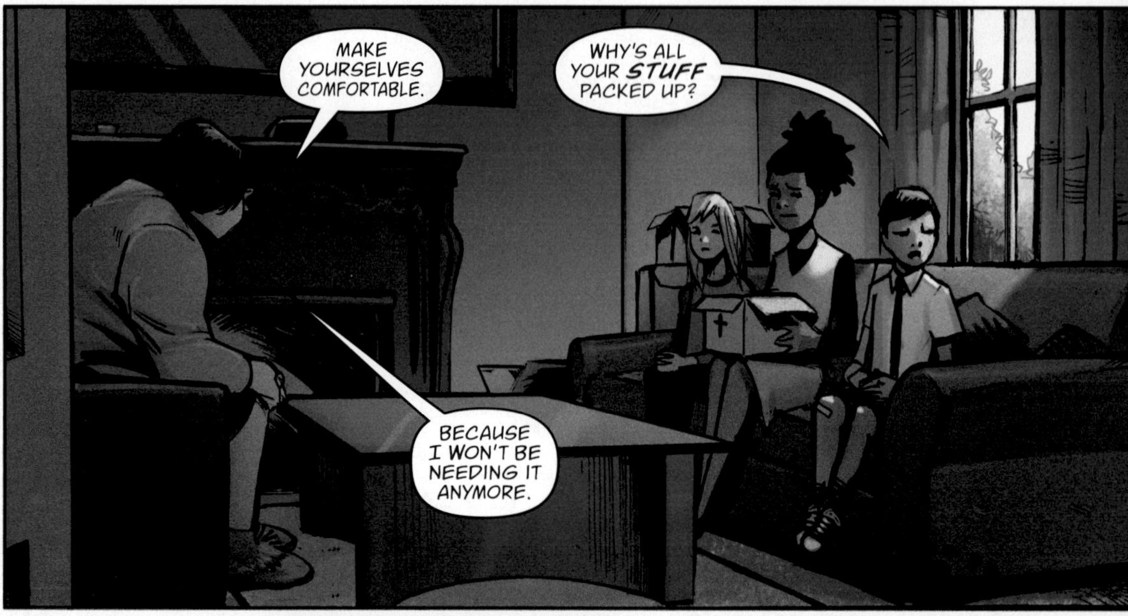
MAKE YOURSELVES COMFORTABLE.
WHY'S ALL YOUR STUFF PACKED UP?
BECAUSE I WON'T BE NEEDING IT ANYMORE.

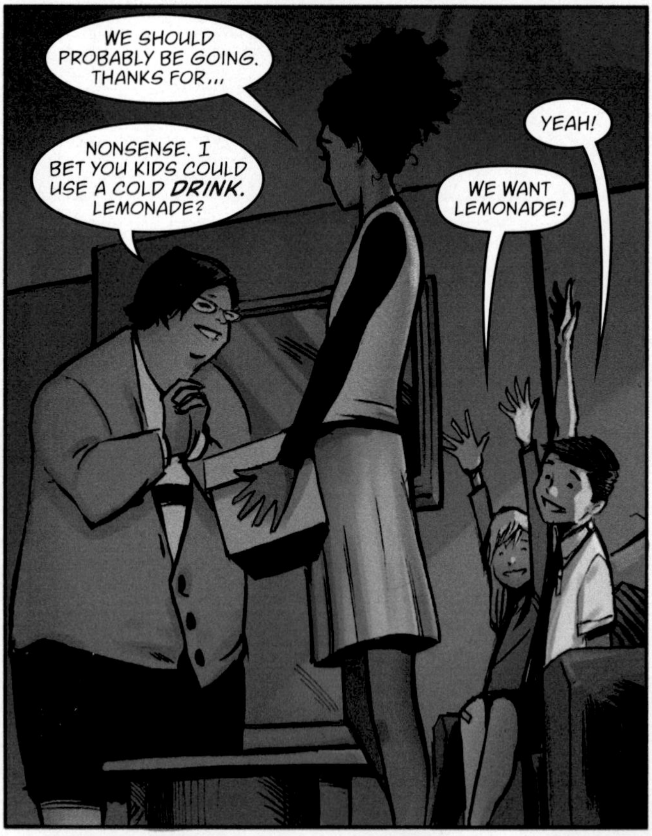
WE SHOULD PROBABLY BE GOING. THANKS FOR...
NONSENSE. I BET YOU KIDS COULD USE A COLD DRINK. LEMONADE?
YEAH!
WE WANT LEMONADE!

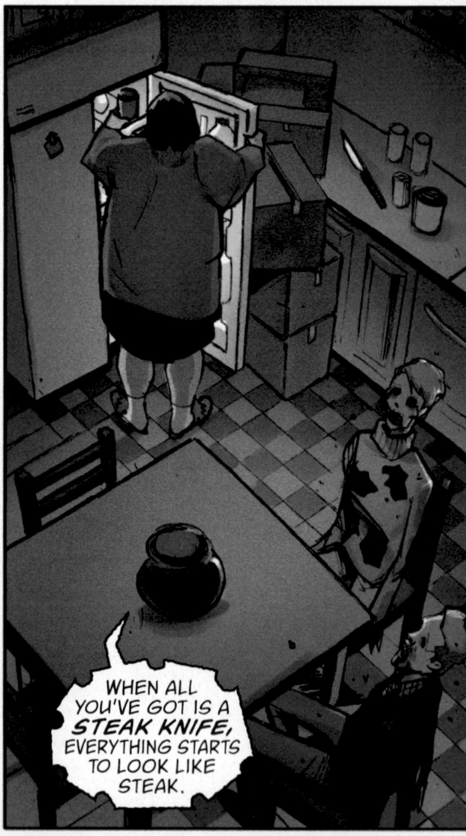
WHEN ALL YOU'VE GOT IS A STEAK KNIFE, EVERYTHING STARTS TO LOOK LIKE STEAK.

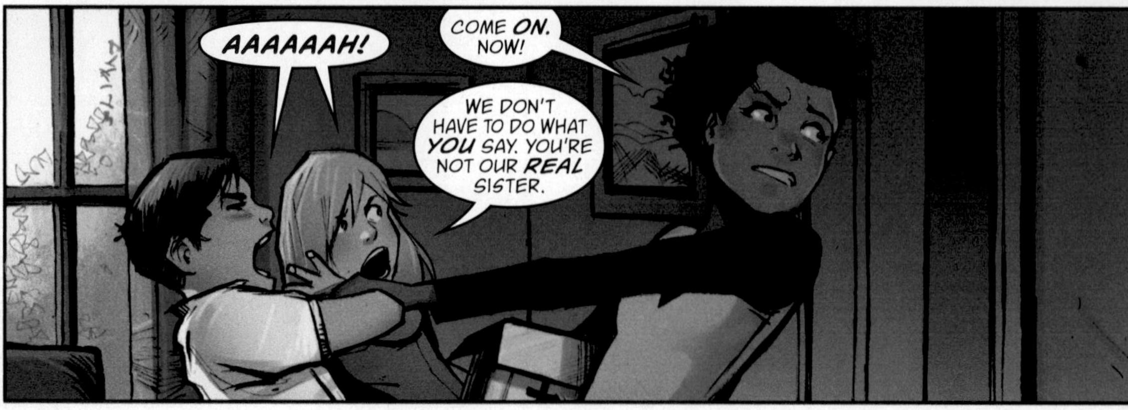
AAAAAAH!
COME ON. NOW!
WE DON'T HAVE TO DO WHAT YOU SAY. YOU'RE NOT OUR REAL SISTER.

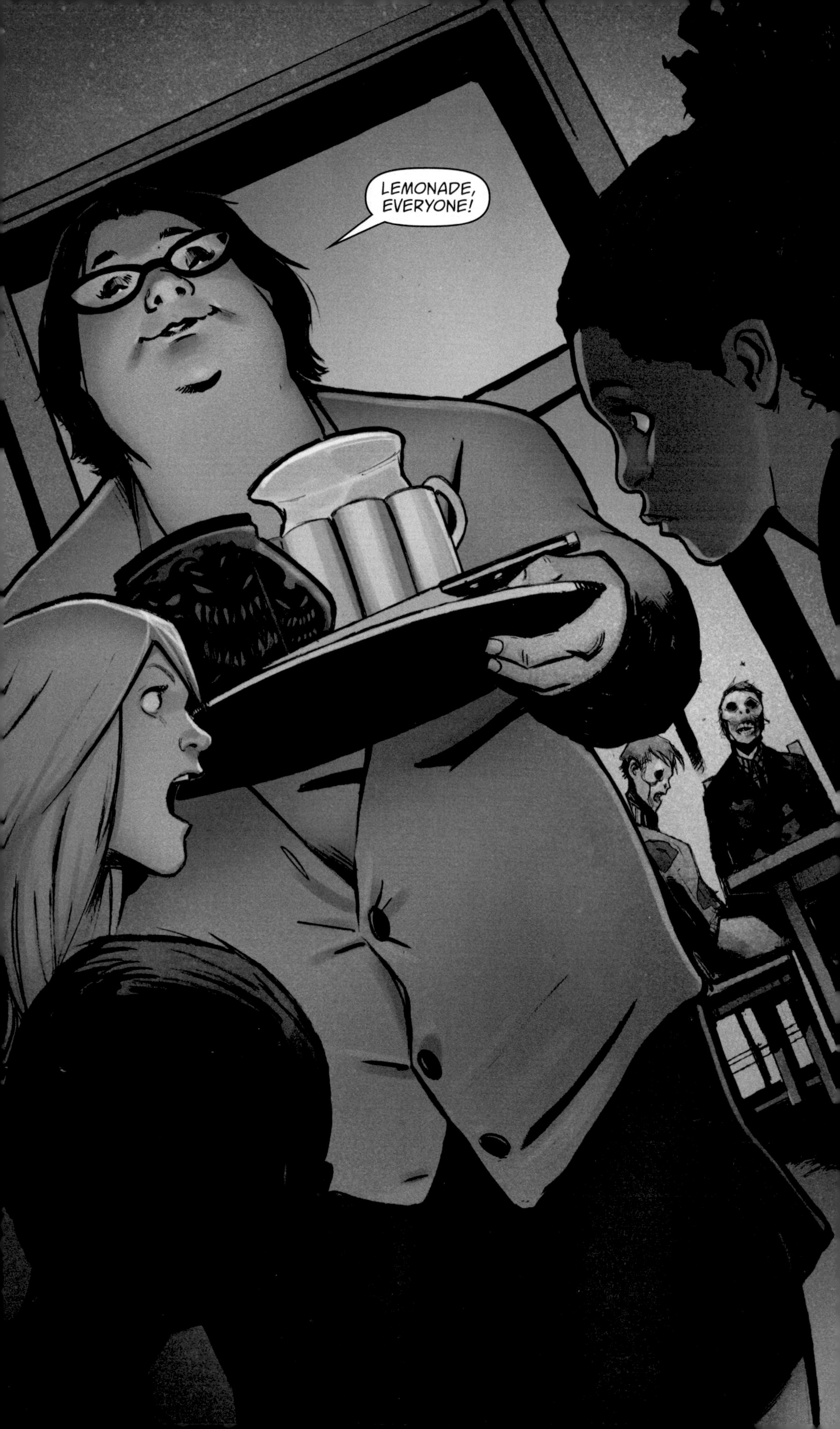
LEMONADE, EVERYONE!

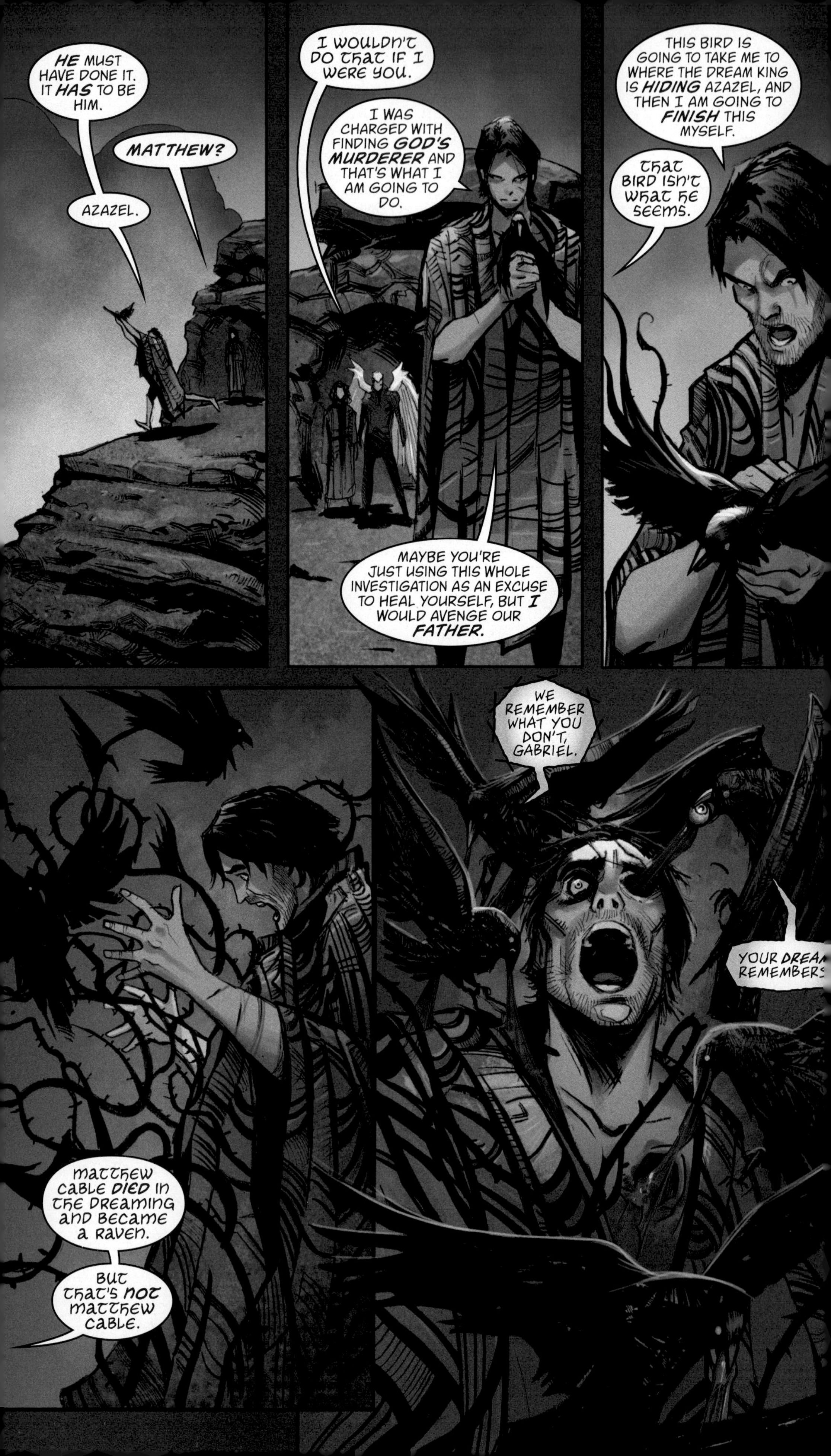

HE MUST HAVE DONE IT. IT HAS TO BE HIM.
MATTHEW?
AZAZEL.
I WOULDN'T DO THAT IF I WERE YOU.
I WAS CHARGED WITH FINDING GOD'S MURDERER AND THAT'S WHAT I AM GOING TO DO.
MAYBE YOU'RE JUST USING THIS WHOLE INVESTIGATION AS AN EXCUSE TO HEAL YOURSELF, BUT I WOULD AVENGE OUR FATHER.
THIS BIRD IS GOING TO TAKE ME TO WHERE THE DREAM KING IS HIDING AZAZEL, AND THEN I AM GOING TO FINISH THIS MYSELF.
THAT BIRD ISN'T WHAT HE SEEMS.
MATTHEW CABLE DIED IN THE DREAMING AND BECAME A RAVEN.
BUT THAT'S NOT MATTHEW CABLE.
WE REMEMBER WHAT YOU DON'T, GABRIEL.

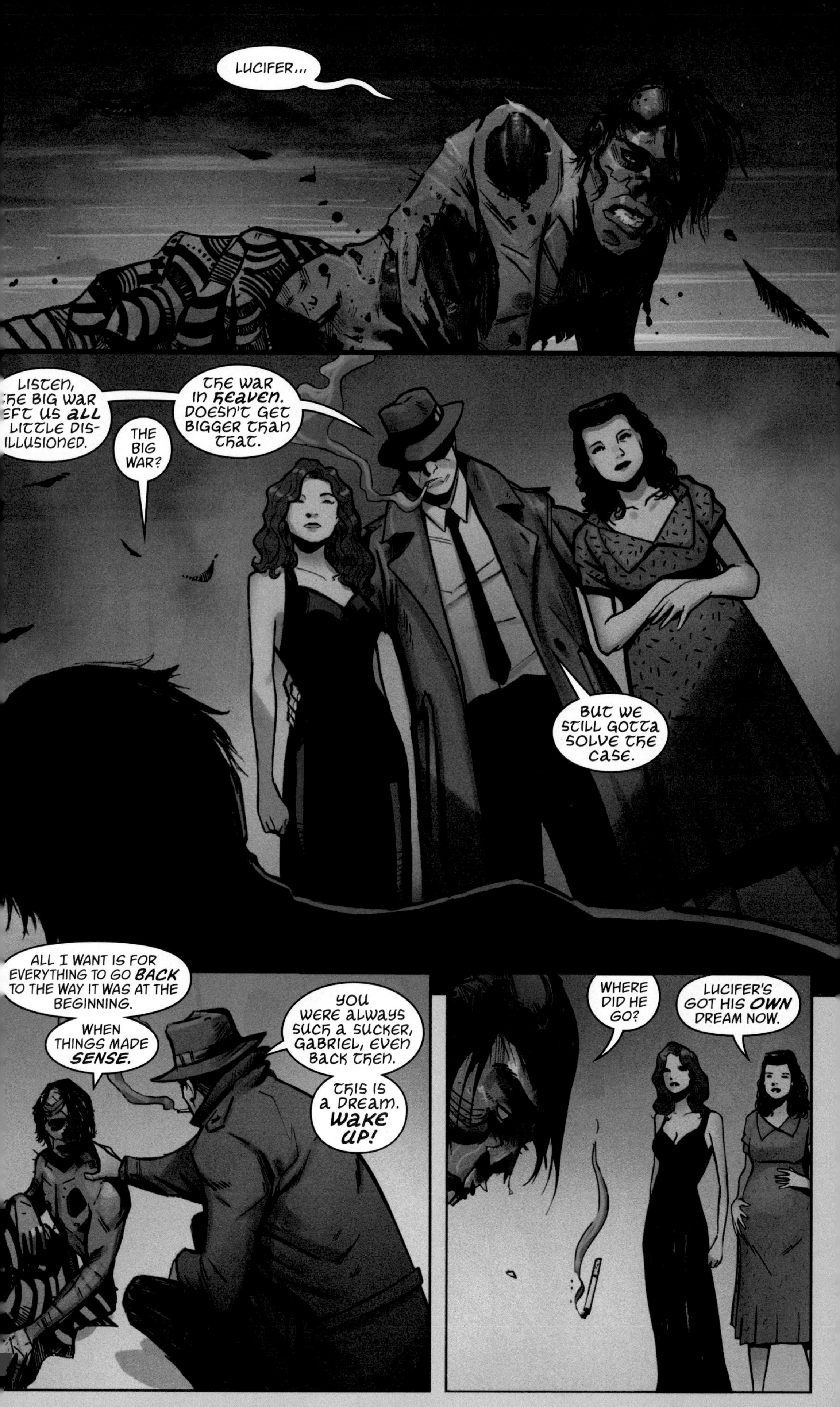
LUCIFER...
LISTEN, THE BIG WAR LEFT US ALL A LITTLE DIS-ILLUSIONED.
THE BIG WAR?
THE WAR IN HEAVEN. DOESN'T GET BIGGER THAN THAT.
BUT WE STILL GOTTA SOLVE THE CASE.
ALL I WANT IS FOR EVERYTHING TO GO BACK TO THE WAY IT WAS AT THE BEGINNING.
WHEN THINGS MADE SENSE.
YOU WERE ALWAYS SUCH A SUCKER, GABRIEL, EVEN BACK THEN.
THIS IS A DREAM. WAKE UP!
WHERE DID HE GO?
LUCIFER'S GOT HIS OWN DREAM NOW.

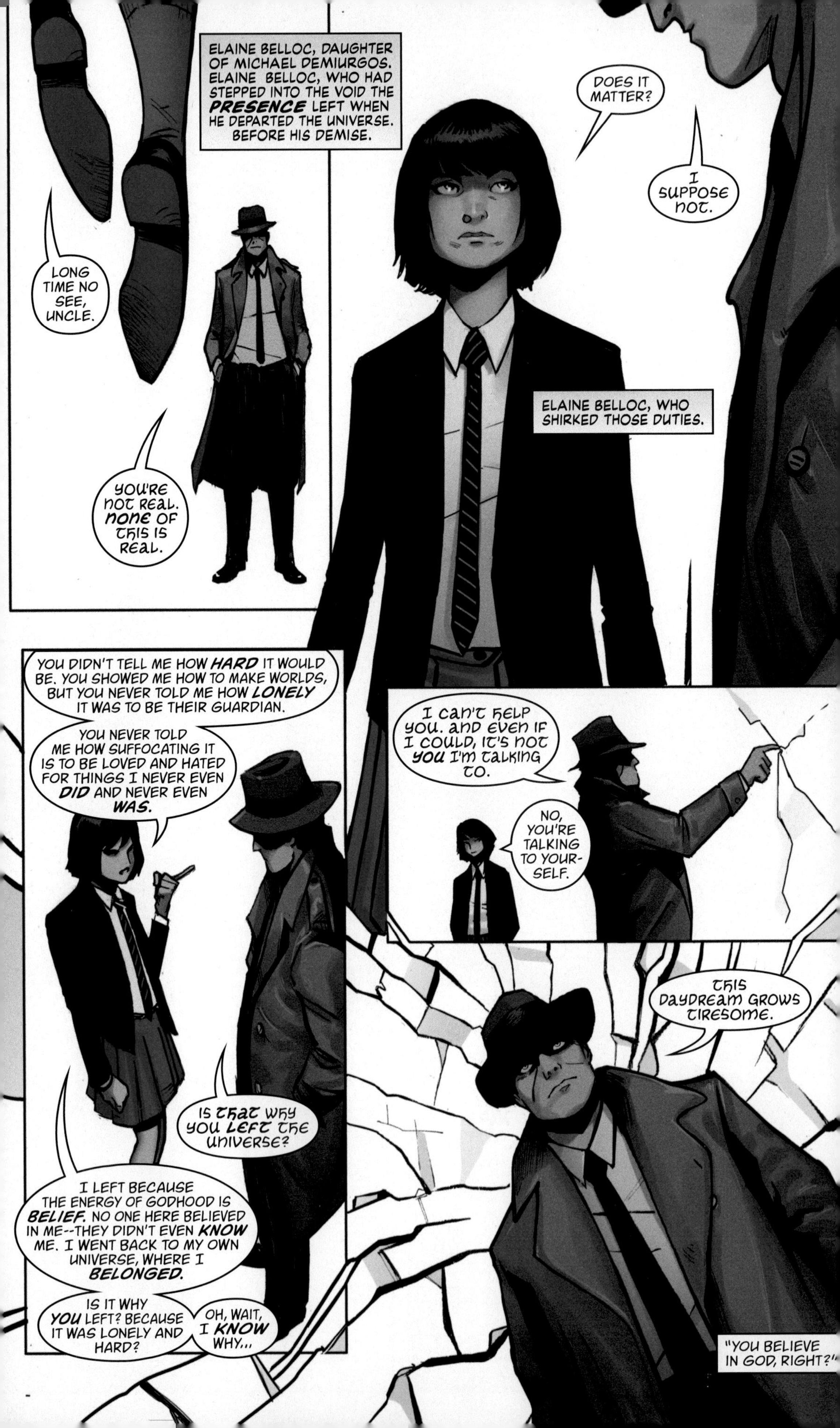
ELAINE BELLOC, DAUGHTER OF MICHAEL DEMIURGOS. ELAINE BELLOC, WHO HAD STEPPED INTO THE VOID THE PRESENCE LEFT WHEN HE DEPARTED THE UNIVERSE. BEFORE HIS DEMISE.
LONG TIME NO SEE, UNCLE.
YOU'RE NOT REAL. NONE OF THIS IS REAL.
DOES IT MATTER?
I SUPPOSE NOT.
ELAINE BELLOC, WHO SHIRKED THOSE DUTIES.
YOU DIDN'T TELL ME HOW HARD IT WOULD BE. YOU SHOWED ME HOW TO MAKE WORLDS, BUT YOU NEVER TOLD ME HOW LONELY IT WAS TO BE THEIR GUARDIAN.
YOU NEVER TOLD ME HOW SUFFOCATING IT IS TO BE LOVED AND HATED FOR THINGS I NEVER EVEN DID AND NEVER EVEN WAS.
IS THAT WHY YOU LEFT THE UNIVERSE?
I LEFT BECAUSE THE ENERGY OF GODHOOD IS BELIEF. NO ONE HERE BELIEVED IN ME--THEY DIDN'T EVEN KNOW ME. I WENT BACK TO MY OWN UNIVERSE, WHERE I BELONGED.
IS IT WHY YOU LEFT? BECAUSE IT WAS LONELY AND HARD?
OH, WAIT, I KNOW WHY...
I CAN'T HELP YOU. AND EVEN IF I COULD, IT'S NOT YOU I'M TALKING TO.
NO, YOU'RE TALKING TO YOURSELF.
THIS DAYDREAM GROWS TIRESOME.
"YOU BELIEVE IN GOD, RIGHT?"

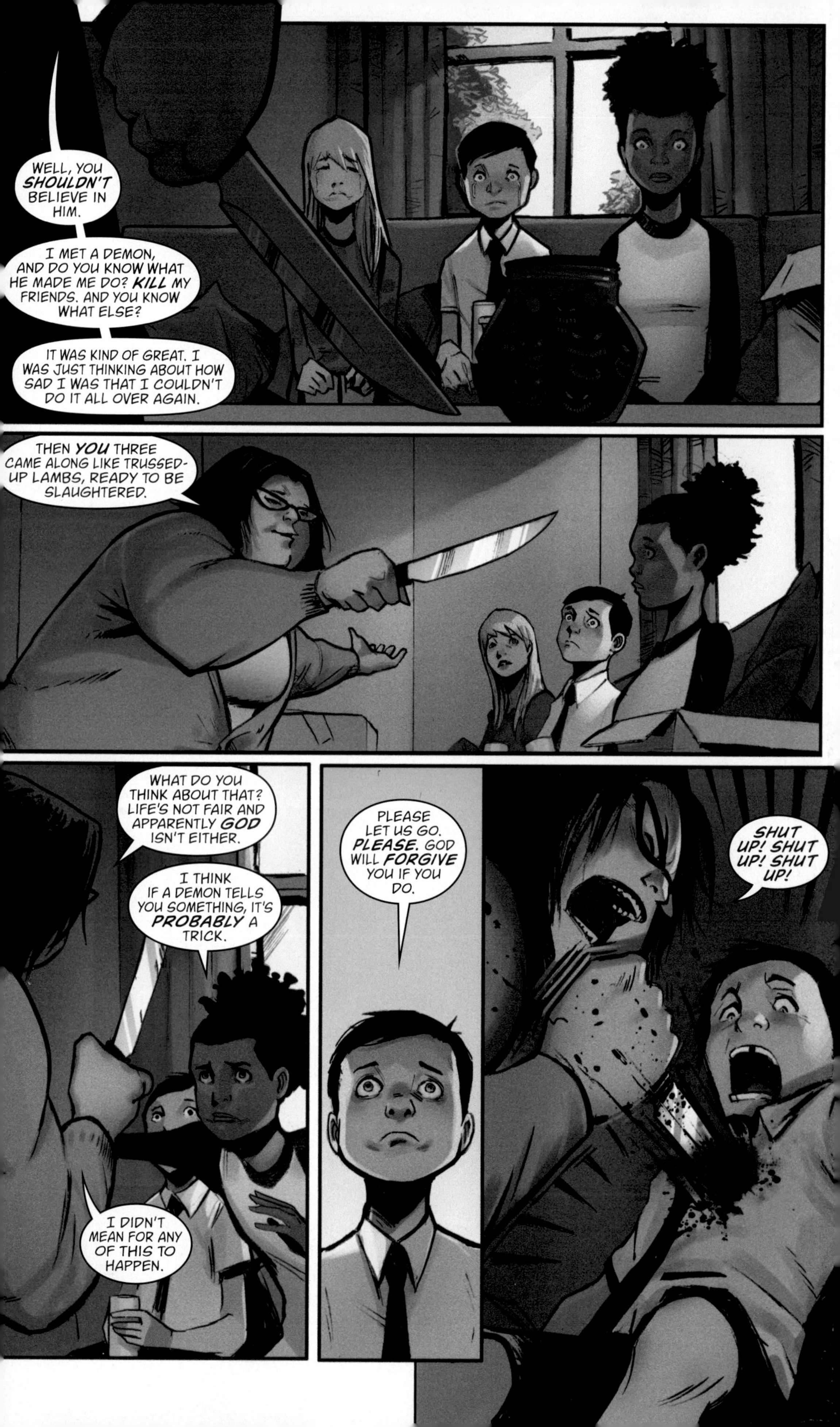
WELL, YOU SHOULDN'T BELIEVE IN HIM.
I MET A DEMON, AND DO YOU KNOW WHAT HE MADE ME DO? KILL MY FRIENDS. AND YOU KNOW WHAT ELSE?
IT WAS KIND OF GREAT. I WAS JUST THINKING ABOUT HOW SAD I WAS THAT I COULDN'T DO IT ALL OVER AGAIN.
THEN YOU THREE CAME ALONG LIKE TRUSSED-UP LAMBS, READY TO BE SLAUGHTERED.
WHAT DO YOU THINK ABOUT THAT? LIFE'S NOT FAIR AND APPARENTLY GOD ISN'T EITHER.
I THINK IF A DEMON TELLS YOU SOMETHING, IT'S PROBABLY A TRICK.
I DIDN'T MEAN FOR ANY OF THIS TO HAPPEN.
PLEASE LET US GO. PLEASE. GOD WILL FORGIVE YOU IF YOU DO.
SHUT UP! SHUT UP! SHUT UP!

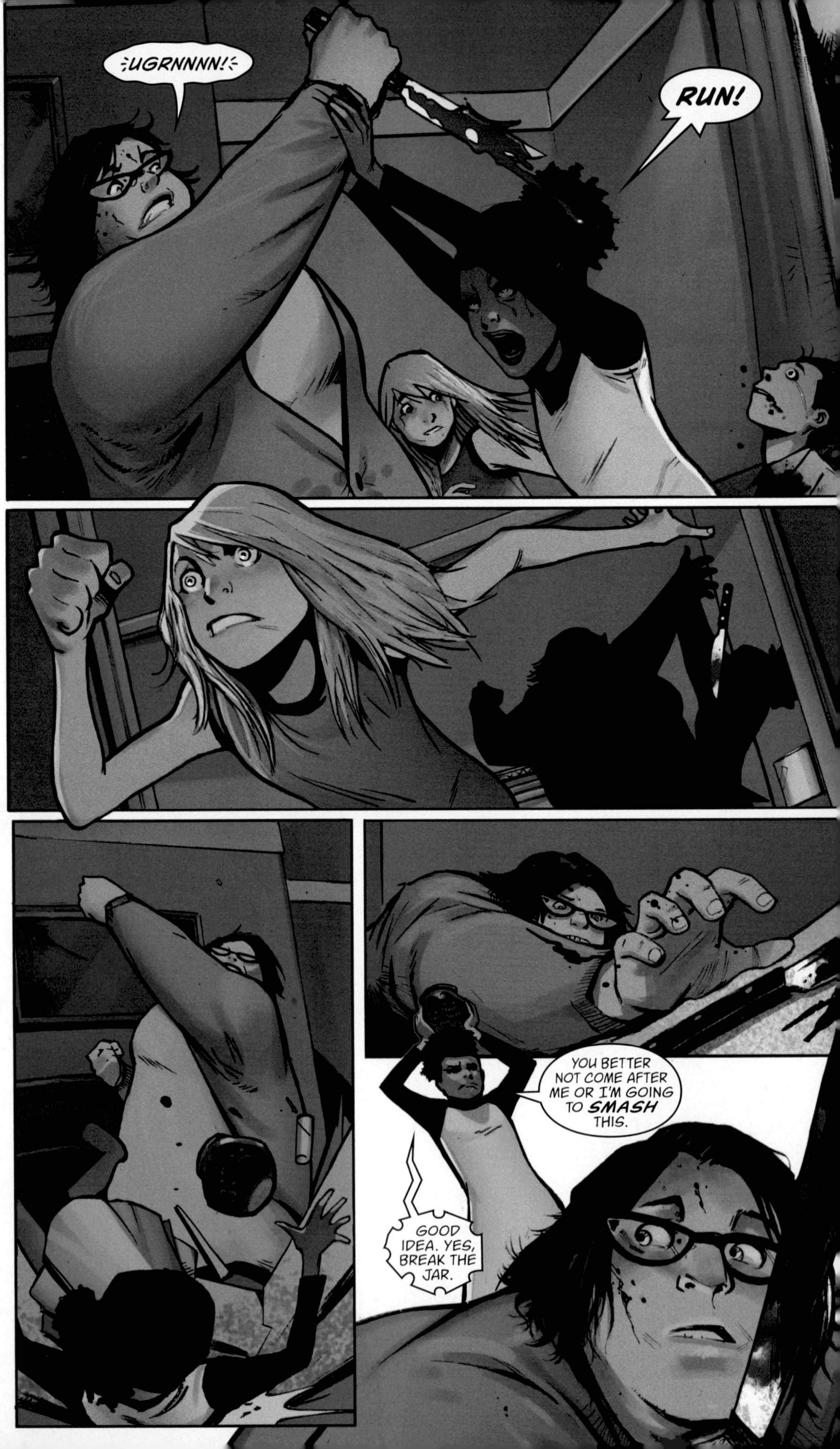
UGRNNNN!
RUN!
YOU BETTER NOT COME AFTER ME OR I'M GOING TO SMASH THIS.
GOOD IDEA. YES, BREAK THE JAR.

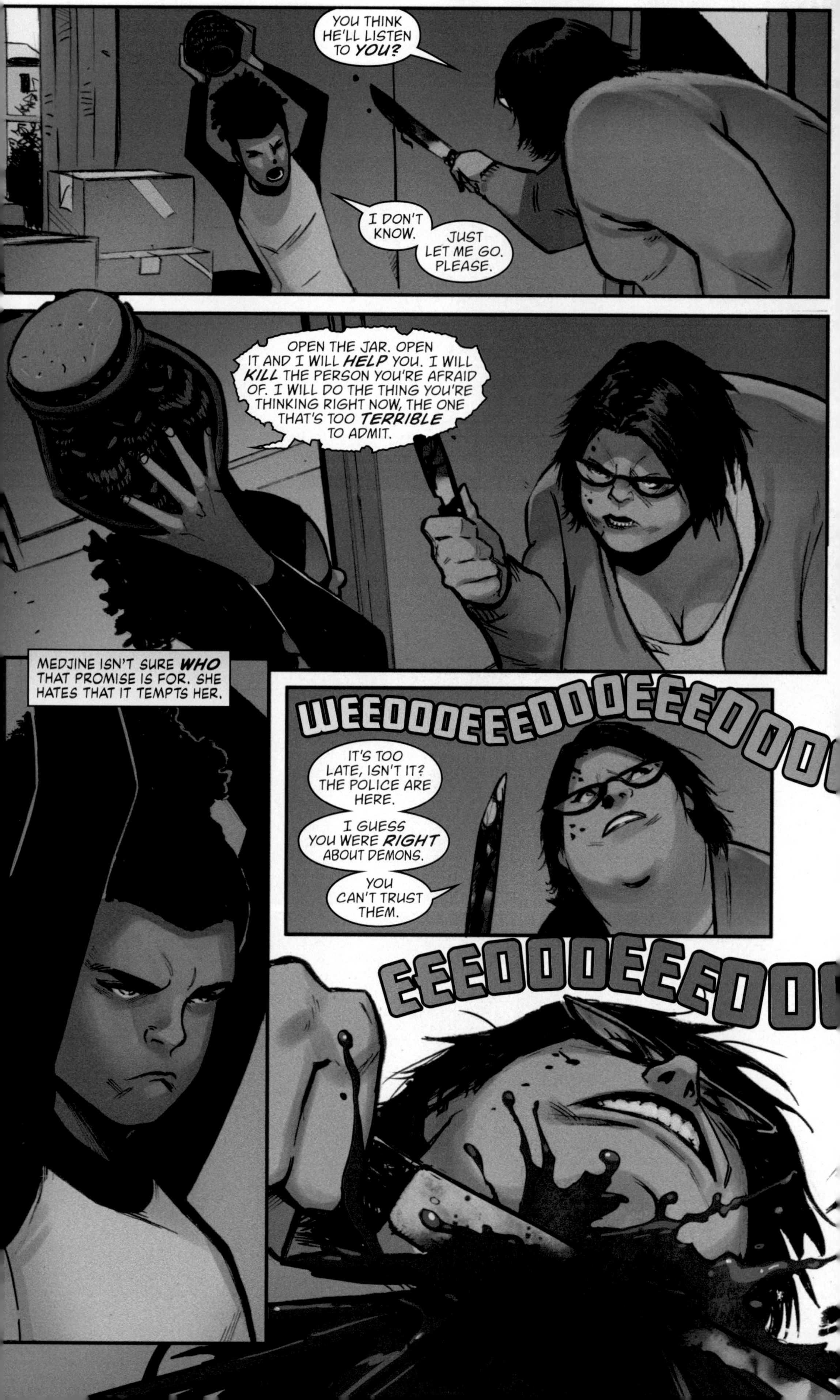
YOU THINK HE'LL LISTEN TO YOU?
I DON'T KNOW.
JUST LET ME GO. PLEASE.
OPEN THE JAR. OPEN IT AND I WILL HELP YOU. I WILL KILL THE PERSON YOU'RE AFRAID OF. I WILL DO THE THING YOU'RE THINKING RIGHT NOW, THE ONE THAT'S TOO TERRIBLE TO ADMIT.
MEDJINE ISN'T SURE WHO THAT PROMISE IS FOR. SHE HATES THAT IT TEMPTS HER.
WEEOOOEEEOOOEEEOOO
IT'S TOO LATE, ISN'T IT? THE POLICE ARE HERE.
I GUESS YOU WERE RIGHT ABOUT DEMONS.
YOU CAN'T TRUST THEM.
EEEOOOEEEOO

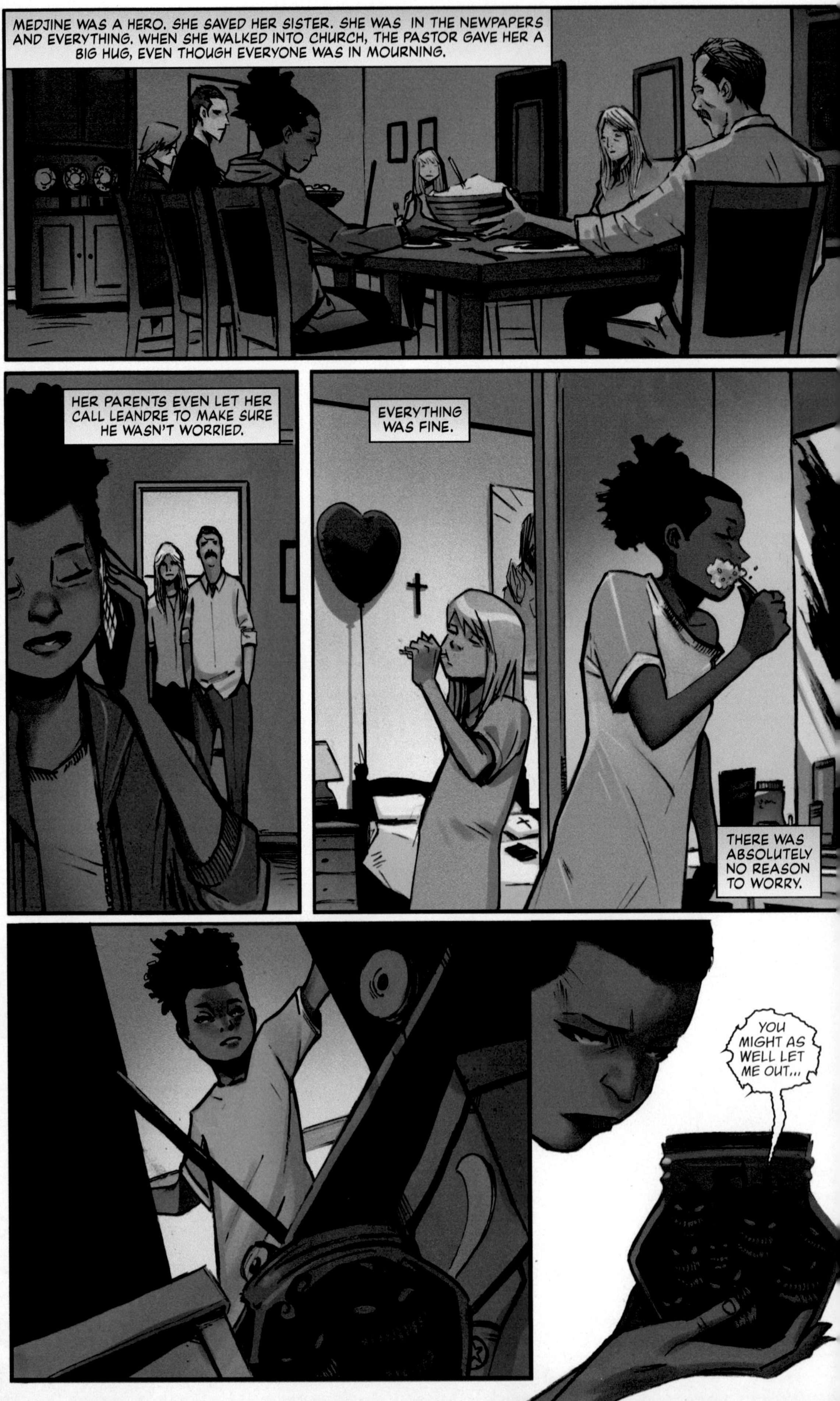
MEDJINE WAS A HERO. SHE SAVED HER SISTER. SHE WAS IN THE NEWPAPERS AND EVERYTHING. WHEN SHE WALKED INTO CHURCH, THE PASTOR GAVE HER A BIG HUG, EVEN THOUGH EVERYONE WAS IN MOURNING.
HER PARENTS EVEN LET HER CALL LEANDRE TO MAKE SURE HE WASN'T WORRIED.
EVERYTHING WAS FINE.
THERE WAS ABSOLUTELY NO REASON TO WORRY.
YOU MIGHT AS WELL LET ME OUT...

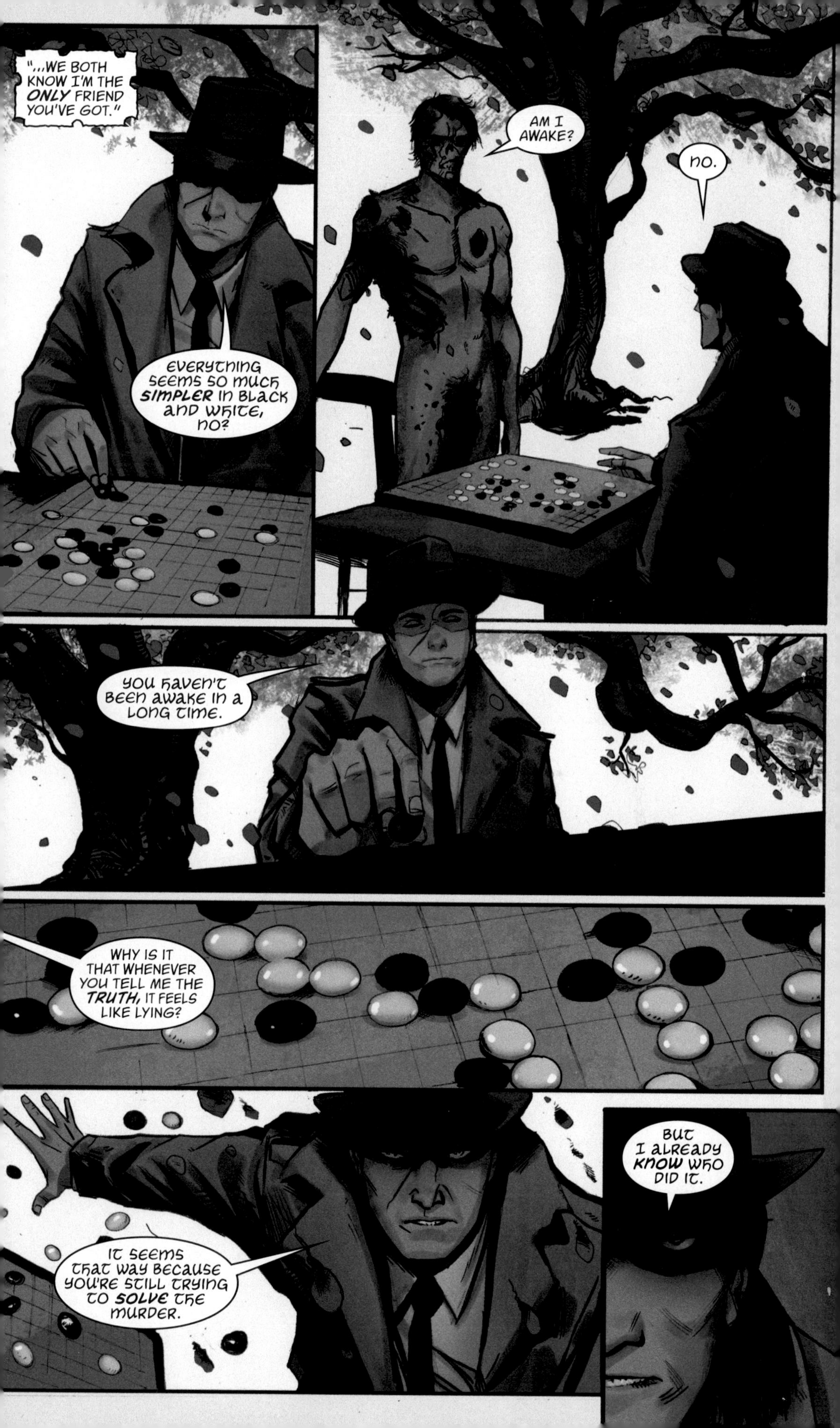
"...WE BOTH KNOW I'M THE ONLY FRIEND YOU'VE GOT."
EVERYTHING SEEMS SO MUCH SIMPLER IN BLACK AND WHITE, NO?
AM I AWAKE?
NO.
YOU HAVEN'T BEEN AWAKE IN A LONG TIME.
WHY IS IT THAT WHENEVER YOU TELL ME THE TRUTH, IT FEELS LIKE LYING?
IT SEEMS THAT WAY BECAUSE YOU'RE STILL TRYING TO SOLVE THE MURDER.
BUT I ALREADY KNOW WHO DID IT.

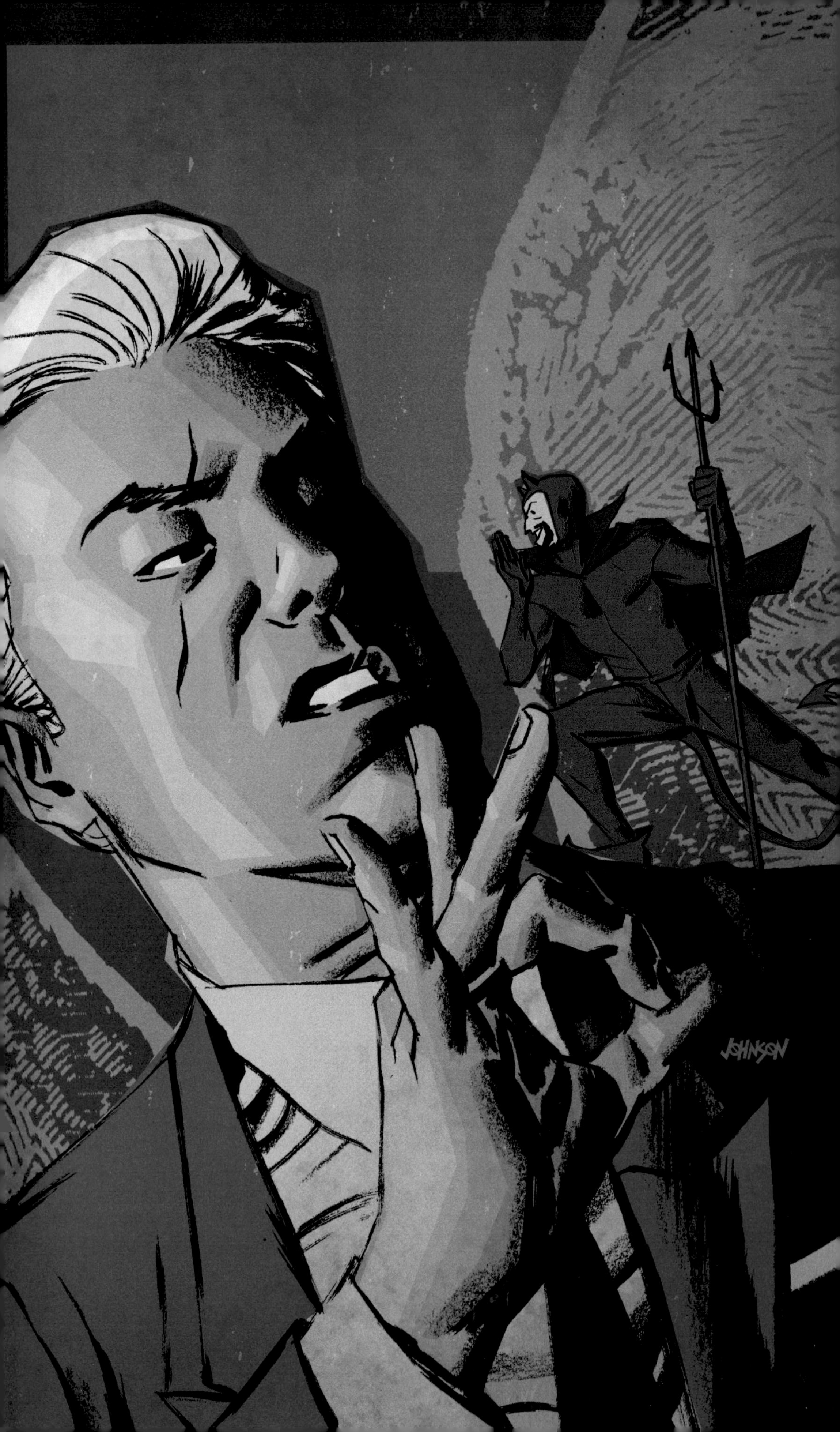
JOHNSON

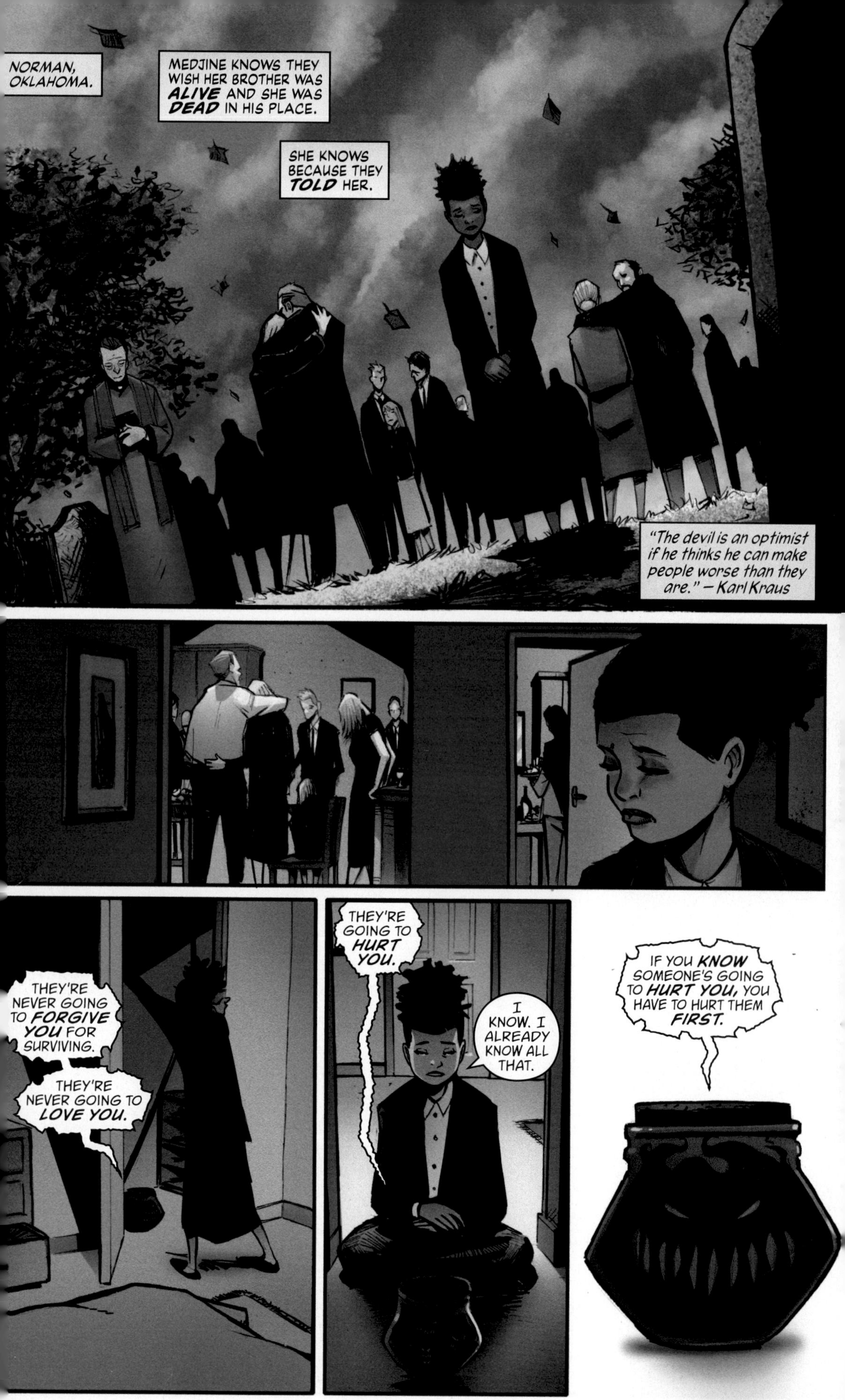
NORMAN, OKLAHOMA.
MEDJINE KNOWS THEY WISH HER BROTHER WAS ALIVE AND SHE WAS DEAD IN HIS PLACE.
SHE KNOWS BECAUSE THEY TOLD HER.
"The devil is an optimist if he thinks he can make people worse than they are." —Karl Kraus
THEY'RE NEVER GOING TO FORGIVE YOU FOR SURVIVING.
THEY'RE NEVER GOING TO LOVE YOU.
THEY'RE GOING TO HURT YOU.
I KNOW. I ALREADY KNOW ALL THAT.
IF YOU KNOW SOMEONE'S GOING TO HURT YOU, YOU HAVE TO HURT THEM FIRST.

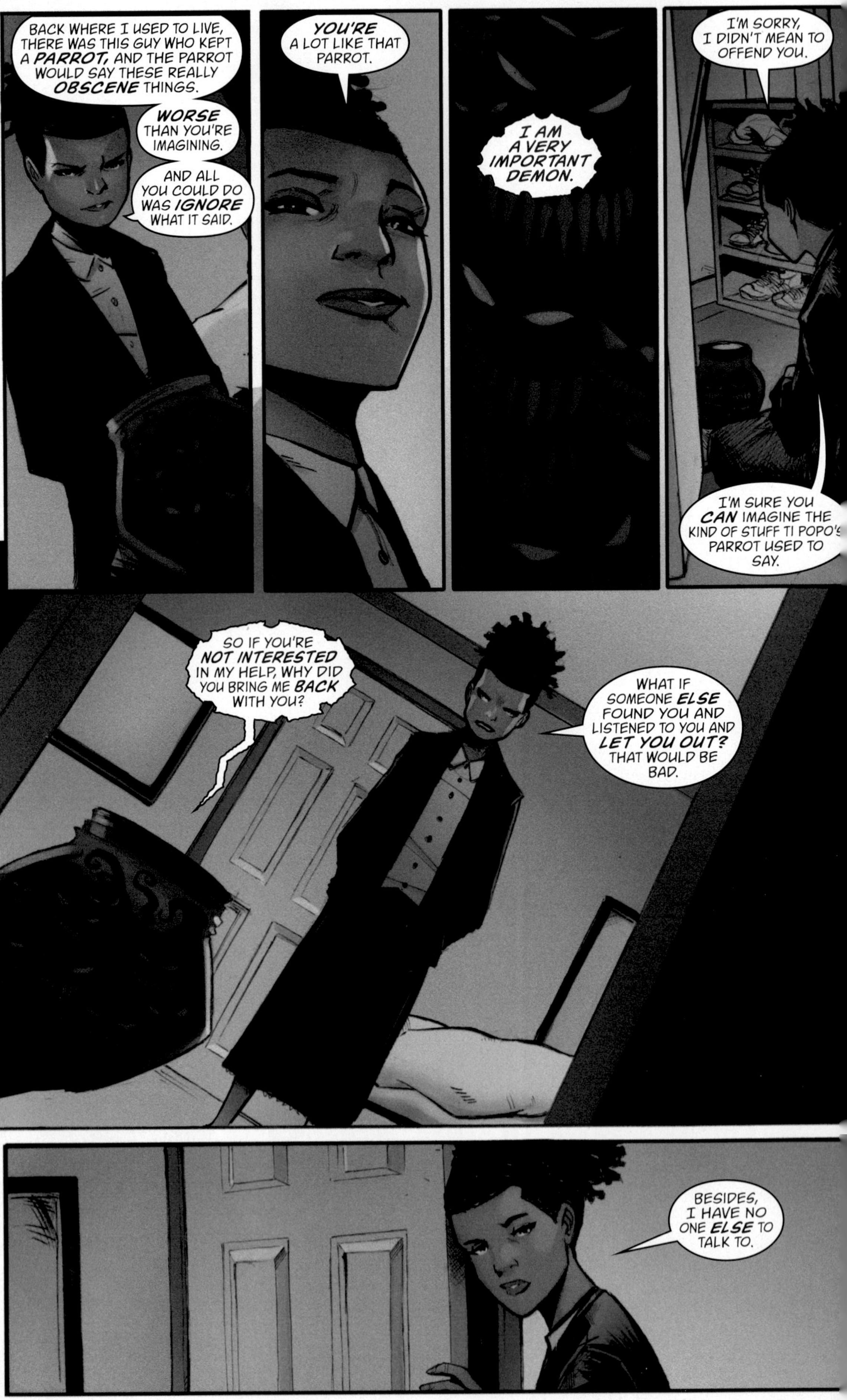
BACK WHERE I USED TO LIVE, THERE WAS THIS GUY WHO KEPT A PARROT, AND THE PARROT WOULD SAY THESE REALLY OBSCENE THINGS.
WORSE THAN YOU'RE IMAGINING.
AND ALL YOU COULD DO WAS IGNORE WHAT IT SAID.
YOU'RE A LOT LIKE THAT PARROT.
I AM A VERY IMPORTANT DEMON.
I'M SORRY, I DIDN'T MEAN TO OFFEND YOU.
I'M SURE YOU CAN IMAGINE THE KIND OF STUFF TI POPO'S PARROT USED TO SAY.
SO IF YOU'RE NOT INTERESTED IN MY HELP, WHY DID YOU BRING ME BACK WITH YOU?
WHAT IF SOMEONE ELSE FOUND YOU AND LISTENED TO YOU AND LET YOU OUT? THAT WOULD BE BAD.
BESIDES, I HAVE NO ONE ELSE TO TALK TO.

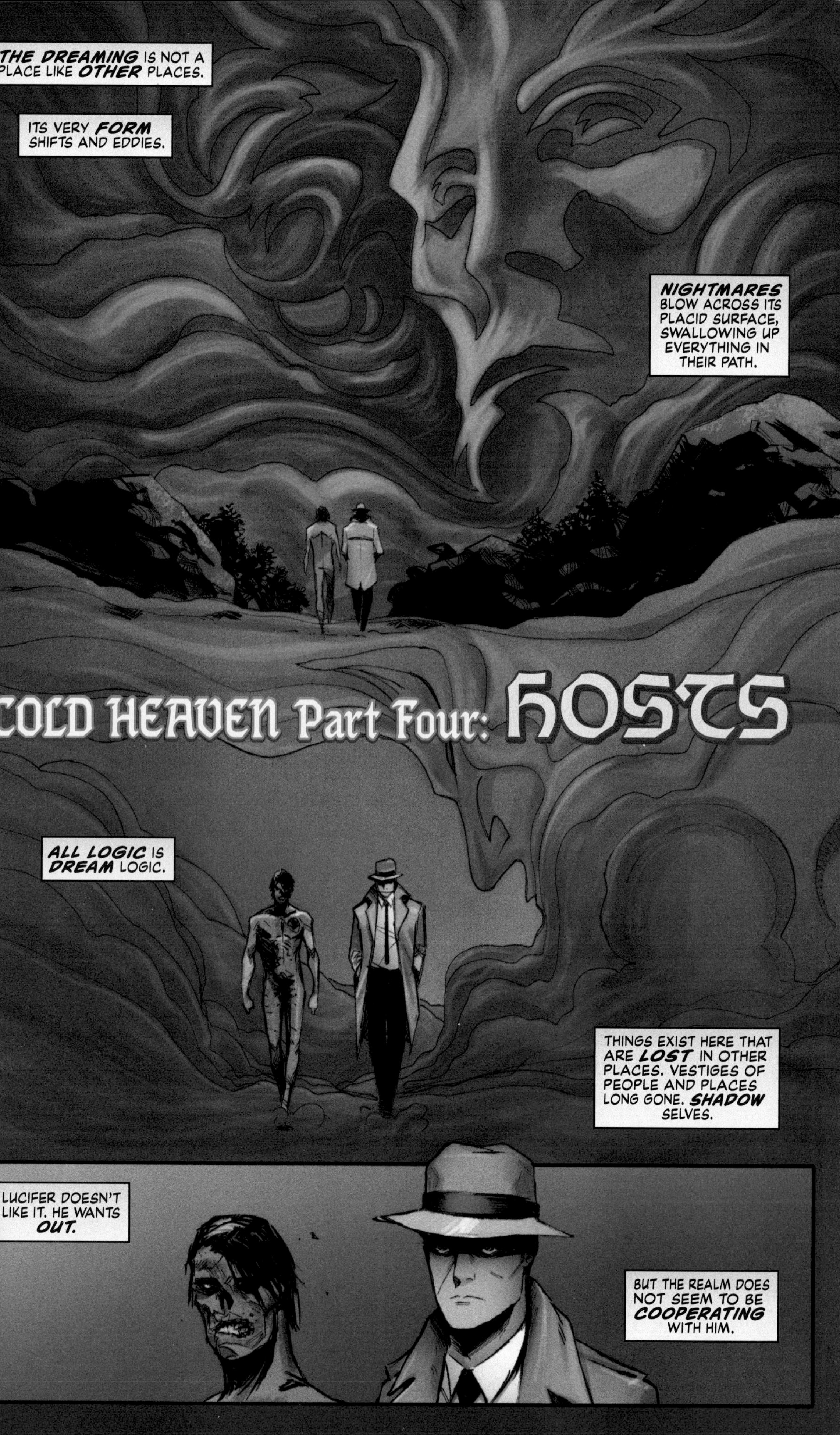
THE DREAMING IS NOT A PLACE LIKE OTHER PLACES.
ITS VERY FORM SHIFTS AND EDDIES.
NIGHTMARES BLOW ACROSS ITS PLACID SURFACE, SWALLOWING UP EVERYTHING IN THEIR PATH.
COLD HEAVEN Part Four: HOSTS
ALL LOGIC IS DREAM LOGIC.
THINGS EXIST HERE THAT ARE LOST IN OTHER PLACES. VESTIGES OF PEOPLE AND PLACES LONG GONE. SHADOW SELVES.
LUCIFER DOESN'T LIKE IT. HE WANTS OUT.
BUT THE REALM DOES NOT SEEM TO BE COOPERATING WITH HIM.

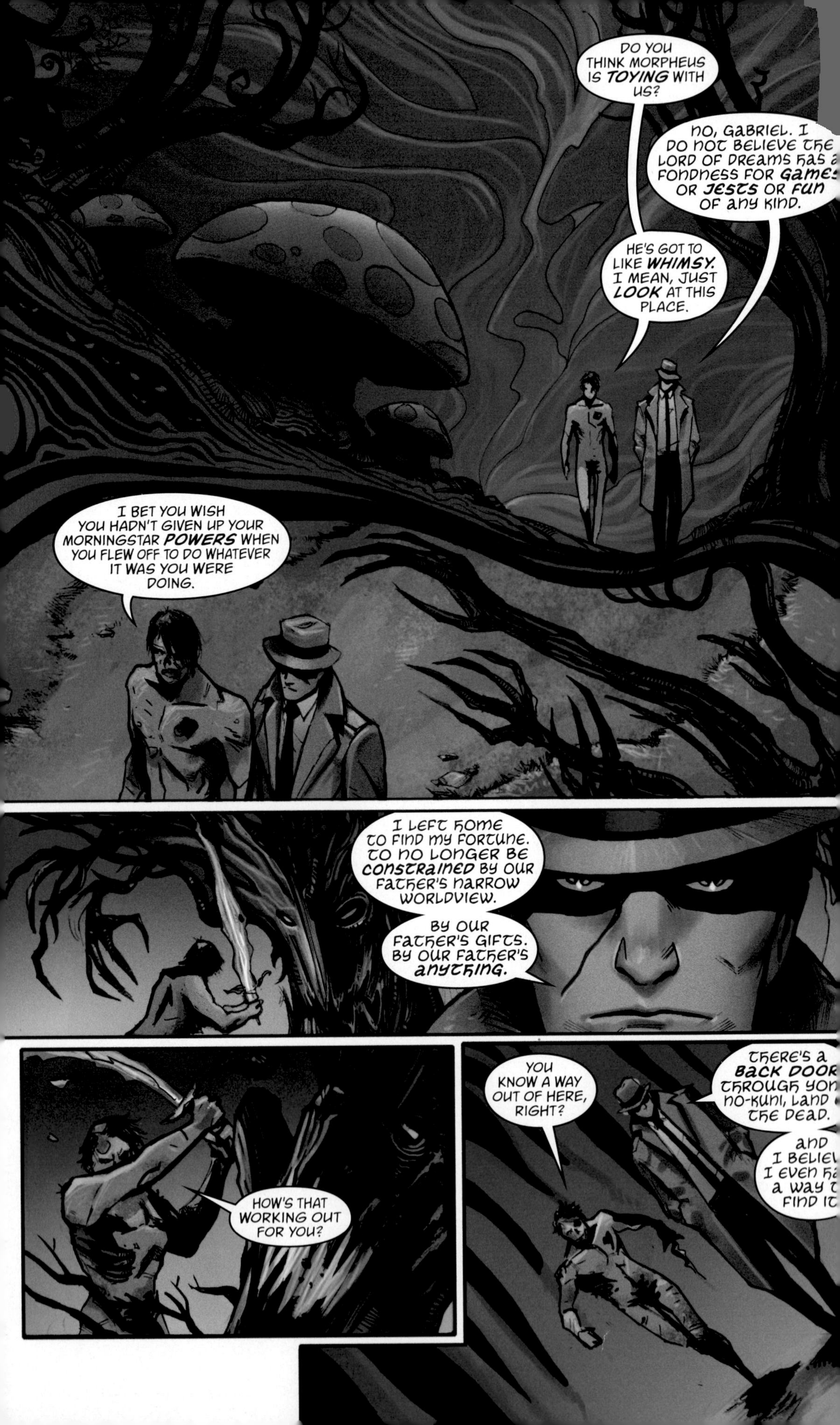
DO YOU THINK MORPHEUS IS TOYING WITH US?
NO, GABRIEL. I DO NOT BELIEVE THE LORD OF DREAMS HAS A FONDNESS FOR GAMES OR JESTS OR FUN OF ANY KIND.
HE'S GOT TO LIKE WHIMSY. I MEAN, JUST LOOK AT THIS PLACE.
I BET YOU WISH YOU HADN'T GIVEN UP YOUR MORNINGSTAR POWERS WHEN YOU FLEW OFF TO DO WHATEVER IT WAS YOU WERE DOING.
I LEFT HOME TO FIND MY FORTUNE. TO NO LONGER BE CONSTRAINED BY OUR FATHER'S NARROW WORLDVIEW.
BY OUR FATHER'S GIFTS. BY OUR FATHER'S ANYTHING.
HOW'S THAT WORKING OUT FOR YOU?
YOU KNOW A WAY OUT OF HERE, RIGHT?

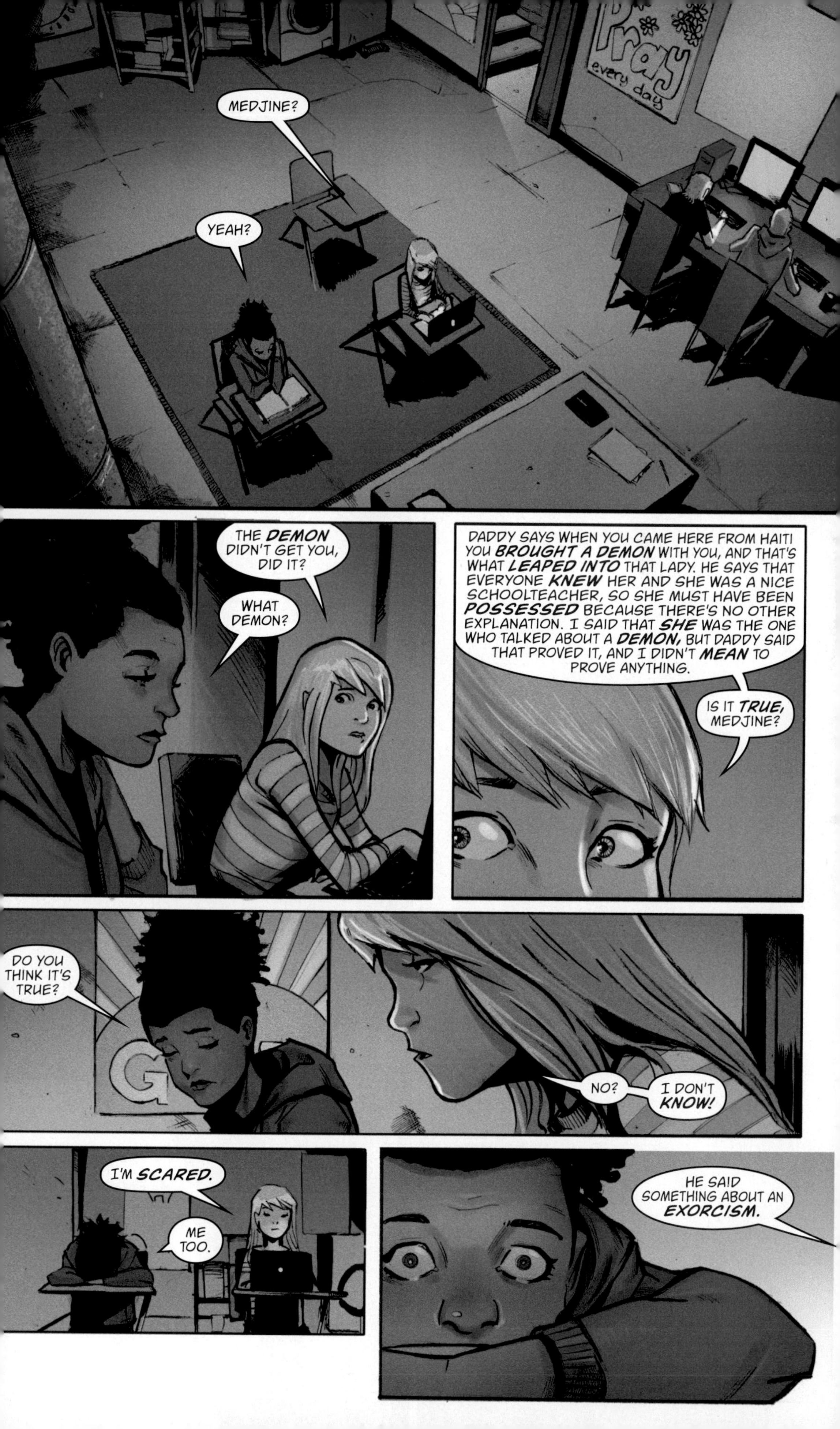
Pray
every day
MEDJINE?
YEAH?
THE DEMON DIDN'T GET YOU, DID IT?
WHAT DEMON?
DADDY SAYS WHEN YOU CAME HERE FROM HAITI YOU BROUGHT A DEMON WITH YOU, AND THAT'S WHAT LEAPED INTO THAT LADY. HE SAYS THAT EVERYONE KNEW HER AND SHE WAS A NICE SCHOOLTEACHER, SO SHE MUST HAVE BEEN POSSESSED BECAUSE THERE'S NO OTHER EXPLANATION. I SAID THAT SHE WAS THE ONE WHO TALKED ABOUT A DEMON, BUT DADDY SAID THAT PROVED IT, AND I DIDN'T MEAN TO PROVE ANYTHING.
IS IT TRUE, MEDJINE?
DO YOU THINK IT'S TRUE?
NO?
I DON'T KNOW!
I'M SCARED.
ME TOO.
HE SAID SOMETHING ABOUT AN EXORCISM.

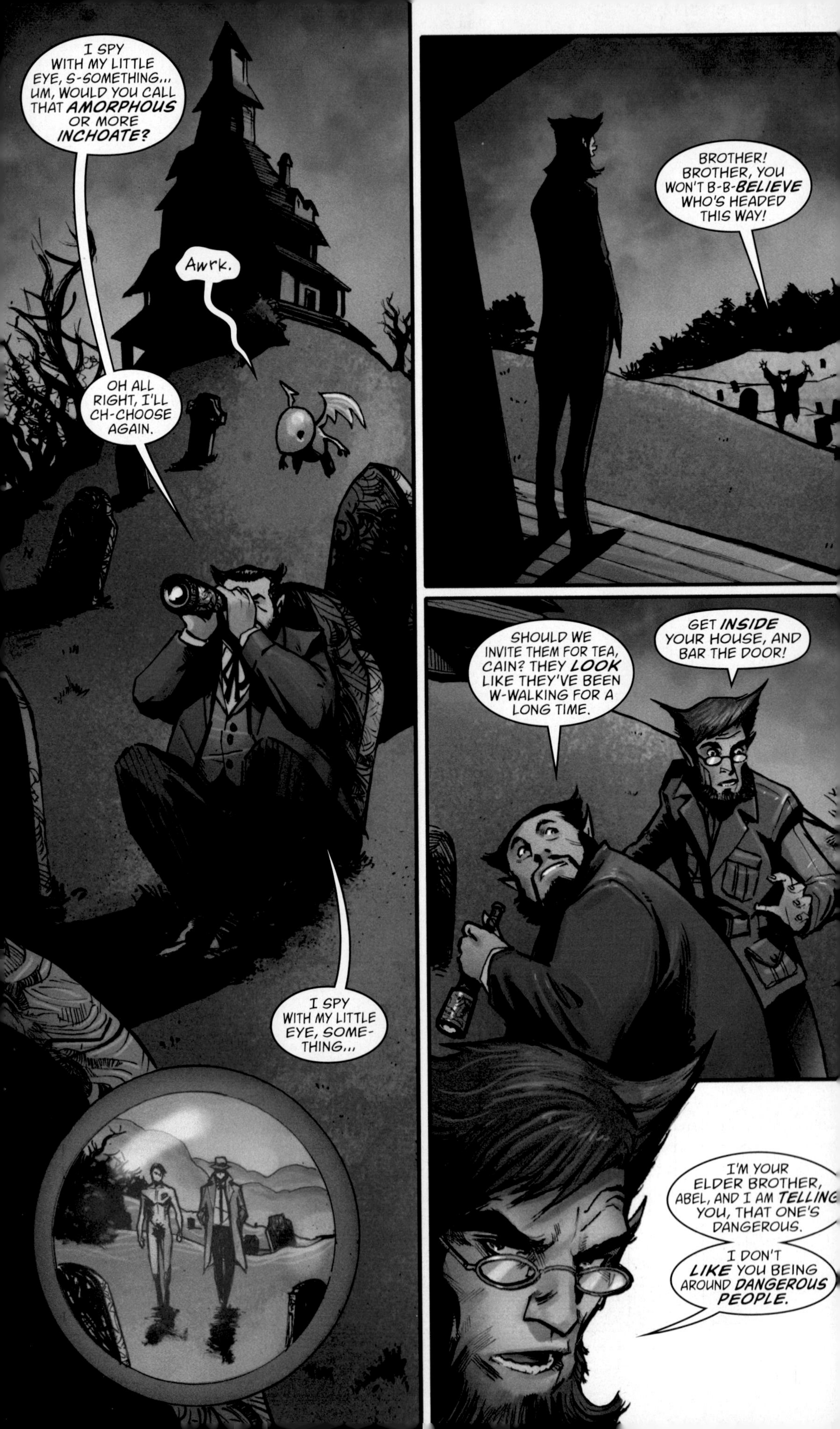

I SPY WITH MY LITTLE EYE, S-SOMETHING... UM, WOULD YOU CALL THAT AMORPHOUS OR MORE INCHOATE?
Awrk.
OH ALL RIGHT, I'LL CH-CHOOSE AGAIN.
I SPY WITH MY LITTLE EYE, SOME-THING...
BROTHER! BROTHER, YOU WON'T B-B-BELIEVE WHO'S HEADED THIS WAY!
SHOULD WE INVITE THEM FOR TEA, CAIN? THEY LOOK LIKE THEY'VE BEEN W-WALKING FOR A LONG TIME.
GET INSIDE YOUR HOUSE, AND BAR THE DOOR!
I'M YOUR ELDER BROTHER, ABEL, AND I AM TELLING YOU, THAT ONE'S DANGEROUS.
I DON'T LIKE YOU BEING AROUND DANGEROUS PEOPLE.

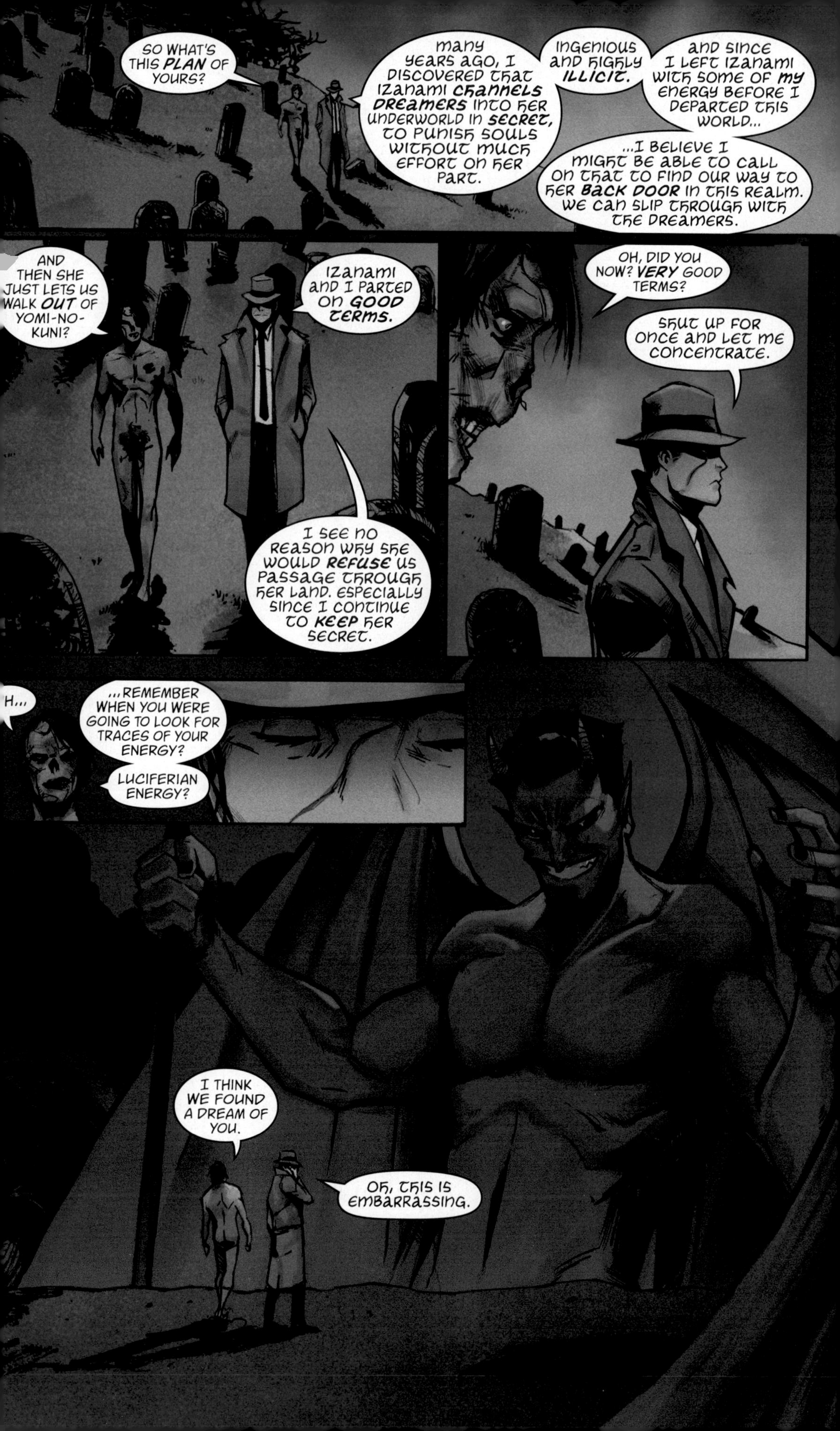
SO WHAT'S THIS PLAN OF YOURS?
MANY YEARS AGO, I DISCOVERED THAT IZANAMI CHANNELS DREAMERS INTO HER UNDERWORLD IN SECRET, TO PUNISH SOULS WITHOUT MUCH EFFORT ON HER PART.
INGENIOUS AND HIGHLY ILLICIT.
AND SINCE I LEFT IZANAMI WITH SOME OF MY ENERGY BEFORE I DEPARTED THIS WORLD...
...I BELIEVE I MIGHT BE ABLE TO CALL ON THAT TO FIND OUR WAY TO HER BACK DOOR IN THIS REALM. WE CAN SLIP THROUGH WITH THE DREAMERS.
AND THEN SHE JUST LETS US WALK OUT OF YOMI-NO-KUNI?
IZANAMI AND I PARTED ON GOOD TERMS.
I SEE NO REASON WHY SHE WOULD REFUSE US PASSAGE THROUGH HER LAND. ESPECIALLY SINCE I CONTINUE TO KEEP HER SECRET.
OH, DID YOU NOW? VERY GOOD TERMS?
SHUT UP FOR ONCE AND LET ME CONCENTRATE.
H...
...REMEMBER WHEN YOU WERE GOING TO LOOK FOR TRACES OF YOUR ENERGY?
LUCIFERIAN ENERGY?
I THINK WE FOUND A DREAM OF YOU.
OH, THIS IS EMBARRASSING.

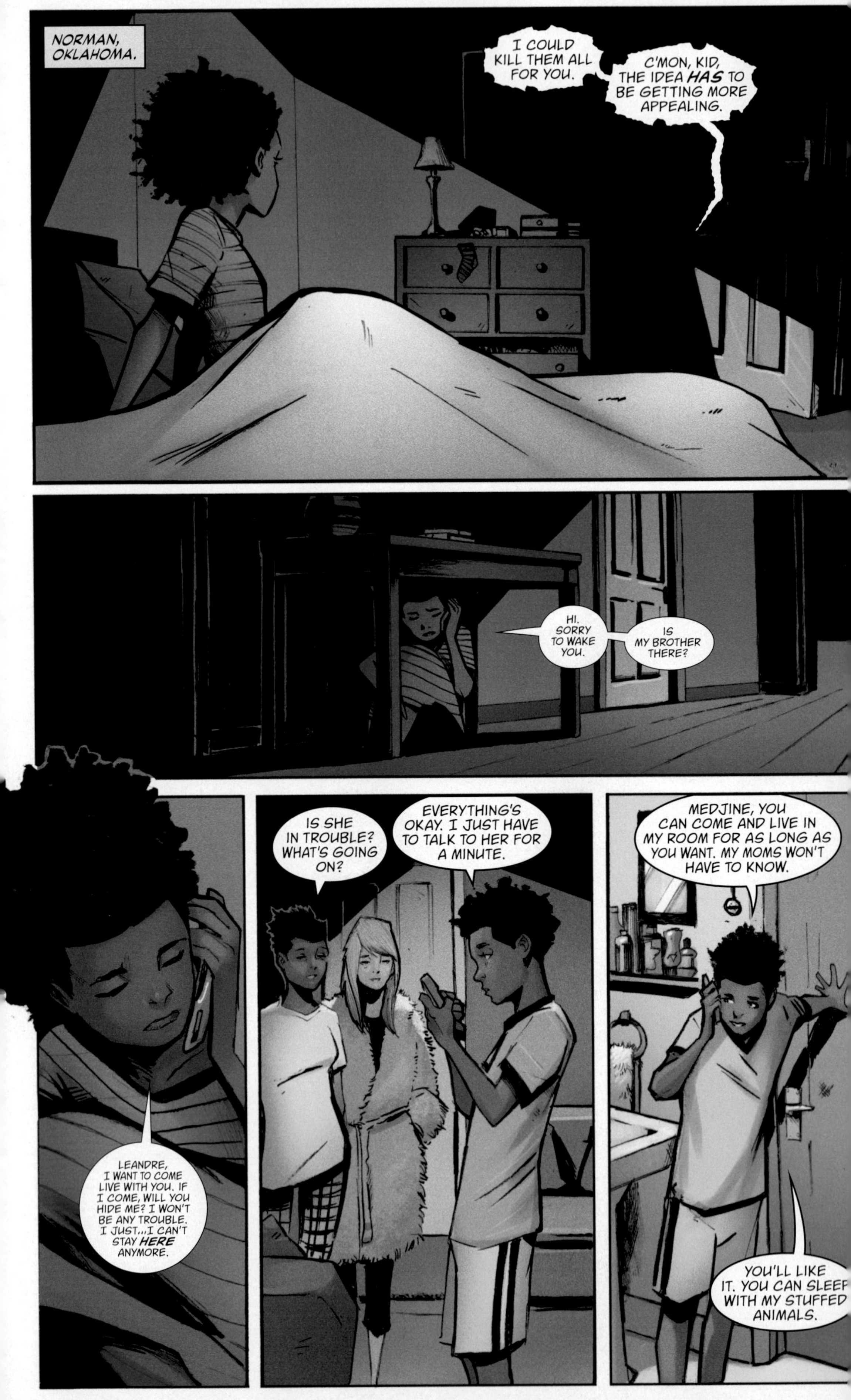
NORMAN, OKLAHOMA.
I COULD KILL THEM ALL FOR YOU.
C'MON, KID, THE IDEA HAS TO BE GETTING MORE APPEALING.
HI. SORRY TO WAKE YOU.
IS MY BROTHER THERE?
LEANDRE, I WANT TO COME LIVE WITH YOU. IF I COME, WILL YOU HIDE ME? I WON'T BE ANY TROUBLE. I JUST...I CAN'T STAY HERE ANYMORE.
IS SHE IN TROUBLE? WHAT'S GOING ON?
EVERYTHING'S OKAY. I JUST HAVE TO TALK TO HER FOR A MINUTE.
MEDJINE, YOU CAN COME AND LIVE IN MY ROOM FOR AS LONG AS YOU WANT. MY MOMS WON'T HAVE TO KNOW.
YOU'LL LIKE IT. YOU CAN SLEEP WITH MY STUFFED ANIMALS.

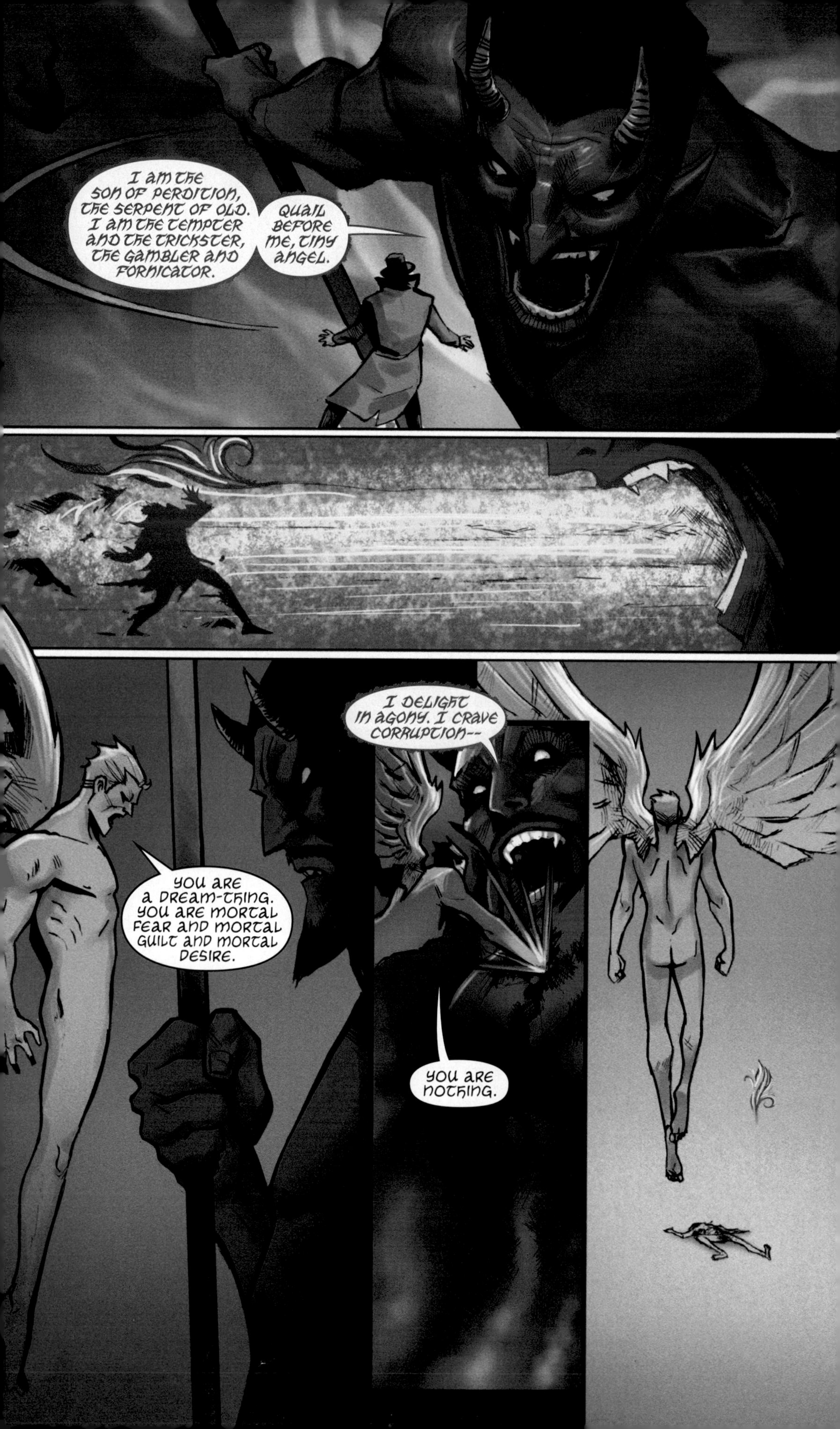
I AM THE SON OF PERDITION, THE SERPENT OF OLD. I AM THE TEMPTER AND THE TRICKSTER, THE GAMBLER AND FORNICATOR.
QUAIL BEFORE ME, TINY ANGEL.
I DELIGHT IN AGONY. I CRAVE CORRUPTION--
YOU ARE A DREAM-THING. YOU ARE MORTAL FEAR AND MORTAL GUILT AND MORTAL DESIRE.
YOU ARE NOTHING.

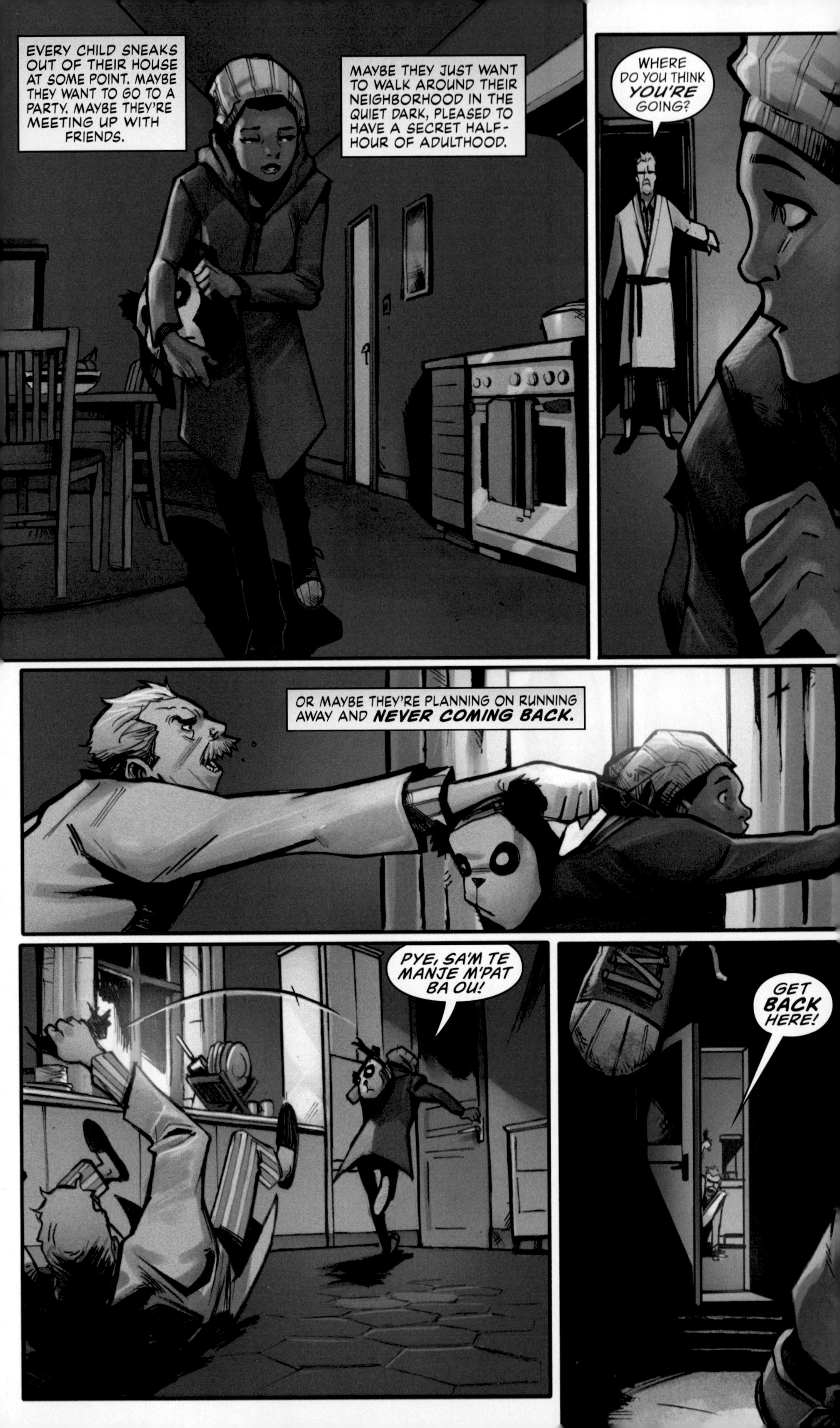
EVERY CHILD SNEAKS OUT OF THEIR HOUSE AT SOME POINT. MAYBE THEY WANT TO GO TO A PARTY. MAYBE THEY'RE MEETING UP WITH FRIENDS.
MAYBE THEY JUST WANT TO WALK AROUND THEIR NEIGHBORHOOD IN THE QUIET DARK, PLEASED TO HAVE A SECRET HALF-HOUR OF ADULTHOOD.
WHERE DO YOU THINK *YOU'RE* GOING?
OR MAYBE THEY'RE PLANNING ON RUNNING AWAY AND ***NEVER COMING BACK.***
PYE, SA'M TE MANJE M'PAT BA OU!
*GET **BACK** HERE!*

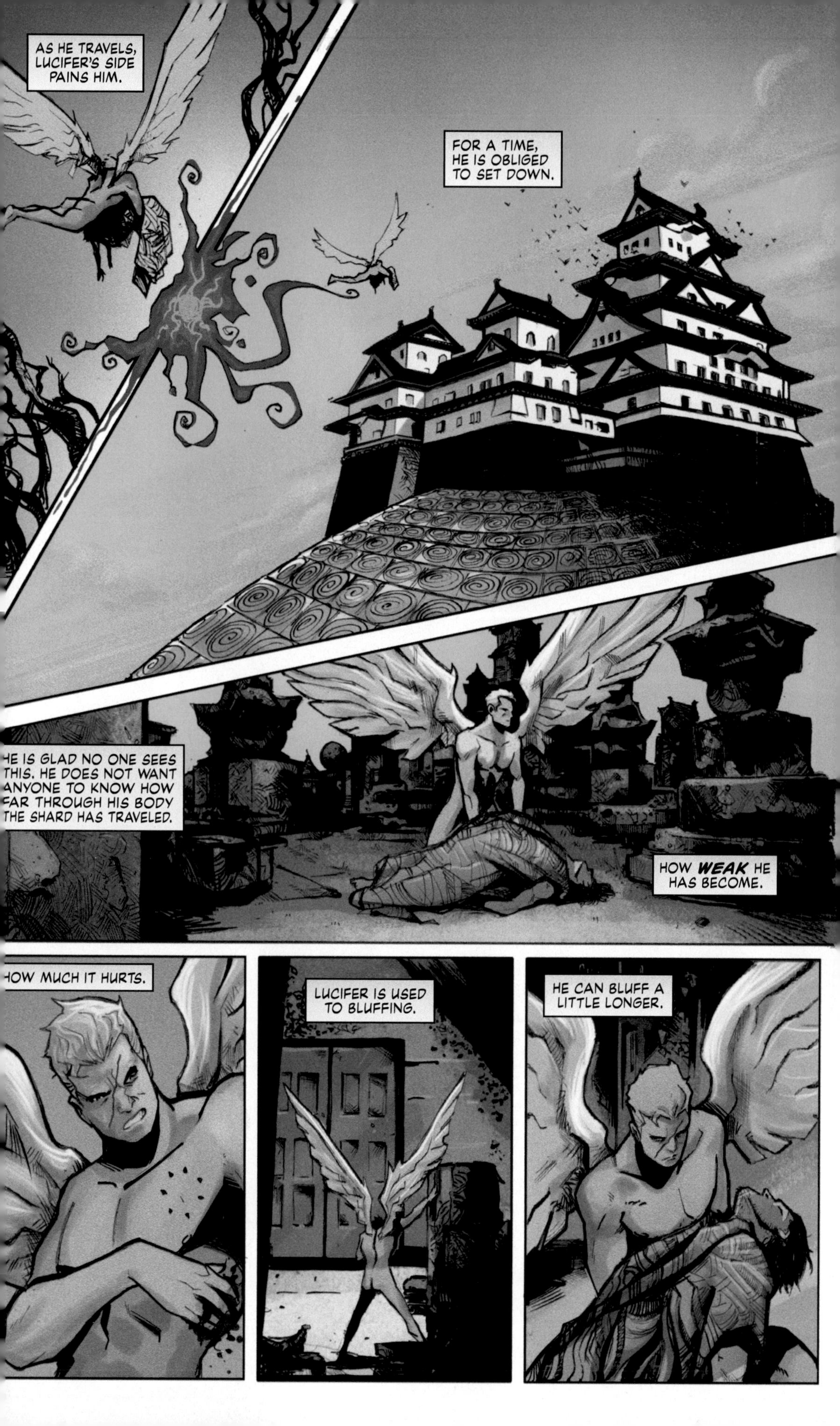
AS HE TRAVELS, LUCIFER'S SIDE PAINS HIM.
FOR A TIME, HE IS OBLIGED TO SET DOWN.
HE IS GLAD NO ONE SEES THIS. HE DOES NOT WANT ANYONE TO KNOW HOW FAR THROUGH HIS BODY THE SHARD HAS TRAVELED.
HOW **WEAK** HE HAS BECOME.
HOW MUCH IT HURTS.
LUCIFER IS USED TO BLUFFING.
HE CAN BLUFF A LITTLE LONGER.

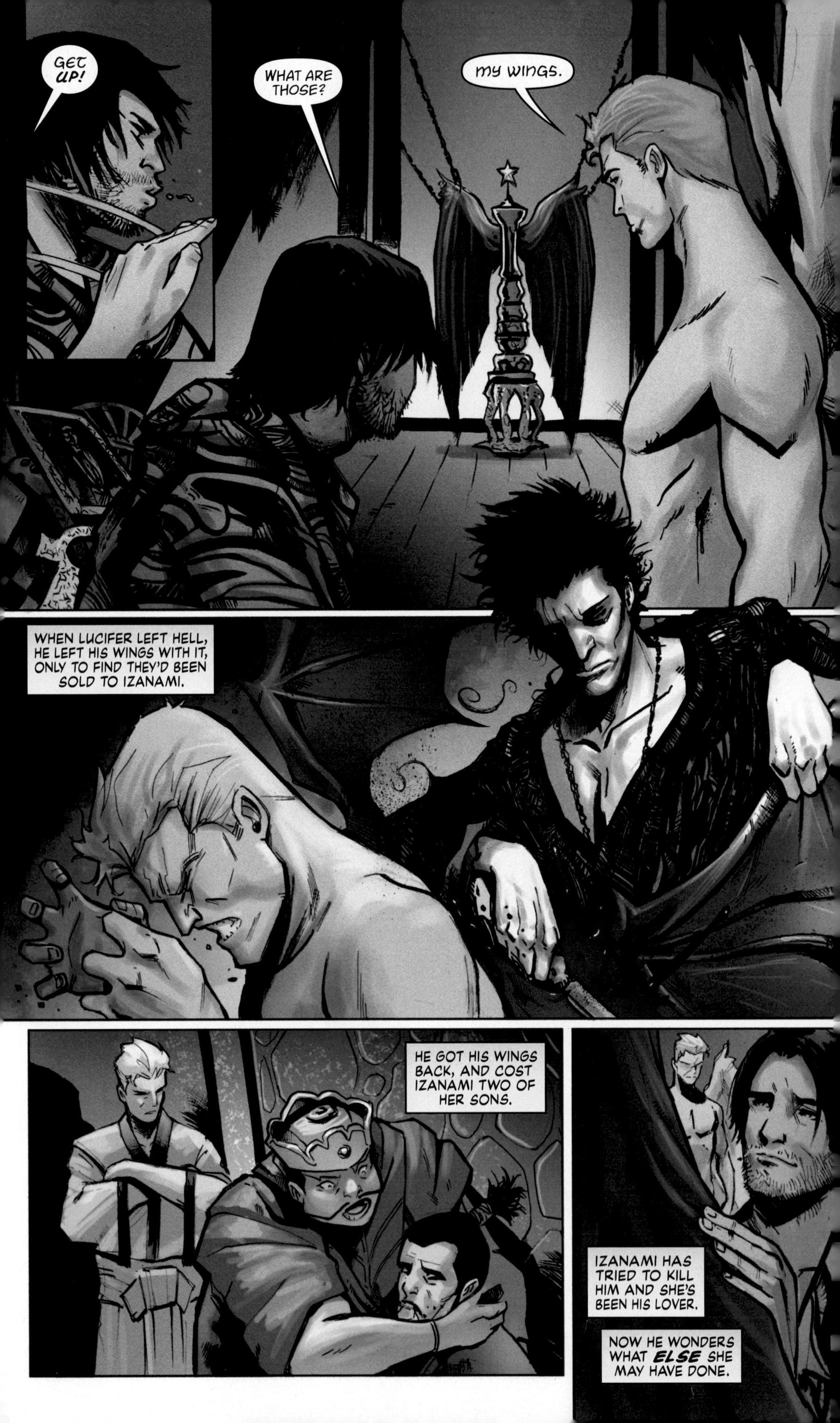
GET UP!
WHAT ARE THOSE?
MY WINGS.
WHEN LUCIFER LEFT HELL, HE LEFT HIS WINGS WITH IT, ONLY TO FIND THEY'D BEEN SOLD TO IZANAMI.
HE GOT HIS WINGS BACK, AND COST IZANAMI TWO OF HER SONS.
IZANAMI HAS TRIED TO KILL HIM AND SHE'S BEEN HIS LOVER.
NOW HE WONDERS WHAT ELSE SHE MAY HAVE DONE.

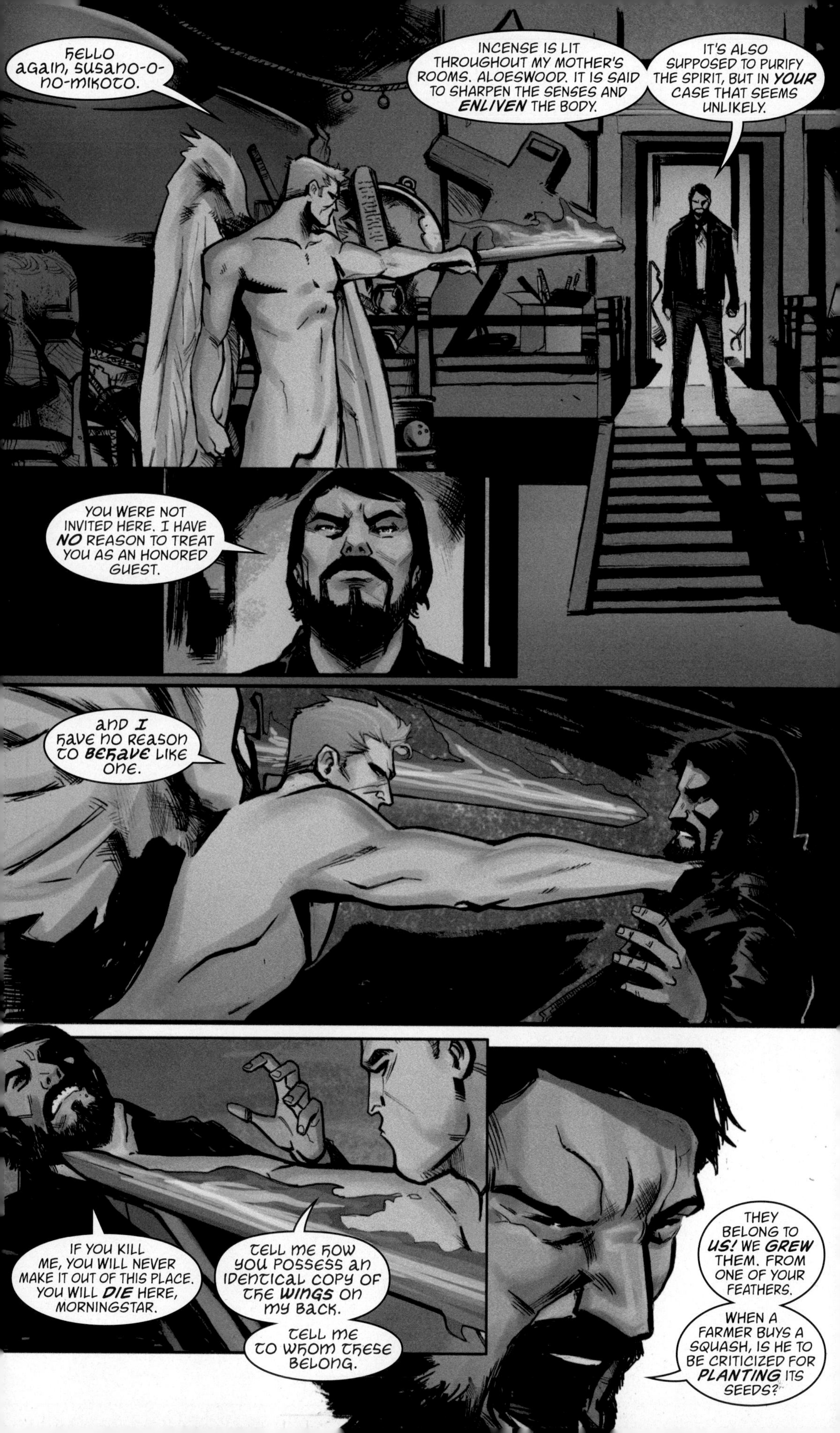
HELLO AGAIN, SUSANO-O-NO-MIKOTO.
INCENSE IS LIT THROUGHOUT MY MOTHER'S ROOMS. ALOESWOOD. IT IS SAID TO SHARPEN THE SENSES AND ENLIVEN THE BODY.
IT'S ALSO SUPPOSED TO PURIFY THE SPIRIT, BUT IN YOUR CASE THAT SEEMS UNLIKELY.
YOU WERE NOT INVITED HERE. I HAVE NO REASON TO TREAT YOU AS AN HONORED GUEST.
AND I HAVE NO REASON TO BEHAVE LIKE ONE.
IF YOU KILL ME, YOU WILL NEVER MAKE IT OUT OF THIS PLACE. YOU WILL DIE HERE, MORNINGSTAR.
TELL ME HOW YOU POSSESS AN IDENTICAL COPY OF THE WINGS ON MY BACK.
TELL ME TO WHOM THESE BELONG.
THEY BELONG TO US! WE GREW THEM. FROM ONE OF YOUR FEATHERS.
WHEN A FARMER BUYS A SQUASH, IS HE TO BE CRITICIZED FOR PLANTING ITS SEEDS?

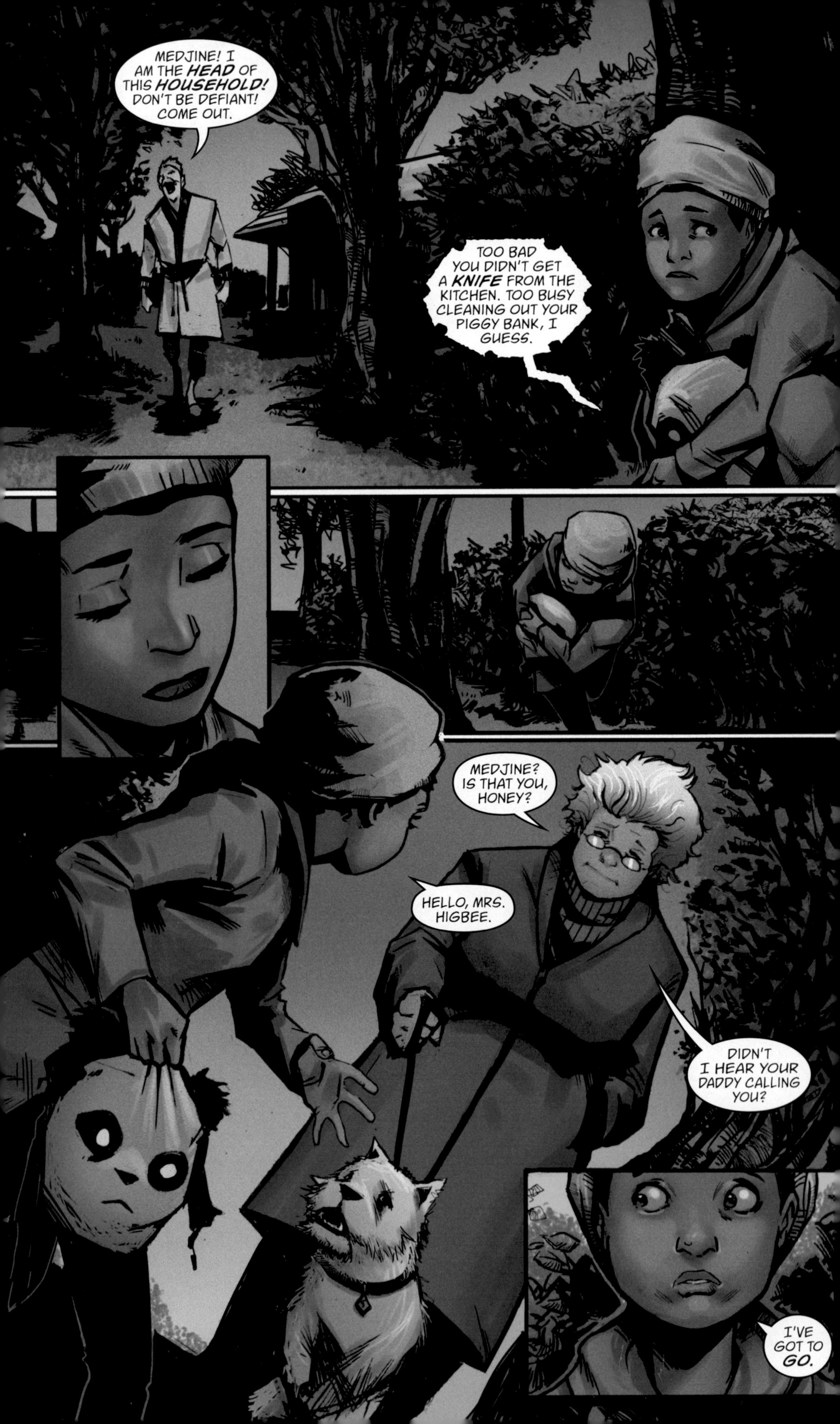
MEDJINE! I AM THE HEAD OF THIS HOUSEHOLD! DON'T BE DEFIANT! COME OUT.
TOO BAD YOU DIDN'T GET A KNIFE FROM THE KITCHEN. TOO BUSY CLEANING OUT YOUR PIGGY BANK, I GUESS.
MEDJINE? IS THAT YOU, HONEY?
HELLO, MRS. HIGBEE.
DIDN'T I HEAR YOUR DADDY CALLING YOU?
I'VE GOT TO GO.

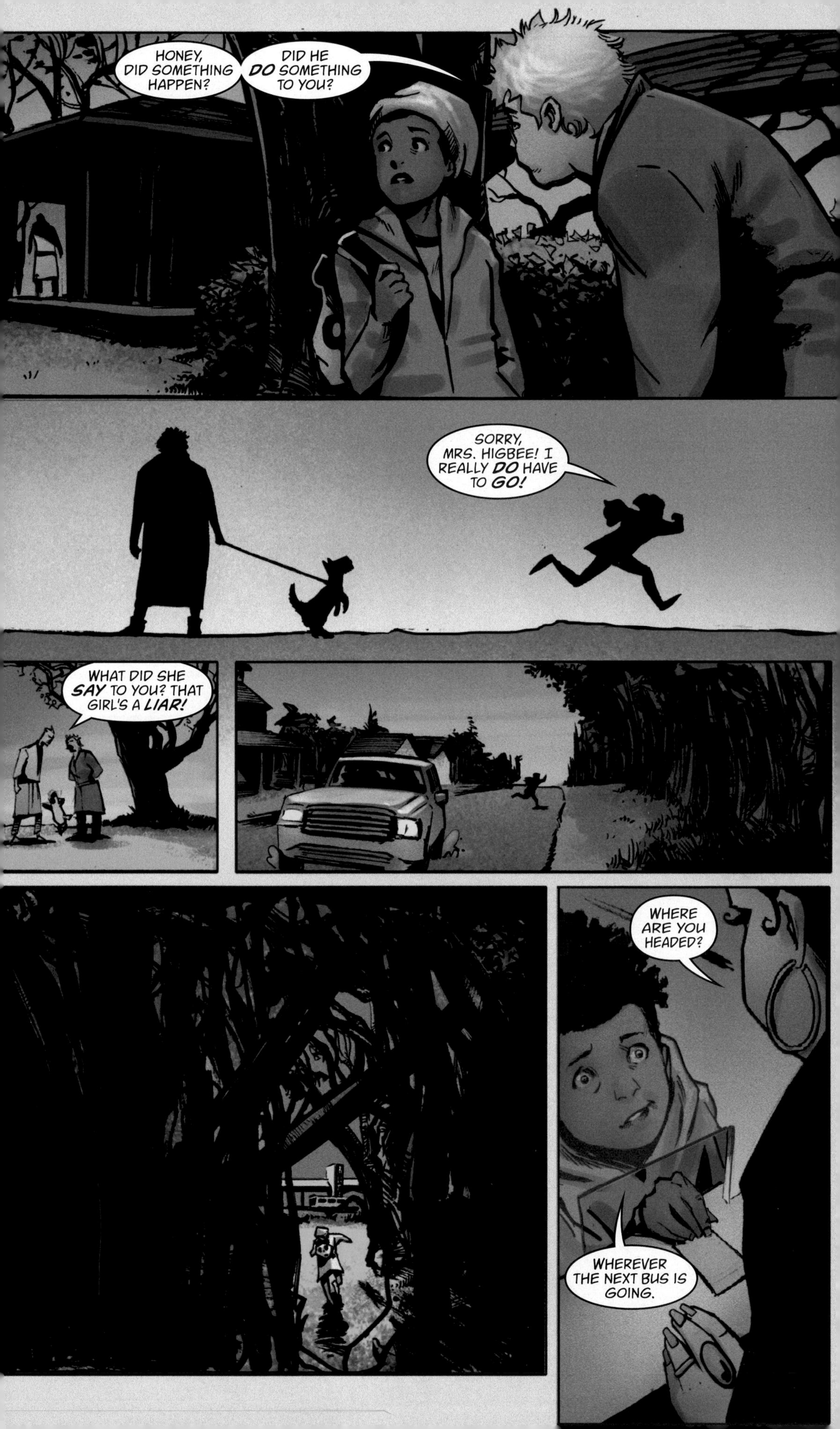
HONEY, DID SOMETHING HAPPEN?
DID HE DO SOMETHING TO YOU?
SORRY, MRS. HIGBEE! I REALLY DO HAVE TO GO!
WHAT DID SHE SAY TO YOU? THAT GIRL'S A LIAR!
WHERE ARE YOU HEADED?
WHEREVER THE NEXT BUS IS GOING.

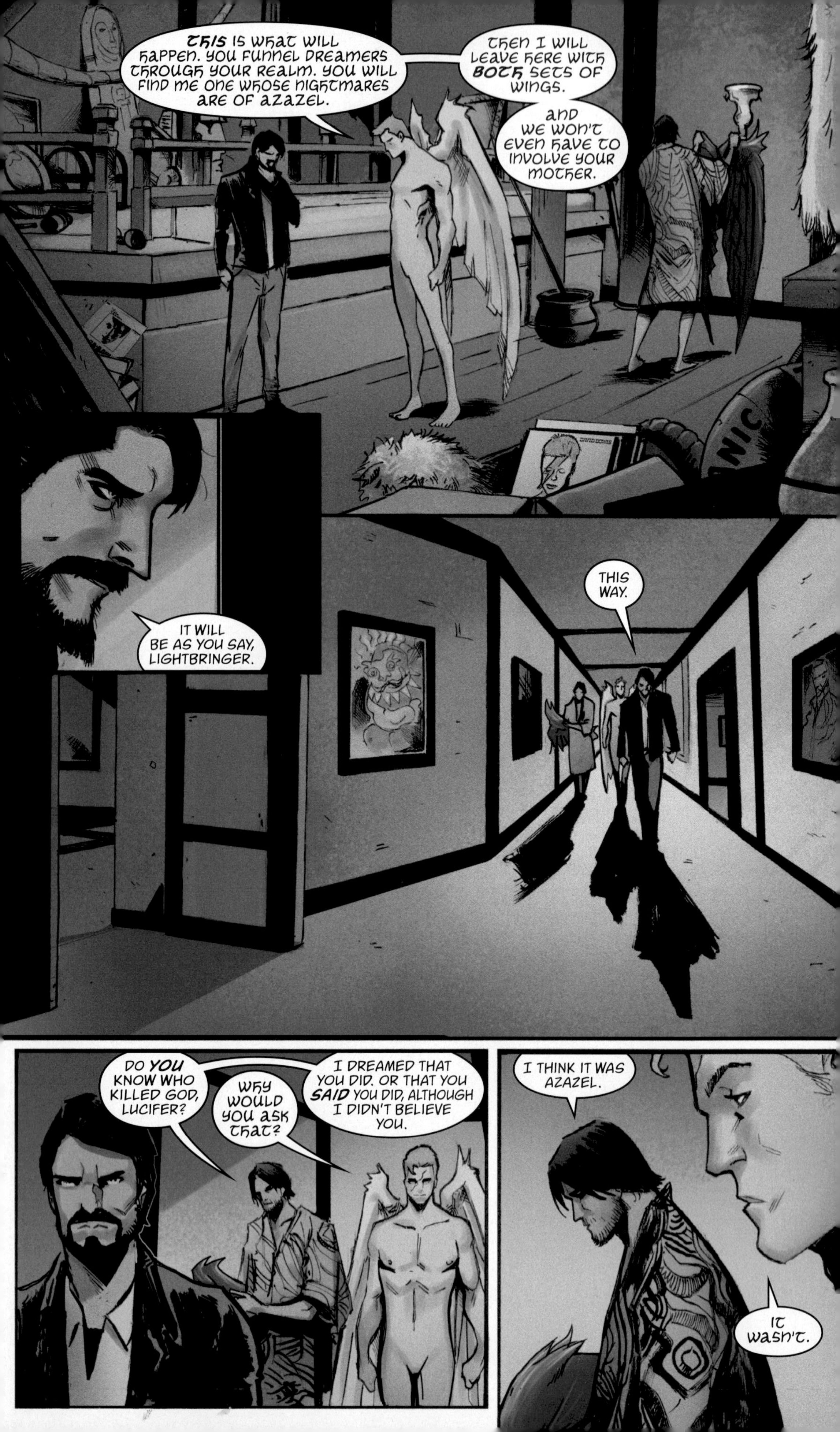
THIS IS WHAT WILL HAPPEN. YOU FUNNEL DREAMERS THROUGH YOUR REALM. YOU WILL FIND ME ONE WHOSE NIGHTMARES ARE OF AZAZEL.
THEN I WILL LEAVE HERE WITH BOTH SETS OF WINGS.
AND WE WON'T EVEN HAVE TO INVOLVE YOUR MOTHER.
IT WILL BE AS YOU SAY, LIGHTBRINGER.
THIS WAY.
DO YOU KNOW WHO KILLED GOD, LUCIFER?
WHY WOULD YOU ASK THAT?
I DREAMED THAT YOU DID. OR THAT YOU SAID YOU DID, ALTHOUGH I DIDN'T BELIEVE YOU.
I THINK IT WAS AZAZEL.
IT WASN'T.

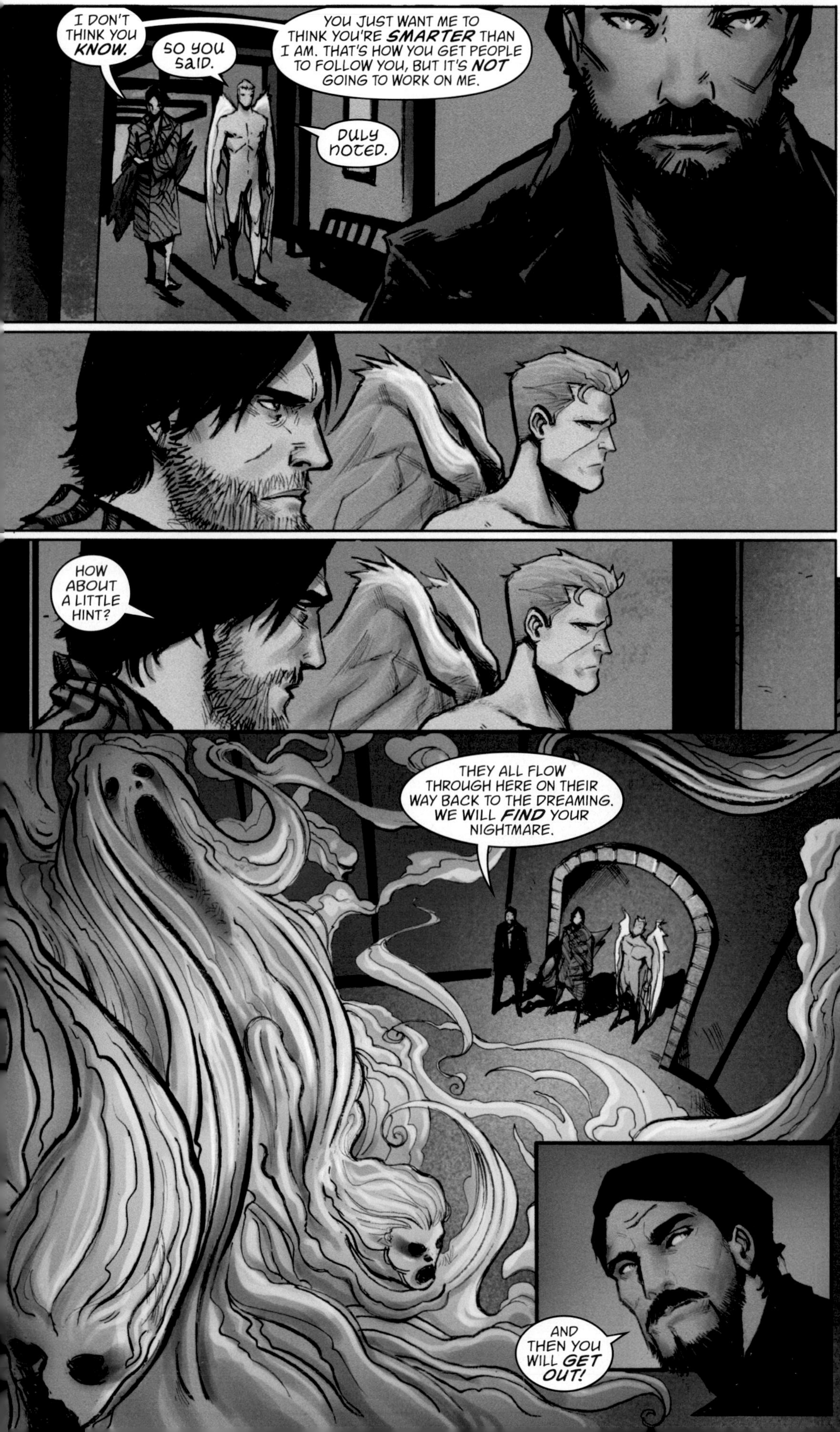
I DON'T THINK YOU **KNOW.**
SO YOU SAID.
YOU JUST WANT ME TO THINK YOU'RE ***SMARTER*** THAN I AM. THAT'S HOW YOU GET PEOPLE TO FOLLOW YOU, BUT IT'S ***NOT*** GOING TO WORK ON ME.
DULY NOTED.
HOW ABOUT A LITTLE HINT?
THEY ALL FLOW THROUGH HERE ON THEIR WAY BACK TO THE DREAMING. WE WILL ***FIND*** YOUR NIGHTMARE.
AND THEN YOU WILL ***GET OUT!***

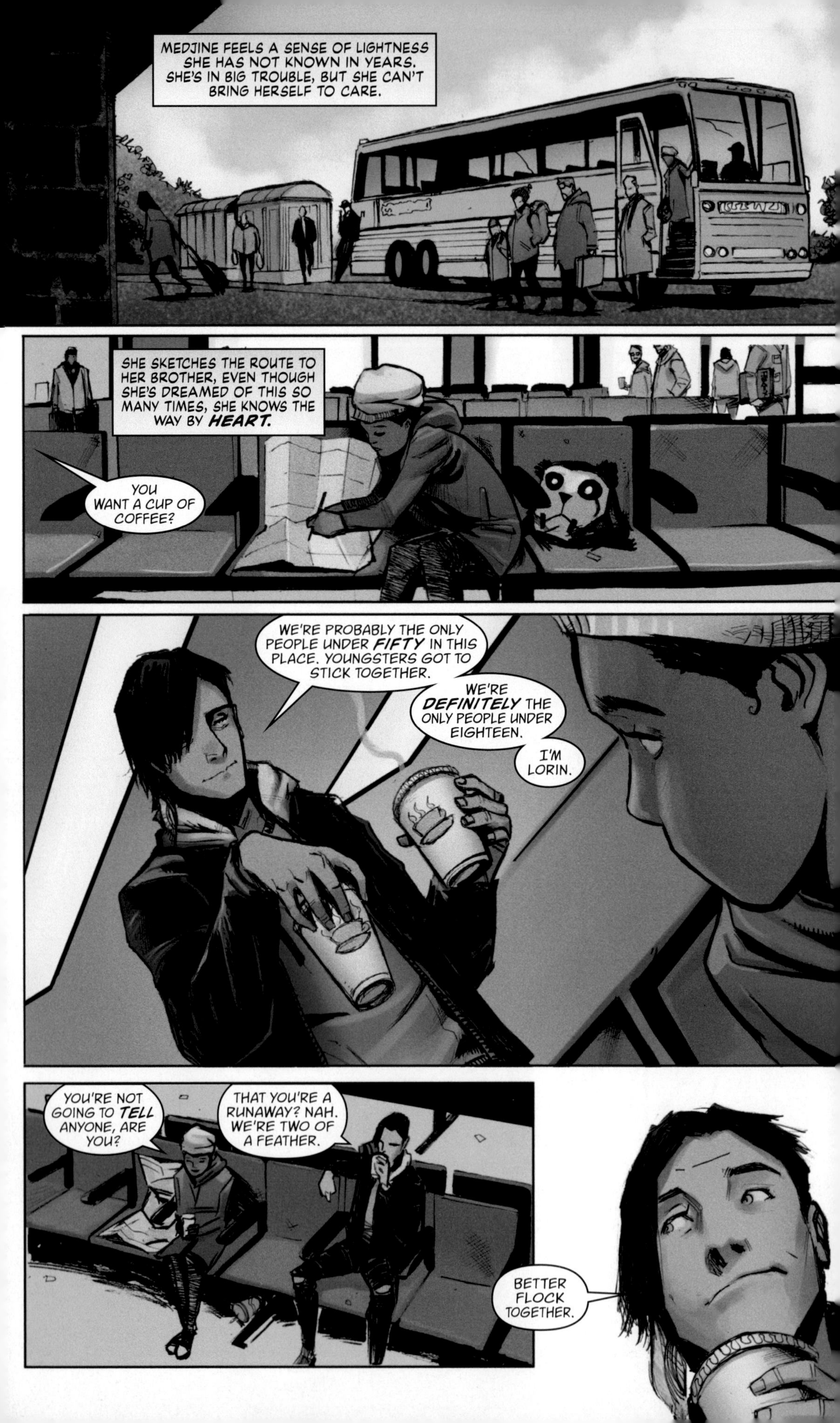
MEDJINE FEELS A SENSE OF LIGHTNESS SHE HAS NOT KNOWN IN YEARS. SHE'S IN BIG TROUBLE, BUT SHE CAN'T BRING HERSELF TO CARE.
SHE SKETCHES THE ROUTE TO HER BROTHER, EVEN THOUGH SHE'S DREAMED OF THIS SO MANY TIMES, SHE KNOWS THE WAY BY HEART.
YOU WANT A CUP OF COFFEE?
WE'RE PROBABLY THE ONLY PEOPLE UNDER FIFTY IN THIS PLACE. YOUNGSTERS GOT TO STICK TOGETHER.
WE'RE DEFINITELY THE ONLY PEOPLE UNDER EIGHTEEN.
I'M LORIN.
YOU'RE NOT GOING TO TELL ANYONE, ARE YOU?
THAT YOU'RE A RUNAWAY? NAH. WE'RE TWO OF A FEATHER.
BETTER FLOCK TOGETHER.

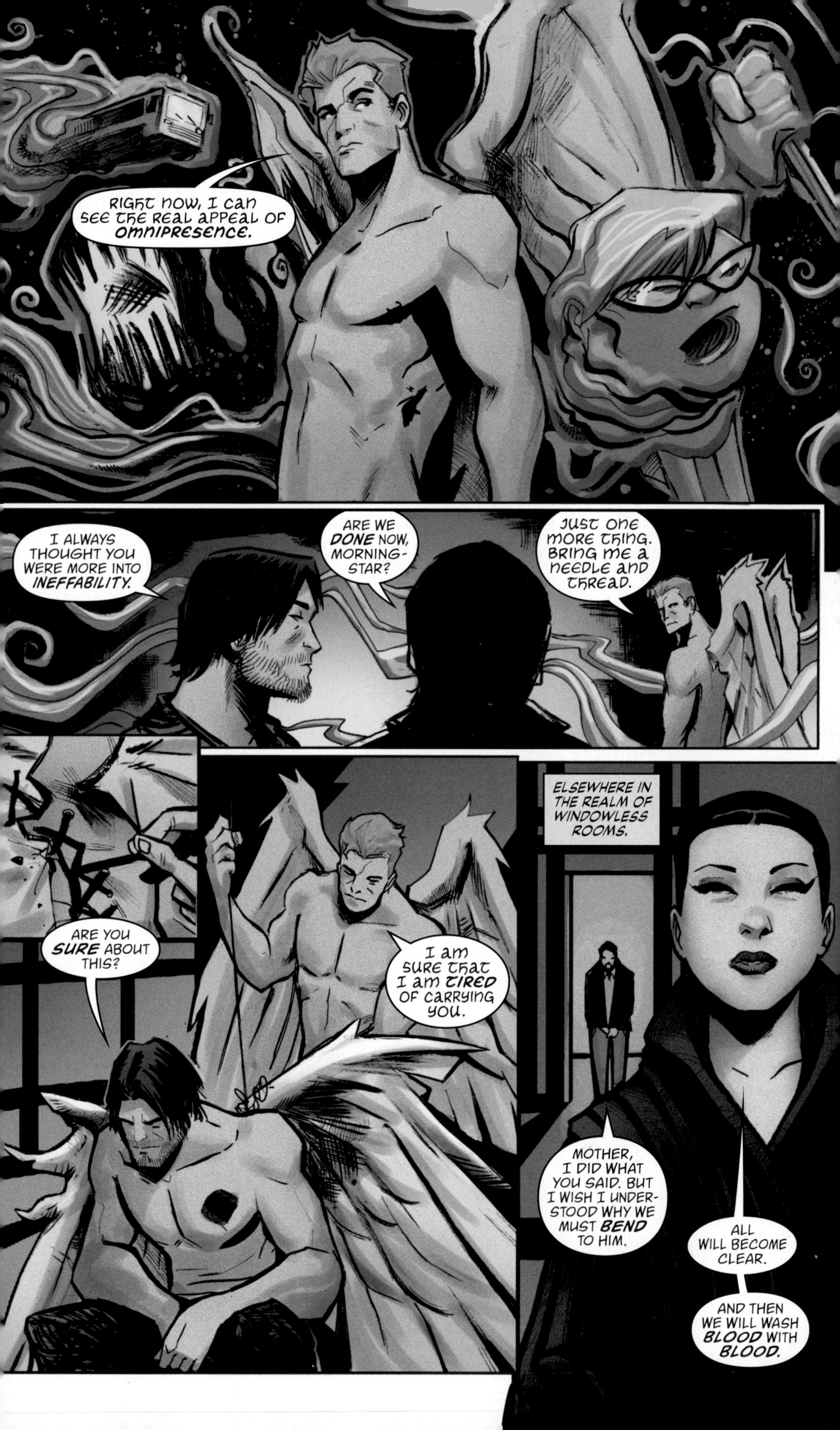
RIGHT NOW, I CAN SEE THE REAL APPEAL OF OMNIPRESENCE.
I ALWAYS THOUGHT YOU WERE MORE INTO INEFFABILITY.
ARE WE DONE NOW, MORNING-STAR?
JUST ONE MORE THING. BRING ME A NEEDLE AND THREAD.
ARE YOU SURE ABOUT THIS?
I AM SURE THAT I AM TIRED OF CARRYING YOU.
ELSEWHERE IN THE REALM OF WINDOWLESS ROOMS.
MOTHER, I DID WHAT YOU SAID. BUT I WISH I UNDER-STOOD WHY WE MUST BEND TO HIM.
ALL WILL BECOME CLEAR.
AND THEN WE WILL WASH BLOOD WITH BLOOD.

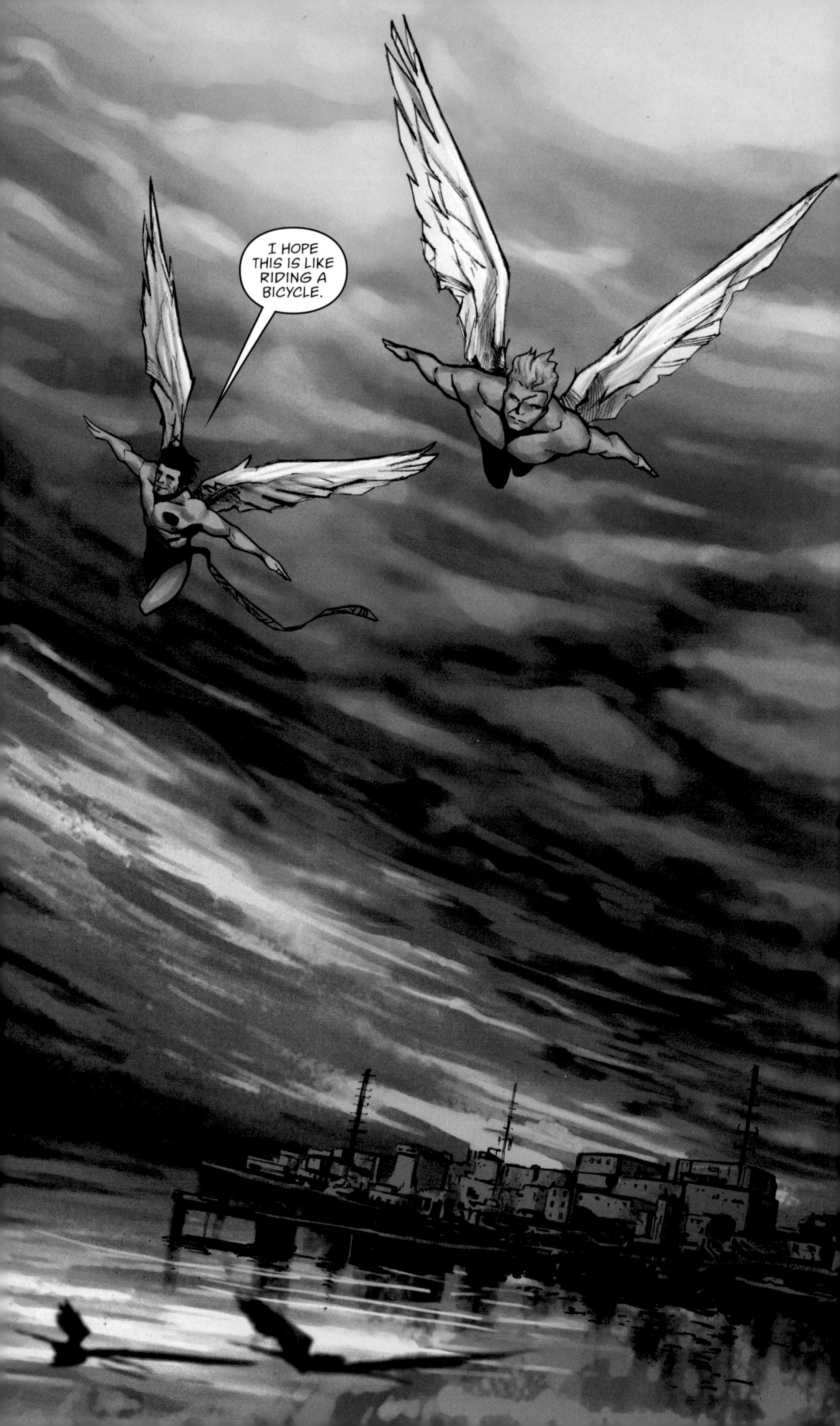
I HOPE THIS IS LIKE RIDING A BICYCLE.

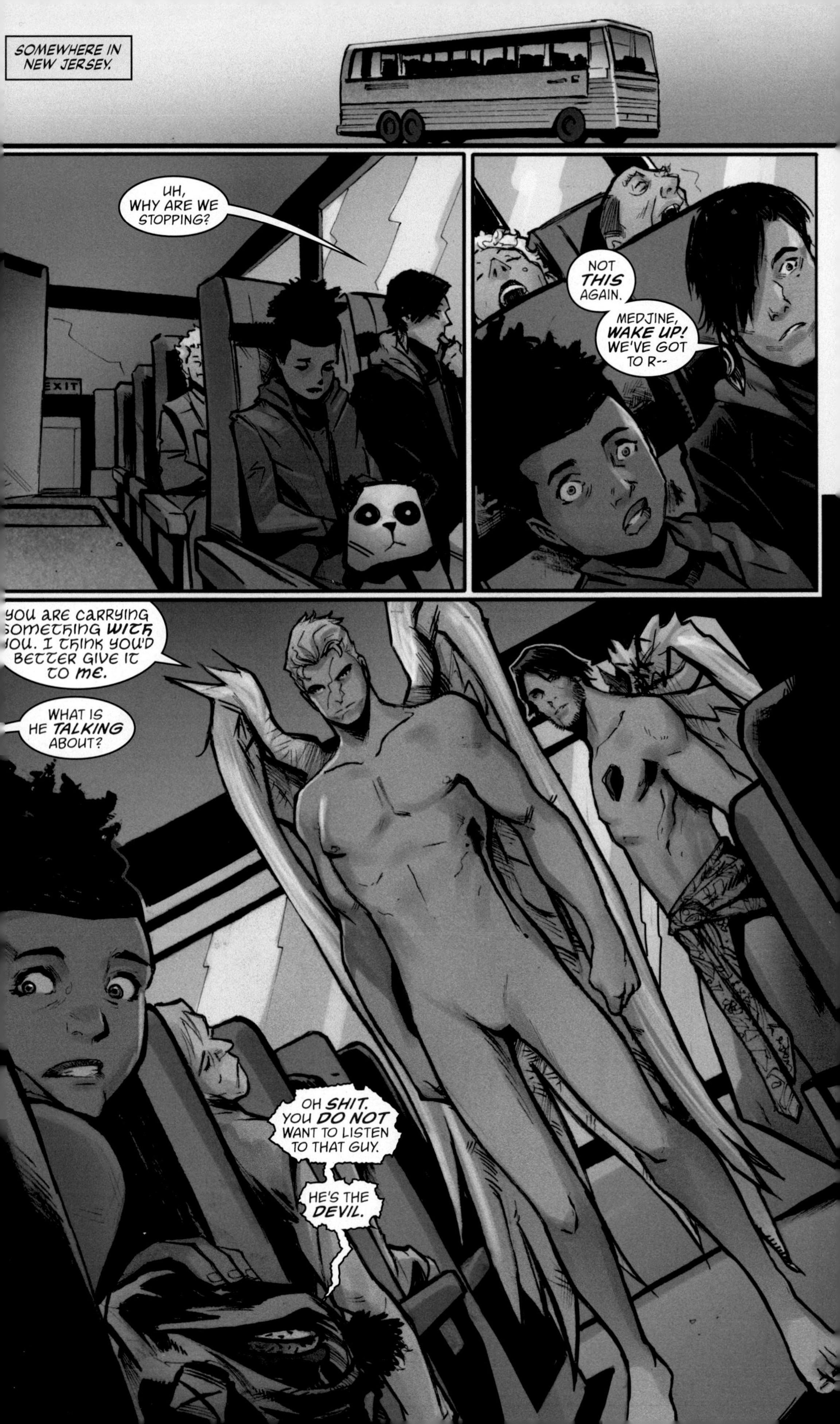
SOMEWHERE IN NEW JERSEY.
UH, WHY ARE WE STOPPING?
NOT THIS AGAIN.
MEDJINE, WAKE UP! WE'VE GOT TO R--
YOU ARE CARRYING SOMETHING WITH YOU. I THINK YOU'D BETTER GIVE IT TO ME.
WHAT IS HE TALKING ABOUT?
OH SHIT. YOU DO NOT WANT TO LISTEN TO THAT GUY.
HE'S THE DEVIL.

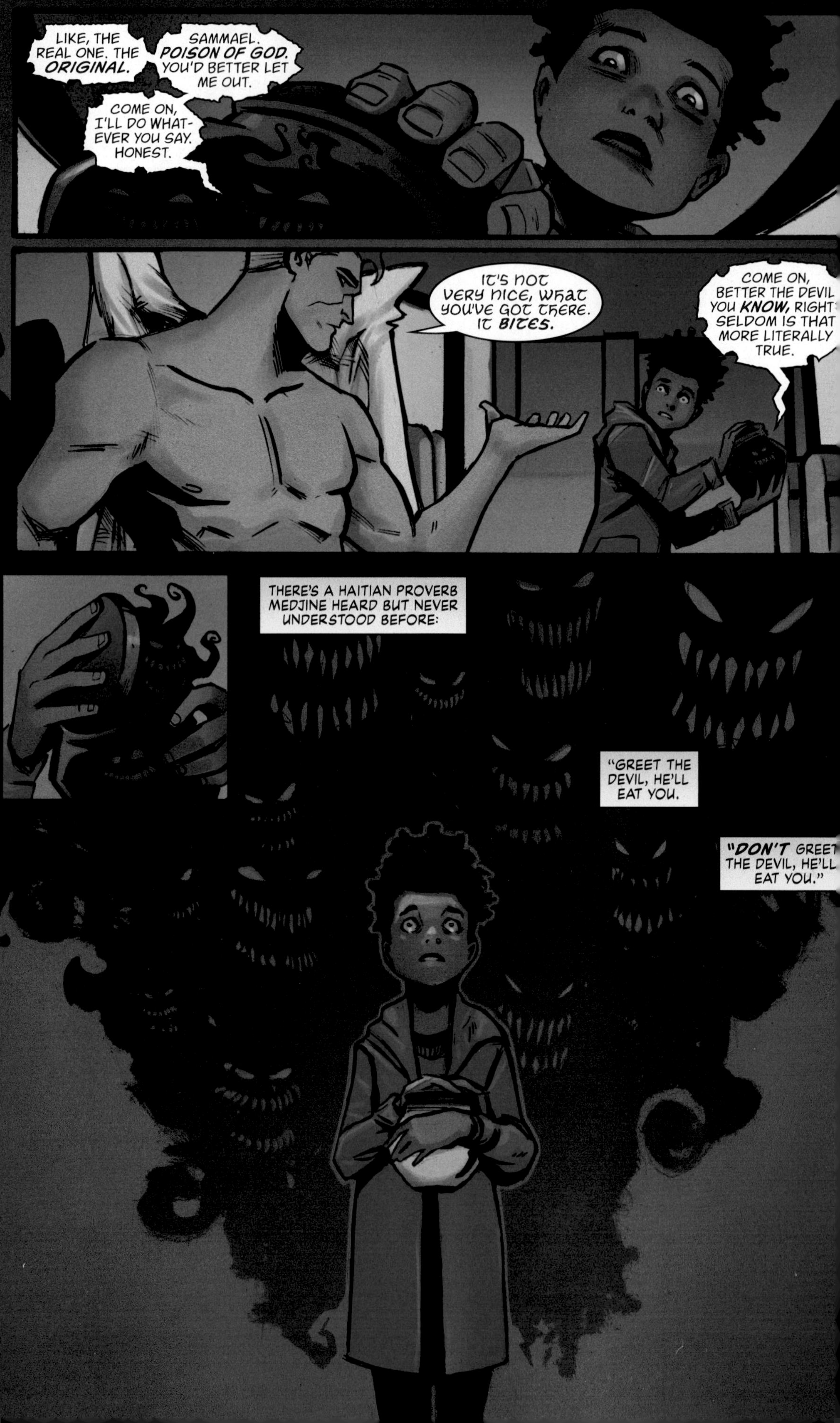
LIKE, THE REAL ONE. THE ORIGINAL.
SAMMAEL. POISON OF GOD. YOU'D BETTER LET ME OUT.
COME ON, I'LL DO WHATEVER YOU SAY. HONEST.
IT'S NOT VERY NICE, WHAT YOU'VE GOT THERE. IT BITES.
COME ON, BETTER THE DEVIL YOU KNOW, RIGHT? SELDOM IS THAT MORE LITERALLY TRUE.
THERE'S A HAITIAN PROVERB MEDJINE HEARD BUT NEVER UNDERSTOOD BEFORE:
"GREET THE DEVIL, HE'LL EAT YOU.
"DON'T GREET THE DEVIL, HE'LL EAT YOU."

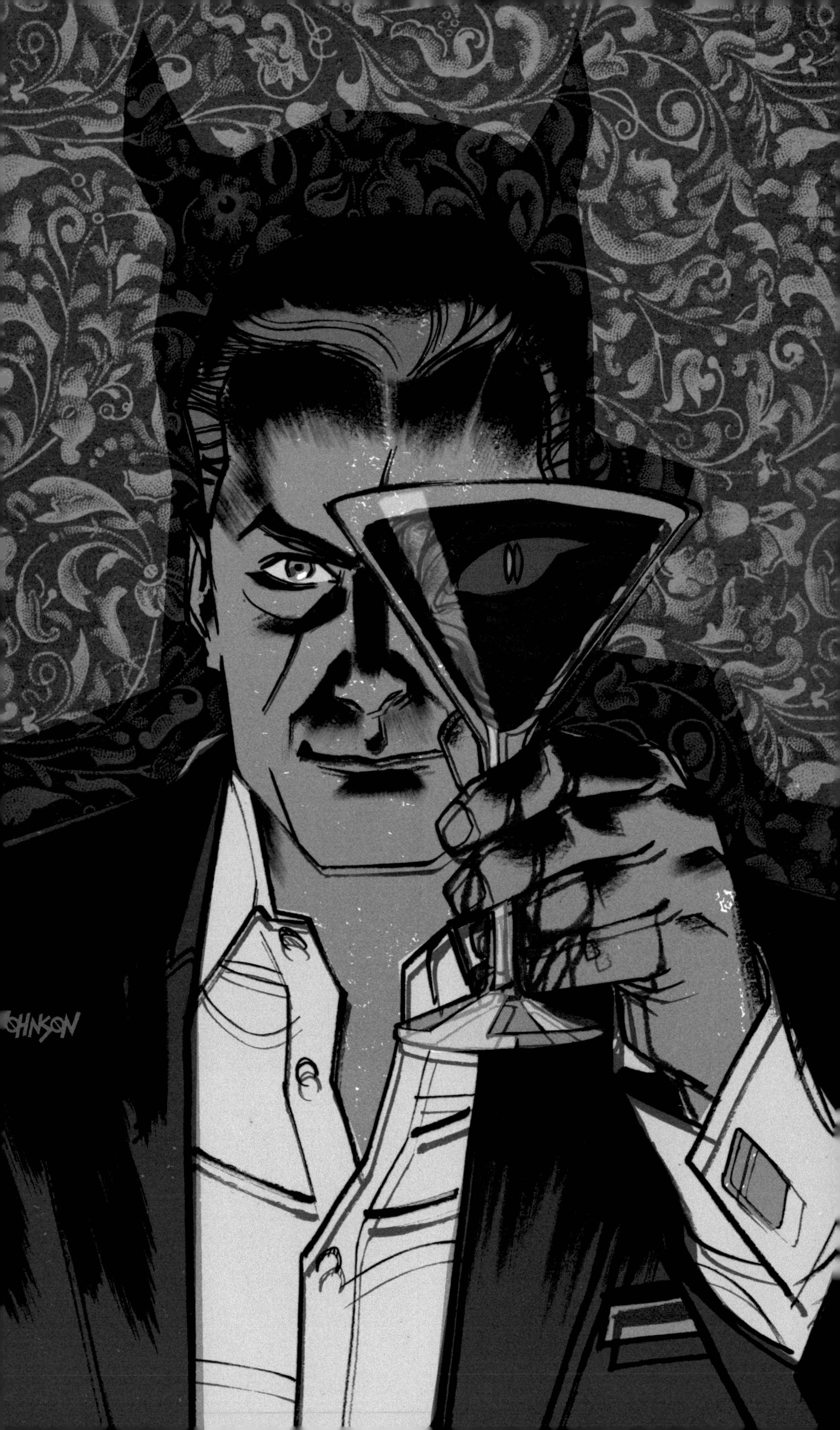
OHNSON

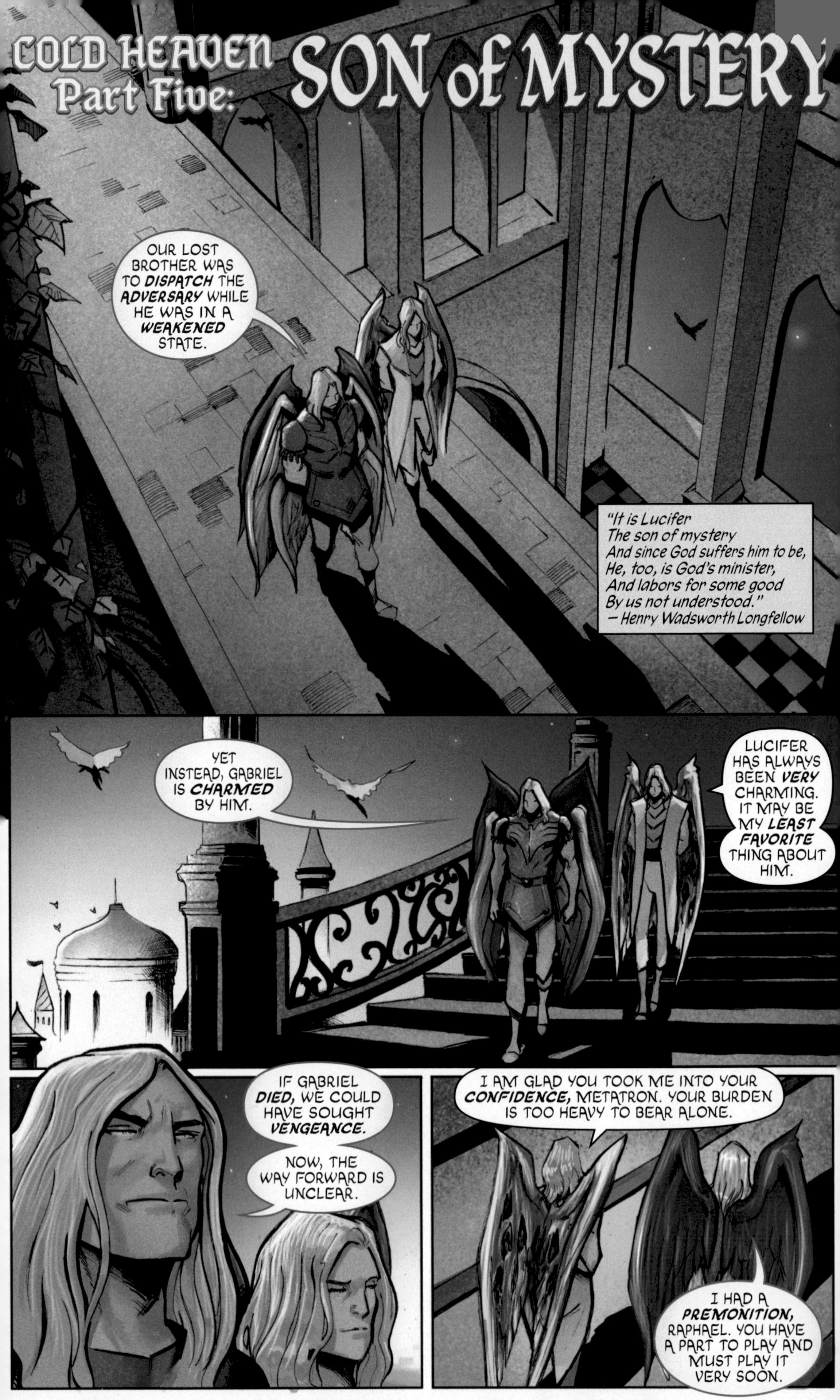
COLD HEAVEN Part Five: SON of MYSTERY
OUR LOST BROTHER WAS TO DISPATCH THE ADVERSARY WHILE HE WAS IN A WEAKENED STATE.
"It is Lucifer
The son of mystery
And since God suffers him to be,
He, too, is God's minister,
And labors for some good
By us not understood."
— Henry Wadsworth Longfellow
YET INSTEAD, GABRIEL IS CHARMED BY HIM.
LUCIFER HAS ALWAYS BEEN VERY CHARMING. IT MAY BE MY LEAST FAVORITE THING ABOUT HIM.
IF GABRIEL DIED, WE COULD HAVE SOUGHT VENGEANCE.
NOW, THE WAY FORWARD IS UNCLEAR.
I AM GLAD YOU TOOK ME INTO YOUR CONFIDENCE, METATRON. YOUR BURDEN IS TOO HEAVY TO BEAR ALONE.
I HAD A PREMONITION, RAPHAEL. YOU HAVE A PART TO PLAY AND MUST PLAY IT VERY SOON.

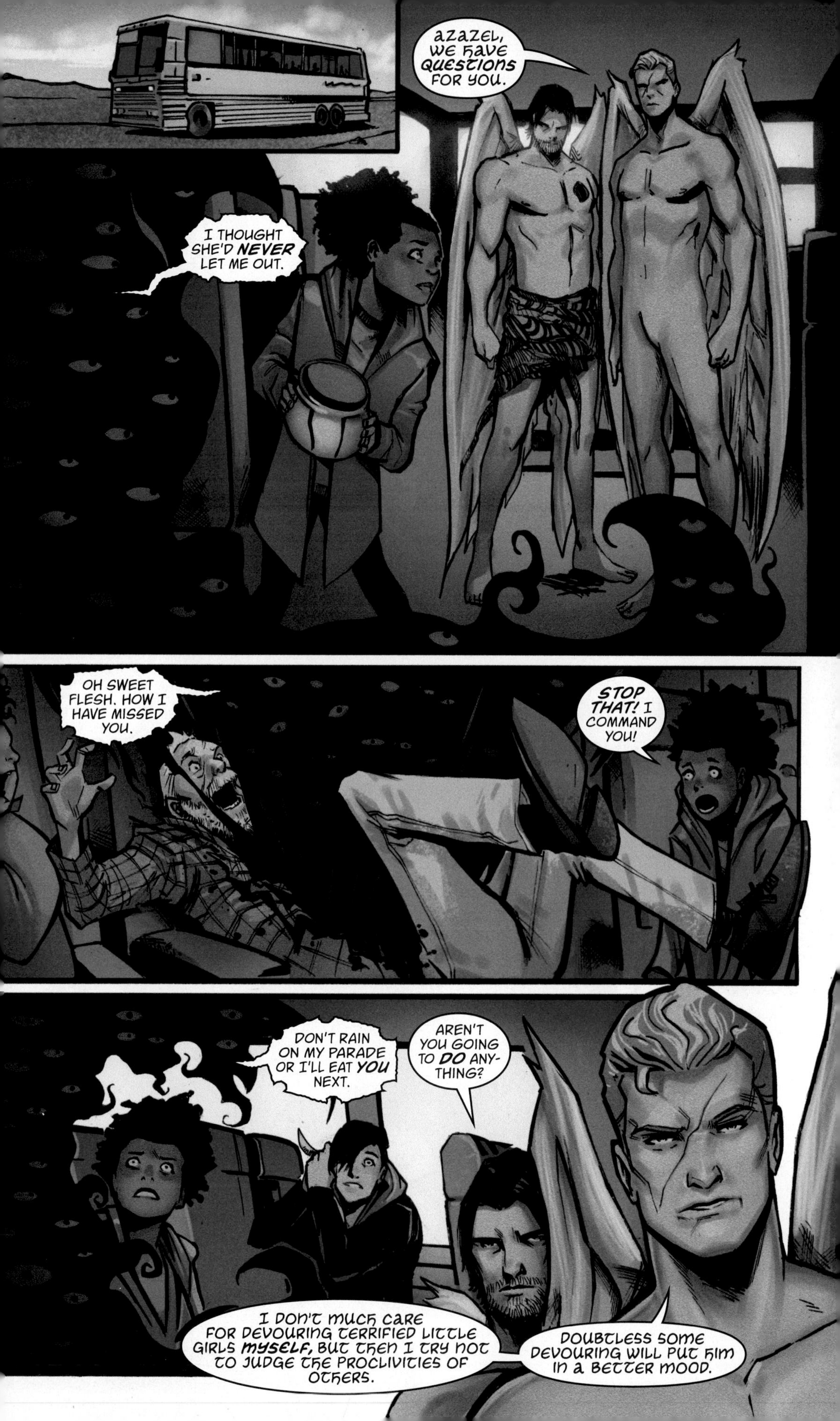
AZAZEL, WE HAVE QUESTIONS FOR YOU.
I THOUGHT SHE'D NEVER LET ME OUT.
OH SWEET FLESH. HOW I HAVE MISSED YOU.
STOP THAT! I COMMAND YOU!
DON'T RAIN ON MY PARADE OR I'LL EAT YOU NEXT.
AREN'T YOU GOING TO DO ANYTHING?
DOUBTLESS SOME DEVOURING WILL PUT HIM IN A BETTER MOOD.
I DON'T MUCH CARE FOR DEVOURING TERRIFIED LITTLE GIRLS MYSELF, BUT THEN I TRY NOT TO JUDGE THE PROCLIVITIES OF OTHERS.

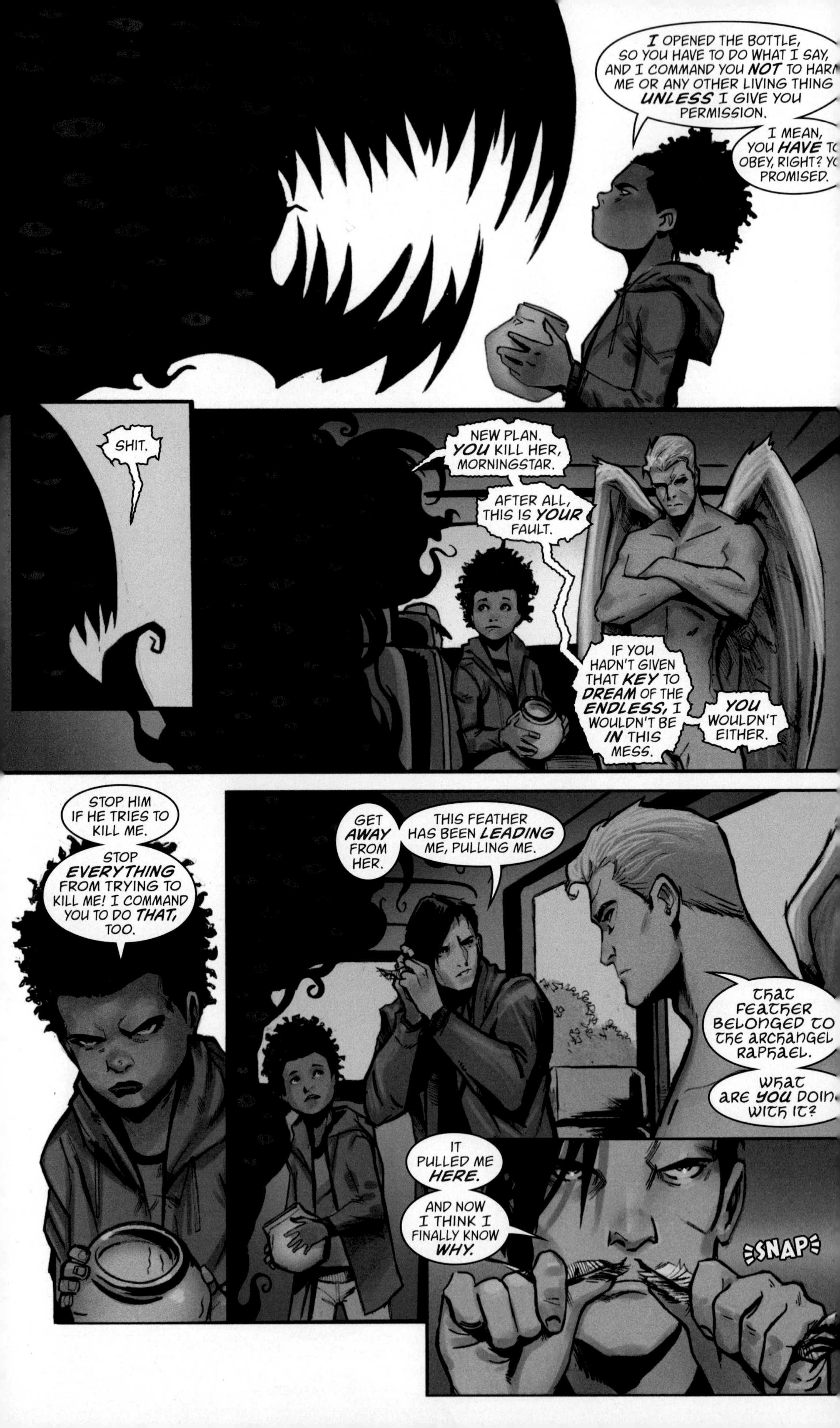
I OPENED THE BOTTLE, SO YOU HAVE TO DO WHAT I SAY, AND I COMMAND YOU NOT TO HARM ME OR ANY OTHER LIVING THING UNLESS I GIVE YOU PERMISSION.
I MEAN, YOU HAVE TO OBEY, RIGHT? YOU PROMISED.
SHIT.
NEW PLAN. YOU KILL HER, MORNINGSTAR.
AFTER ALL, THIS IS YOUR FAULT.
IF YOU HADN'T GIVEN THAT KEY TO DREAM OF THE ENDLESS, I WOULDN'T BE IN THIS MESS.
YOU WOULDN'T EITHER.
STOP HIM IF HE TRIES TO KILL ME.
STOP EVERYTHING FROM TRYING TO KILL ME! I COMMAND YOU TO DO THAT, TOO.
GET AWAY FROM HER.
THIS FEATHER HAS BEEN LEADING ME, PULLING ME.
THAT FEATHER BELONGED TO THE ARCHANGEL RAPHAEL.
WHAT ARE YOU DOIN WITH IT?
IT PULLED ME HERE.
AND NOW I THINK I FINALLY KNOW WHY.
SNAP

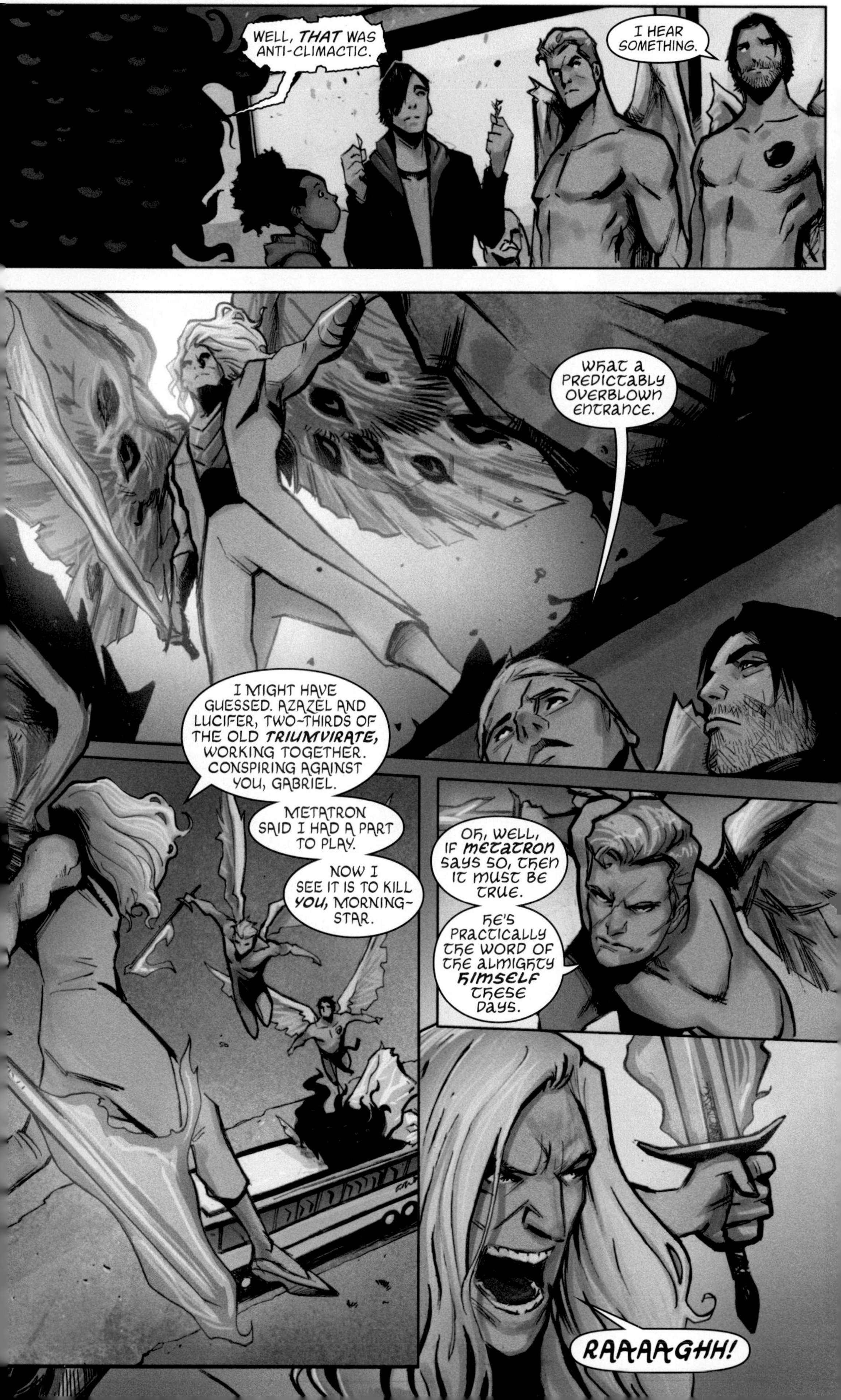

WELL, *THAT* WAS ANTI-CLIMACTIC.
I HEAR SOMETHING.
WHAT A PREDICTABLY OVERBLOWN ENTRANCE.
I MIGHT HAVE GUESSED. AZAZEL AND LUCIFER, TWO-THIRDS OF THE OLD *TRIUMVIRATE,* WORKING TOGETHER. CONSPIRING AGAINST YOU, GABRIEL.
METATRON SAID I HAD A PART TO PLAY.
NOW I SEE IT IS TO KILL *YOU,* MORNING-STAR.
OH, WELL, IF *METATRON* SAYS SO, THEN IT MUST BE TRUE.
HE'S PRACTICALLY THE WORD OF THE ALMIGHTY *HIMSELF* THESE DAYS.
RAAAAGHH!

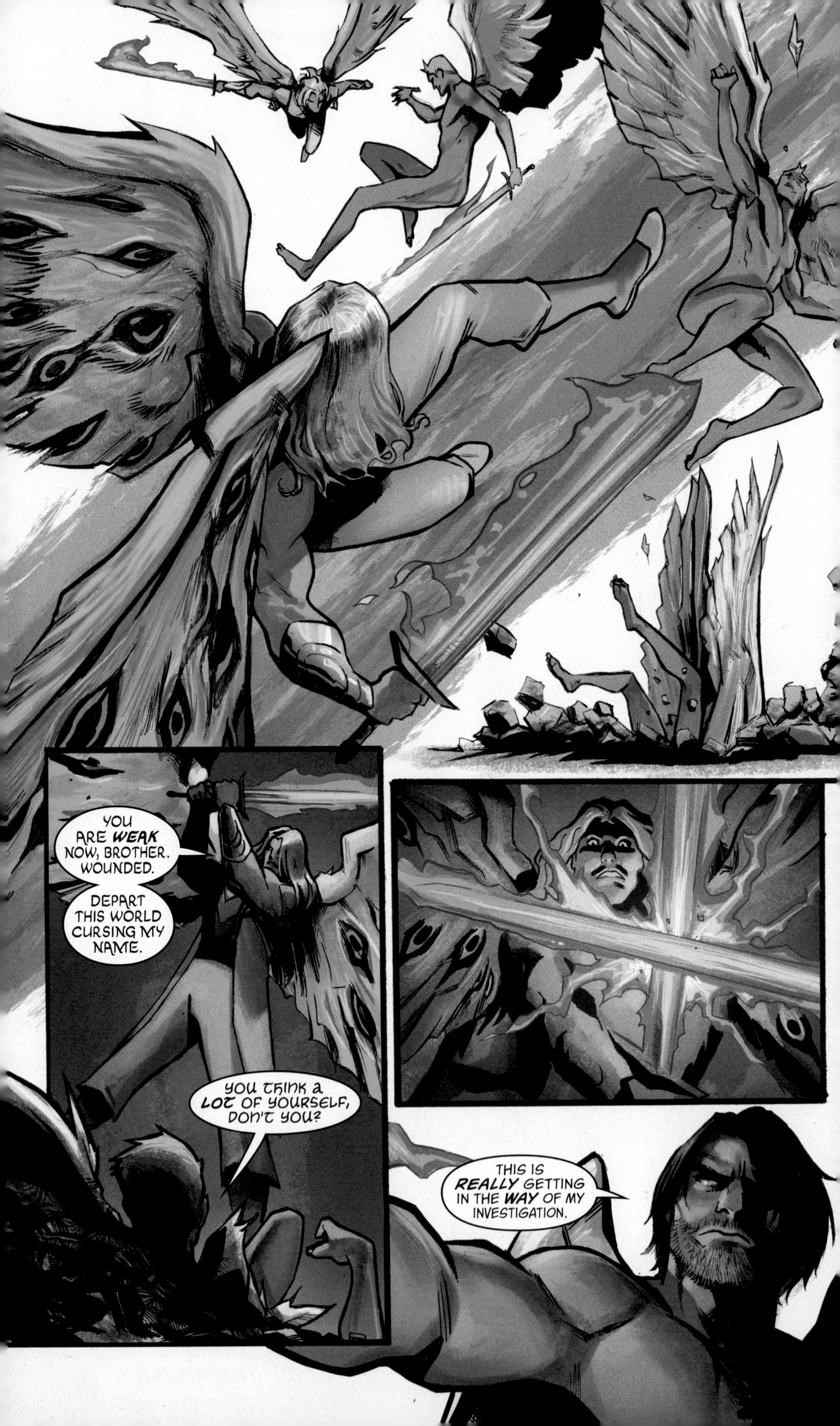
YOU ARE WEAK NOW, BROTHER. WOUNDED.
DEPART THIS WORLD CURSING MY NAME.
YOU THINK A LOT OF YOURSELF, DON'T YOU?
THIS IS REALLY GETTING IN THE WAY OF MY INVESTIGATION.

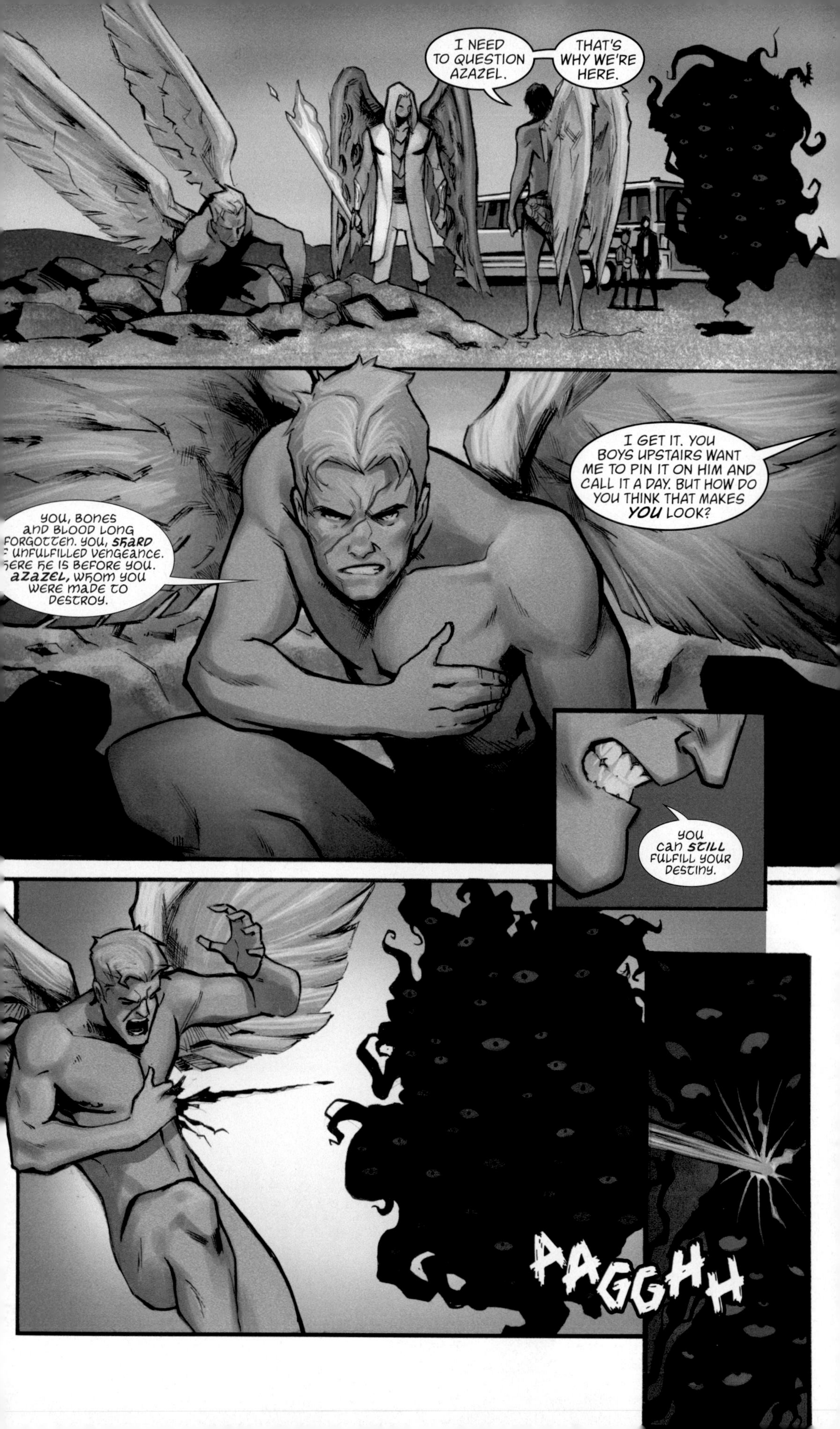
I NEED TO QUESTION AZAZEL.
THAT'S WHY WE'RE HERE.
I GET IT. YOU BOYS UPSTAIRS WANT ME TO PIN IT ON HIM AND CALL IT A DAY. BUT HOW DO YOU THINK THAT MAKES YOU LOOK?
YOU, BONES AND BLOOD LONG FORGOTTEN. YOU, SHARD F UNFULFILLED VENGEANCE. ERE HE IS BEFORE YOU. AZAZEL, WHOM YOU WERE MADE TO DESTROY.
YOU CAN STILL FULFILL YOUR DESTINY.
AAGGHH

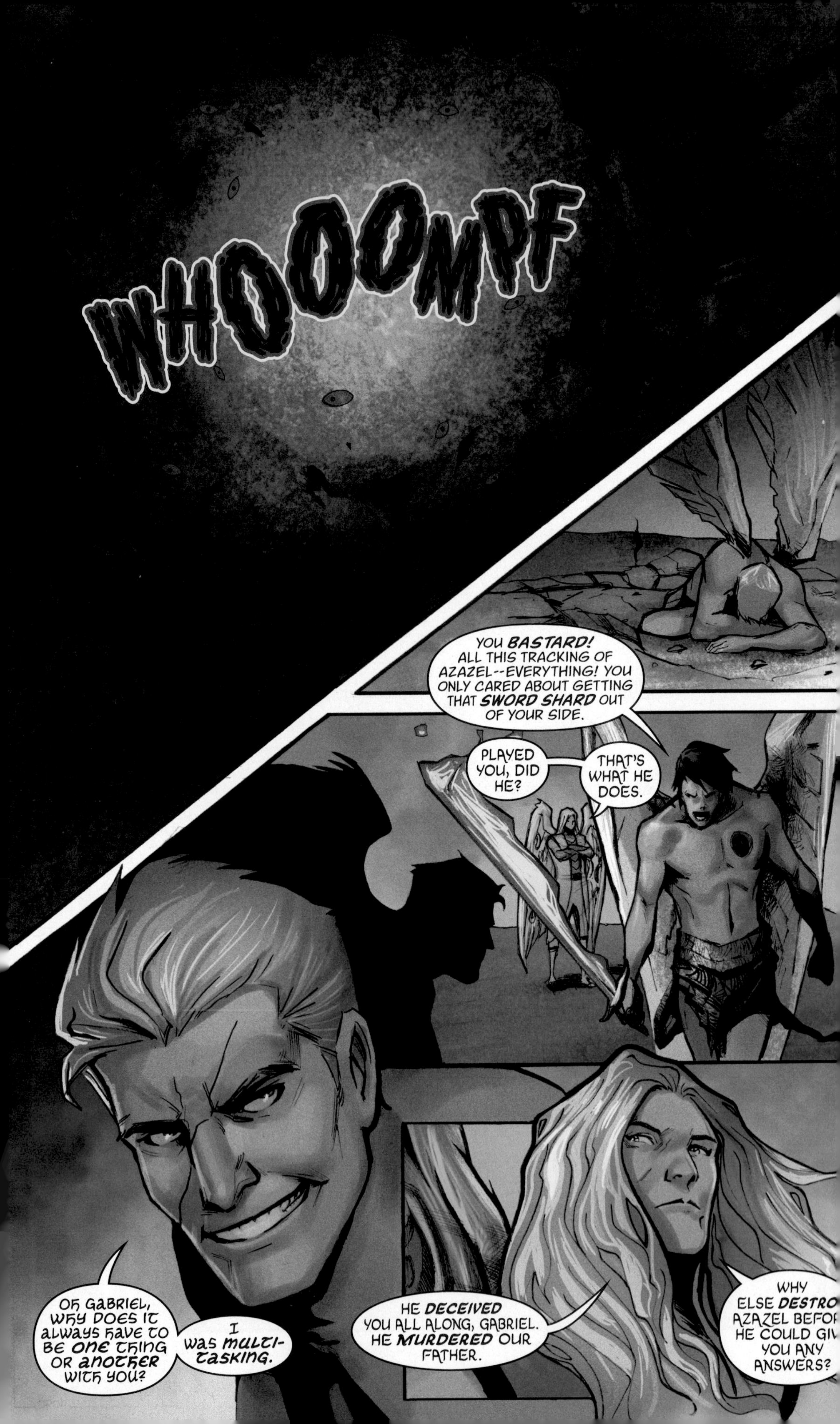
WHOOOOMPF
YOU BASTARD! ALL THIS TRACKING OF AZAZEL--EVERYTHING! YOU ONLY CARED ABOUT GETTING THAT SWORD SHARD OUT OF YOUR SIDE.
PLAYED YOU, DID HE?
THAT'S WHAT HE DOES.
OH GABRIEL, WHY DOES IT ALWAYS HAVE TO BE ONE THING OR ANOTHER WITH YOU?
I WAS MULTI-TASKING.
HE DECEIVED YOU ALL ALONG, GABRIEL. HE MURDERED OUR FATHER.
WHY ELSE DESTRO AZAZEL BEFOR HE COULD GIV YOU ANY ANSWERS?

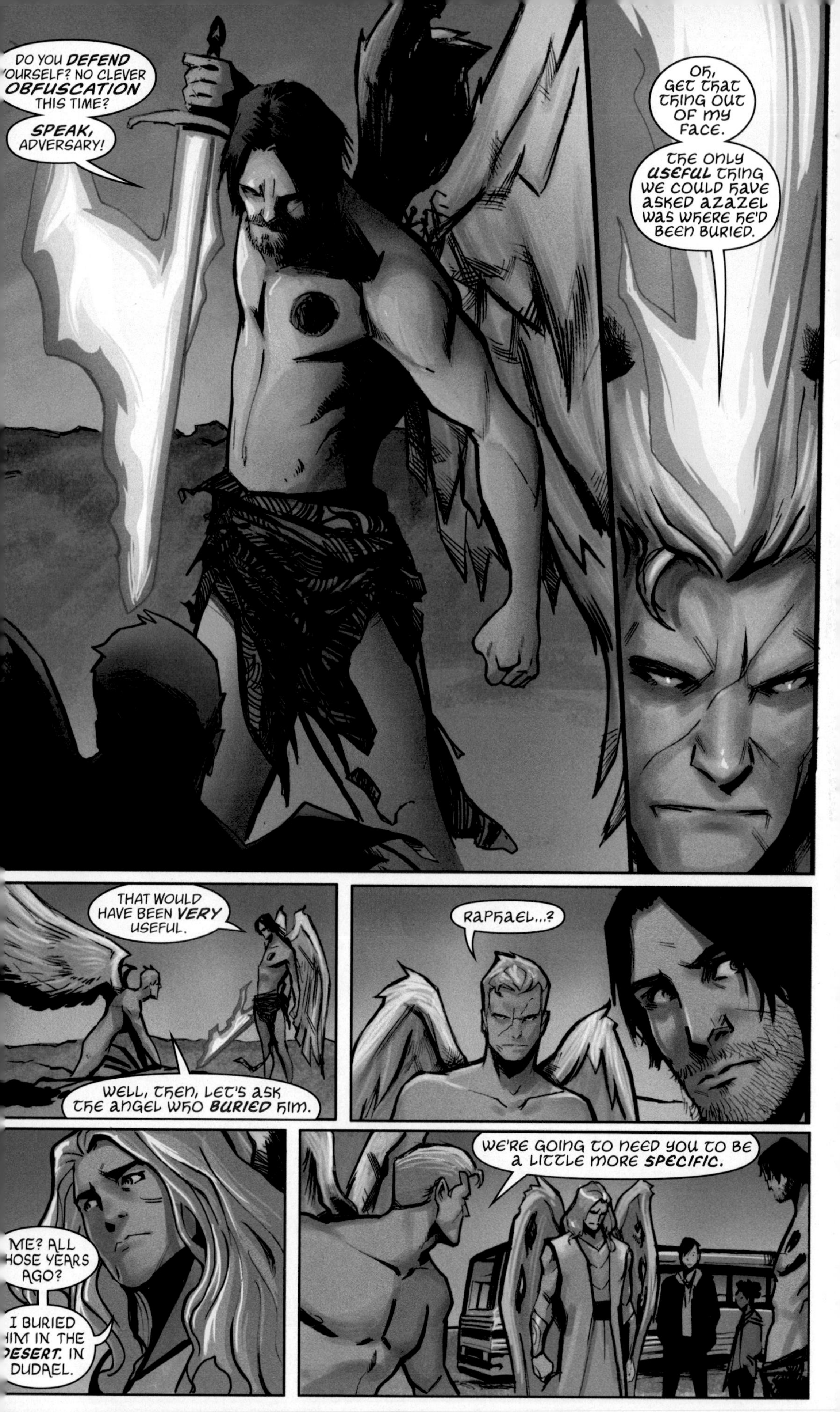
DO YOU DEFEND YOURSELF? NO CLEVER OBFUSCATION THIS TIME?
SPEAK, ADVERSARY!
OH, GET THAT THING OUT OF MY FACE.
THE ONLY USEFUL THING WE COULD HAVE ASKED AZAZEL WAS WHERE HE'D BEEN BURIED.
THAT WOULD HAVE BEEN VERY USEFUL.
WELL, THEN, LET'S ASK THE ANGEL WHO BURIED HIM.
RAPHAEL...?
ME? ALL THOSE YEARS AGO?
I BURIED HIM IN THE DESERT. IN DUDAEL.
WE'RE GOING TO NEED YOU TO BE A LITTLE MORE SPECIFIC.

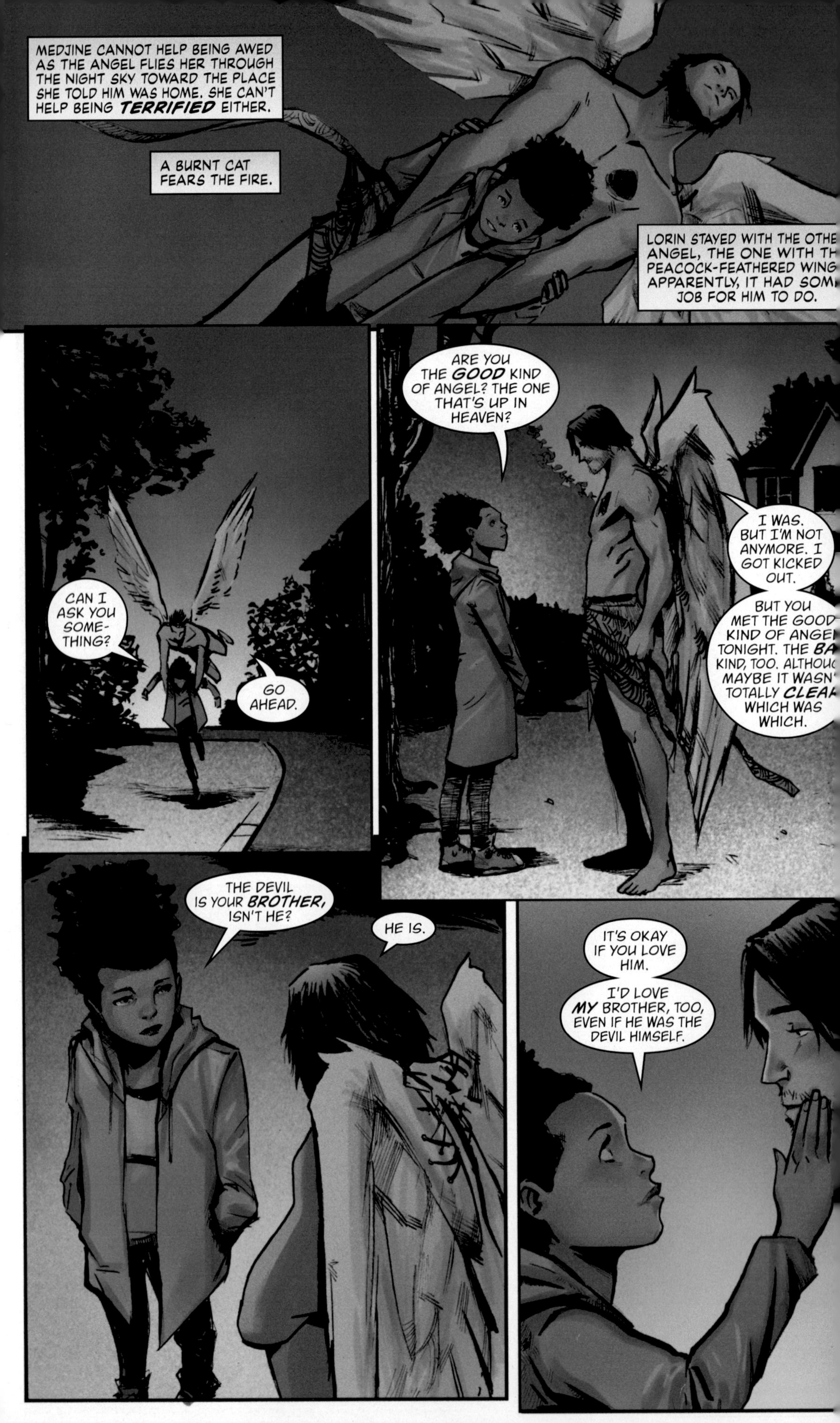
MEDJINE CANNOT HELP BEING AWED AS THE ANGEL FLIES HER THROUGH THE NIGHT SKY TOWARD THE PLACE SHE TOLD HIM WAS HOME. SHE CAN'T HELP BEING TERRIFIED EITHER.
A BURNT CAT FEARS THE FIRE.
LORIN STAYED WITH THE OTHE ANGEL, THE ONE WITH TH PEACOCK-FEATHERED WING APPARENTLY, IT HAD SOM JOB FOR HIM TO DO.
CAN I ASK YOU SOME-THING?
GO AHEAD.
ARE YOU THE GOOD KIND OF ANGEL? THE ONE THAT'S UP IN HEAVEN?
I WAS. BUT I'M NOT ANYMORE. I GOT KICKED OUT.
BUT YOU MET THE GOOD KIND OF ANGE TONIGHT. THE BA KIND, TOO. ALTHOU MAYBE IT WASN TOTALLY CLEA WHICH WAS WHICH.
THE DEVIL IS YOUR BROTHER, ISN'T HE?
HE IS.
IT'S OKAY IF YOU LOVE HIM.
I'D LOVE MY BROTHER, TOO, EVEN IF HE WAS THE DEVIL HIMSELF.

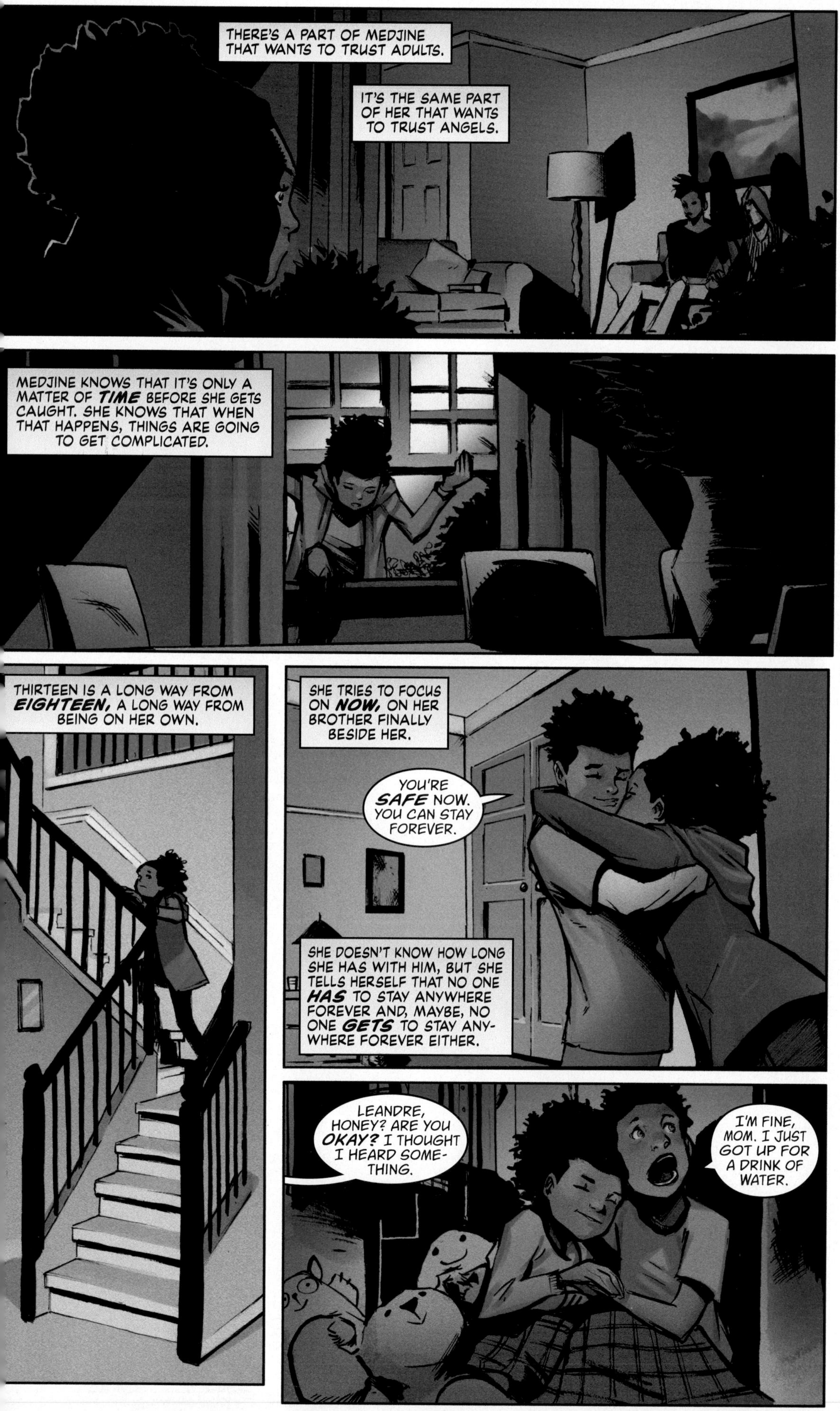
THERE'S A PART OF MEDJINE THAT WANTS TO TRUST ADULTS.
IT'S THE SAME PART OF HER THAT WANTS TO TRUST ANGELS.
MEDJINE KNOWS THAT IT'S ONLY A MATTER OF TIME BEFORE SHE GETS CAUGHT. SHE KNOWS THAT WHEN THAT HAPPENS, THINGS ARE GOING TO GET COMPLICATED.
THIRTEEN IS A LONG WAY FROM EIGHTEEN, A LONG WAY FROM BEING ON HER OWN.
SHE TRIES TO FOCUS ON NOW, ON HER BROTHER FINALLY BESIDE HER.
YOU'RE SAFE NOW. YOU CAN STAY FOREVER.
SHE DOESN'T KNOW HOW LONG SHE HAS WITH HIM, BUT SHE TELLS HERSELF THAT NO ONE HAS TO STAY ANYWHERE FOREVER AND, MAYBE, NO ONE GETS TO STAY ANY-WHERE FOREVER EITHER.
LEANDRE, HONEY? ARE YOU OKAY? I THOUGHT I HEARD SOME-THING.
I'M FINE, MOM. I JUST GOT UP FOR A DRINK OF WATER.

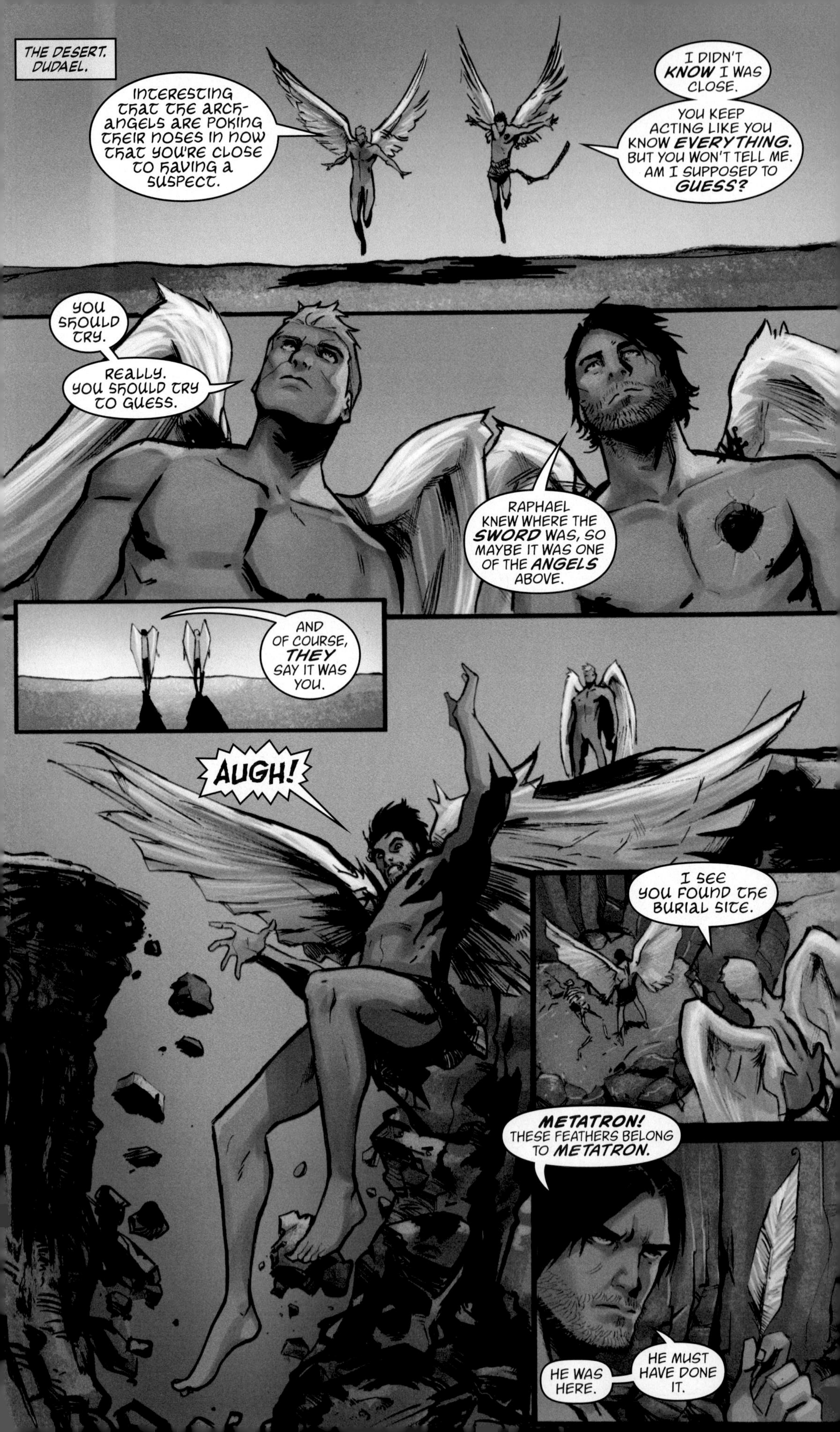
THE DESERT. DUDAEL.
INTERESTING THAT THE ARCH-ANGELS ARE POKING THEIR NOSES IN NOW THAT YOU'RE CLOSE TO HAVING A SUSPECT.
I DIDN'T KNOW I WAS CLOSE.
YOU KEEP ACTING LIKE YOU KNOW EVERYTHING. BUT YOU WON'T TELL ME. AM I SUPPOSED TO GUESS?
YOU SHOULD TRY.
REALLY. YOU SHOULD TRY TO GUESS.
RAPHAEL KNEW WHERE THE SWORD WAS, SO MAYBE IT WAS ONE OF THE ANGELS ABOVE.
AND OF COURSE, THEY SAY IT WAS YOU.
AUGH!
I SEE YOU FOUND THE BURIAL SITE.
METATRON! THESE FEATHERS BELONG TO METATRON.
HE WAS HERE.
HE MUST HAVE DONE IT.

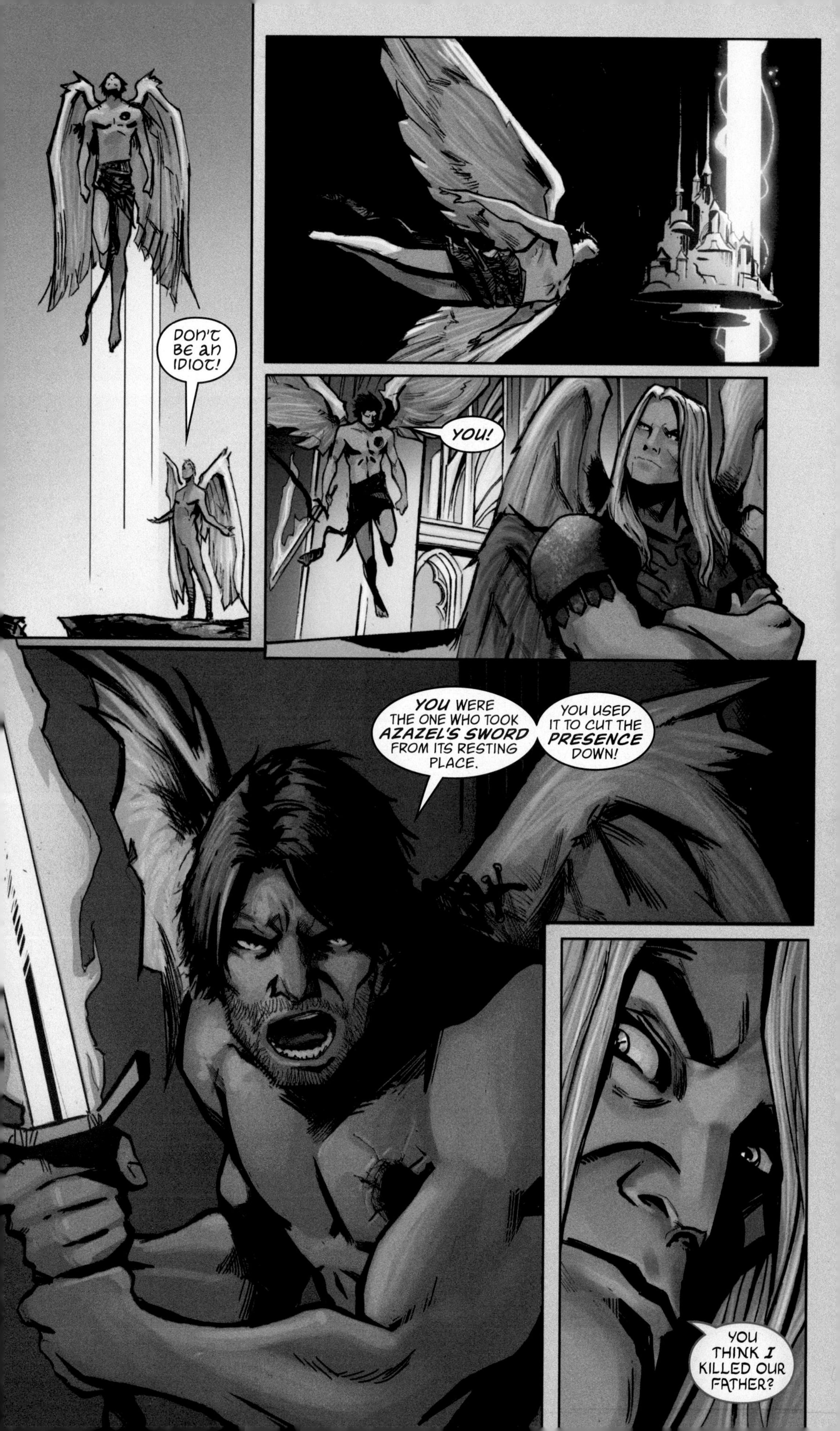
DON'T BE AN IDIOT!
YOU!
YOU WERE THE ONE WHO TOOK AZAZEL'S SWORD FROM ITS RESTING PLACE.
YOU USED IT TO CUT THE PRESENCE DOWN!
YOU THINK I KILLED OUR FATHER?

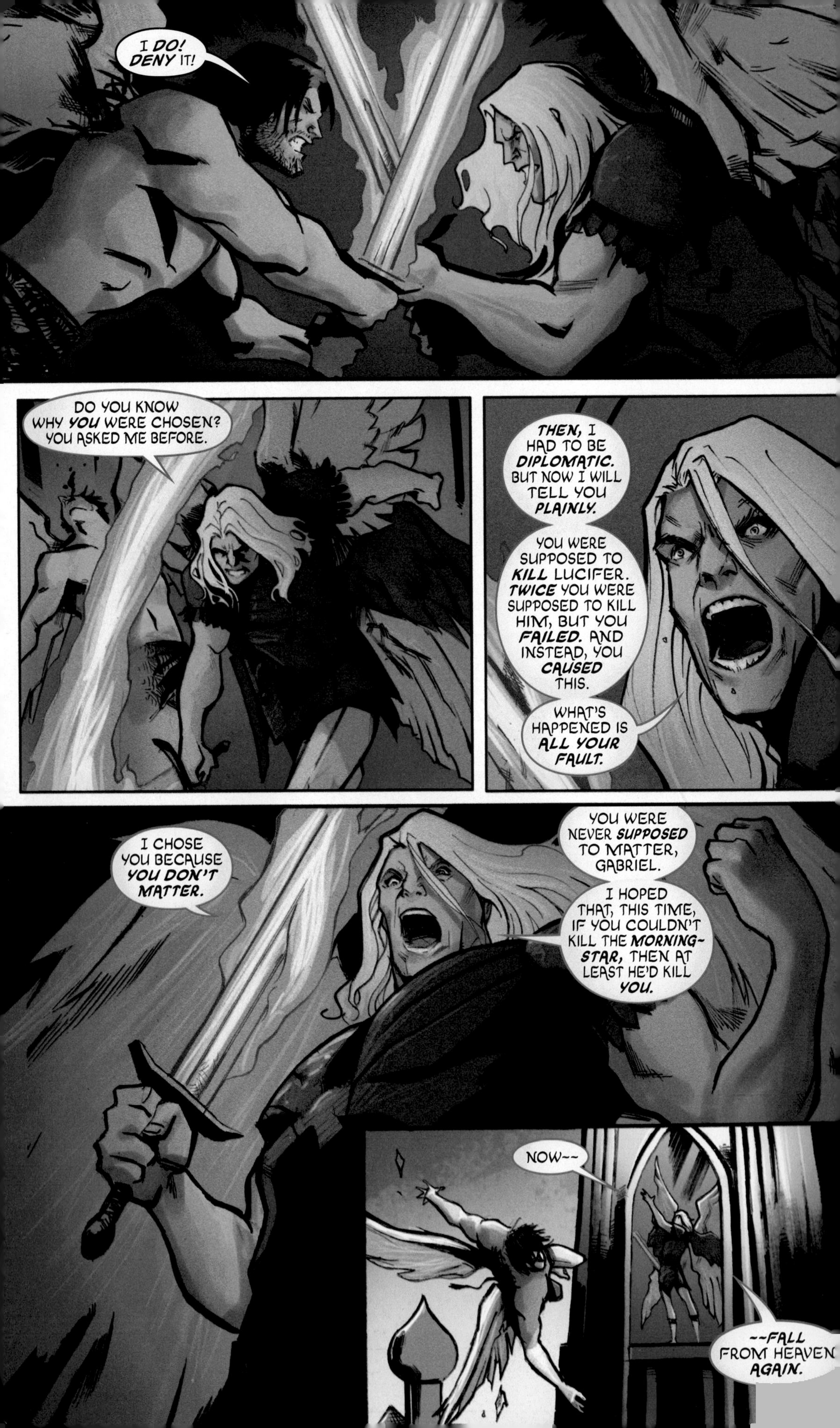
I DO! DENY IT!
DO YOU KNOW WHY YOU WERE CHOSEN? YOU ASKED ME BEFORE.
THEN, I HAD TO BE DIPLOMATIC. BUT NOW I WILL TELL YOU PLAINLY.
YOU WERE SUPPOSED TO KILL LUCIFER. TWICE YOU WERE SUPPOSED TO KILL HIM, BUT YOU FAILED. AND INSTEAD, YOU CAUSED THIS.
WHAT'S HAPPENED IS ALL YOUR FAULT.
I CHOSE YOU BECAUSE YOU DON'T MATTER.
YOU WERE NEVER SUPPOSED TO MATTER, GABRIEL.
I HOPED THAT, THIS TIME, IF YOU COULDN'T KILL THE MORNING-STAR, THEN AT LEAST HE'D KILL YOU.
NOW--
--FALL FROM HEAVEN AGAIN.

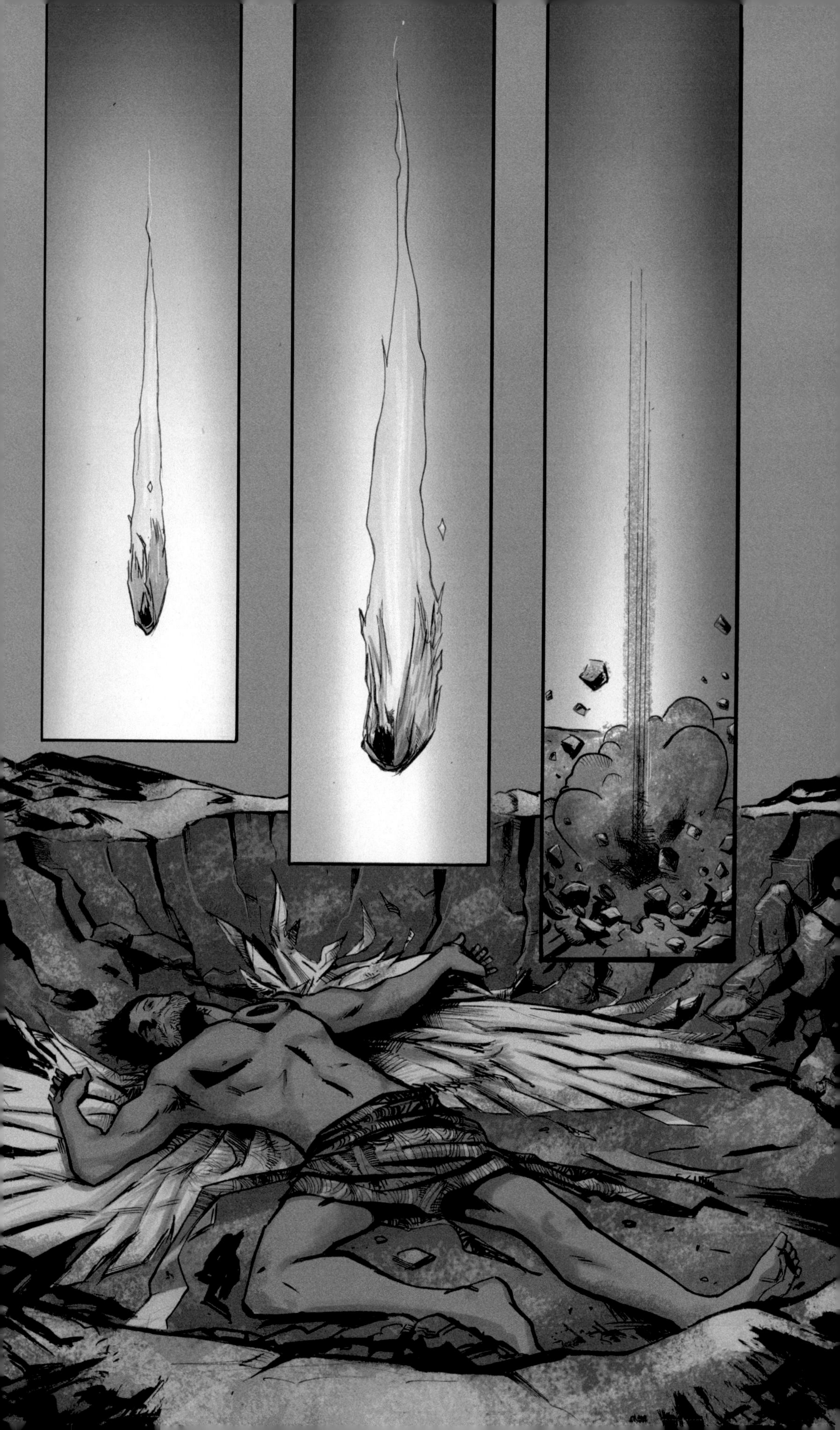

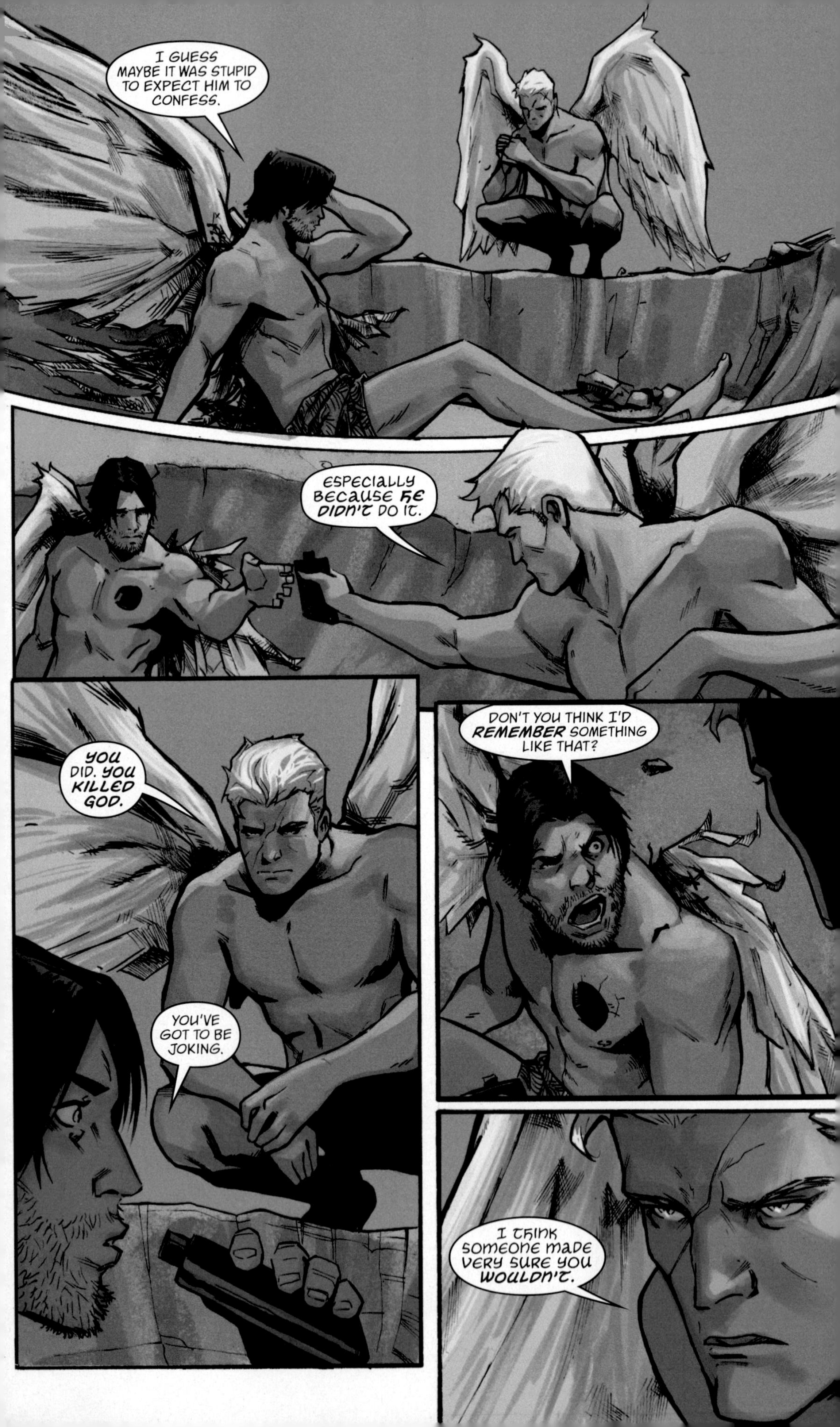
I GUESS MAYBE IT WAS STUPID TO EXPECT HIM TO CONFESS.
ESPECIALLY BECAUSE HE DIDN'T DO IT.
YOU DID. YOU KILLED GOD.
YOU'VE GOT TO BE JOKING.
DON'T YOU THINK I'D REMEMBER SOMETHING LIKE THAT?
I THINK SOMEONE MADE VERY SURE YOU WOULDN'T.

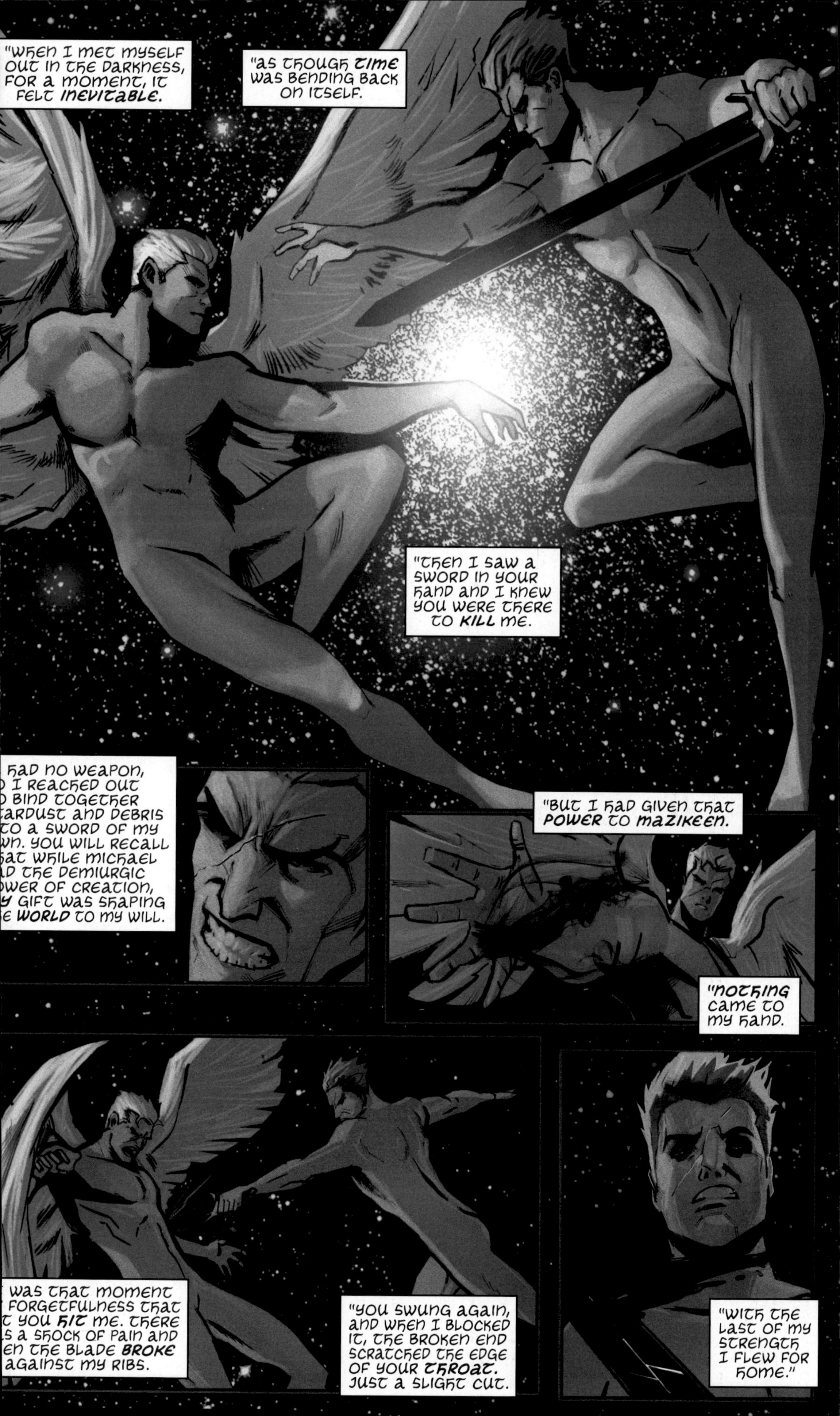
"WHEN I MET MYSELF OUT IN THE DARKNESS, FOR A MOMENT, IT FELT INEVITABLE.
"AS THOUGH TIME WAS BENDING BACK ON ITSELF.
"THEN I SAW A SWORD IN YOUR HAND AND I KNEW YOU WERE THERE TO KILL ME.
HAD NO WEAPON, I REACHED OUT BIND TOGETHER TARDUST AND DEBRIS TO A SWORD OF MY WN. YOU WILL RECALL HAT WHILE MICHAEL AD THE DEMIURGIC OWER OF CREATION, GIFT WAS SHAPING E WORLD TO MY WILL.
"BUT I HAD GIVEN THAT POWER TO MAZIKEEN.
"NOTHING CAME TO MY HAND.
WAS THAT MOMENT FORGETFULNESS THAT T YOU HIT ME. THERE S A SHOCK OF PAIN AND EN THE BLADE BROKE AGAINST MY RIBS.
"YOU SWUNG AGAIN, AND WHEN I BLOCKED IT, THE BROKEN END SCRATCHED THE EDGE OF YOUR THROAT. JUST A SLIGHT CUT.
"WITH THE LAST OF MY STRENGTH I FLEW FOR HOME."

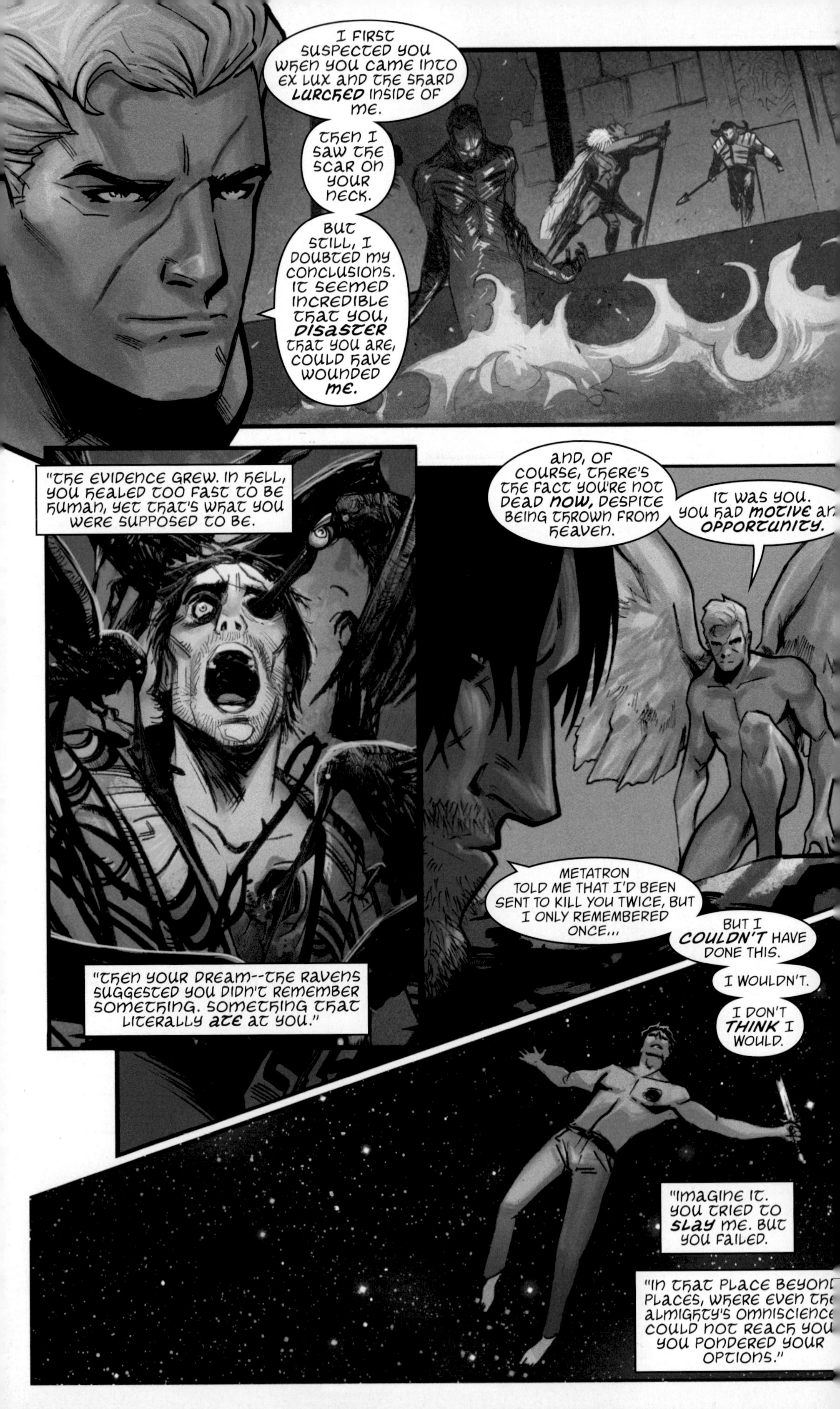
I FIRST SUSPECTED YOU WHEN YOU CAME INTO EX LUX AND THE SHARD **LURCHED** INSIDE OF ME.
THEN I SAW THE SCAR ON YOUR NECK.
BUT STILL, I DOUBTED MY CONCLUSIONS. IT SEEMED INCREDIBLE THAT YOU, **DISASTER** THAT YOU ARE, COULD HAVE WOUNDED **ME.**
"THE EVIDENCE GREW. IN HELL, YOU HEALED TOO FAST TO BE HUMAN, YET THAT'S WHAT YOU WERE SUPPOSED TO BE.
"THEN YOUR DREAM--THE RAVENS SUGGESTED YOU DIDN'T REMEMBER SOMETHING. SOMETHING THAT LITERALLY **ATE** AT YOU."
AND, OF COURSE, THERE'S THE FACT YOU'RE NOT DEAD **NOW,** DESPITE BEING THROWN FROM HEAVEN.
IT WAS YOU. YOU HAD **MOTIVE** AN **OPPORTUNITY.**
METATRON TOLD ME THAT I'D BEEN SENT TO KILL YOU TWICE, BUT I ONLY REMEMBERED ONCE...
BUT I **COULDN'T** HAVE DONE THIS.
I WOULDN'T.
I DON'T **THINK** I WOULD.
"IMAGINE IT. YOU TRIED TO **SLAY** ME. BUT YOU FAILED.
"IN THAT PLACE BEYOND PLACES, WHERE EVEN THE ALMIGHTY'S OMNISCIENCE COULD NOT REACH YOU YOU PONDERED YOUR OPTIONS."

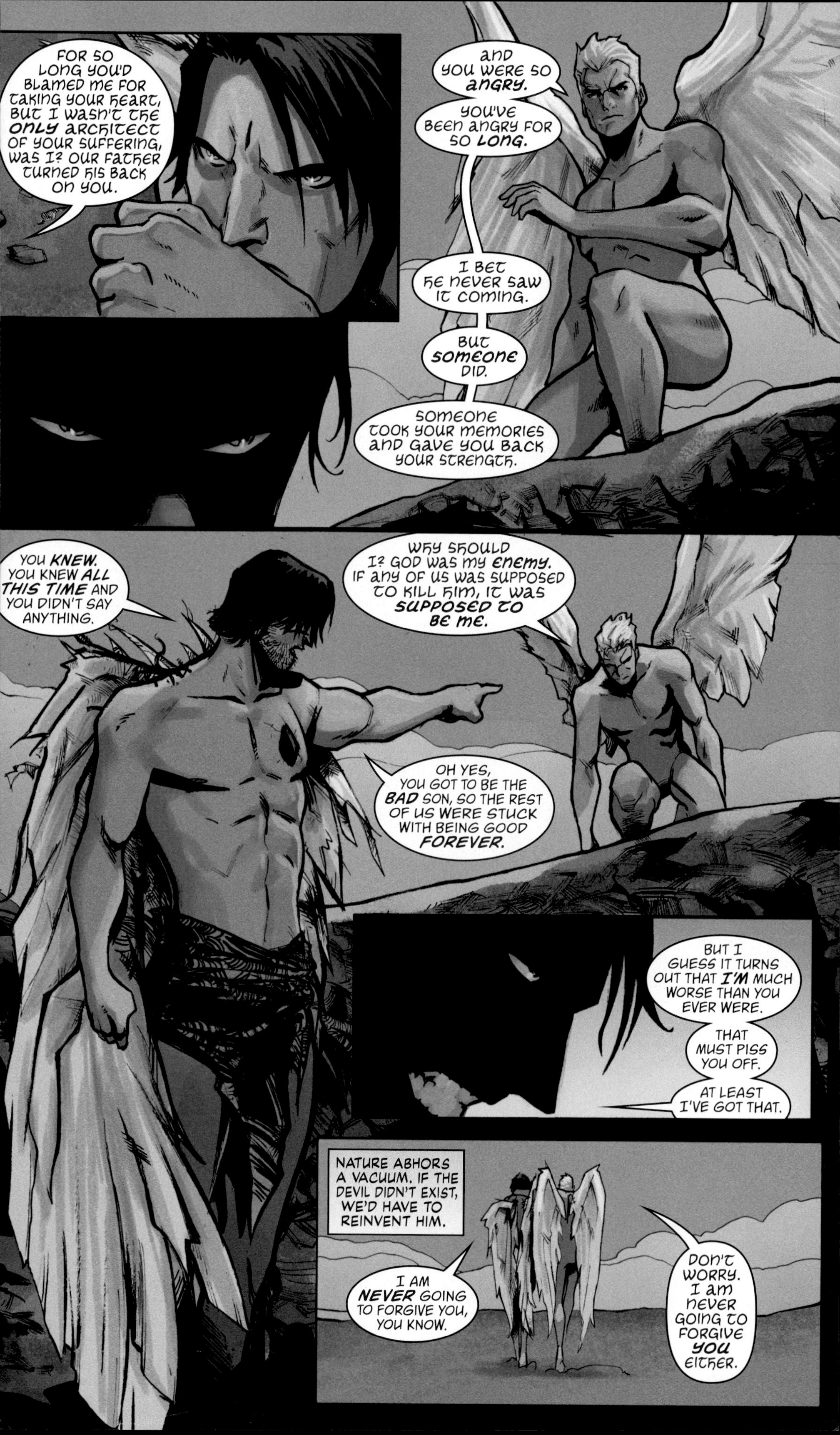

FOR SO LONG YOU'D BLAMED ME FOR TAKING YOUR HEART, BUT I WASN'T THE ONLY ARCHITECT OF YOUR SUFFERING, WAS I? OUR FATHER TURNED HIS BACK ON YOU.
AND YOU WERE SO ANGRY.
YOU'VE BEEN ANGRY FOR SO LONG.
I BET HE NEVER SAW IT COMING.
BUT SOMEONE DID.
SOMEONE TOOK YOUR MEMORIES AND GAVE YOU BACK YOUR STRENGTH.
YOU KNEW. YOU KNEW ALL THIS TIME AND YOU DIDN'T SAY ANYTHING.
WHY SHOULD I? GOD WAS MY ENEMY. IF ANY OF US WAS SUPPOSED TO KILL HIM, IT WAS SUPPOSED TO BE ME.
OH YES, YOU GOT TO BE THE BAD SON, SO THE REST OF US WERE STUCK WITH BEING GOOD FOREVER.
BUT I GUESS IT TURNS OUT THAT I'M MUCH WORSE THAN YOU EVER WERE.
THAT MUST PISS YOU OFF.
AT LEAST I'VE GOT THAT.
NATURE ABHORS A VACUUM. IF THE DEVIL DIDN'T EXIST, WE'D HAVE TO REINVENT HIM.
I AM NEVER GOING TO FORGIVE YOU, YOU KNOW.
DON'T WORRY. I AM NEVER GOING TO FORGIVE YOU EITHER.

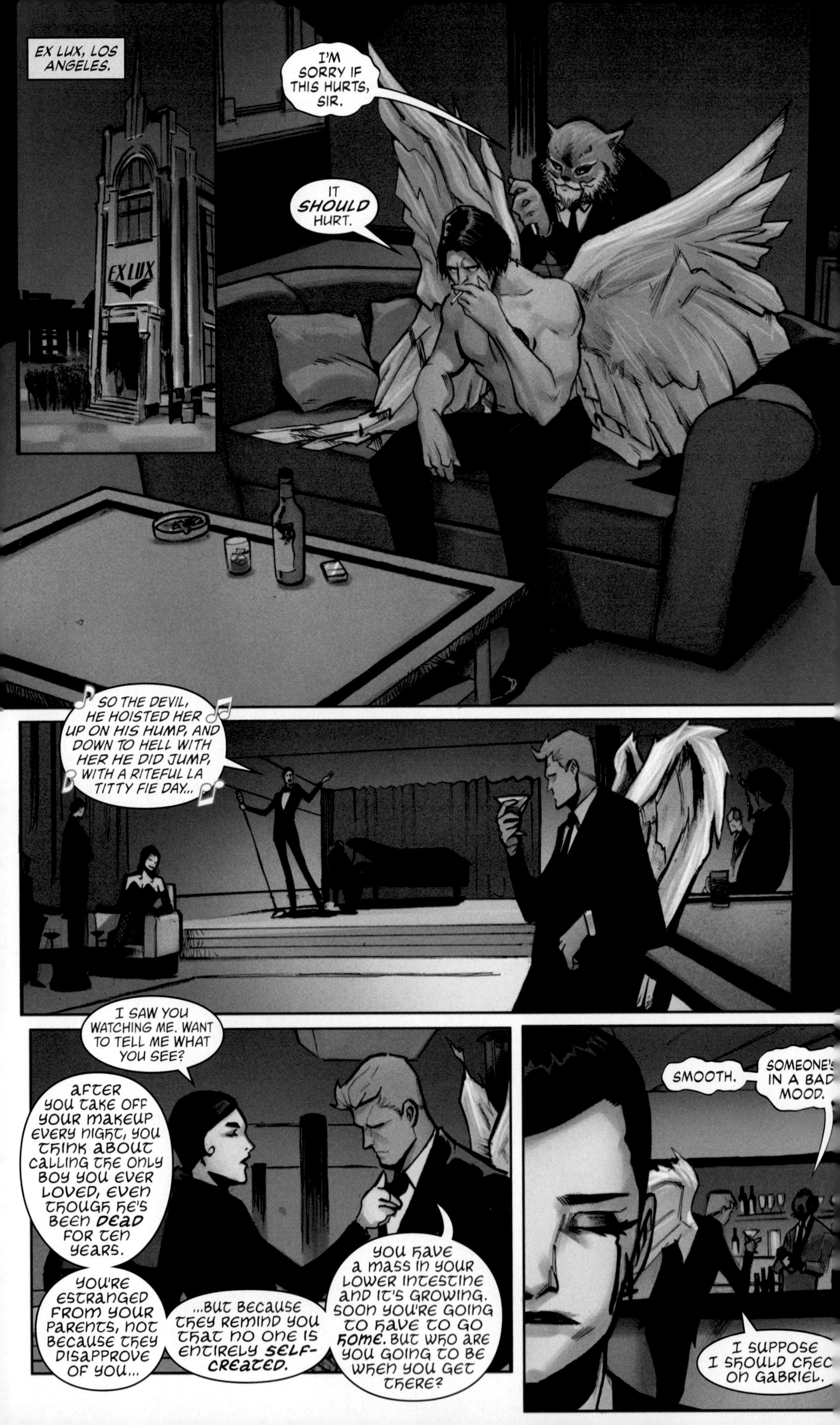
EX LUX, LOS ANGELES.
EX LUX
I'M SORRY IF THIS HURTS, SIR.
IT SHOULD HURT.
SO THE DEVIL, HE HOISTED HER UP ON HIS HUMP, AND DOWN TO HELL WITH HER HE DID JUMP, WITH A RITEFUL LA TITTY FIE DAY...
I SAW YOU WATCHING ME. WANT TO TELL ME WHAT YOU SEE?
AFTER YOU TAKE OFF YOUR MAKEUP EVERY NIGHT, YOU THINK ABOUT CALLING THE ONLY BOY YOU EVER LOVED, EVEN THOUGH HE'S BEEN DEAD FOR TEN YEARS.
YOU'RE ESTRANGED FROM YOUR PARENTS, NOT BECAUSE THEY DISAPPROVE OF YOU...
...BUT BECAUSE THEY REMIND YOU THAT NO ONE IS ENTIRELY SELF-CREATED.
YOU HAVE A MASS IN YOUR LOWER INTESTINE AND IT'S GROWING. SOON YOU'RE GOING TO HAVE TO GO HOME. BUT WHO ARE YOU GOING TO BE WHEN YOU GET THERE?
SMOOTH.
SOMEONE'S IN A BAD MOOD.
I SUPPOSE I SHOULD CHEC ON GABRIEL.

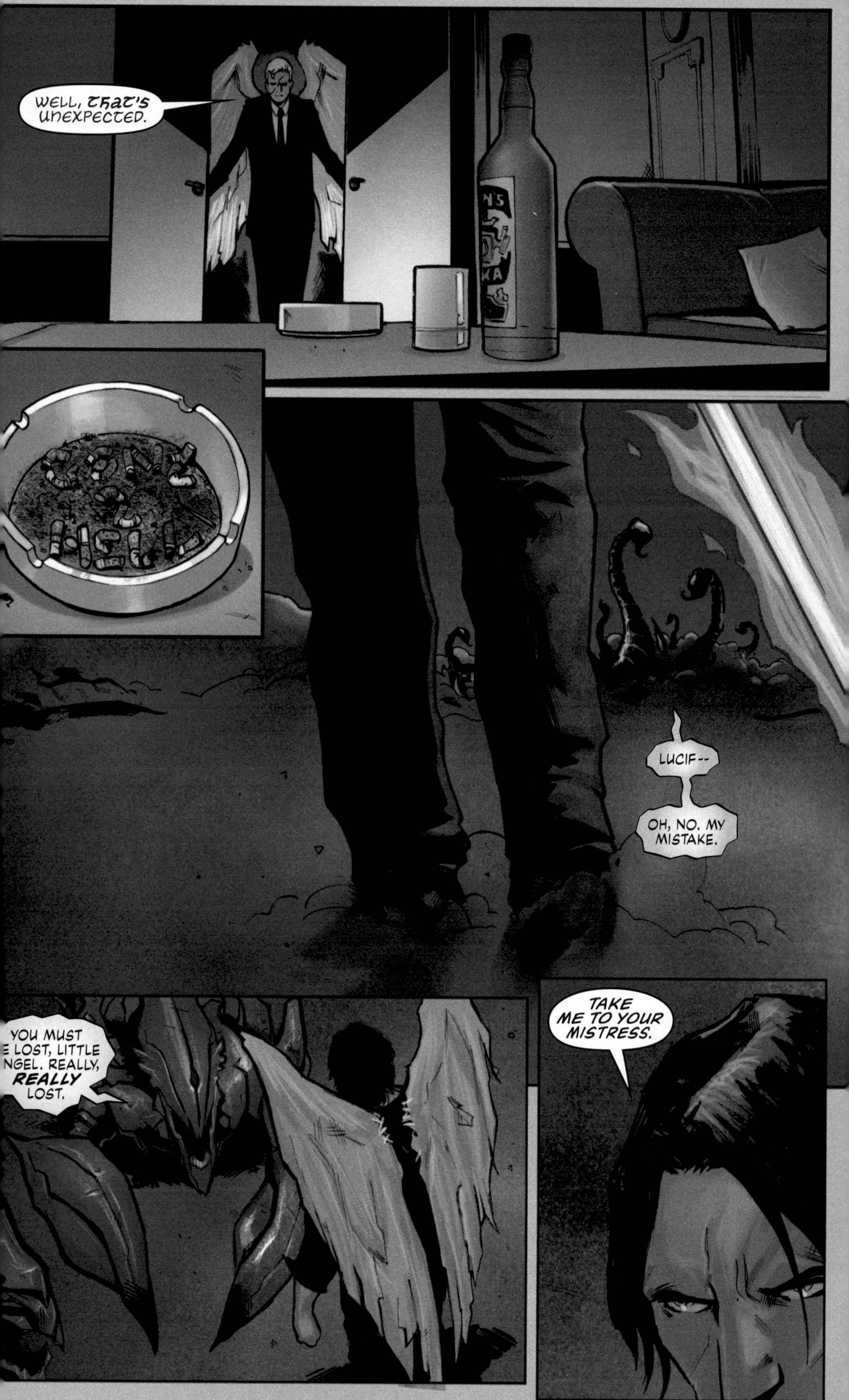

WELL, THAT'S UNEXPECTED.
LUCIF--
OH, NO. MY MISTAKE.
YOU MUST E LOST, LITTLE NGEL. REALLY, REALLY LOST.
TAKE ME TO YOUR MISTRESS.

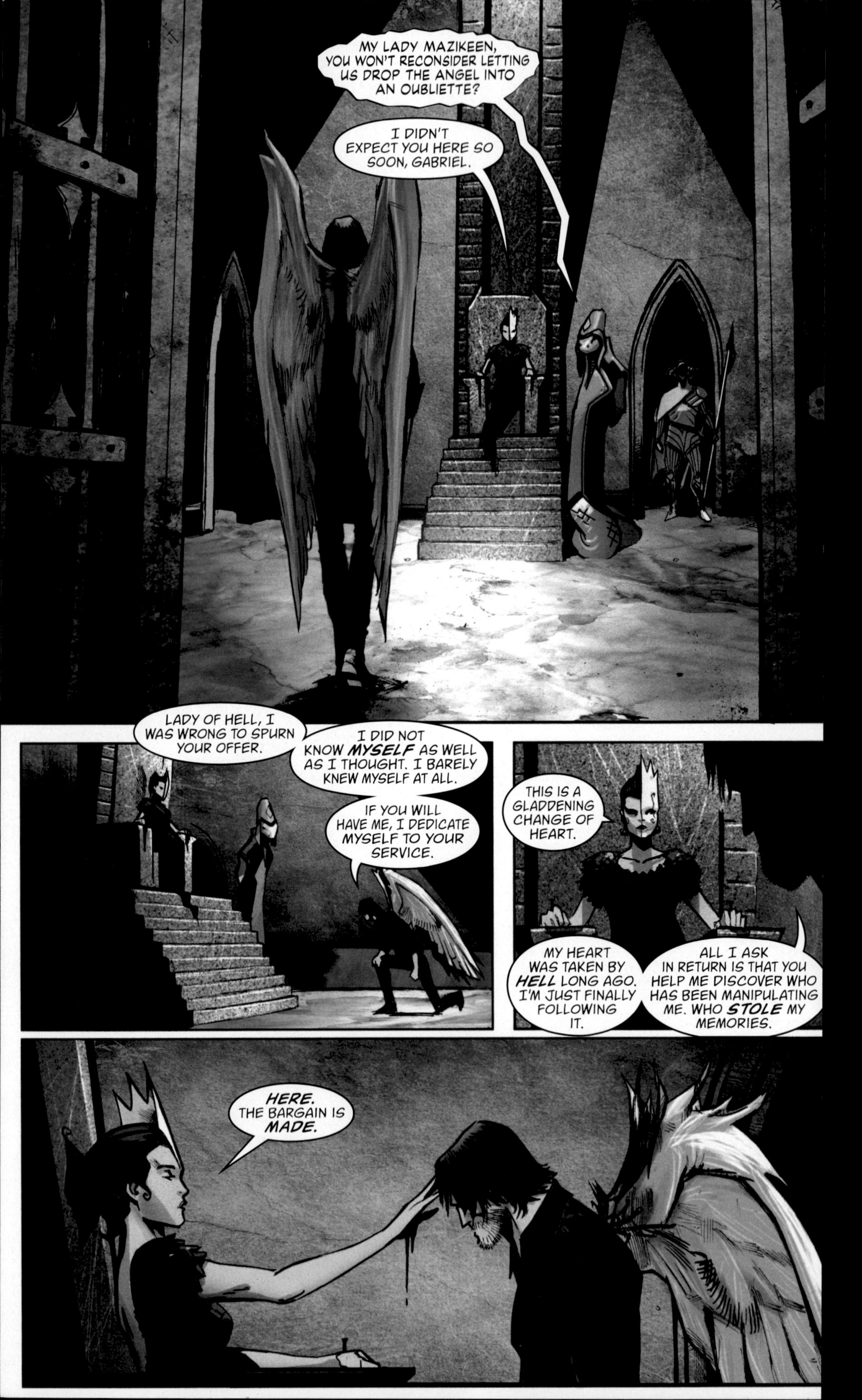
MY LADY MAZIKEEN, YOU WON'T RECONSIDER LETTING US DROP THE ANGEL INTO AN OUBLIETTE?
I DIDN'T EXPECT YOU HERE SO SOON, GABRIEL.
LADY OF HELL, I WAS WRONG TO SPURN YOUR OFFER.
I DID NOT KNOW MYSELF AS WELL AS I THOUGHT. I BARELY KNEW MYSELF AT ALL.
IF YOU WILL HAVE ME, I DEDICATE MYSELF TO YOUR SERVICE.
THIS IS A GLADDENING CHANGE OF HEART.
MY HEART WAS TAKEN BY HELL LONG AGO. I'M JUST FINALLY FOLLOWING IT.
ALL I ASK IN RETURN IS THAT YOU HELP ME DISCOVER WHO HAS BEEN MANIPULATING ME. WHO STOLE MY MEMORIES.
HERE. THE BARGAIN IS MADE.

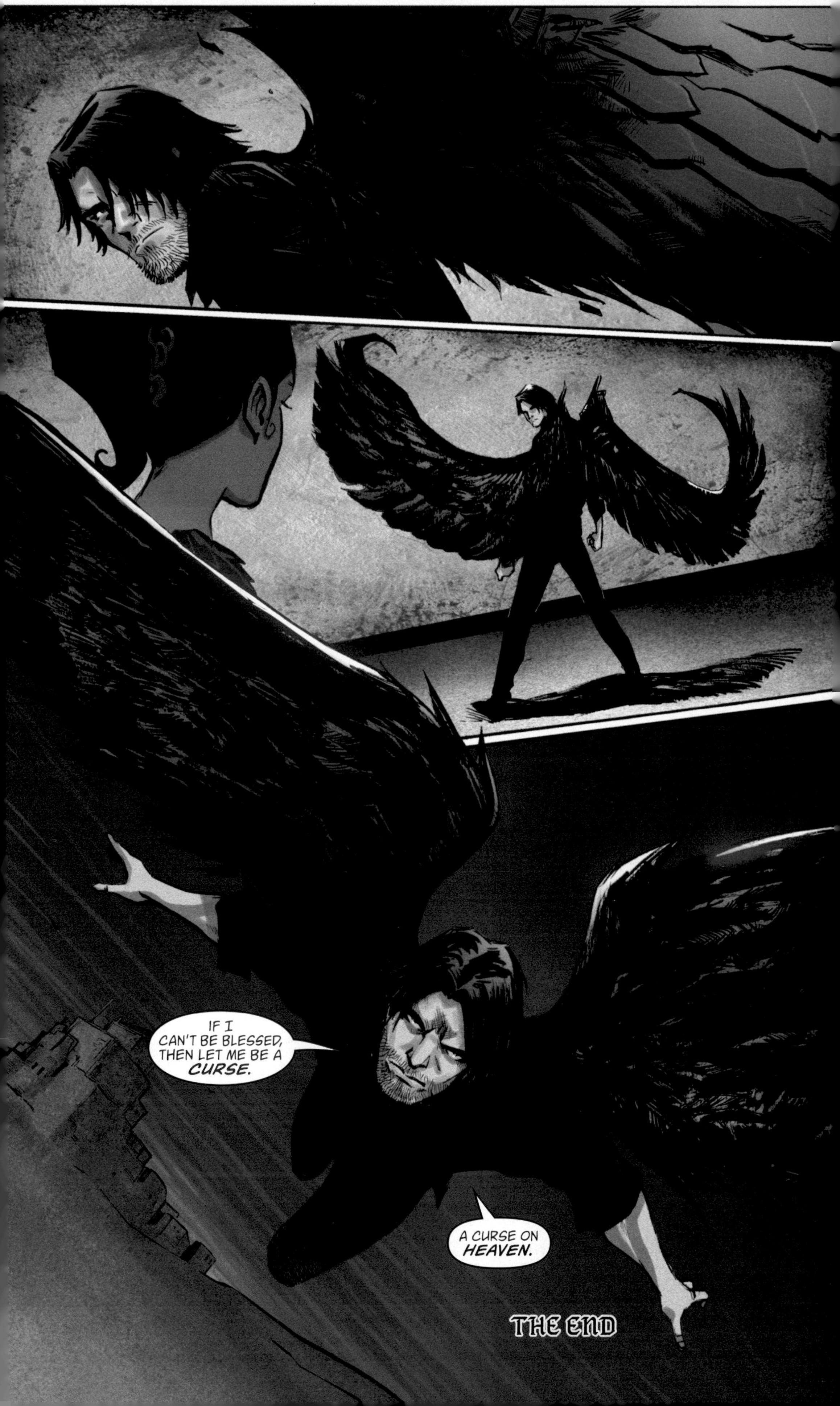
IF I CAN'T BE BLESSED, THEN LET ME BE A CURSE.
A CURSE ON HEAVEN.
THE END

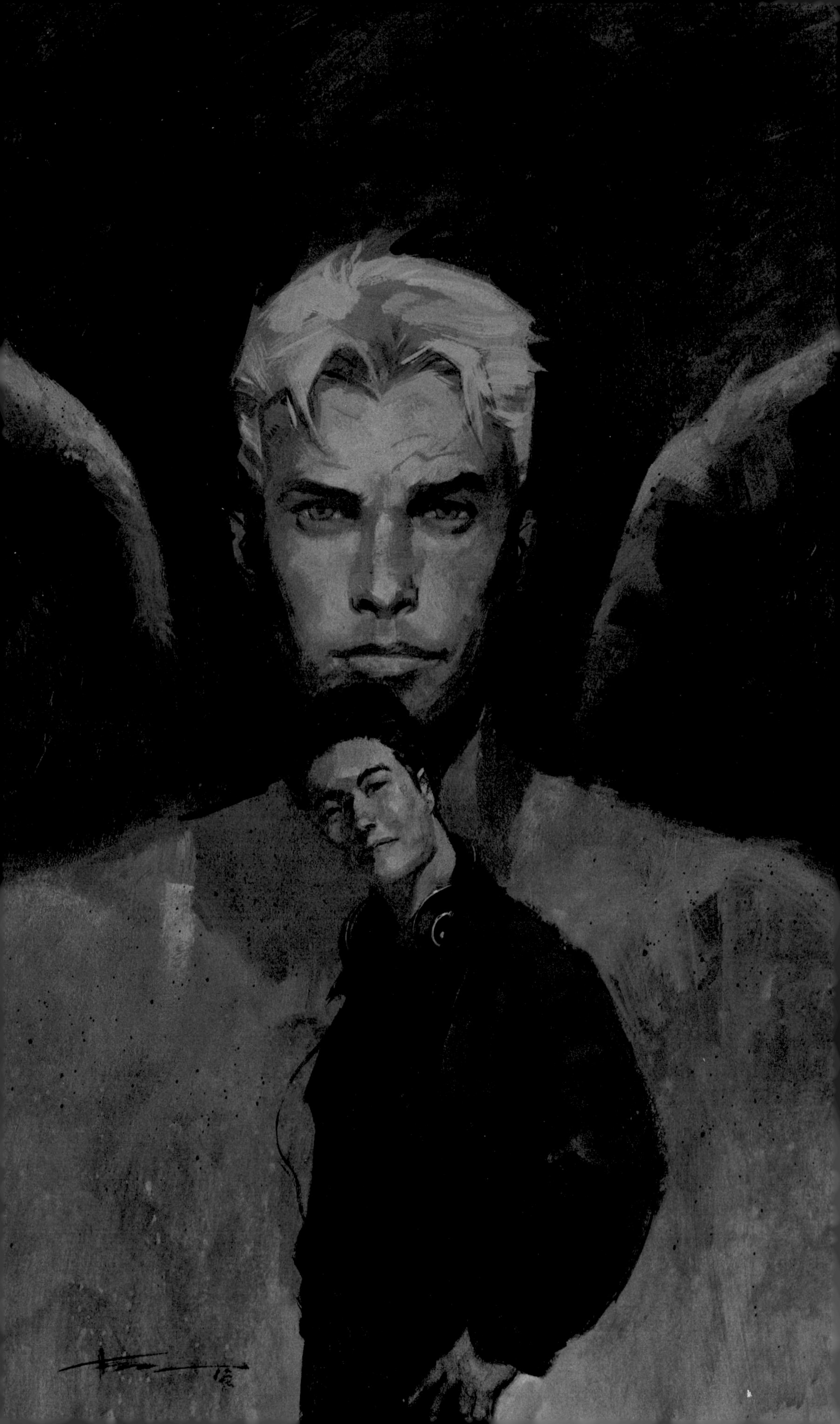

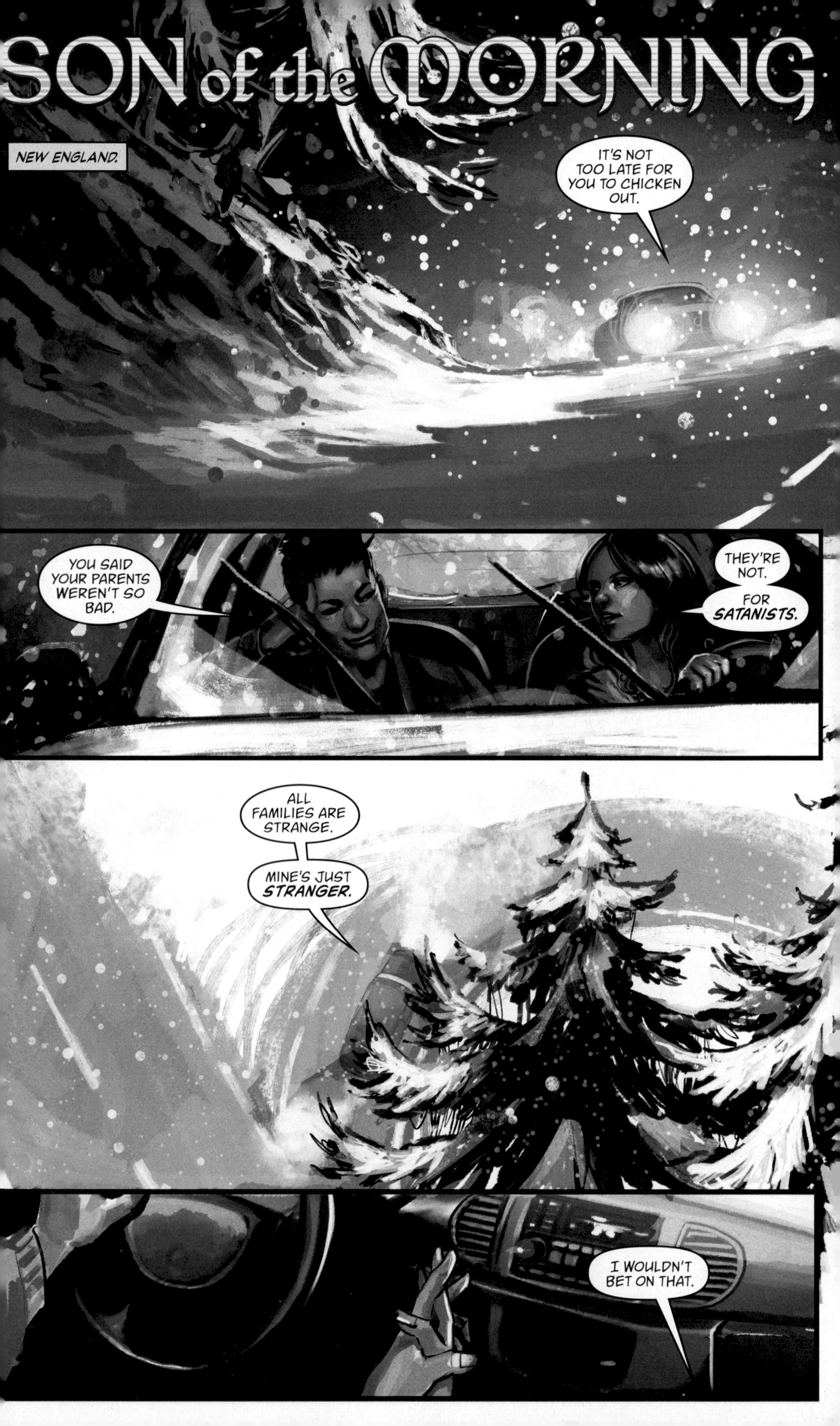
SON of the MORNING
NEW ENGLAND.
IT'S NOT TOO LATE FOR YOU TO CHICKEN OUT.
YOU SAID YOUR PARENTS WEREN'T SO BAD.
THEY'RE NOT.
FOR SATANISTS.
ALL FAMILIES ARE STRANGE.
MINE'S JUST STRANGER.
I WOULDN'T BET ON THAT.

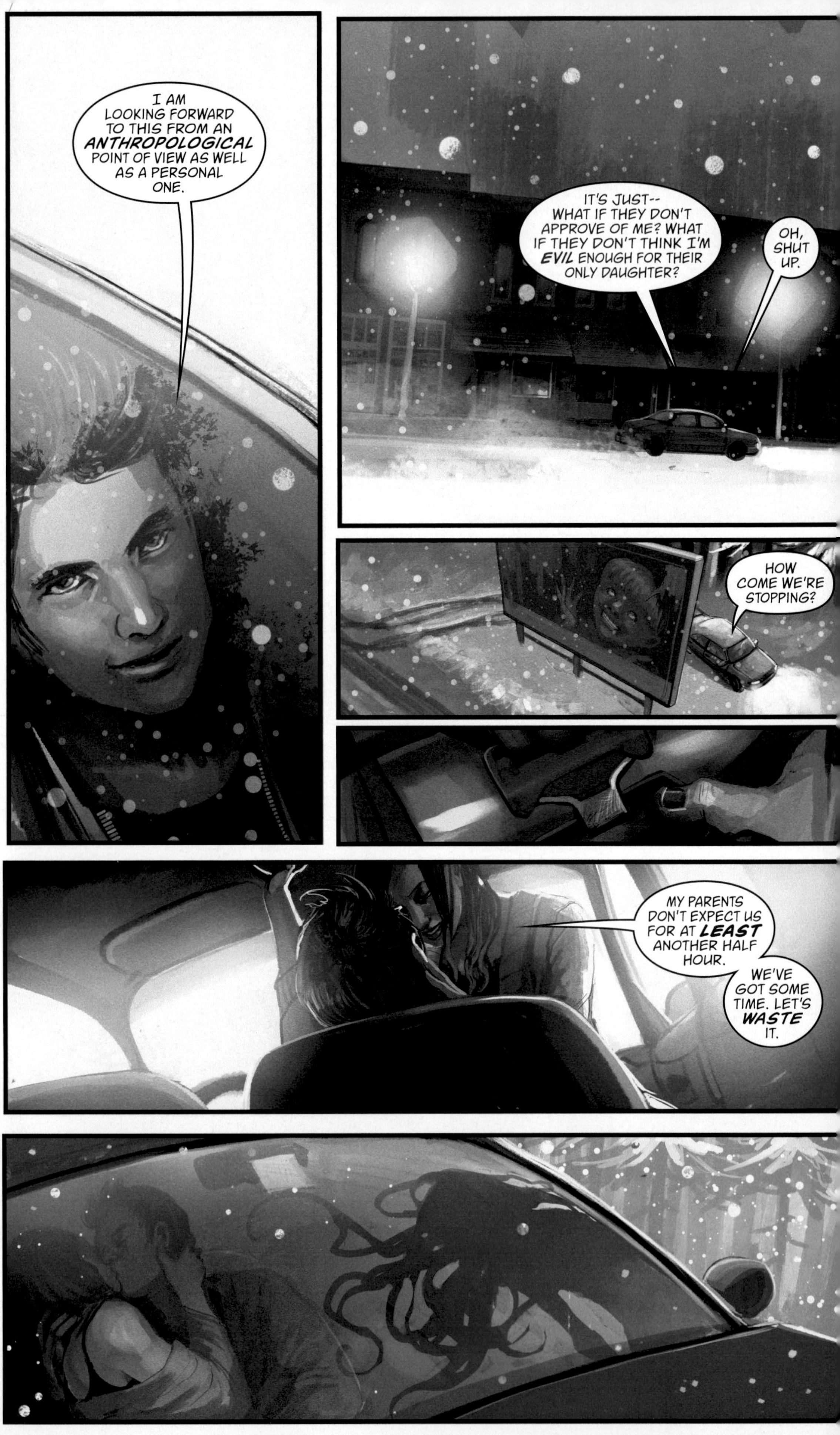
I AM LOOKING FORWARD TO THIS FROM AN ANTHROPOLOGICAL POINT OF VIEW AS WELL AS A PERSONAL ONE.
IT'S JUST-- WHAT IF THEY DON'T APPROVE OF ME? WHAT IF THEY DON'T THINK I'M EVIL ENOUGH FOR THEIR ONLY DAUGHTER?
OH, SHUT UP.
HOW COME WE'RE STOPPING?
MY PARENTS DON'T EXPECT US FOR AT LEAST ANOTHER HALF HOUR.
WE'VE GOT SOME TIME. LET'S WASTE IT.

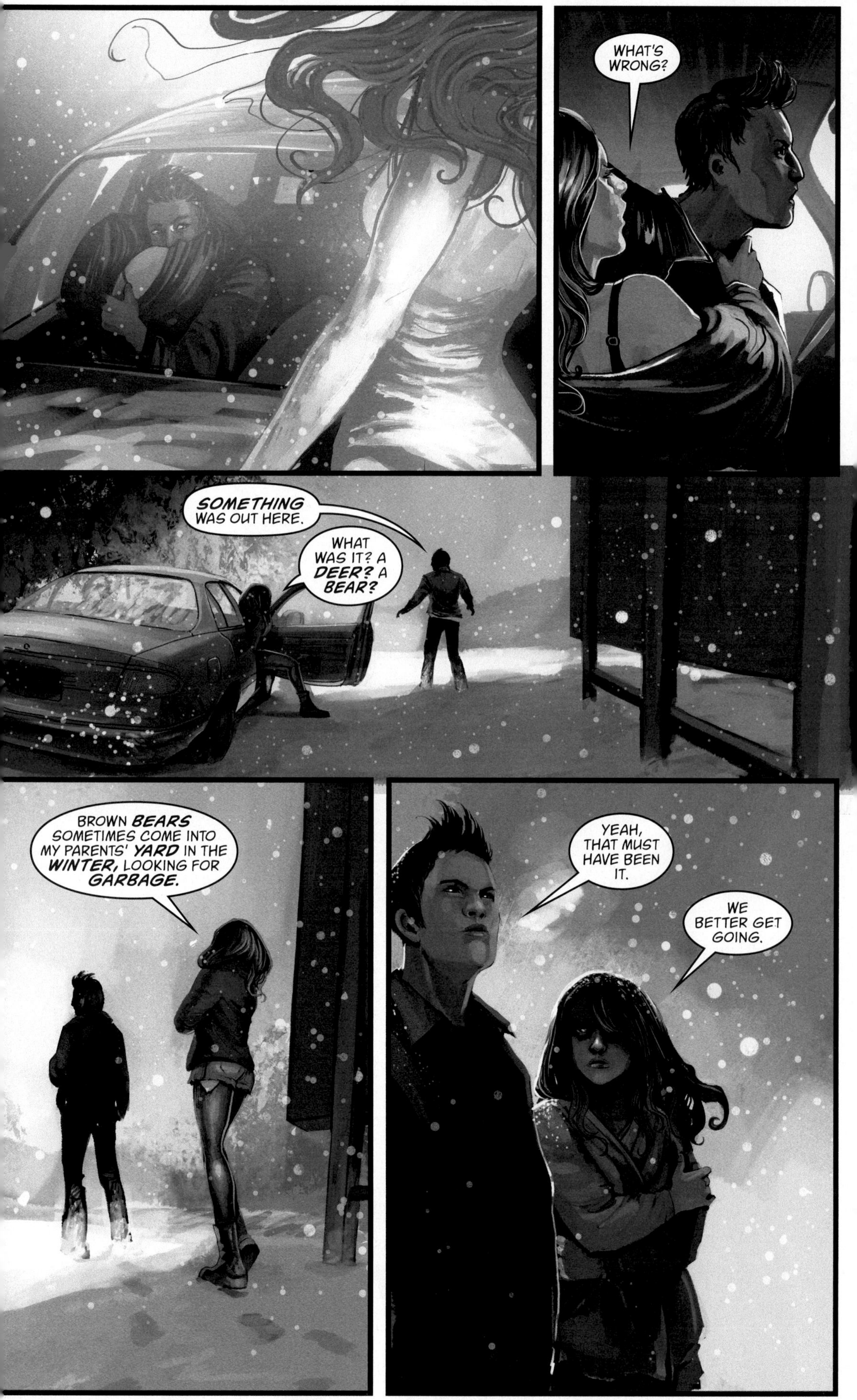
WHAT'S WRONG?
SOMETHING WAS OUT HERE.
WHAT WAS IT? A DEER? A BEAR?
BROWN BEARS SOMETIMES COME INTO MY PARENTS' YARD IN THE WINTER, LOOKING FOR GARBAGE.
YEAH, THAT MUST HAVE BEEN IT.
WE BETTER GET GOING.

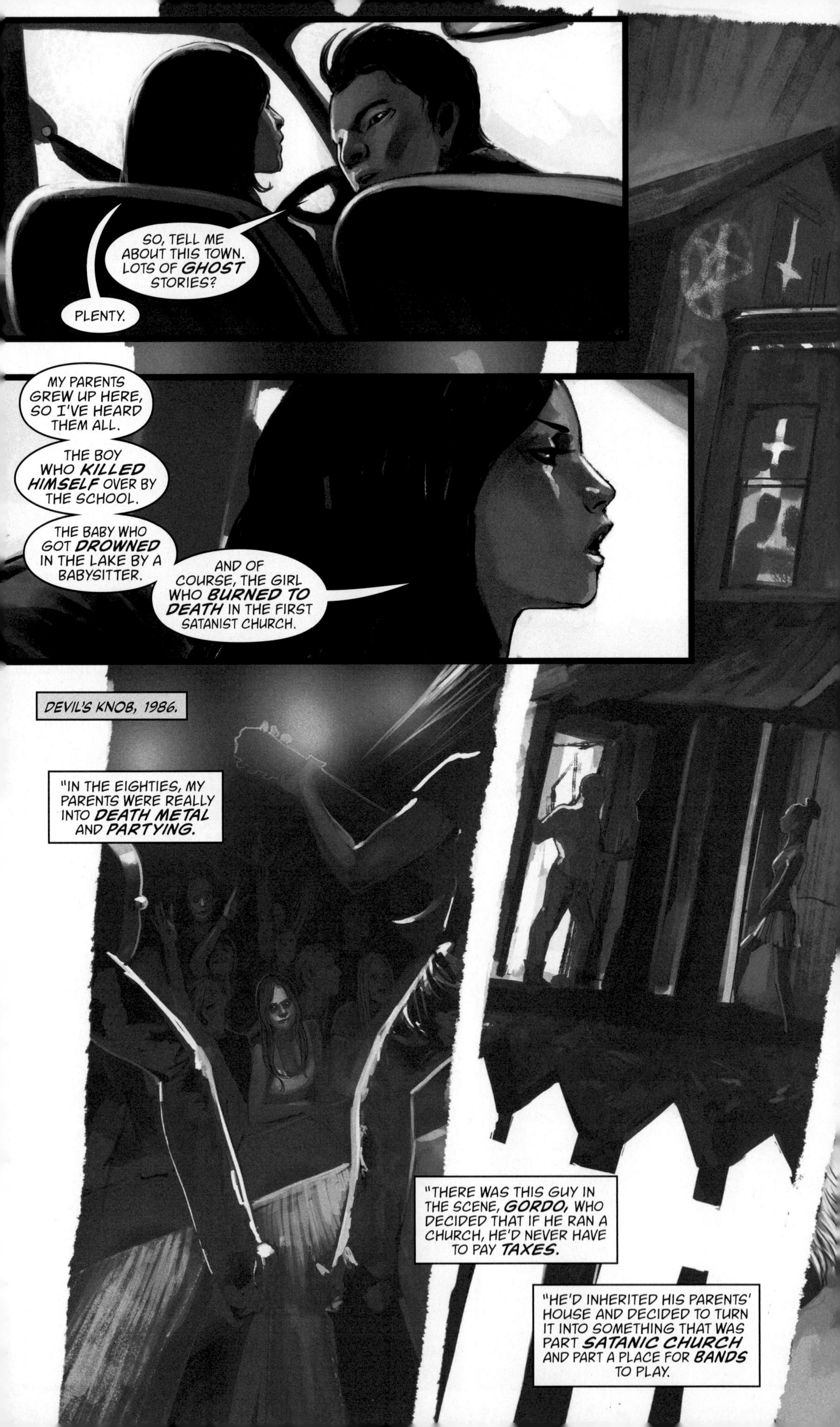
SO, TELL ME ABOUT THIS TOWN. LOTS OF GHOST STORIES?
PLENTY.
MY PARENTS GREW UP HERE, SO I'VE HEARD THEM ALL.
THE BOY WHO KILLED HIMSELF OVER BY THE SCHOOL.
THE BABY WHO GOT DROWNED IN THE LAKE BY A BABYSITTER.
AND OF COURSE, THE GIRL WHO BURNED TO DEATH IN THE FIRST SATANIST CHURCH.
DEVIL'S KNOB, 1986.
"IN THE EIGHTIES, MY PARENTS WERE REALLY INTO DEATH METAL AND PARTYING.
"THERE WAS THIS GUY IN THE SCENE, GORDO, WHO DECIDED THAT IF HE RAN A CHURCH, HE'D NEVER HAVE TO PAY TAXES.
"HE'D INHERITED HIS PARENTS' HOUSE AND DECIDED TO TURN IT INTO SOMETHING THAT WAS PART SATANIC CHURCH AND PART A PLACE FOR BANDS TO PLAY.

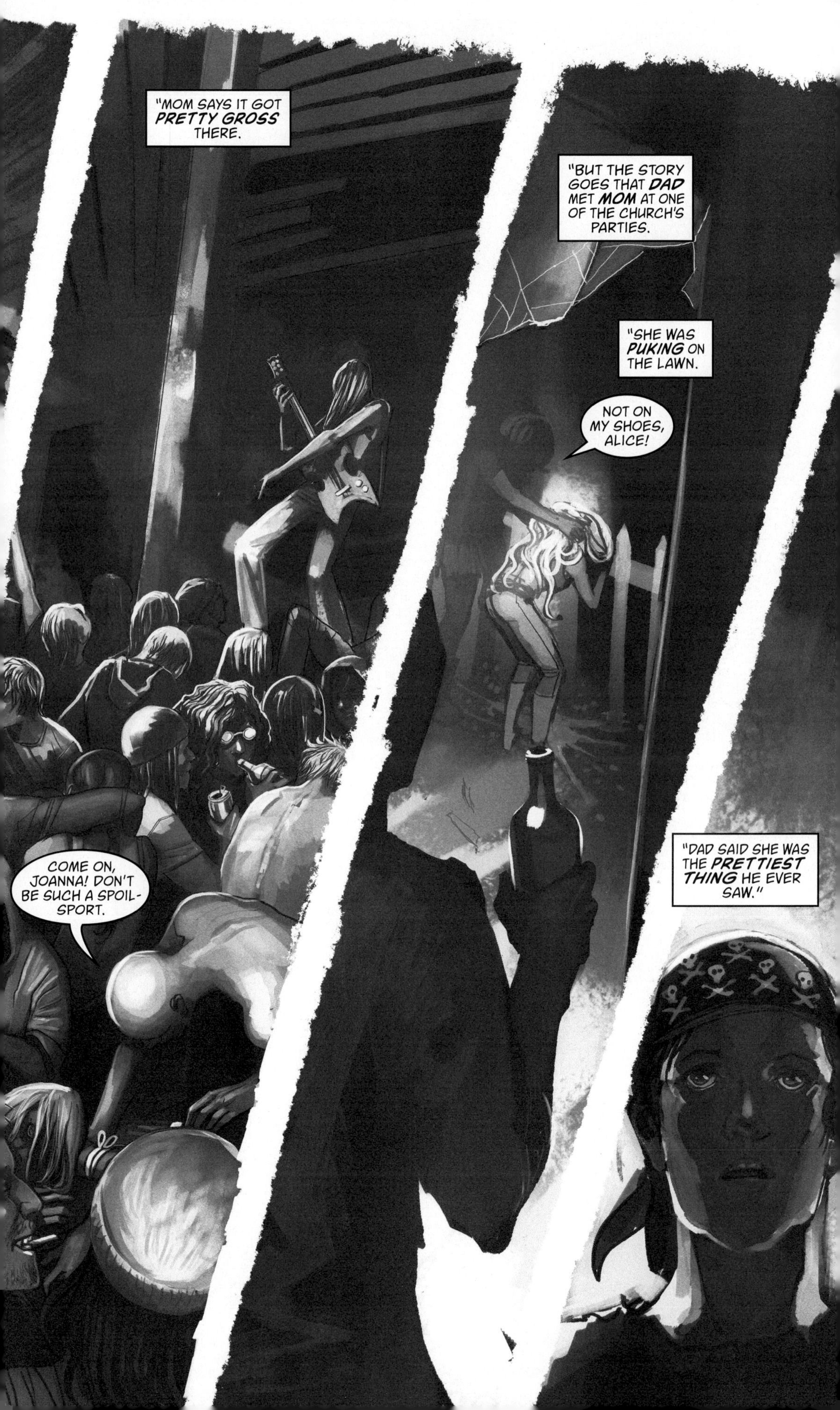
"MOM SAYS IT GOT PRETTY GROSS THERE.
COME ON, JOANNA! DON'T BE SUCH A SPOIL-SPORT.
"BUT THE STORY GOES THAT DAD MET MOM AT ONE OF THE CHURCH'S PARTIES.
"SHE WAS PUKING ON THE LAWN.
NOT ON MY SHOES, ALICE!
"DAD SAID SHE WAS THE PRETTIEST THING HE EVER SAW."

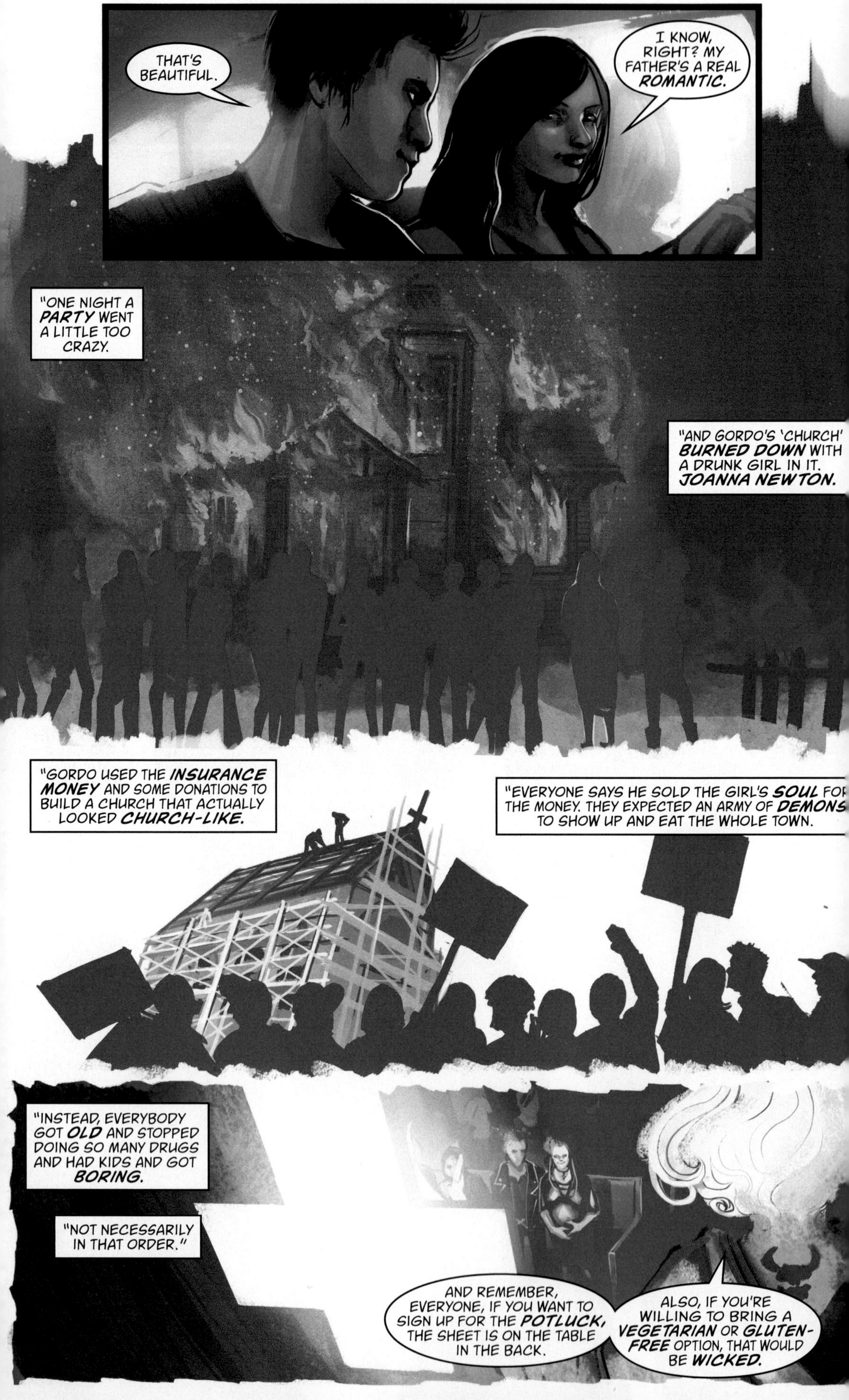

THAT'S BEAUTIFUL.
I KNOW, RIGHT? MY FATHER'S A REAL ROMANTIC.
"ONE NIGHT A PARTY WENT A LITTLE TOO CRAZY.
"AND GORDO'S 'CHURCH' BURNED DOWN WITH A DRUNK GIRL IN IT. JOANNA NEWTON.
"GORDO USED THE INSURANCE MONEY AND SOME DONATIONS TO BUILD A CHURCH THAT ACTUALLY LOOKED CHURCH-LIKE.
"EVERYONE SAYS HE SOLD THE GIRL'S SOUL FOR THE MONEY. THEY EXPECTED AN ARMY OF DEMONS TO SHOW UP AND EAT THE WHOLE TOWN.
"INSTEAD, EVERYBODY GOT OLD AND STOPPED DOING SO MANY DRUGS AND HAD KIDS AND GOT BORING.
"NOT NECESSARILY IN THAT ORDER."
AND REMEMBER, EVERYONE, IF YOU WANT TO SIGN UP FOR THE POTLUCK, THE SHEET IS ON THE TABLE IN THE BACK.
ALSO, IF YOU'RE WILLING TO BRING A VEGETARIAN OR GLUTEN-FREE OPTION, THAT WOULD BE WICKED.

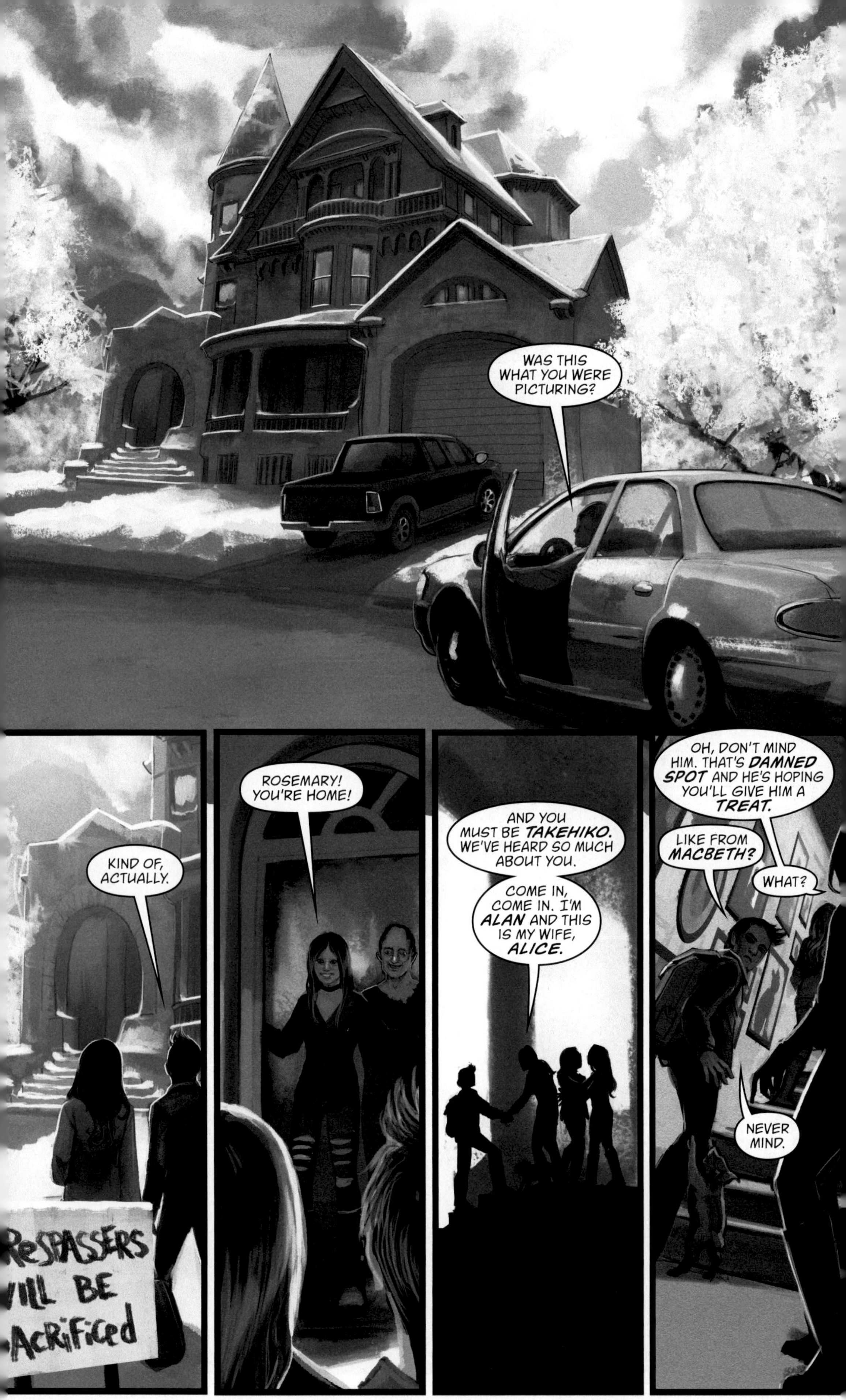
WAS THIS WHAT YOU WERE PICTURING?
KIND OF, ACTUALLY.
ReSPASSERS VILL BE ACRIFICED
ROSEMARY! YOU'RE HOME!
AND YOU MUST BE TAKEHIKO. WE'VE HEARD SO MUCH ABOUT YOU.
COME IN, COME IN. I'M ALAN AND THIS IS MY WIFE, ALICE.
OH, DON'T MIND HIM. THAT'S DAMNED SPOT AND HE'S HOPING YOU'LL GIVE HIM A TREAT.
LIKE FROM MACBETH?
WHAT?
NEVER MIND.

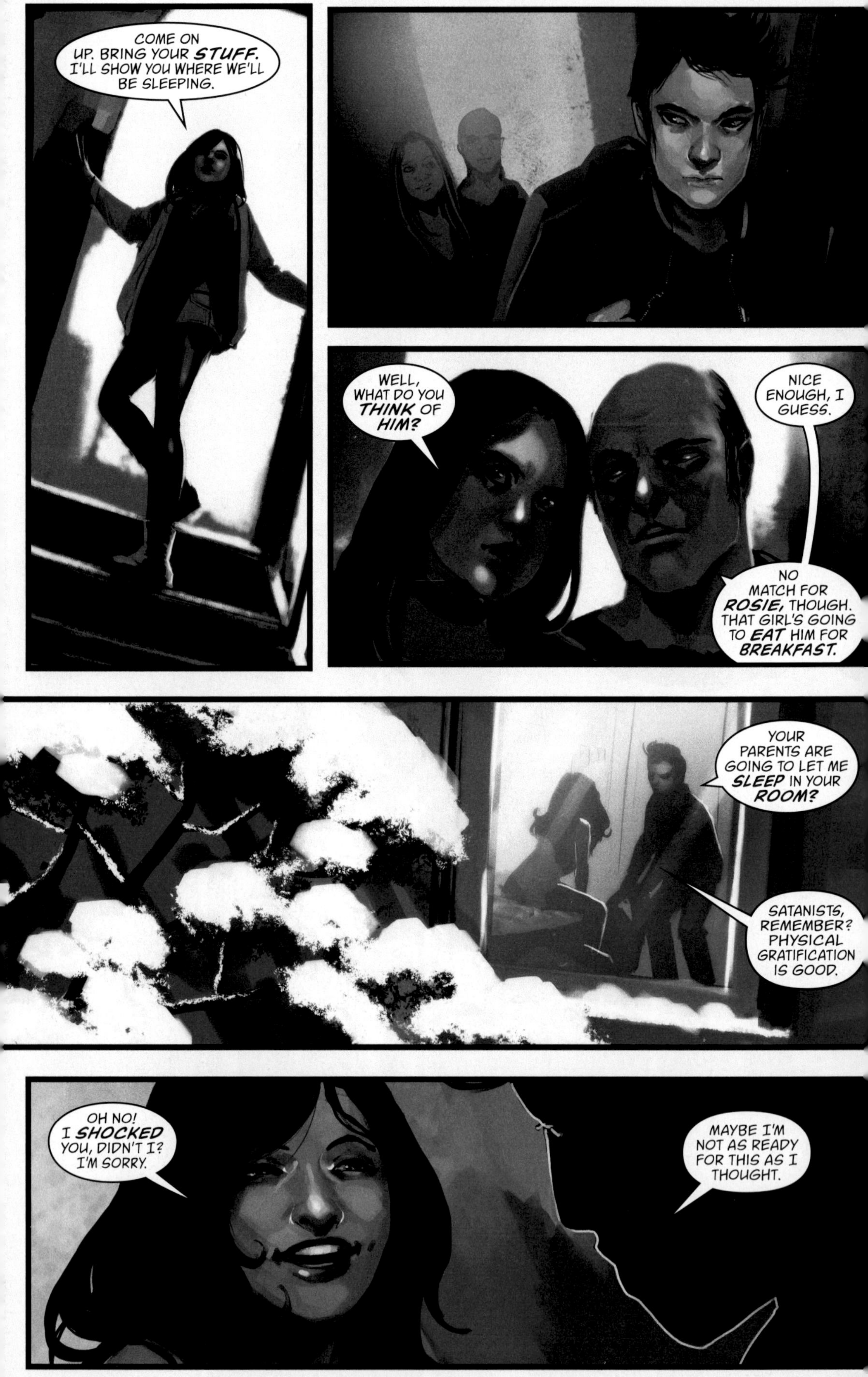
COME ON UP. BRING YOUR STUFF. I'LL SHOW YOU WHERE WE'LL BE SLEEPING.
WELL, WHAT DO YOU THINK OF HIM?
NICE ENOUGH, I GUESS.
NO MATCH FOR ROSIE, THOUGH. THAT GIRL'S GOING TO EAT HIM FOR BREAKFAST.
YOUR PARENTS ARE GOING TO LET ME SLEEP IN YOUR ROOM?
SATANISTS, REMEMBER? PHYSICAL GRATIFICATION IS GOOD.
OH NO! I SHOCKED YOU, DIDN'T I? I'M SORRY.
MAYBE I'M NOT AS READY FOR THIS AS I THOUGHT.

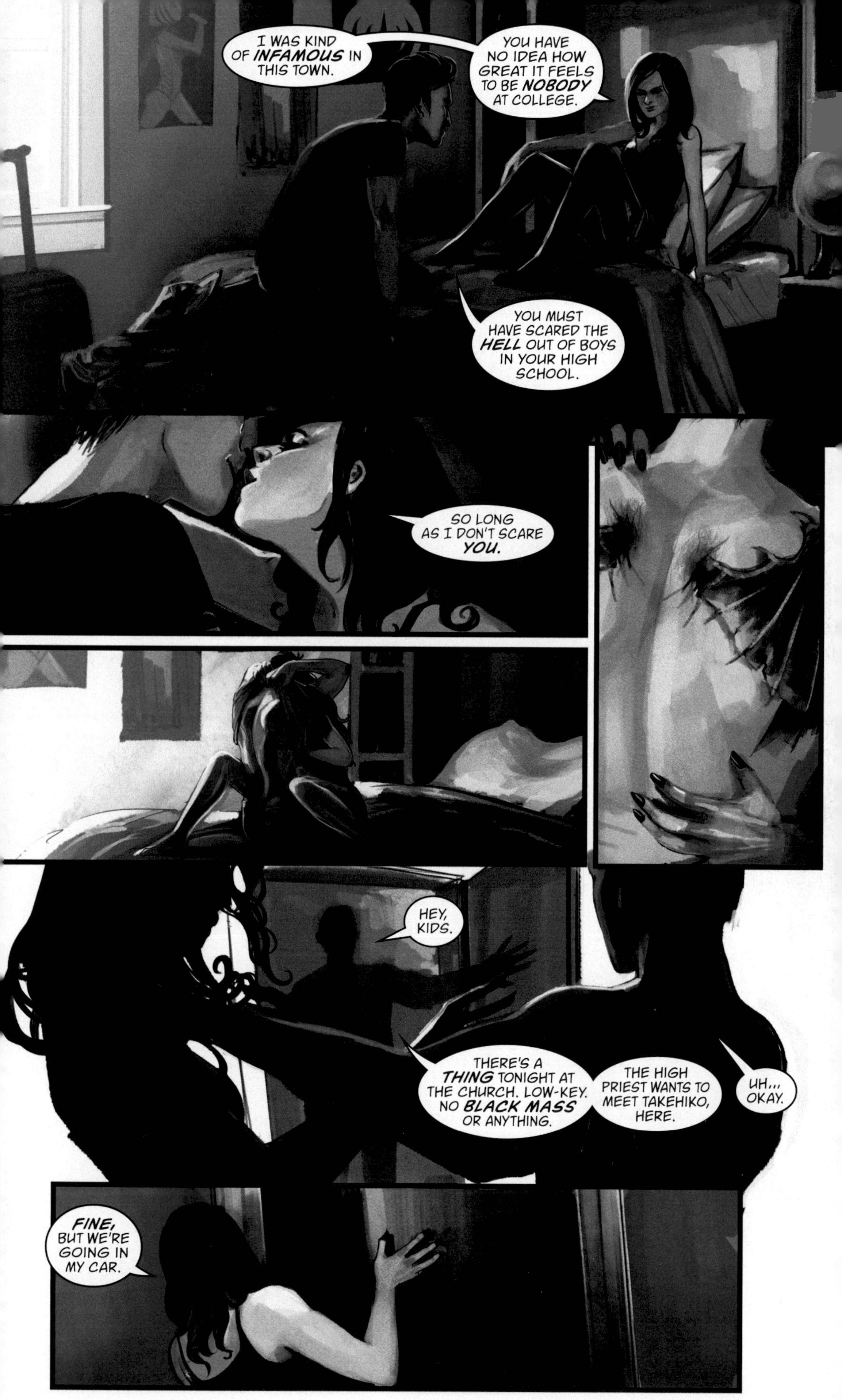
I WAS KIND OF INFAMOUS IN THIS TOWN.
YOU HAVE NO IDEA HOW GREAT IT FEELS TO BE NOBODY AT COLLEGE.
YOU MUST HAVE SCARED THE HELL OUT OF BOYS IN YOUR HIGH SCHOOL.
SO LONG AS I DON'T SCARE YOU.
HEY, KIDS.
THERE'S A THING TONIGHT AT THE CHURCH. LOW-KEY. NO BLACK MASS OR ANYTHING.
THE HIGH PRIEST WANTS TO MEET TAKEHIKO, HERE.
UH... OKAY.
FINE, BUT WE'RE GOING IN MY CAR.

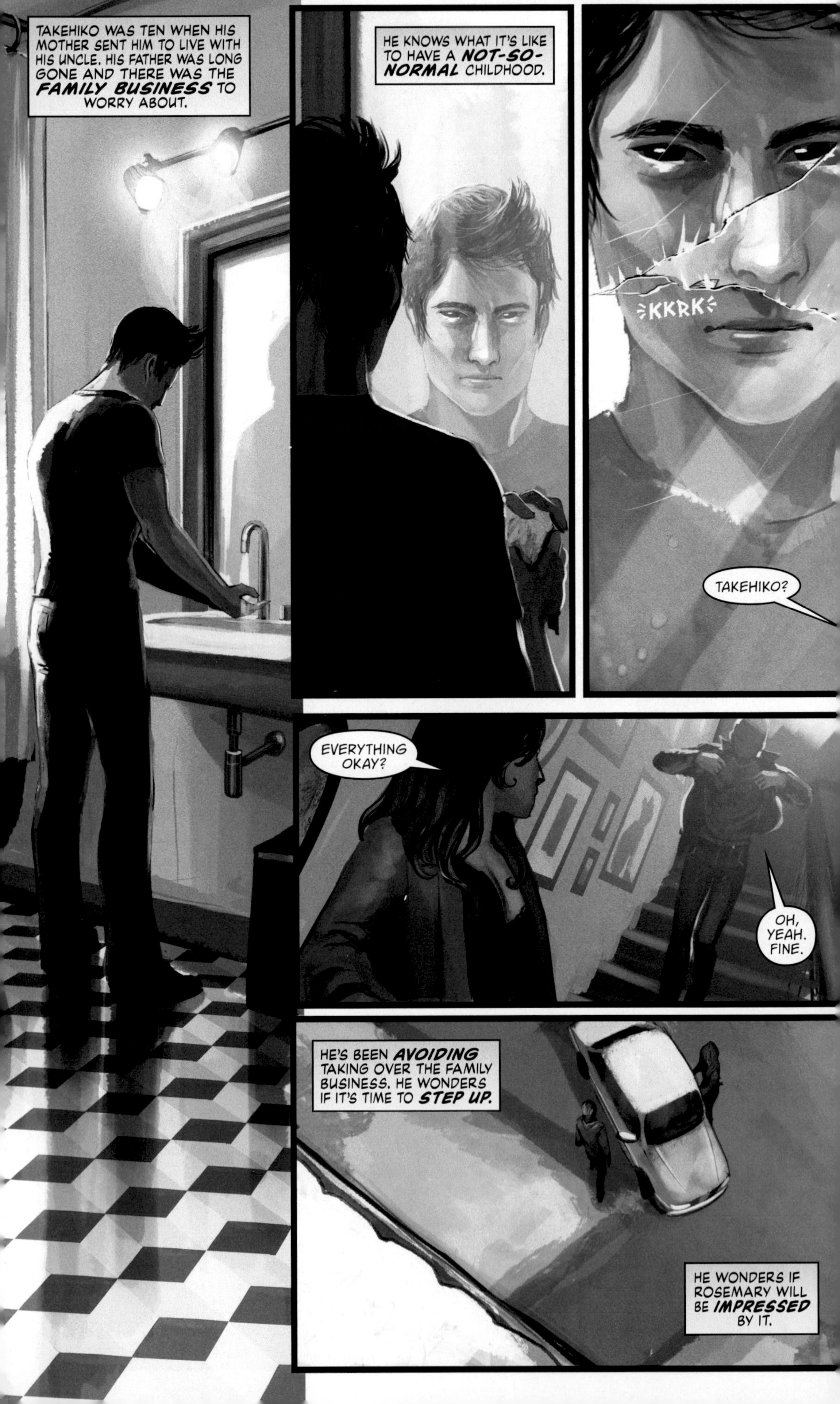
TAKEHIKO WAS TEN WHEN HIS MOTHER SENT HIM TO LIVE WITH HIS UNCLE. HIS FATHER WAS LONG GONE AND THERE WAS THE **FAMILY BUSINESS** TO WORRY ABOUT.
HE KNOWS WHAT IT'S LIKE TO HAVE A **NOT-SO-NORMAL** CHILDHOOD.
KKRK
TAKEHIKO?
EVERYTHING OKAY?
OH, YEAH. FINE.
HE'S BEEN **AVOIDING** TAKING OVER THE FAMILY BUSINESS. HE WONDERS IF IT'S TIME TO **STEP UP.**
HE WONDERS IF ROSEMARY WILL BE **IMPRESSED** BY IT.

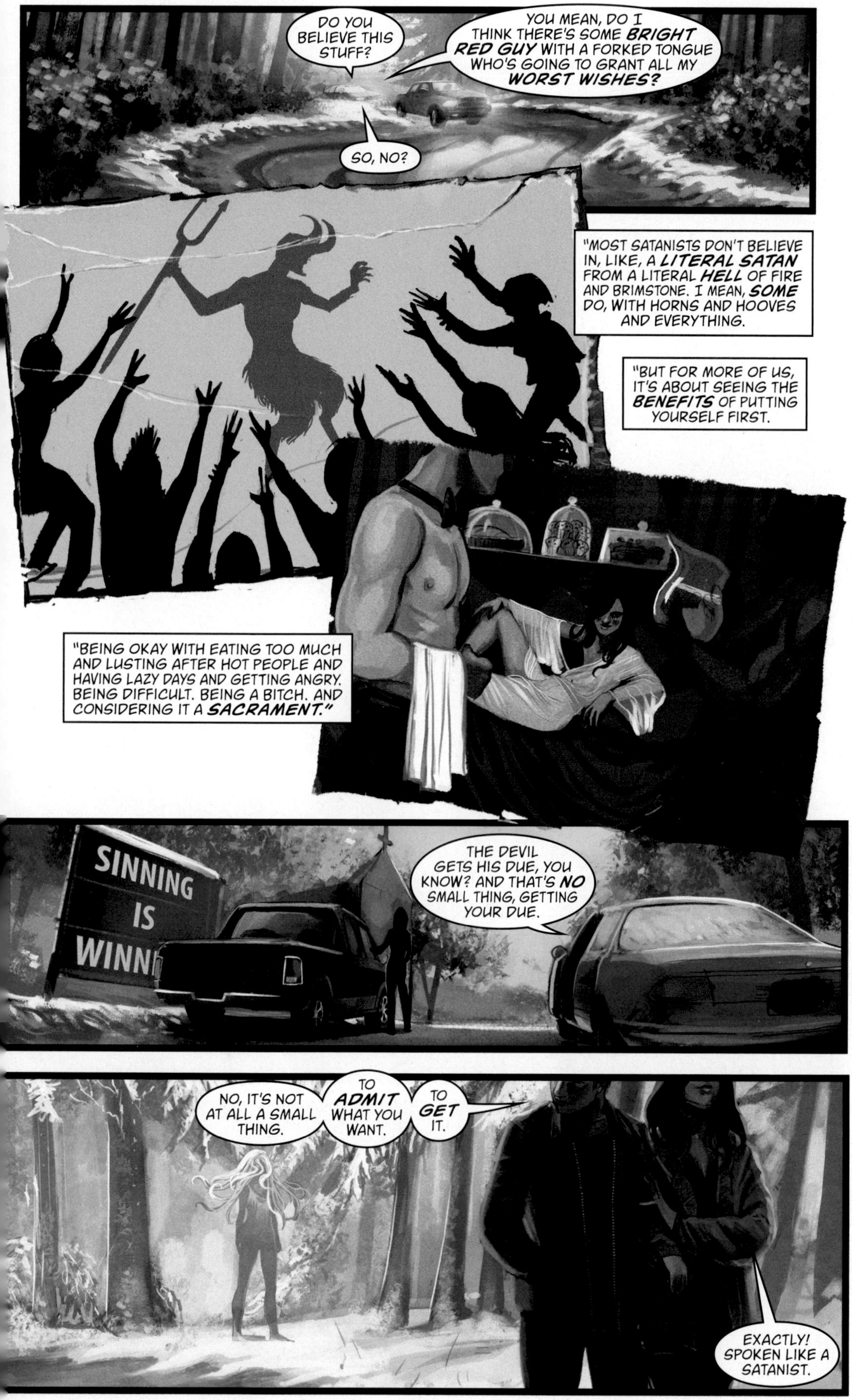
DO YOU BELIEVE THIS STUFF?
YOU MEAN, DO I THINK THERE'S SOME BRIGHT RED GUY WITH A FORKED TONGUE WHO'S GOING TO GRANT ALL MY WORST WISHES?
SO, NO?
"MOST SATANISTS DON'T BELIEVE IN, LIKE, A LITERAL SATAN FROM A LITERAL HELL OF FIRE AND BRIMSTONE. I MEAN, SOME DO, WITH HORNS AND HOOVES AND EVERYTHING.
"BUT FOR MORE OF US, IT'S ABOUT SEEING THE BENEFITS OF PUTTING YOURSELF FIRST.
"BEING OKAY WITH EATING TOO MUCH AND LUSTING AFTER HOT PEOPLE AND HAVING LAZY DAYS AND GETTING ANGRY. BEING DIFFICULT. BEING A BITCH. AND CONSIDERING IT A SACRAMENT."
SINNING IS WINN
THE DEVIL GETS HIS DUE, YOU KNOW? AND THAT'S NO SMALL THING, GETTING YOUR DUE.
NO, IT'S NOT AT ALL A SMALL THING.
TO ADMIT WHAT YOU WANT.
TO GET IT.
EXACTLY! SPOKEN LIKE A SATANIST.

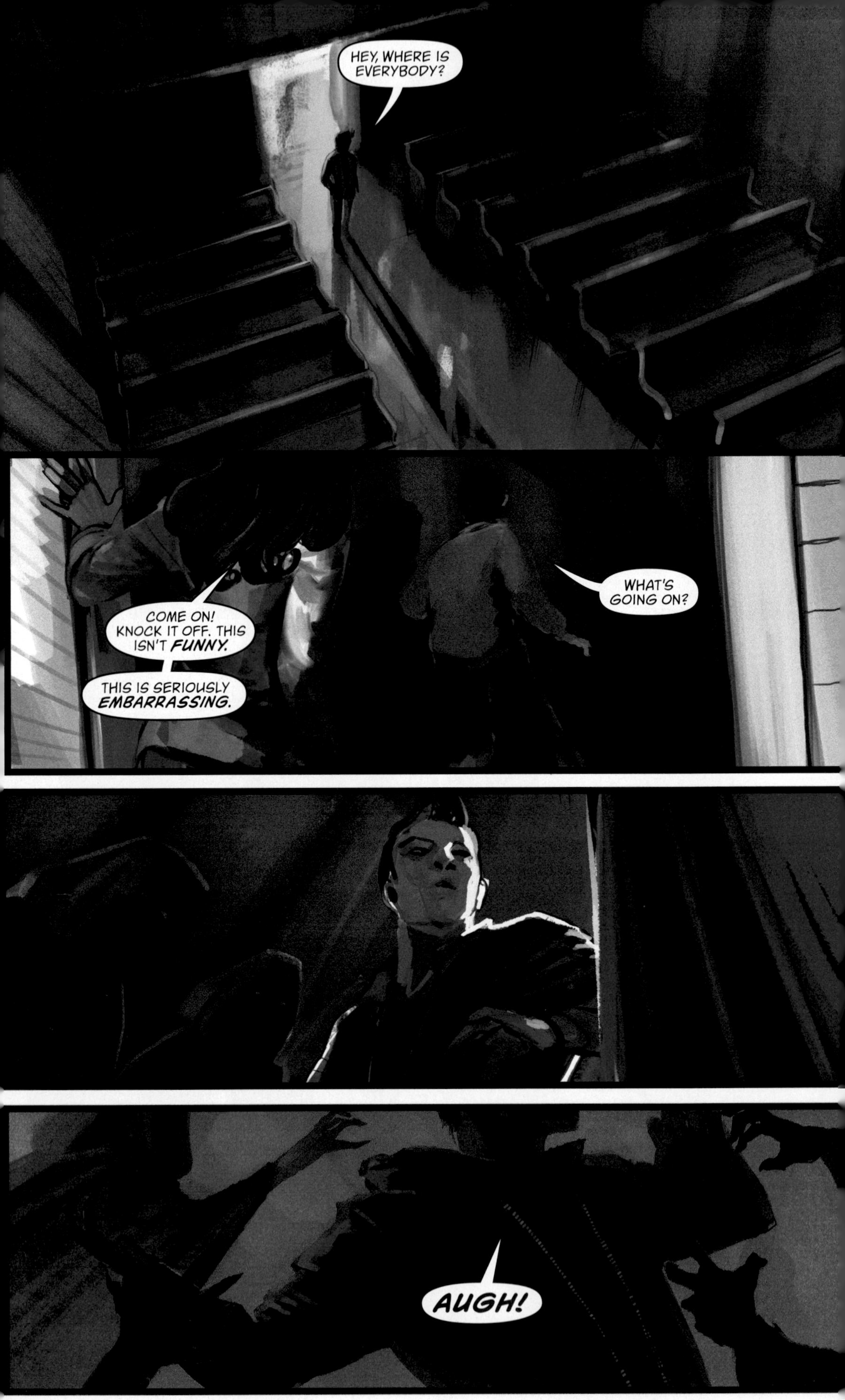
HEY, WHERE IS EVERYBODY?
COME ON! KNOCK IT OFF. THIS ISN'T *FUNNY.*
THIS IS SERIOUSLY *EMBARRASSING.*
WHAT'S GOING ON?
AUGH!

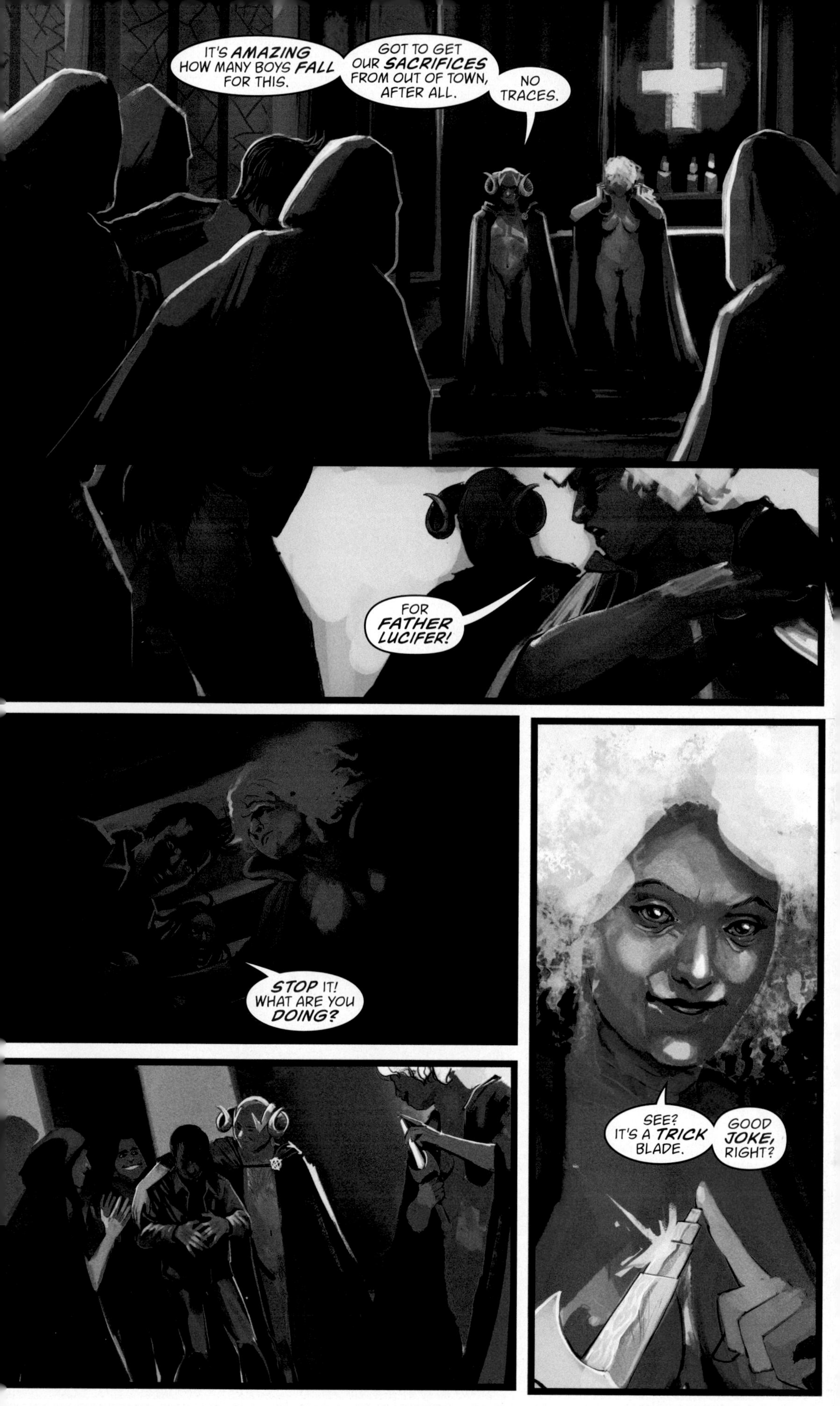
IT'S AMAZING HOW MANY BOYS FALL FOR THIS.
GOT TO GET OUR SACRIFICES FROM OUT OF TOWN, AFTER ALL.
NO TRACES.
FOR FATHER LUCIFER!
STOP IT! WHAT ARE YOU DOING?
SEE? IT'S A TRICK BLADE.
GOOD JOKE, RIGHT?

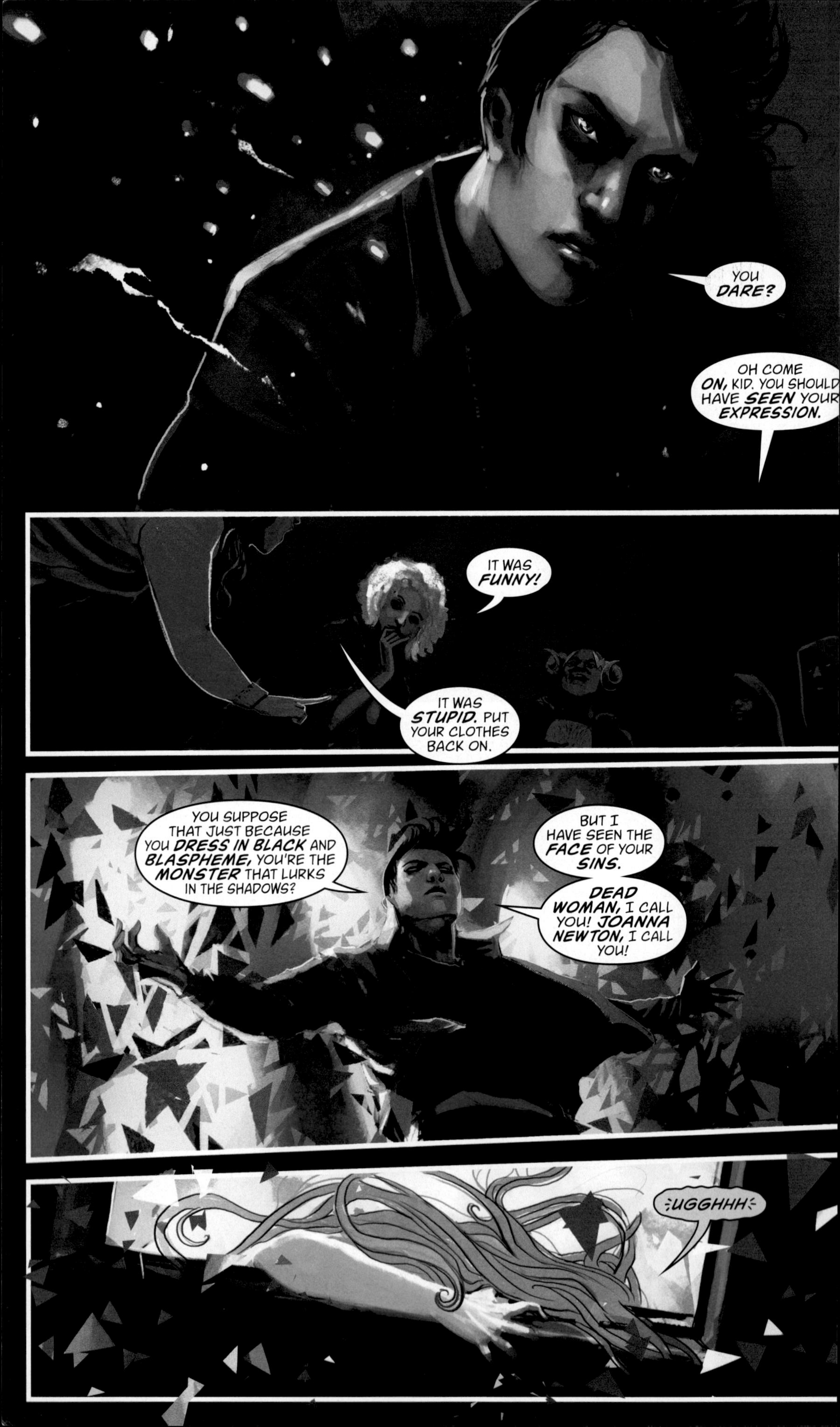
YOU DARE?
OH COME ON, KID. YOU SHOULD HAVE SEEN YOUR EXPRESSION.
IT WAS FUNNY!
IT WAS STUPID. PUT YOUR CLOTHES BACK ON.
YOU SUPPOSE THAT JUST BECAUSE YOU DRESS IN BLACK AND BLASPHEME, YOU'RE THE MONSTER THAT LURKS IN THE SHADOWS?
BUT I HAVE SEEN THE FACE OF YOUR SINS.
DEAD WOMAN, I CALL YOU! JOANNA NEWTON, I CALL YOU!
UGGHHH

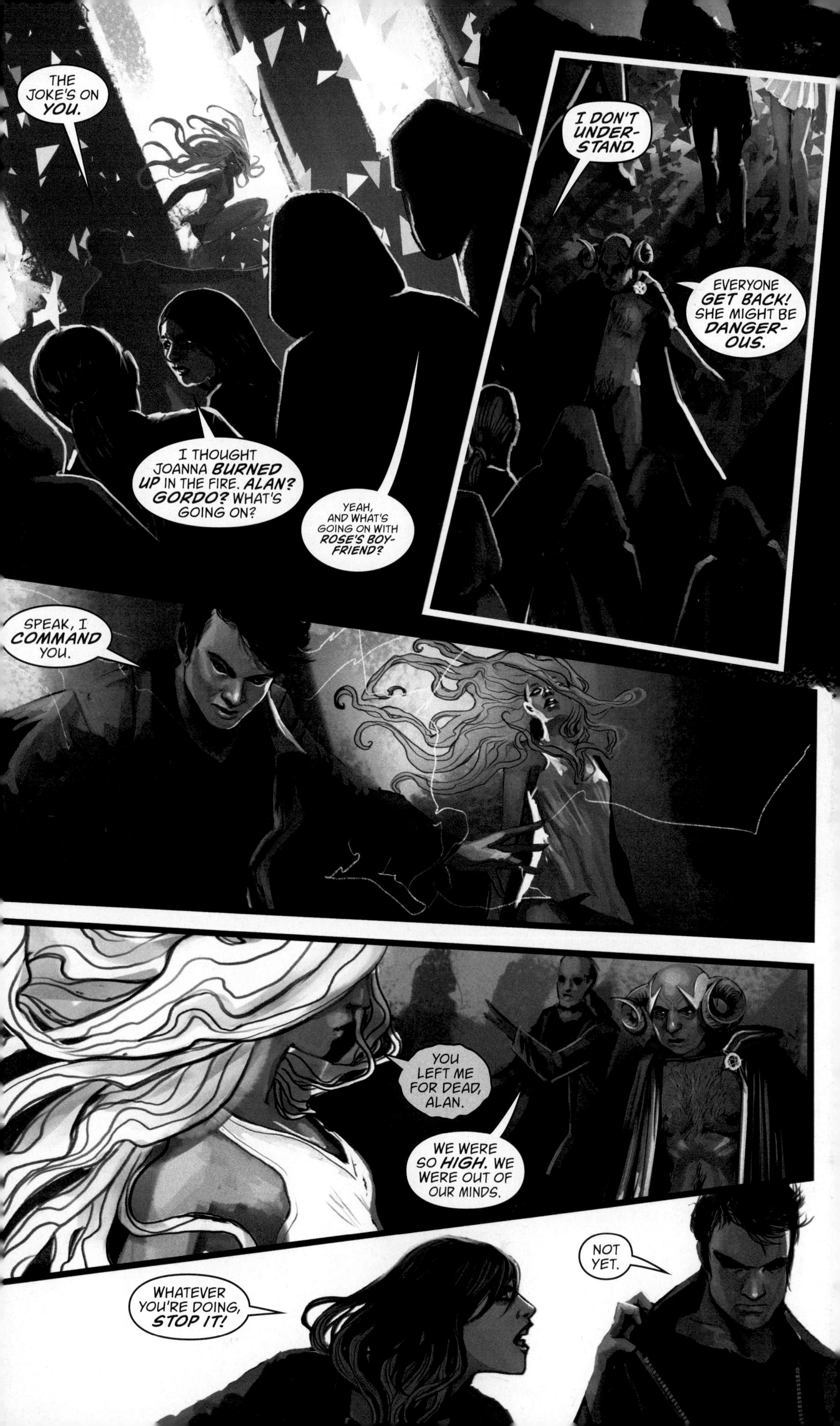
THE JOKE'S ON YOU.
I THOUGHT JOANNA BURNED UP IN THE FIRE. ALAN? GORDO? WHAT'S GOING ON?
YEAH, AND WHAT'S GOING ON WITH ROSE'S BOY-FRIEND?
I DON'T UNDER-STAND.
EVERYONE GET BACK! SHE MIGHT BE DANGER-OUS.
SPEAK, I COMMAND YOU.
YOU LEFT ME FOR DEAD, ALAN.
WE WERE SO HIGH. WE WERE OUT OF OUR MINDS.
WHATEVER YOU'RE DOING, STOP IT!
NOT YET.

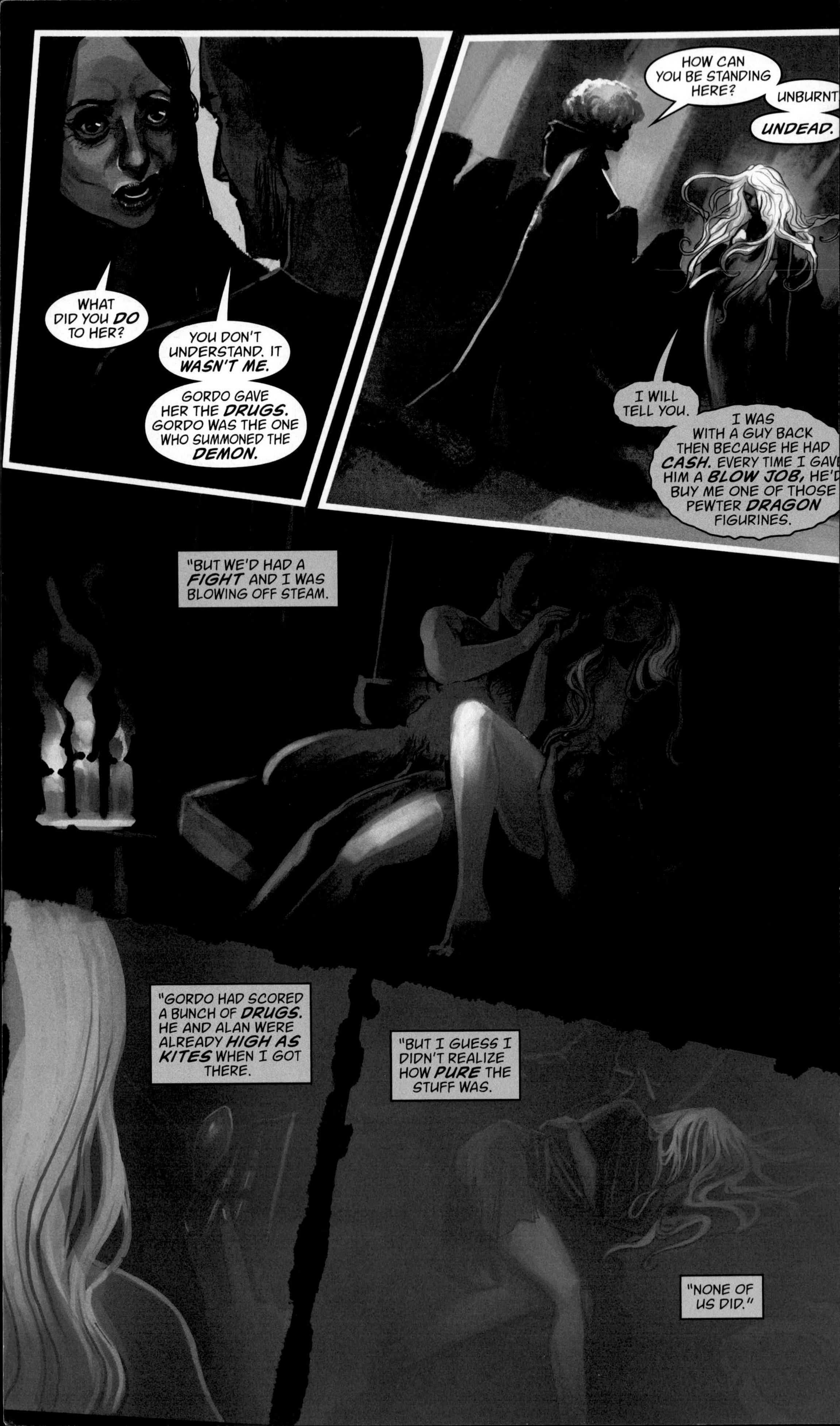
WHAT DID YOU DO TO HER?
YOU DON'T UNDERSTAND. IT WASN'T ME.
GORDO GAVE HER THE DRUGS. GORDO WAS THE ONE WHO SUMMONED THE DEMON.
HOW CAN YOU BE STANDING HERE?
UNBURNT
UNDEAD.
I WILL TELL YOU.
I WAS WITH A GUY BACK THEN BECAUSE HE HAD CASH. EVERY TIME I GAVE HIM A BLOW JOB, HE'D BUY ME ONE OF THOSE PEWTER DRAGON FIGURINES.
"BUT WE'D HAD A FIGHT AND I WAS BLOWING OFF STEAM.
"GORDO HAD SCORED A BUNCH OF DRUGS. HE AND ALAN WERE ALREADY HIGH AS KITES WHEN I GOT THERE.
"BUT I GUESS I DIDN'T REALIZE HOW PURE THE STUFF WAS.
"NONE OF US DID."

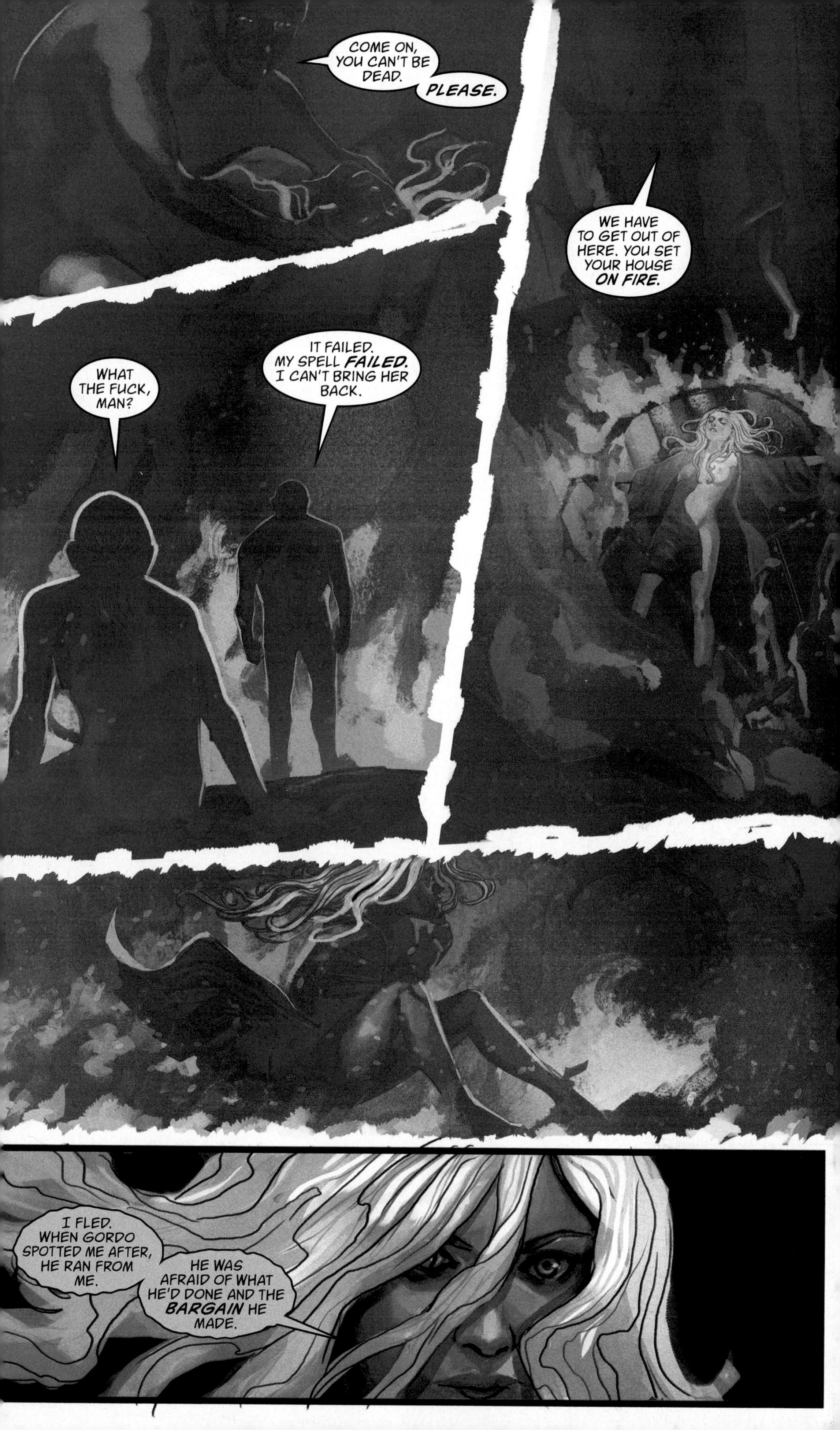
COME ON, YOU CAN'T BE DEAD.
PLEASE.
WE HAVE TO GET OUT OF HERE. YOU SET YOUR HOUSE ON FIRE.
WHAT THE FUCK, MAN?
IT FAILED. MY SPELL FAILED. I CAN'T BRING HER BACK.
I FLED. WHEN GORDO SPOTTED ME AFTER, HE RAN FROM ME.
HE WAS AFRAID OF WHAT HE'D DONE AND THE BARGAIN HE MADE.

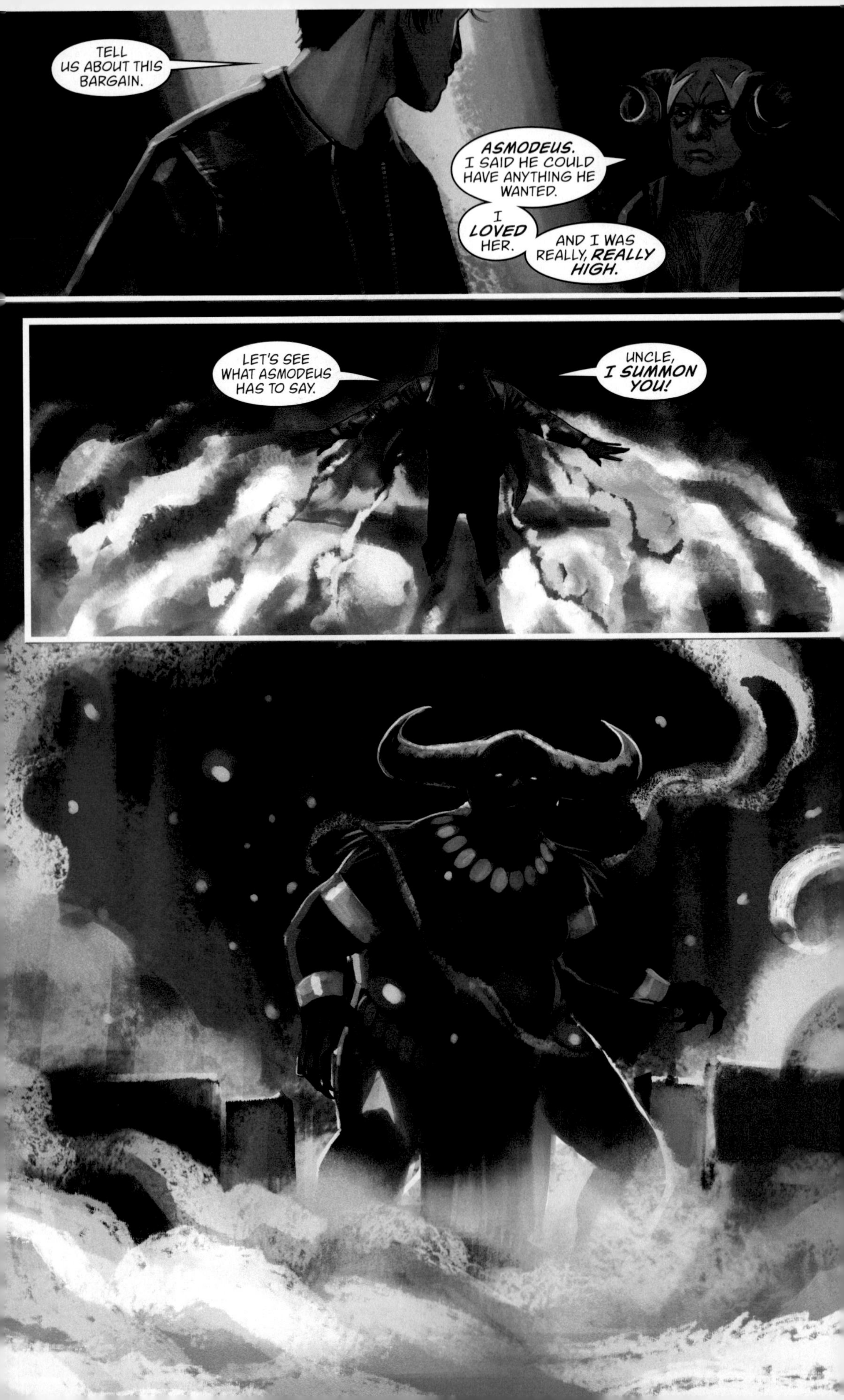
TELL US ABOUT THIS BARGAIN.
ASMODEUS. I SAID HE COULD HAVE ANYTHING HE WANTED.
I LOVED HER.
AND I WAS REALLY, REALLY HIGH.
LET'S SEE WHAT ASMODEUS HAS TO SAY.
UNCLE, I SUMMON YOU!

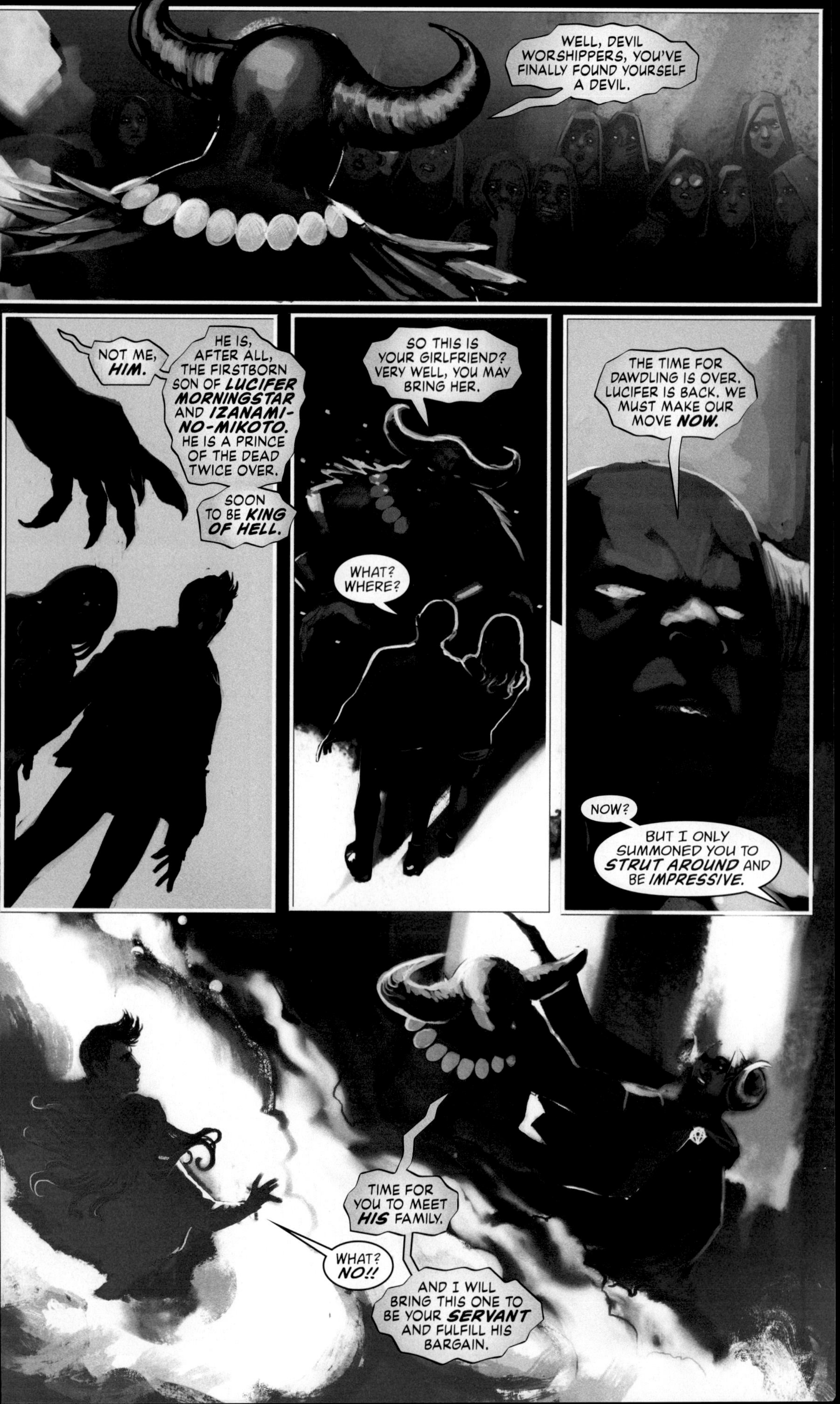
WELL, DEVIL WORSHIPPERS, YOU'VE FINALLY FOUND YOURSELF A DEVIL.
NOT ME, HIM.
HE IS, AFTER ALL, THE FIRSTBORN SON OF LUCIFER MORNINGSTAR AND IZANAMI-NO-MIKOTO. HE IS A PRINCE OF THE DEAD TWICE OVER.
SOON TO BE KING OF HELL.
SO THIS IS YOUR GIRLFRIEND? VERY WELL, YOU MAY BRING HER.
WHAT? WHERE?
THE TIME FOR DAWDLING IS OVER. LUCIFER IS BACK. WE MUST MAKE OUR MOVE NOW.
NOW?
BUT I ONLY SUMMONED YOU TO STRUT AROUND AND BE IMPRESSIVE.
TIME FOR YOU TO MEET HIS FAMILY.
WHAT? NO!!
AND I WILL BRING THIS ONE TO BE YOUR SERVANT AND FULFILL HIS BARGAIN.

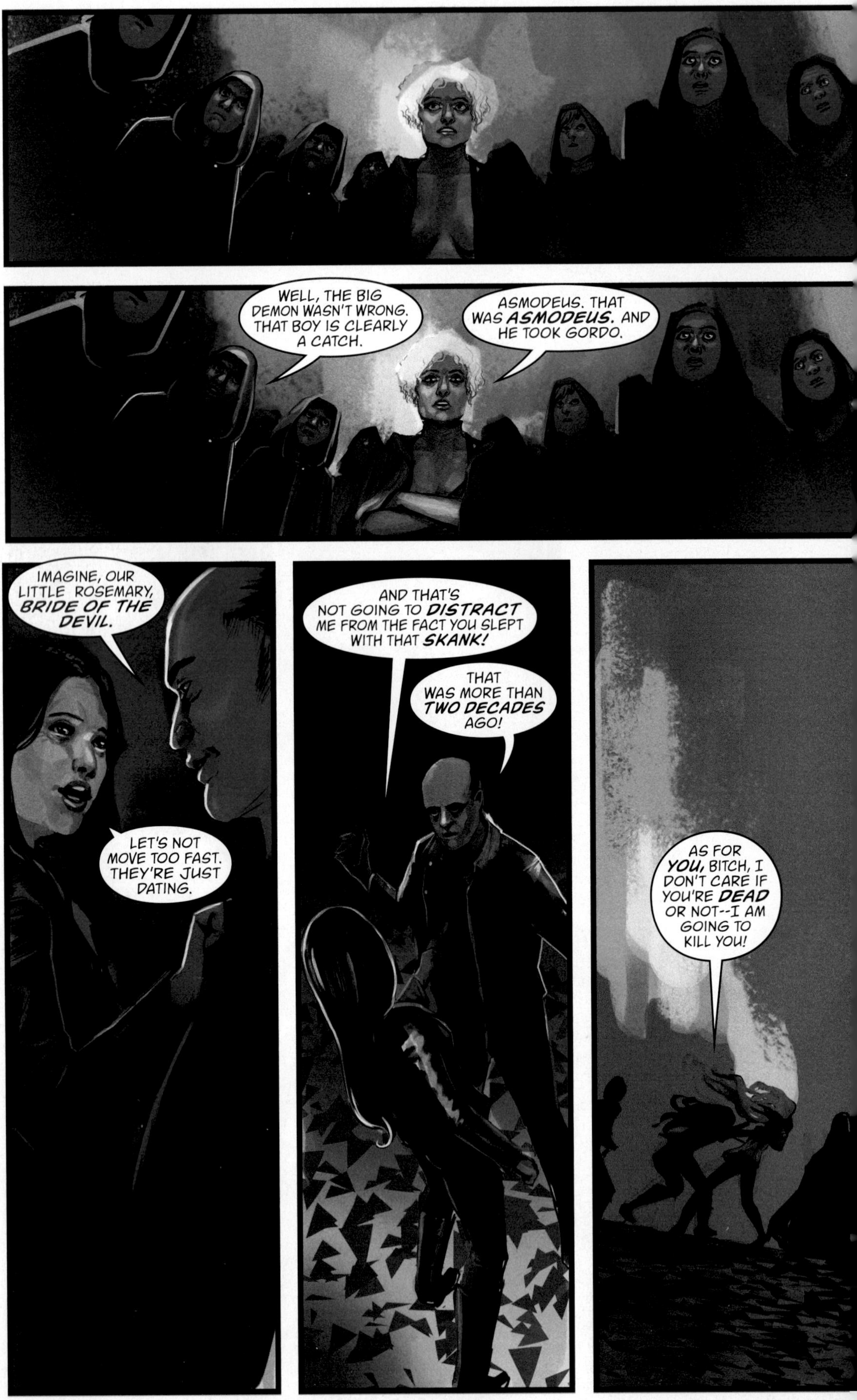
WELL, THE BIG DEMON WASN'T WRONG. THAT BOY IS CLEARLY A CATCH.
ASMODEUS. THAT WAS ASMODEUS. AND HE TOOK GORDO.
IMAGINE, OUR LITTLE ROSEMARY, BRIDE OF THE DEVIL.
LET'S NOT MOVE TOO FAST. THEY'RE JUST DATING.
AND THAT'S NOT GOING TO DISTRACT ME FROM THE FACT YOU SLEPT WITH THAT SKANK!
THAT WAS MORE THAN TWO DECADES AGO!
AS FOR YOU, BITCH, I DON'T CARE IF YOU'RE DEAD OR NOT--I AM GOING TO KILL YOU!

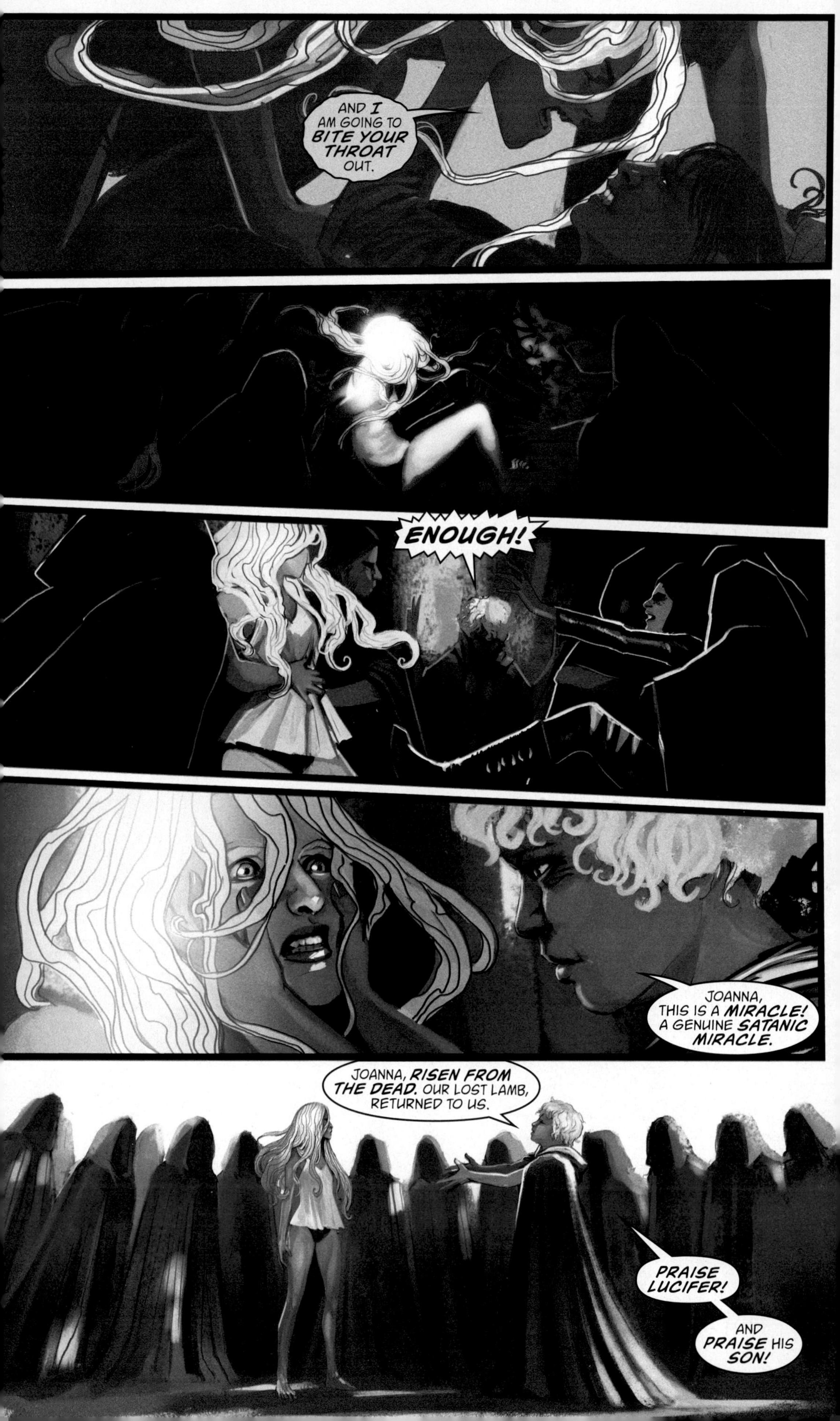
AND I AM GOING TO BITE YOUR THROAT OUT.
ENOUGH!
JOANNA, THIS IS A MIRACLE! A GENUINE SATANIC MIRACLE.
JOANNA, RISEN FROM THE DEAD. OUR LOST LAMB, RETURNED TO US.
PRAISE LUCIFER!
AND PRAISE HIS SON!

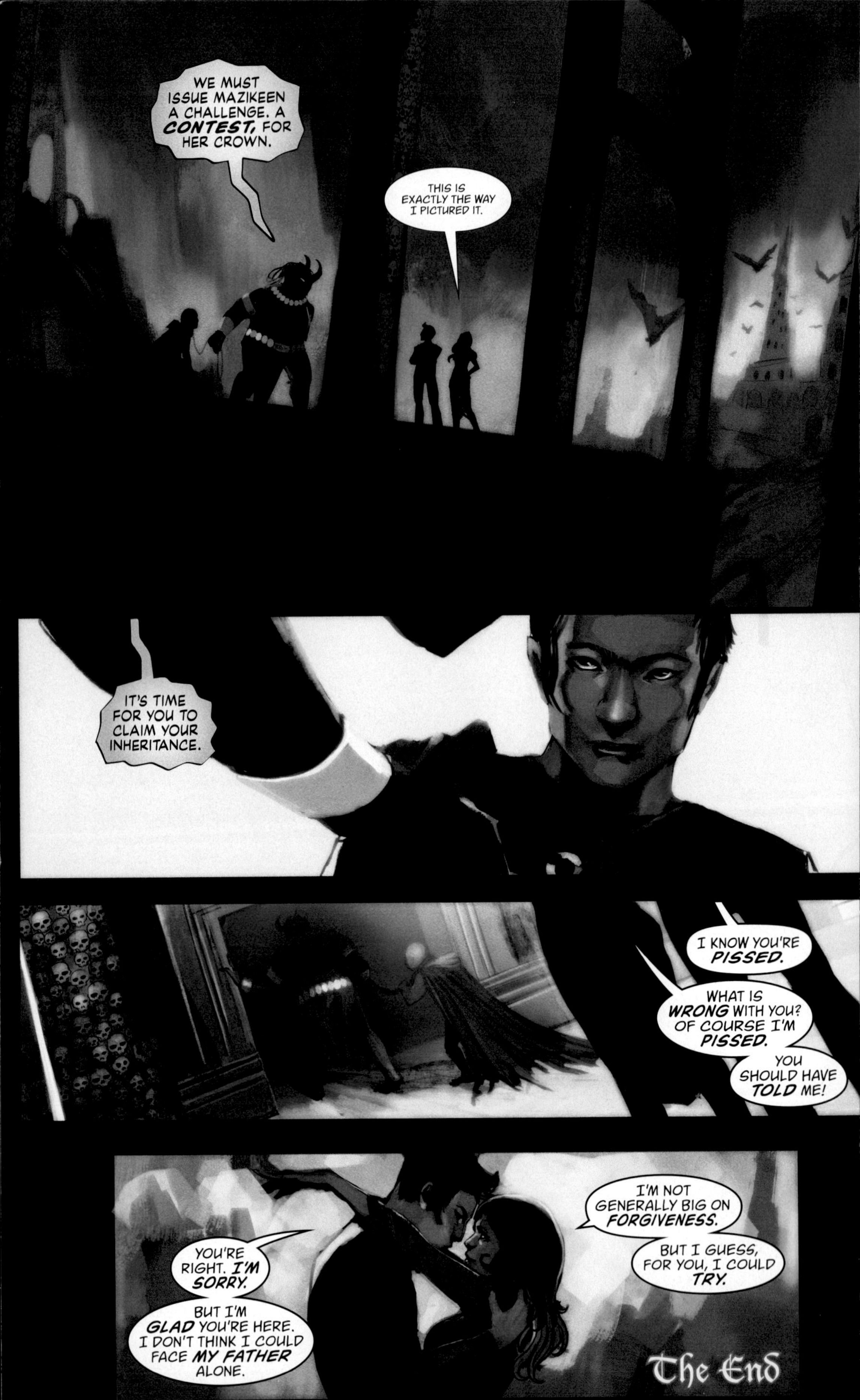
WE MUST ISSUE MAZIKEEN A CHALLENGE. A CONTEST, FOR HER CROWN.
THIS IS EXACTLY THE WAY I PICTURED IT.
IT'S TIME FOR YOU TO CLAIM YOUR INHERITANCE.
I KNOW YOU'RE PISSED.
WHAT IS WRONG WITH YOU? OF COURSE I'M PISSED.
YOU SHOULD HAVE TOLD ME!
YOU'RE RIGHT. I'M SORRY.
BUT I'M GLAD YOU'RE HERE. I DON'T THINK I COULD FACE MY FATHER ALONE.
I'M NOT GENERALLY BIG ON FORGIVENESS.
BUT I GUESS, FOR YOU, I COULD TRY.
The End

VERTIGO

"Moving, funny, insightful."
—*POPMATTERS*

"A compelling protagonist worthy of his own series."
—*THE A.V. CLUB*

"It's no easy task to make a reader root for the bad guy—in this case, the Devil himself—something Carey handles with much care and skill."
—*EXAMINER*

FROM THE WRITER OF *HELLBLAZER*

MIKE CAREY

with PETER GROSS

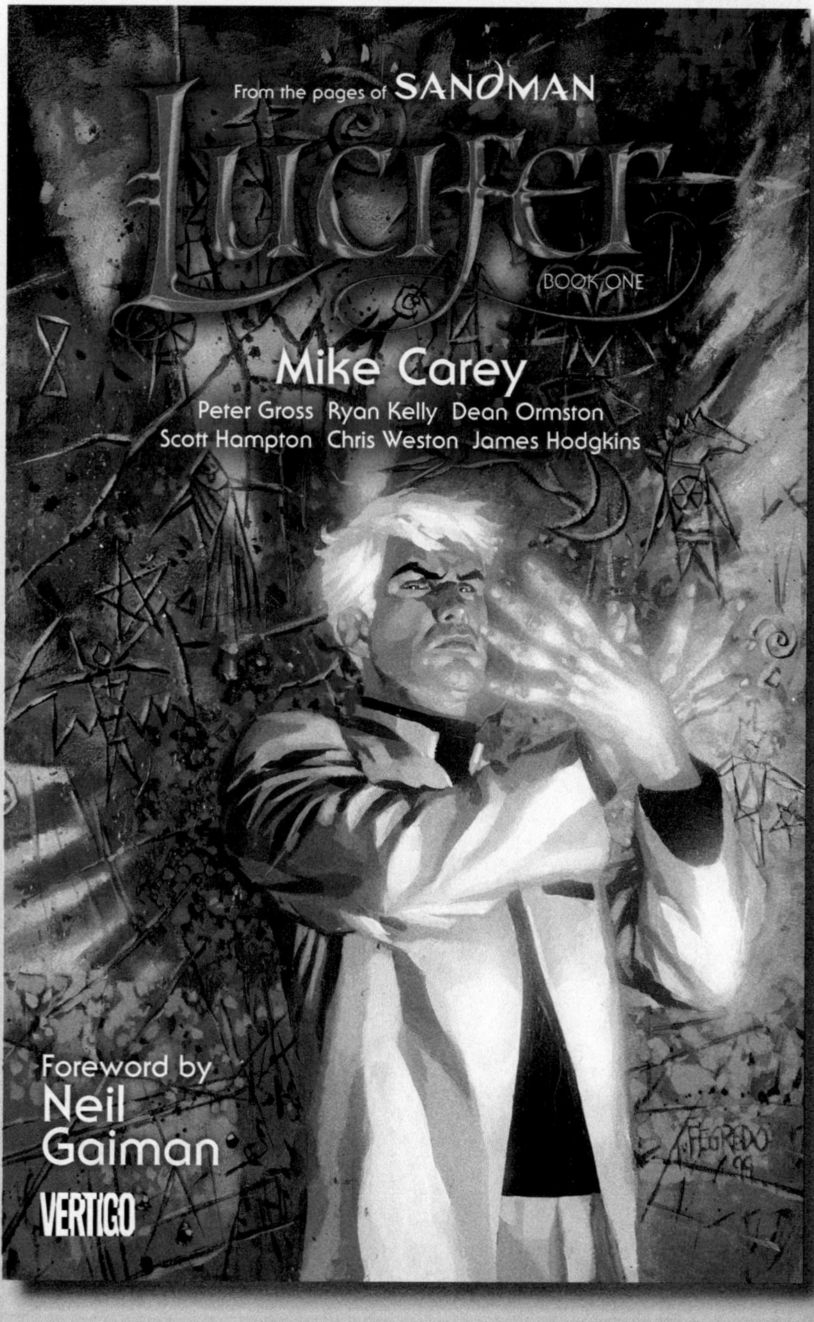
From the pages of SANDMAN
Lucifer
BOOK ONE
Mike Carey
Peter Gross Ryan Kelly Dean Ormston
Scott Hampton Chris Weston James Hodgkins
Foreword by Neil Gaiman
VERTIGO

LUCIFER BOOK TWO

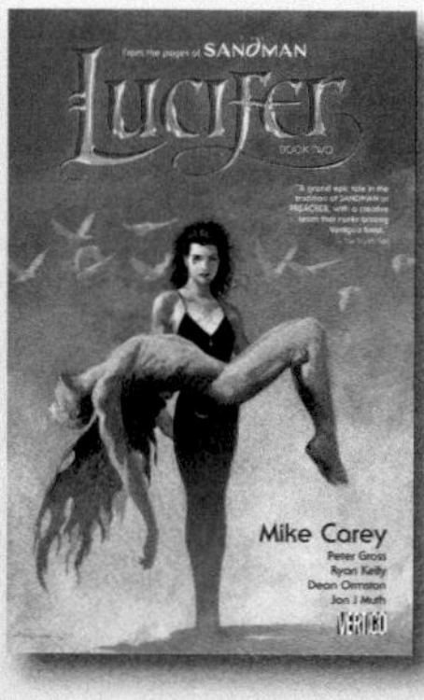
From the pages of SANDMAN
Lucifer
BOOK TWO
Mike Carey
VERTIGO

LUCIFER BOOK THREE

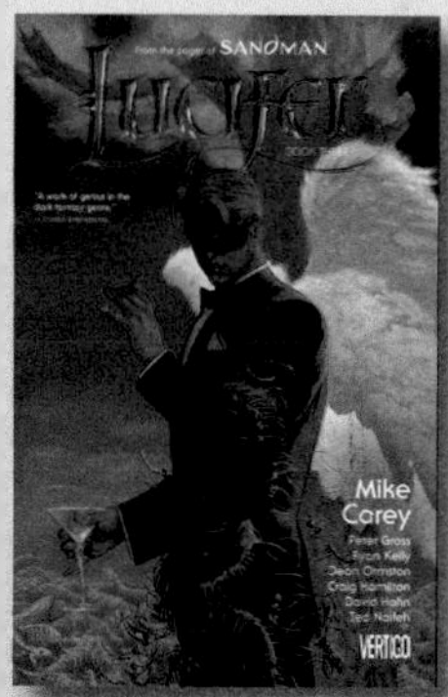
From the pages of SANDMAN
Lucifer
Mike Carey
VERTIGO

LUCIFER BOOK FOUR

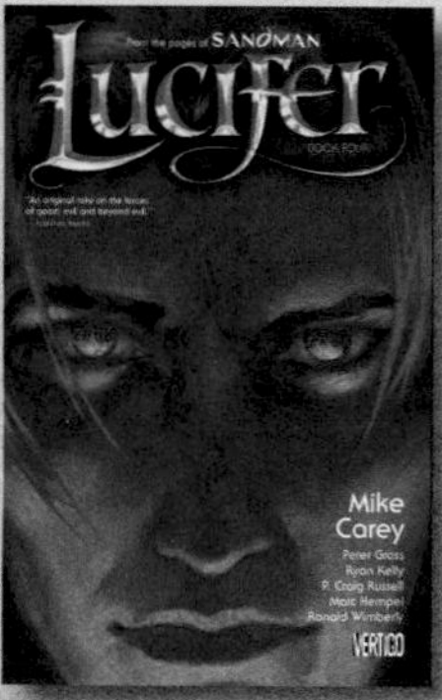
From the pages of SANDMAN
Lucifer
Mike Carey
VERTIGO

VERTIGO

"What Gaiman has written is a comics masterpiece." —PUBLISHERS WEEKLY

"The smartest comic book ever written." —USA TODAY

"The landmark comic-book series that actually made death seem cool." —ENTERTAINMENT WEEKLY

FROM THE *NEW YORK TIMES* # 1 BEST-SELLING AUTHOR

NEIL GAIMAN

THE SANDMAN VOL. 4: SEASON OF MISTS

READ THE COMPLETE SERIES!

THE SANDMAN VOL. 1: PRELUDES & NOCTURNES

THE SANDMAN VOL. 2: THE DOLL'S HOUSE

THE SANDMAN VOL. 3: DREAM COUNTRY

THE SANDMAN VOL. 4: SEASON OF MISTS

THE SANDMAN VOL. 5: A GAME OF YOU

THE SANDMAN VOL. 6: FABLES & REFLECTIONS

THE SANDMAN VOL. 7: BRIEF LIVES

THE SANDMAN VOL. 8: WORLDS' END

THE SANDMAN VOL. 9: THE KINDLY ONES

THE SANDMAN VOL. 10: THE WAKE

THE SANDMAN: ENDLESS NIGHTS

THE SANDMAN: THE DREAM HUNTERS

NOW WITH FULLY REMASTERED COLORING

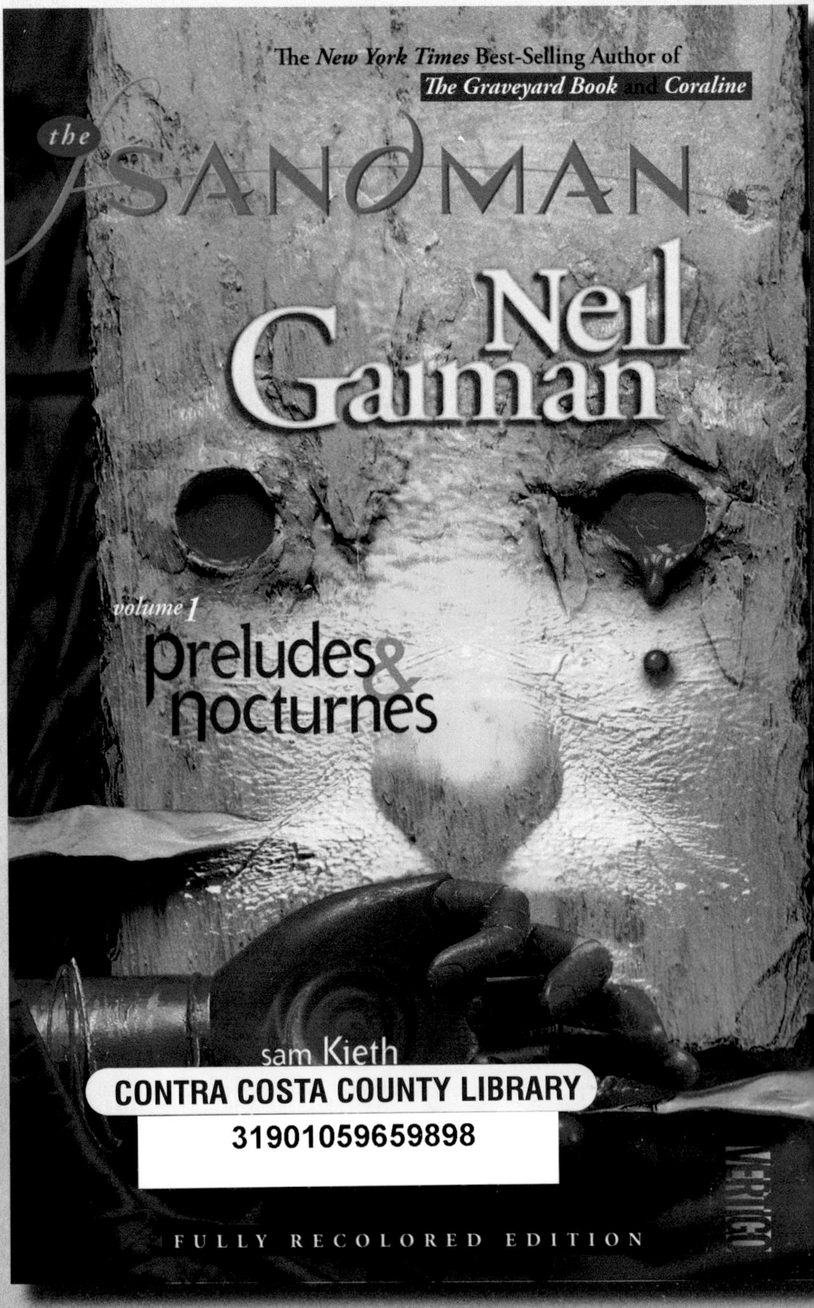

The *New York Times* Best-Selling Author of *The Graveyard Book* and *Coraline*

the SANDMAN

Neil Gaiman

volume 1
preludes & nocturnes

sam Kieth

FULLY RECOLORED EDITION

CONTRA COSTA COUNTY LIBRARY

31901059659898